BOILERPLATE CLAUSES, INTERNATIONAL COMMERCIAL CONTRACTS AND THE APPLICABLE LAW

With the aim of creating an autonomous regime for the interpretation and application of the contract, boilerplate clauses are often inserted into international commercial contracts without negotiations or regard for their legal effects. The assumption that sufficiently detailed and clear language will ensure that the legal effects of the contract will only be based on the contract, as opposed to the applicable law, was originally encouraged by English courts, and today most international contracts have these clauses, irrespective of the governing law.

This collection of essays demonstrates that this assumption is not fully applicable under systems of civil law, because these systems are based on principles, such as good faith and loyalty, which contradict this approach.

GIUDITTA CORDERO-MOSS is a professor at the Institute of Private Law, University of Oslo, where her main areas of expertise are international commercial law, comparative law and private international law. She is also an international arbitrator and has in the past practised as an international commercial lawyer in Italy, Norway and Russia.

BOILERPLATE CLAUSES, INTERNATIONAL COMMERCIAL CONTRACTS AND THE APPLICABLE LAW

Edited by
GIUDITTA CORDERO-MOSS

CAMBRIDGE
UNIVERSITY PRESS

CAMBRIDGE UNIVERSITY PRESS
Cambridge, New York, Melbourne, Madrid, Cape Town,
Singapore, São Paulo, Delhi, Tokyo, Mexico City

Cambridge University Press
The Edinburgh Building, Cambridge CB2 8RU, UK

Published in the United States of America by Cambridge University Press, New York

www.cambridge.org
Information on this title: www.cambridge.org/9780521197892

First published 2011

Printed in the United Kingdom at the University Press, Cambridge

A catalogue record for this publication is available from the British Library

Library of Congress Cataloguing in Publication data
Boilerplate clauses, international commercial contracts and the applicable
law / edited by Giuditta Cordero-Moss.
p. cm.
ISBN 978-0-521-19789-2 (hardback)
1. Standardized terms of contract. 2. Contracts – Language. 3. Foreign trade
regulation. I. Cordero-Moss, Giuditta. II. Title.
K845.S7B65 2011
346.02′2–dc22
2010037106

ISBN 978-0-521-19789-2 Hardback

CONTENTS

List of contributors   *page* xvii
Preface   xxi

Introduction   1
GIUDITTA CORDERO-MOSS

1   Overview of the book   1

2   The findings   3

3   Acknowledgments   4

PART 1   **How contracts are written in practice**   7

Introduction to Part 1   9

1.   Negotiating international contracts: does the process
     invite a review of standard contracts from the point
     of view of national legal requirements?   11
     DAVID ECHENBERG

1   How it all got started   12
     1.1   Not all contractual terms are created equal   12
     1.2   Imperfect information   15
     1.3   Non-negotiated contracts   17

2   The end result   18
     2.1   The contract as an imperfect compromise   18
     2.2   Consequences   18

2.   Multinational companies and national contracts   20
     MARIA CELESTE VETTESE

1   Introduction   20

2   Standard contractual structures, their impact on national
    legislations and the expectations of the parties   22

3   The in-house lawyer perspective   29

PART 2   **Methodological challenges**   33

Introduction to Part 2   35

3. Does the use of common law contract models give rise
    to a tacit choice of law or to a harmonised, transnational
    interpretation?   37
    GIUDITTA CORDERO-MOSS

    1   Does the drafting style imply a choice of the applicable
        law?   37
        1.1   Tacit choice of law   39
        1.2   Closest connection   41
        1.3   Conclusion   43

    2   Is a uniform interpretation of international contracts that
        is independent from the applicable law possible?   43
        2.1   Transnational sources   44
        2.2   Does transnational law have the force of law?   45
        2.3   Does transnational law exclude the applicable law?   47
              2.3.1   Specific contract regulations   47
              2.3.2   General contract regulations   48
        2.4   Does transnational law provide a uniform standard?   52

    3   Conclusion   60

4. Common law-based contracts under German law   62
    GERHARD DANNEMANN

    1   Introduction   62

    2   Likely problems   64

    3   Court practice   67
        3.1   Shipping contracts, exclusion and penalty clauses   68
        3.2   Financial securities and good faith   74
        3.3   Brokerage and good faith   75
        3.4   Construction contracts, warnings and fault   75
        3.5   Control of standard terms and exclusion clauses   76

    4   Conclusions   77

5. Comparing exculpatory clauses under Anglo-American law:
    testing total legal convergence   80
    EDWARD T. CANUEL

    1   Introducing the comparative legal method: the first step
        in evaluating total legal convergence   81
        1.1   Legal convergence theory: discussion points   83

    2   Exculpatory clauses: background, interaction with
        contractual theories and duties   85
        2.1   The role of unconscionability   86
        2.2   Assent, duty to read   87

    3   Testing convergence within the Anglo-American
        family: towage contracts and exculpatory
        clauses   93
        3.1   The development of US law: *Bisso* and beyond   93
        3.2   The common law family comparison: English law   95
        3.3   The role of legal technicalities   98

    4   Conclusion: a step away from total legal
        convergence   101

6. Circulation of common law contract models in Europe: the
    impact of the European Union system   104
    JEAN-SYLVESTRE BERGÉ

    1   The European Union system and circulation of common
        law contract models   104

    2   An almost perfect example: the *Courage* case   104

    3   The context of the case in EU law   105

    4   The three lessons drawn from the *Courage* case   106

    5   First lesson: in contract law, the use of the principle
        of procedural autonomy is rather exceptional and
        of a subsidiary nature   107

    6   Second lesson: the European framework governing the
        principle of procedural autonomy aims at establishing a
        correlation between partly autonomous and partly
        hierarchised legal systems   108

7 Third lesson: the intervention of EU law leads to a rereading of national laws, which is rather nuanced and has a broad meaning 110

8 Conclusion 112

PART 3 **The applicable law's effects on boilerplate clauses** 113

Introduction to Part 3 115

1 Clauses analysed in Part 3 118
    1.1 Entire agreement 119
    1.2 No waiver 119
    1.3 No oral amendments 119
    1.4 Severability 119
    1.5 Conditions/essential terms 119
    1.6 Sole remedy 119
    1.7 Subject to contract 120
    1.8 Material adverse change 120
    1.9 Liquidated damages 120
    1.10 Indemnity 121
    1.11 Representations and warranties 122
    1.12 Hardship 122
    1.13 *Force majeure* 123

2 Cases illustrating the need for coordination with the applicable law 125
    2.1 Clauses aiming at fully detaching the contract from the applicable law 125
    2.2 Clauses using a terminology with legal effects not known to the applicable law 127
    2.3 Clauses regulating matters already regulated in the applicable law 127

7. The common law tradition: application of boilerplate clauses under English law 129
EDWIN PEEL

1 Introduction 129
    1.1 Content 129
    1.2 Interpretation 132
    1.3 Good faith 134
    1.4 Conclusion and methodology 135

2   The clauses   136

   2.1   Entire agreement   136

   2.2   No waiver   144

   2.3   No oral amendments   146

   2.4   Conditions   148

   2.5   Sole remedy   152

   2.6   Subject to contract   154

   2.7   Liquidated damages   160

   2.8   Indemnity   165

   2.9   Representations and warranties   170

   2.10   Hardship/*force majeure*   175

3   Conclusion   178

8.   The Germanic tradition: application of boilerplate clauses under German law   179

ULRICH MAGNUS

1   Introduction   179

2   General method of interpretation of contracts   180

3   Law applicable to the interpretation of international commercial contracts   182

   3.1   Generally applicable law   182

      3.1.1   Applicability of the *lex contractus*   182

      3.1.2   Choice of law   183

      3.1.3   Construction clauses   184

      3.1.4   Applicable law in the absence of a choice of law   184

   3.2   Contract interpretation under international conventions   184

   3.3   Use of international trade terms   186

   3.4   Use of international standard contracts   187

   3.5   Terms specific for a certain law   187

   3.6   Mid-summary   188

4   'Acting under wrong law'   188

   4.1   A well-known phenomenon   188

   4.2   The courts' view   189

   4.3   Critique and solution   190

5   Discussion of specific clauses   192

    5.1   Clauses aiming at fully detaching the contract from
          the applicable law   192
          5.1.1   Entire agreement clauses   192
          5.1.2   No oral amendments clauses   197
    5.2   Clauses that use a terminology with legal effects not known
          to the applicable law   199
          5.2.1   Indemnity clauses   200
          5.2.2   Liquidated damages clauses   202
          5.2.3   Conclusion   203
    5.3. Contract clauses that regulate matters already regulated
          in the applicable law   203
          5.3.1   *Force majeure* clauses   204
          5.3.2   Hardship clauses   206

6.   Final conclusions   207

9.   The Romanistic tradition: application of boilerplate clauses
     under French law   210
     XAVIER LAGARDE, DAVID MÉHEUT AND JEAN-MICHEL
     REVERSAC

     1   Preliminary observations   210

     2   Entire agreement ('clause d'intégralité')   214

     3   No waiver   215

     4   No oral amendments   216

     5   Severability   216

     6   Conditions   217

     7   Sole remedy   218

     8   Subject to contract   220

     9   Material adverse change   221

    10   Liquidated damages   222

    11   Indemnity   222

    12   Representations and warranties   223

13 Hardship   225

14 *Force majeure*   226

10. The Romanistic tradition: application of boilerplate clauses
     under Italian law   227
     GIORGIO DE NOVA

     1 Entire agreement clauses and no oral amendments clauses
        as clauses provided in alien contracts   227

     2 Entire agreement clauses and no oral amendments clauses
        as 'stylistic clauses'?   228

     3 No oral amendments clauses under Italian law   228

     4 Entire agreement clauses under Italian law   229

     5 Entire agreement clauses under the CISG   230

     6 Articles 2722 and 2723 of the Italian Civil Code
        with respect to interpreting the contract   231

     7 Entire agreement clauses and implied
        conditions   232

11. The Nordic tradition: application of boilerplate clauses
     under Danish law   233
     PETER MØGELVANG-HANSEN

     1 Danish contract law in general   233

     2 Clauses aimed at fully detaching the contract from the
        applicable law   236
        2.1 Entire agreement   236
        2.2 No oral amendments   237
        2.3 No waiver   238
        2.4 Severability   239
        2.5 Conditions   239
        2.6 Sole remedy   241
        2.7 Subject to contract   242
        2.8 Material adverse change   244

     3 Clauses that use a terminology with legal effects not
        known to the applicable law   245
        3.1 Liquidated damages   246

4 Clauses that regulate matters already regulated in the applicable law 247

4.1 Representations and warranties 247

4.2 Hardship and *force majeure* 248

4.3 Clauses on contractual liability and/or product liability 249

12. The Nordic tradition: application of boilerplate clauses under Finnish law 254

GUSTAF MÖLLER

1 Introduction 254

2 Clauses aiming at fully detaching the contract from the applicable law 256

2.1 Entire agreement 256

2.2 No waiver 257

2.3 No oral amendments 257

2.4 Severability 258

2.5 Conditions 258

2.6 Sole remedy 259

2.7 Subject to contract 259

2.8 Material adverse change 260

3 Clauses that use a terminology with legal effects not known to the applicable law 260

3.1 Liquidated damages 260

3.2 Indemnity 261

4 Clauses that regulate matters already regulated in the applicable law 262

4.1 Representations and warranties 262

4.2 Hardship 263

4.3 *Force majeure* 263

13. The Nordic tradition: application of boilerplate clauses under Norwegian law 265

VIGGO HAGSTRØM

1 The Scandinavian law of obligations – and of contracts – is a part of the law with old traditions 265

2 The way commercial contracts are drafted in Norway has changed considerably during the past twenty to thirty years   266

3 Clauses aimed at fully detaching the contract from the applicable law   268

   3.1 Entire agreement   268

   3.2 No waiver   269

   3.3 No oral amendments   269

   3.4 Severability   270

   3.5 Conditions   270

   3.6 Sole remedy   271

   3.7 Subject to contract   271

   3.8 Material adverse change   272

4 Clauses with legal effects not known to the applicable law   272

   4.1 Liquidated damages   272

   4.2 Indemnity   273

5 Clauses that regulate matters already regulated in the applicable law and how these interact with each other   273

   5.1 Representations and warranties   273

   5.2 Hardship   274

   5.3 *Force majeure*   274

14. The Nordic tradition: application of boilerplate clauses under Swedish law   276

LARS GORTON

1 General background   276

2 Contractual principles and contractual considerations   278

3 Different parameters   280

4 The organisational/agency aspect – the use of representatives   281

5 Contract phases   282

   5.1 Some general points   282

   5.2 Negotiation phase   283

5.2.1   General remarks   283
5.2.2   Conditions precedent and subject to approval   284
5.2.3   No oral contracts   284
5.2.4   Entire agreement   285
5.3   Performance phase   289
5.3.1   Some general remarks   289
5.3.2   No oral amendments   290
5.3.3   Change of circumstances   290

6   Compensation clauses   294
6.1   General background   294
6.2   Liquidated damages and penalties   295
6.3   The use of compensation clauses   295
6.4   Delay interest   298

7   Conclusion   299

15.   The East European tradition: application of boilerplate clauses under Hungarian law   302
ATTILA MENYHÁRD

1   Introduction   302

2   Entire agreement   306

3   No waiver   307

4   No oral amendments   308

5   Severability   309

6   Conditions   309

7   Sole remedy   311

8   Subject to contract   314

9   Material adverse change   319

10   Liquidated damages   319

11   Indemnity   321

12   Representations and warranties   322

13   Hardship   326

14   *Force majeure*   327

16. The East European tradition: application of boilerplate clauses
     under Russian law   329

     IVAN S. ZYKIN

     1 Introductory remarks   329

     2 Some particular contract clauses   333
        2.1 Entire agreement   333
        2.2 No waiver   334
        2.3 No oral amendments   335
        2.4 Conditions   335
        2.5 Liquidated damages   336
        2.6 Sole remedy   338
        2.7 Subject to contract   338
        2.8 Representations and warranties   339
        2.9 *Force majeure* and hardship   341

     Conclusion: the self-sufficient contract, uniformly
     interpreted on the basis of its own terms: an illusion,
     but not fully useless   344

     GIUDITTA CORDERO-MOSS

     1 International commerce fosters self-sufficient
        contracts   344

     2 Detailed drafting as an attempt to enhance the
        self-sufficiency of contracts   346

     3 No real alternative to the applicable law   350

     4 The differing legal effects of boilerplate
        clauses   353
        4.1 Clauses aiming at fully detaching the contract from
             the applicable law   353
             4.1.1 Entire agreement   353
             4.1.2 No waiver   355
             4.1.3 No oral amendments   356
             4.1.4 Severability   358
             4.1.5 Conditions/essential terms   358
             4.1.6 Sole remedy   359
             4.1.7 Subject to contract   361
             4.1.8 Material adverse change   362

4.2 Clauses using terminology with legal effects not known to the applicable law 362

    4.2.1 Liquidated damages 362

    4.2.2 Indemnity 365

4.3 Clauses regulating matters already regulated in the applicable law 365

    4.3.1 Representations and warranties 365

    4.3.2 Hardship 367

    4.3.3 *Force majeure* 368

5 The drafting style does not achieve self-sufficiency, but has a certain merit 370

6 Conclusion 372

Bibliography 374

Index 388

CONTRIBUTORS

JEAN-SYLVESTRE BERGÉ is a professor at Université Paris Ouest Nanterre La Défense. He specialises in European law, international law and private law, and co-directs the Centre for European and Comparative Law (CEJEC) and the PhD programme at Paris Ouest. He has written several books in French on international and European protection of intellectual property (1996), European law and national private law (2003) and an introduction to European law (2008).

EDWARD T. CANUEL holds the position of European Liaison in the US State Department's climate office and is Regional Hub Officer in Copenhagen. Previously he served, inter alia, as Energy and Economic Officer in Oslo, leading the US Embassy's energy, finance, trade, economic, trade and commercial issues. Prior to joining the US Foreign Service, he practised commercial and government relations law at the international law firm McDermott, Will & Emery.

GIUDITTA CORDERO-MOSS, J.D. (Rome), PhD (Moscow), D. Jur. (Oslo), is a professor at the Institute of Private Law, University of Oslo and is Principal Research Fellow at the Centre for Energy, Petroleum and Mineral Law and Policy, University of Dundee, Scotland. She teaches and publishes within international commercial law, arbitration, comparative law and private international law. A former corporate lawyer, she acts as arbitrator in international commercial and investment disputes.

GERHARD DANNEMANN is a professor at the Humboldt University of Berlin. He is active in the field of comparative law and is, among other things, Fellow of the Institute of European and Comparative Law at the University of Oxford, where he has been a lecturer for several years and eventually became a reader in comparative law. He is general editor and founder of the Oxford University Comparative Law Forum and publishes actively. Since 2005, he has held the position of Chair of the Redaction Committee and Chair of the Terminology Group of the European Research Group on Existing EU Private Law (Acquis Group). He is also Door Tenant at 3 Pump Court Chambers, London.

GIORGIO DE NOVA is a professor at the University of Milan. He is the author of numerous publications on Italian private and contract law, many of which are generally recognised as fundamental works in their respective fields. He is the editor of various prestigious legal reviews in Italy. In addition, he is a practising lawyer with wide experience of commercial contracts, and he is often appointed as arbitrator in international and domestic arbitrations.

DAVID ECHENBERG is Senior Contract Risk Manager, Energy Infrastructure, General Electric, Milan. He is a qualified attorney-at-law in New York and a solicitor in England and Wales, and has worked in private practice in Sao Paulo, Brussels and Washington DC, as well as in-house in Florence, Italy. In addition, he previously acted as an expert legal consultant evaluating the body of law developed by UNCITRAL at the United Nations in New York. His areas of specialisation include international contract and commercial law, M&A and international dispute resolution.

LARS GORTON is a professor emeritus at the University of Lund, is presently a visiting professor at the Center for Kreditret og kapitalmarkedsret (Copenhagen Business School) and is tied to the Stockholm Center for Commercial Law at the Faculty of Law, Stockholm University. He is active in the fields of contract law, maritime law and banking law. In addition to publishing mainly in these areas of law, he has also been a corporate lawyer. He is also presently a board member of the Scandinavian Institute of Maritime law.

VIGGO HAGSTRØM is a professor at the University of Oslo. He is the author of numerous publications on Norwegian private and contract law that are recognised as fundamental in Norwegian legal doctrine. He is the general editor of the most recognised Scandinavian legal doctrinal review and has significant commercial experience, among other things, as a commercial arbitrator.

XAVIER LAGARDE is a professor at Université Paris Ouest Nanterre La Défense. He specialises in contract law, civil procedure and alternative dispute resolution, as well as in law and economics. He has written numerous books in his fields of interest. As a partner in the law firm of Peisse-Dupichot-Zirah and Co (Paris Bar), he pleads before court on commercial matters.

ULRICH MAGNUS is a professor at the University of Hamburg. He is active, among other things, in the fields of private and contract law, private international law and comparative law. He is editor of a number of recognised legal reviews and publications series and, until 2009, also acted as a Court of Appeal judge. He participates in a number of international working groups and commissions, including UNCITRAL.

DAVID MÉHEUT is an attorney-at-law at Clyde and Co, Paris. He received an LLB in French and English law from King's College London and the University of Paris I – Panthéon-Sorbonne and an LLM in European Union Law from the University of Paris II – Panthé on-Assas. He specialises in international arbitration and advises clients on multi-jurisdictional issues in relation to insurance, reinsurance and shipping disputes and operations.

ATTILA MENYHÁRD is an associate professor at the ELTE Faculty of Law, Budapest. He is Head of the Civil Law Department in the Faculty of Law at Eötvös Loránd University (Budapest) and is active in the fields of contract law, tort law, property law and company law. He is the author of various books and has contributed to the project for a new Hungarian Civil Code. He participates in several international research projects and programmes and is a listed member of the Arbitration Court attached to the Hungarian Chamber of Commerce and Industry, Budapest.

PETER MØGELVANG-HANSEN is a professor at the Copenhagen Business School. He is active within the fields of contract, marketing and civil enforcement law, and has participated actively in the legislative process in respect of numerous acts within these areas. He is co-editor on the most important Danish law commentary.

GUSTAF MÖLLER is counsel at Krogerus, Finland. He is a former Justice at the Supreme Court of Finland and has been actively contributing to international work in fields relating to, among other things, international contracts – acting as the Finnish delegate to the Hague Conference on Private International Law and UNCITRAL. He is the author of numerous publications and is often invited to present papers at international conferences. He is also the Chairman of the Board of Arbitration of the Finnish Chamber of Commerce.

EDWIN PEEL is Fellow and Tutor in Law at Keble College, University of Oxford. He publishes actively in the field of contract law and conflict of laws and is, among other things, the author of the revised editions of *Treitel on the Law of Contract* and the editor of various Oxford University Press books on contracts, including, most recently, *Contract Terms* (2007). He is a qualified solicitor and acts as a consultant to Clifford Chance LLP.

JEAN-MICHEL REVERSAC is an attorney-at-Law at Clyde and Co, Paris, where he is in charge of the Corporate and Commercial Team. He is active in advising foreign investors in France regarding the acquisition of share capital and mergers or acquisitions of ongoing businesses. He also pleads before court on commercial matters, including insurance and banking litigations.

MARIA CELESTE VETTESE holds the position of Senior Legal Counsel at Group Function Legal and Compliance ABB S.p.A. She has been practising for over a decade in the fields of international arbitration, private international law and commercial law. She has been actively involved in the closing of several project financing projects in the power generation business, and for the past ten years she has been lecturing on contract law for the Project Management Institute in Italy.

IVAN S. ZYKIN, Dr. Sc. (Law), is a professor and is Head of the Centre for Legal Problems of International Economic Relations at the Institute of State and Law, Russian Academy of Sciences. He has published extensively within the fields of commercial law, private international law and arbitration. He has been actively involved in drafting the legislation of the Russian Federation and has represented Russia in several international negotiations and conferences, inter alia, in the frame of UNCTAD, UNCITRAL and UNIDROIT. He is also Vice-President of the International Commercial Arbitration Court at the Chamber of Commerce and Industry of the Russian Federation and is Partner of Andrey Gorodissky & Partners.

PREFACE

This book applies the method of comparative law to the practice of international commercial contract drafting and therefore gives a quite unusual combination of theory and practice. The underlying idea reflects my own path in the world of international commercial contracts.

For the first part of my career I was, for more than a decade, an in-house lawyer of multinational companies, first in Italy and then in Norway. For all those years I have been drafting and negotiating financial and commercial contracts that were meant to be operative in a variety of countries, from various continental European countries to Russia and what has become the former Soviet Union. It struck me that all contracts were written mainly on the basis of the same models, quite irrespective of the law to which they would be subject. The models were obviously inspired by the common law contract practice, even though the contracts were not meant to be governed by English law. Queries arising out of this observation would be quickly dismissed on account of the expectation by the other contractual party, and even more by involved financial institutions, that recognisable models would be used. Also, these models were deemed to have proven successful in the past. Any ambition to verify the compatibility of the models with the applicable law would be limited to asking local lawyers to render a legal opinion on the enforceability of the contract. These legal opinions would focus on the absence of conflict with mandatory rules of the applicable law, but would normally not consider the drafting style. Any attempt to adjust the drafting style to the applicable legal tradition would be to no avail – in part because contracts are, most of the time, written under time pressure and in part due to the reluctance to modify proven models. Therefore, I went on drafting and negotiating clauses that I suspected would not always be enforceable according to their terms.

As soon as I started working full time in academia, I took up all the unanswered questions that had accumulated during my years as a corporate lawyer. The result was a research project financed by the Norwegian Research Council that, in turn, resulted in this book.

The just-mentioned practice of structuring international contracts according to the common law legal tradition, and not according to the applicable law, is analysed here according to the following lines. First, it is explained how international contracts are written, and why the drafters often disregard the applicable law. This shows that the drafter does not necessarily intend to subject the contract to English law: rather, the drafter adopts the style typical for English contracts because, with its high degree of detail and apparent exhaustiveness, it suggests that the contract may be interpreted on the basis of its own terms and without having to take into consideration the applicable law. This impression of self-sufficiency is enhanced by the use of boilerplate clauses, contract regulations that recur in all types of contract and aim at creating an autonomous regime for the interpretation and application of the contract.

Secondly, some methodological questions are addressed: should the inspiring common law also be given a central role in the interpretation of international contracts? Should contracts be governed by general principles that do not belong to a specific national law, since national laws are not taken into particular consideration when contracts are drafted? The analysis will show that these alternatives are not feasible and that, therefore, international contracts have to be governed by the national law that is applicable according to the general conflict rules. This may lead to the applicability of a law not belonging to the common law tradition.

The third issue addressed is: will the governing law influence the interpretation and application of the contract? A series of boilerplate clauses often recurring in international contracts will be analysed first from the point of view of English law, which is the system underlying the original drafting style, and then from the point of view of a number of laws, representing various sub-families of the civilian tradition. The analysis will show how contract clauses may be affected by the governing law.

The material contained in this book is updated as of June 2010.

Giuditta Cordero-Moss

~

Introduction

GIUDITTA CORDERO-MOSS

1 Overview of the book

This book addresses the question of whether the drafting style of inter-national contracts may actually achieve rendering the contract self-sufficient. The drafting style, including the recurrence of boilerplate clauses in all types of contracts and irrespective of the governing law, seems to aim at detaching the contract from any elements external to the contract itself, including the applicable law. This drafting style is origi-nally based on the common law approach to contracts, but is now adopted in most international contracts even when they are not subject to a law belonging to the common law family. The analysis follows three different stages, each dealt with in a different part of the book.

Part 1 of this book contains contributions by attorneys practising in international business, who explain the circumstances that lead to writing commercial contracts in a way that disregards the structure and tradition of the applicable law. This may be explained first of all in light of the fact that commercial contracts are often the result of an extensive process of negotiations. In Chapter 1, David Echenberg describes how the dynamics of negotiations contribute to the development of contracts that are not tailored to any specific state law. Lawyers drafting contracts for multinational companies will often be subject to the company's internal policy that tends to be standardised in order to facilitate internal risk assessment and knowledge management. An internal standardisa-tion opposes adjustments of model contracts even though they might be necessary in order to comply with the applicable law. Maria Celeste Vettese reports in Chapter 2 on the internal standardisation and the impact that it has on contract drafting.

Part 2 of this book analyses some methodological questions that arise out of the described contract practice. If international contracts are written without giving much consideration to the applicable law, it

1

may seem legitimate to enquire whether they have to be interpreted under principles that do not belong to the applicable law. There are two possible approaches to this situation, each traditionally dealt with in a different branch of the law: private international law and international commercial law. The former makes it possible to verify whether adopting a contract model developed under a certain legal system may imply that that system's law governs the contract. The latter aims at giving a uniform interpretation to contracts, irrespective of the governing law. In Chapter 3, Giuditta Cordero-Moss analyses the implications that the style of contract drafting may have when choosing the governing law. The chapter then verifies whether, and if so to what extent, generally acknowledged rules, trade usages or transnational restatements of principles may contribute to overcome the tension between the style of the contract and the law governing it. Gerhard Dannemann reports in Chapter 4 how German courts have been coping with the methodological challenges of contracts modelled on a foreign legal tradition. In Chapter 5, Edward T. Canuel verifies whether convergence among different legal systems may be relied upon to such an extent that contracts may be drafted without needing to have regard to the governing law. He analyses how common law courts interpret and apply the contractual mechanism of exculpatory clauses and finds that these clauses have varying legal effects even within the same legal family. Jean-Sylvestre Bergé observes in Chapter 6 that the circulation of legal models is a phenomenon occurring on different levels and shows that the system of the European Union forces the acceptance of legal concepts belonging to different legal traditions.

The analysis undertaken in Part 2 shows that contracts have to be interpreted under the domestic law that is applicable to them. Hence, contract terms that were originally developed to meet the requirements and criteria of the common law often have to be interpreted under an applicable law belonging to the civil law family. As is well known, common law and civil law systems present various differences in respect of regulation and interpretation of contracts. Therefore, when an international contract governed by a civil law system is written in the common law style, a tension may arise between the different legal traditions.

Part 3 of this book thus analyses how the wording of the contract terms (inspired by the common law) reacts when it is subject to a civilian governing law: will it be interpreted literally or in the light of underlying principles of the governing law? Will it have legal effects comparable to those that it would have under the common law? Will the same wording have different legal effects depending on the applicable law? The analysis is made on the basis of a series of so-called boilerplate clauses, common contract terms and recurring legal concepts that are frequently found in commercial contracts irrespective of the type of legal relationship regulated by the contract. These are listed in the introduction to Part 3. The criteria for the analysis, also listed in the introduction to Part 3, are intended to highlight the possible tension between the contract's language and the applicable law. In Chapter 7, Edwin Peel analyses the originally intended effects of the listed clauses and verifies to what extent these effects may actually be achieved under English law.

Because within the civil law there is no uniform approach to many aspects of contract law, the effects that the listed clauses may achieve under a civilian governing law will be analysed from the point of view of several legal systems deemed to represent the various sub-families of the civil law: the Germanic, Romanistic, Scandinavian and East European families. Thus, in Chapter 8, the analysis is made under German law by Ulrich Magnus; in Chapter 9, under French law by Xavier Lagarde, together with David Méheut and Jean-Michel Reversac; in Chapter 10, under Italian law by Giorgio De Nova; in Chapter 11, under Danish law by Peter Møgelvang-Hansen; in Chapter 12, under Finnish law by Gustaf Möller; in Chapter 13, under Norwegian law by Viggo Hagstrøm; in Chapter 14, under Swedish law by Lars Gorton; in Chapter 15, under Hungarian law by Attila Menyhárd; and in Chapter 16, under Russian law by Ivan S. Zykin.

2 The findings

The expectation that the contract is a self-sufficient unit independent of the applicable law, upon which the drafting of international contracts seems to rely, does not necessarily correspond to the legal effects of the contract. Many recurrent clauses have the function of exhaustively regulating the contract's interpretation and application, thus detaching it from the influence of any external elements, such as the applicable law. This apparent expectation of the drafters may originally have been based on the drafting technique developed under English contract law, which delegates most of the regulation to the parties in the contract and features a low degree of interference by the courts. However, these clauses may not be expected to achieve a full detachment from the applicable law when this belongs to a civil law system, where the general contract law and the courts have a much more active role. Chapter 7 shows that even under English law, the expectation of total detachment may not always be fulfilled.

In brief, the drafters of international contracts seem to have an excessive trust in the self-sufficiency of the instruments that they write. In reality, the sophisticated contract drafter is aware of this assumption's fallacy. Contracts are nevertheless written in this way because the drafters consider it too burdensome to adjust all clauses of every single contract model to the circumstances of the specific case. Based on a cost-benefit evaluation of the resources needed to adjust the contract to the applicable law, the drafters accept a calculated legal risk.

The less aware drafter will rely on a literal and full implementation of the contract's wording, and this reliance will be enhanced by the use of boilerplate clauses aiming at regulating interpretation and application irrespective of the applicable legal tradition. To the extent that the contract's wording turns out not to be literally and fully enforceable under the applicable law, its presence may nevertheless be useful: not all differences of interpretation end up in court, and in the process leading to the settlement of the dispute, a harsh clause may give a stronger negotiating position even though it may on closer inspection be recognised as unenforceable.

3   Acknowledgments

This book is the result of the research project 'Anglo-American Contract Models and Norwegian or other Civil Law Governing Law' (www.jus. uio.no/ifp/english/research/projects/anglo/index.html) that I ran from 2004 to 2010 at the Department of Private Law of the Law Faculty at the University of Oslo. The project was financed by this Department and the Research Council of Norway. Research assistant positions were also financed by the Norwegian office of the law firm DLA Piper. Some research on specific maritime law topics was financed by the Nordic Institute of Maritime Law.

The aim of the project was to achieve a systematic overview of the frictions that might run counter to the expectations of each of the parties when a common law-inspired contract is governed by a civilian law: this includes the party that had relied on the effects of the (common law-inspired) contractual formulation, as well as the party that had relied on the applicability of the (Norwegian or other civilian) governing law.

Research was done by research assistants at the Department of Private Law of the Law Faculty at the University of Oslo, who each wrote a paper on selected clauses or contract practices that form the origin of these frictions. The papers assessed the specific function of each clause or contract practice in the contract model under the original common law system and verified the extent to which the clause is capable of exercising the same function once the contract is inserted into the context of a different governing law (primarily Norwegian law). These papers are published in the Publication Series of the Department of Private Law, in a separate series called 'Anglo-American Contract Models'. Eight issues belong to this series: No. 1, Introduction and Method (No. 169/ 2007, by Giuditta Cordero-Moss); No. 2, No Waiver (No. 176/2009, by Fredrik Skribeland); No. 3, Entire Agreement (No. 177/2009, by Henrik Wærsted Bjørnstad); No. 4, No Oral Amendments (No. 178/2009, by Jens Christian Westly); No. 5, Conditions, Warranties, Representations, Covenants (No. 179/2009, by Tor Sandsbraaten); No. 6, Liquidated Damages (No. 180/2010, by Kyrre Kielland); No. 7, Indemnity (No. 181/2010, by André Bjerketveit); and No. 8, Material Adverse Change (No. 183/2010, by Lars Ole Sikkeland).

In addition, three PhD theses were written in the framework of the project: on liquidated damages under the US and Norwegian law, by Edward T. Canuel; on hardship clauses, by Herman Bruserud; and on *force majeure* clauses, by Anders Mikelsen.

The project enjoyed the permanent cooperation of English and American academics and practitioners, who participated in the project's workshops, commented on each paper and contributed with their knowledge and insight: Edwin Peel, Fellow and Tutor in Law, Keble College, University of Oxford, Mr Jim Percival, at that time Head of Dispute Resolution, British Nuclear Fuels plc, and Mr Edward T. Canuel, at that time Energy and Economic Officer at the US Embassy in Oslo. Mr Peel contributes to this book with the chapter on the interpretation and application of contract clauses under English law and Mr Canuel with the chapter on the diverging interpretation of certain contract clauses within the common law legal family.

The interaction of contract models and governing law is a topic of interest for the academy and for the legislator (in view of possible reforms to enhance the unification of the contract law), as it has a considerable amount of relevance to the practice of international business. Practising lawyers, both those in private practice and in-house company lawyers, are confronted with this matter on a daily basis, and the project's research is of immediate and direct relevance to their practice. To take advantage of this common interest, a users' group was established, with representatives from the main Norwegian law firms and legal departments of Norwegian companies who are active in the field of international contracts. A list may be found at www.jus.uio.no/ifp/ forskning/prosjekter/anglo/usergroup.html. The users' group has worked as an advisory forum, providing input on the identification and formulation of research themes, as well as contributing practical insight to ensure the relevance of the perspectives chosen for the research.

The practice of adopting common law-inspired contract models is not limited to Norway, and the tension that may arise between the common law system of origin of the contract and the law governing the contract becomes relevant whenever the latter belongs to the civil law family. Numerous academics and practitioners from a number of civilian countries have contributed to the project's seminars and workshops. Their papers are collected in this book.

The copy-editing of the material collected in this book was made by Miriam Hatoum of Boston University.

A special acknowledgement goes to Cambridge University Press and, particularly, to Finola O'Sullivan, Editorial Director, Law, whose understanding of the subject matter and farsightedness have made this book possible and whose friendly support has made it a pleasant enterprise.

All those mentioned above, as well as those who are not specifically mentioned here but contributed to the smooth performance of the project, are deeply thanked.

PART 1

How contracts are written in practice

~

Introduction to Part 1

Using a certain language to write a contract does not necessarily mean that the legal system that is expressed in that idiom is applied. This is clearly shown by the fact that often the parties to a contract that is written in the English language expressly choose a governing law that is not expressed in English, be it the law of the state to which one of the parties belongs, the law of the state where the contract shall be performed or the law of a third state, which is deemed to be neutral and therefore preferred by both parties. Therefore, it should not be surprising to see commercial contracts written in English, but structured in the same way as a contract would be structured under the law that the parties have chosen to govern their relationship. These contracts would be developed and written according to the legal technique and legal tradition of the governing law, and only from a linguistic point of view would they be expressed in English. The process of drafting would not necessarily have to take place in two tiers, first writing the contract in the original language and then translating it into English. It could very well be possible to think and structure the contract according to the criteria of the governing law and write it directly in English, although the difficulties of expressing legal concepts in a foreign language are well known, that is, of separating the means of expression from the object that is expressed.

However, international commercial contract practice does not seem to follow this path. Not only does the drafter of the contract use the English language, it also applies contract models that are developed in England, the USA or other common law jurisdictions. Separating the use of the English language from the adoption of the underlying legal structures would assume: (i) a thorough knowledge of the English or other common law system under which the model has been developed; (ii) an understanding of the function of the various contract clauses in that legal system; (iii) a systematic comparison with the governing legal system; and (iv) an exclusion or correction of the contract clauses that turn out to be tailored to the legal system under which the model was developed and not to the governing legal system. Such an extensive process cannot always be expected in the framework of a commercial case and, as a result, contract models are often simply adopted as they are. Hence, contracts often reflect the requirements and structure of a contract law that will not govern them.

It may apparently seem unreasonable to disregard the legal tradition under which the contract will be interpreted and applied. Experienced practitioners who are active in the drafting of international commercial contracts have been asked to explain the rationale behind this commercial practice. In Part 1, David Echenberg and Maria Celeste Vettese show how the dynamics of negotiations, considerations of efficiency and organisational matters affect the process of drafting contracts and lead to contracts that are not tailored to any specific state law.

Negotiating international contracts: does the process invite a review of standard contracts from the point of view of national legal requirements?

DAVID ECHENBERG[*]

The range of legal entities contracting internationally, as well as the range of types of agreements entered into by companies, is very broad indeed. This introductory chapter will focus generally on companies transacting internationally for one-off contracts for the sale and purchase of goods and services.[1]

Business is about assuming and managing risks, including legal risk. This reality is mirrored in the negotiation process. Contracts can be viewed as the final result of a dynamic process seeking to take into consideration all the imponderabilities of transnational business. Of course, the negotiation process contemplates the enforceability of contractual provisions under the relevant applicable law. That said, the reality is that not all contractual provisions are created equal and there are factors that will impede a complete review, including time restraints and budgetary concerns. There are also the 'unknown' factors, stemming from cultural gaps or linguistic limitations in some cases, or simply from the state of the law in others, to mention only a few. Finally, there are contracts that can be considered as the 'unseen unknowns'.

Section 1 of this chapter outlines the starting point and some of the elements of the negotiation process, seeking to explain why, in practice,

---

[*] The views and opinions in this chapter are solely those of the author and should in no way be construed to represent in whole or in part those of General Electric or any other person or legal entity. The author would like to thank Kai-Uwe Karl, whose suggestions and edits were invaluable.

[1] While there are different 'processes' for different types of contracts, this chapter will focus on one-off transactions and will only touch upon others, be they public tenders, frame agreements or other forms of contractual arrangements.

there may be gaps between 'standard contracts' and 'national legal requirements'. Section 2 briefly reviews the findings.

1   How it all got started

While there is no 'prescribed' procedure for negotiating high-value or strategic international contracts, companies normally initiate the process by exchanging their respective standard terms of purchase and sale. Following generally accepted commercial practice, the starting point for the negotiations are the buyer's terms of purchase. After the initial exchange, the buyer will generally be in the position to insist on the usage of its contractual template subject to the rules of supply and demand and some general exceptions. For example, in some markets a seller may possess a particularly strong bargaining position, such as that of a sole supplier. In addition, there are some sectors that do not follow this general rule, including software, IT and telephony providers when contracting outside their internal markets, who are commonly able to insist on the use of their respective terms of sale. However, in general, the seller normally accepts the buyer's terms as the starting point of the negotiation process and will thereafter reply with a number of counterproposals modifying the buyer's original contractual language.

A distinction should be drawn between large-scale companies and their smaller counterparts. The former will normally have legal counsel 'in house' and the quantity and type of counterproposals will reflect this fact, whereas smaller companies normally do not have easy access to such additional resources (at least without incurring additional costs) and generally provide fewer counterproposals. Furthermore, in the latter case, as the reviewer is likely to possess a commercial rather than a legal background, the comments will reflect this fact and normally emphasise the commercial rather than the legal contractual provisions.

1.1   Not all contractual terms are created equal

Setting the commercial and technical aspects of the contract aside, the negotiation process typically focuses on a few select legal issues, such as warranty, limitation of liability, termination, dispute resolution and the governing law provisions of the contract. The extent to which individual contractual provisions are reviewed from the point of view of national legal requirements will depend on the importance of the individual provision to one or the other party.

While most contractual provisions are negotiable, specifically meaning in this context that a party would be willing to assume additional risks including the risk of enforceability if it receives benefits elsewhere in the contract or by price adjustment, others will be considered as 'deal breakers'. In the latter case, a party would rather walk away from the negotiations than accept certain contractual terms and the associated risk.

> The author was involved in a transaction where the parties were negotiating a long-term international maintenance contract with an expected duration of fifteen years. When the buyer insisted on having the right to terminate the contract for convenience on very short notice and at no cost, the seller elected to break off the negotiations. Granting the buyer such a right would have undermined the long-term nature of the transaction and in effect would have allocated a significant degree of risk to the seller. This situation was exacerbated by the fact that the seller's business model caused it to assume greater costs in the initial stages of the contract that it planned to have offset by the long-term nature of the agreement.

Whether a contractual provision shall constitute a 'deal breaker' or an acceptable risk that can be mitigated will depend on the risk tolerance of the individual company. For example, under French law, it is inherently difficult to enforce a limitation of liability clause in case of latent defects. To avoid this issue, an international seller may attempt to nominate New York or English law as the governing law where a limitation of liability for latent defects generally stands. However, there will often be strong commercial pressure on the seller to accept French law when contracting with a French buyer insisting on the application of the laws of its home country. In such a scenario, the seller will be compelled to determine whether it is willing to accept this particular allocation of risk that is difficult to mitigate. There are circumstances where the buyer, in turn, will consider the application of its governing law as a deal breaker, as is often the case when it is a state-controlled or state-owned legal entity. Using the same example of latent defects, it may be the case that both parties would consider French law as a deal breaker, the buyer insisting on its usage and the seller rejecting it.

In any event, irrespective of whether or not a contractual provision constitutes a deal breaker, one party will typically have a considerable interest in ensuring that the provision in question is enforceable in case of a dispute. If this cannot be determined in-house, a corporation will often seek advice from outside counsel.

> *The author was involved in a transaction with a French state-owned company buying equipment from a non-French company. The French party insisted on the application of French law and rejected English law, and, as a compromise proposal, accepted the application of Swiss law. Before signing the contract, the non-French party made a considerable investment in analysing the risks relating to the enforceability of the relevant limitation of liability and how such risks could be mitigated.*

On the other hand, there are a number of boilerplate provisions that take second place in the negotiations process, such as inspection, access and audit rights. The parties may not even have an active interest in negotiating some of these provisions and will be less concerned as to whether any such provisions are in line with the national legal requirements under whatever governing law may be applicable.

> *The author was involved in a number of transactions where the governing law was changed in the course of the negotiations without a full review being conducted as to the repercussions of the change of the governing law on certain standard clauses.*

In addition, second rank provisions are often used as bargaining chips during the negotiations process.

> *For example, in an international contract for the purchase of industrial pumps for integration into the buyer's equipment, the buyer required the seller to provide access to its facilities to inspect equipment from a safety perspective, to ensure the seller was making progress under a production schedule and to perform testing. The seller counterproposed a certain amount of advance notice to be provided prior to allowing access and attempted to define the limits of testing to ensure any additional testing would be at the buyer's expense. While safety, access and testing form part of the standard contractual obligations and both parties had an interest in avoiding disruptions and ensuring timely performance, the seller made 'concessions' regarding access rights with the view of receiving other concessions for provisions it valued more highly.*

In fact, granting concessions on issues of minor importance with the view of receiving them on what a party considers as the important contractual clauses should properly be viewed as a negotiation strategy. Even under the circumstances where a party is in a very strong bargaining position, it will generally give a little ground on issues of lesser importance in order to not appear to misuse its strong position. In addition, there are a number of cultural factors to be considered in the interplay of the give-and-take process that varies considerably according to custom and region.

A party may also insist on including certain legal provisions in the contract without being overly concerned as to whether such rules would be enforceable before a court of law. The sole purpose of such contractual provisions may be to influence the behaviour of the other party, and the simple insertion of the clause may be sufficient to achieve compliance in the majority of cases, without that party ever having to enforce such a rule in front of a court or arbitral tribunal.

> For example, contractual terms often reference or include business and ethical codes of conduct. While such codes form part of the contractual obligations assumed by the parties, their main purpose is to put the other party on notice of ethical rather than legal responsibilities.

Finally, the negotiation process is an active and dynamic process, and there are many moving parts when the parties negotiate the terms and conditions for a particular transaction. While parties normally attempt to narrow down the open points as they go through the process and thereafter try to not go back on matters that have been agreed as 'closed', there are no hard and fast rules. Often the personnel negotiating the contract must seek approval at the end of the process from senior management, who may have a different opinion on the acceptable allocation of contractual risk.

> For example, the author was involved in a multimillion-dollar transaction between a European buyer and a South American seller for construction services to be performed in South America. The parties agreed to use a modified version of the buyer's contract with its client as the starting point for the negotiations. Such supply contracts are commonly known as 'flow down contracts' as they seek to align the contractual responsibilities of the supply base with those of the buyer under the client-facing contract. The flow down contract contained a choice of the governing law of the State of New York. In a final business meeting where no lawyers were present, the question of the law governing the transaction was revisited and became part of a wider negotiation. It was agreed to change the governing law, and there was no time to fully review the impact of the new governing law on each contractual provision so that the review was limited to determining whether assuming any additional contractual risk was acceptable in light of the commercial benefits that were achieved.

1.2 Imperfect information

In practice, parties negotiate contracts based on imperfect information, whether it is because of linguistic barriers, the actual state of the law or simply due to a lack of time and resources.

One significant factor is that of language. While the English language is generally considered as the *lingua franca* of international contracts, the corresponding performance may occur anywhere on the globe. Where performance occurs in locations where neither the buyer nor the seller have the requisite ability to efficiently conduct business in the local language, not all of the relevant national legal requirements may form part of the negotiations.

> For example, for an EPC project to be performed in Angola on behalf of a US oil major with an associated contract governed by US law, the supply contract was divided into two parts, as commonly is the case. One part was the offshore or international contract for the work to be performed outside of Angola and the other part was a local contract for the work to be performed in country. All three of the contracts were written in the English language. However, as both the buyer and the seller in the supply contract only had a very limited local presence in Angola, neither had the necessary language capabilities to review the local Angolan legal requirements written in Portuguese.

A related issue is the actual state of law in the relevant national legal system. Legislation, decrees and special laws may in some cases create a myriad of rules that can cause the actual state of the law to be ambiguous or contradictory and, as a result, unknown to the parties. This difficulty is heightened by the fact that many complex issues will never have been brought before the courts and, as a result, there may be no indication on how a law or a series of different laws would be applied in practice. Furthermore, even where companies are willing to pay local counsel for opinions on certain aspects of the law, the answers provided may not be conclusive. Another issue is that in the author's experience, it has proved extremely difficult to access legal texts in some countries, for example, in certain countries in the Middle East.

> In a contract between a state-controlled Tunisian entity and a foreign seller, the buyer insisted that the warranty provisions should include the relevant Tunisian warranty law in addition to the warranties specifically agreed to under the contract. This apparently innocuous request caused the foreign seller a great deal of difficulty, as it was unclear as to how the request impacted the contractual obligations. In particular, the question arose as to which Tunisian laws were being referred to. Was the reference limited to the warranties set out in the Tunisian code of obligations or did it also include all warranty provisions under all Tunisian laws? What would occur if there were discrepancies between the contract and the Code Civile or other relevant Tunisian law? In the end, this issue was resolved not by a complete analysis of Tunisian law that would have been

time-consuming and potentially inconclusive, but rather by stating that the only Tunisian warranty laws that would apply would be statutory laws from which the parties could not derogate.

Another set of factors that will commonly impact the consideration and implementation of the relevant national requirements are the time, resources and collective effort parties dedicate to the contract negotiation process. Parties may not be afforded sufficient time or allocate the necessary resources to negotiate all the terms and conditions. In other cases, parties simply do not take into consideration some national legal requirements that they are (or were previously) aware of, fail to keep their knowledge of national laws up-to-date or, alternatively, do not have the economic resources to take such legal requirements into consideration in the first place.

> *To take a pertinent example, state-owned public entities often issue public tenders for high-value and complex infrastructure projects with very tight deadlines. In one such project in South America, the bidders were international consortiums of engineering and construction companies along with their historic supply base and local companies providing materials and services in-country. The time constraints were severe on the parties forming consortiums to agree to contractual terms and conditions, as they were required to simultaneously prepare the technical aspects of the bid. Faced with this scenario, it was therefore not practicable for the bidders to consider all aspects of the applicable national law. Rather, the parties' past contractual dealings, along with their experience in-country, determined the extent of the inclusion of the national legal requirements. The parties that had a pre-existing contractual agreement relationship, where they worked together on a very similar project in-country, were able to save a great deal of time and could perform a more indepth review of the relevant national law. For the other bidders who did not have a past relationship, the time constraints effectively precluded the examination and inclusion of some aspects of the relevant national legal requirements, in particular, the local mandatory law.*

1.3   Non-negotiated contracts

Another point is worthwhile noting. In actual practice, the large majority of contracts placed by companies are automatically generated and performed without the parties ever reaching a final written agreement or complying with the formal legal requirements regarding acceptance. While such a state of affairs may cause a certain degree of astonishment, it can be explained as being due to the sheer volume of contracts generated by companies that are necessary for the performance of day-to day-operations. Most of these contracts are for small values and often are repetitive in nature, making negotiation a practical impossibility. While a great majority of these contracts are domestic in scope, a certain number are international. Needless to say, in these cases there is no review of the relevant national legal requirements and its inclusion will be entirely dependent upon whether the boilerplate language accurately captured the law in the first place and the formal requirements of the relevant governing law.

2   The end result

2.1   The contract as an imperfect compromise

Where the parties come from different legal systems, the final negotiated contract will often reflect this fact and contain a mixture of principles from both the buyer's and seller's respective legal traditions. This fact alone will often not cause difficulties in the performance of the parties' respective contractual obligations. In the event of a dispute, however, such issues, along with the extent to which national legal requirements were incorporated into the final agreement, may have serious consequences.

2.2   Consequences

The legal and commercial consequences vary when the parties' final agreement does not incorporate all of the relevant national legal requirements.

In one sub-set, the party that has assumed the contractual responsibility in question will bear the associated costs. Taking the example of a seller performing services in Angola, if, in the final contract, the seller contractually agreed to take responsibility for all taxes related to its performance, it follows that it will be held to bear any additional costs imposed under Angolan law. This will be the case regardless as to whether the seller was unaware of the particular service tax during the negotiation phase.

In other cases, both parties will assume the consequences of the failure to include the relevant national law requirements, such as the requirement for international Russian contracts to be written in Russian and English. Should the parties fail to respect this particular obligation, they collectively run the risk of the contract being found to be null and void by the competent legal authority. In such cases, the parties' rights and obligations under the final contract may, in fact, be very different from what the parties actually intended, and the validity of the contract itself may be put into question. Such a result would come as a surprise even to sophisticated parties.

2

Multinational companies and national contracts

MARIA CELESTE VETTESE

1 Introduction

Using a critical approach, the aim of this chapter is to analyse the use of international contracts in day-to-day business in order to assess the limits and the enforceability of clauses contained in standard documents with respect to local legislation.The use of common structures becomes the normal way of drafting international contracts, and these documents are the basis for the discussion between the parties. But where do those standard documents come from? It is important, especially for in-house lawyers, to critically understand the origin of these common contractual structures in order to assess problems that may be related to their use. This analysis will then start by explaining the origin of such standardisation practice and the reasoning behind it.

The globalisation of business, due to the global footprint of corporate transactions, allowed the development of standard international contracts. Terminology and legal concepts related to these international contracts do, in fact, come more often from common law environments rather than from civil law systems. The reason for this influence by the common law system can be found in the strong economic push given in the last century to the development of business[1] by the Anglo-American system. The continuous use of the same type of international contracts creates standard documentation for day-to-day business.

On the other hand, companies have a strong need for internal standardisation, which in turn enhances the use of standard documentation in day-to-day working life. Standardisation means a reduction of internal costs because the complexity in the exchange of information is

---

[1] G. Cordero-Moss, 'Harmonized Contract Clauses in Different Business Cultures', in T. Wihelmsson, E. Paunio, A. Pohjolainen (eds.), *Private Law and the Main Cultures of Europe* (Kluwer International, 2007), pp. 221–239.

a very costly activity. In the legal field, the discussion over interpretations and the definition of applicable rules are costs that can cause losses in terms of competitiveness and/or economic perspectives. As a matter of fact, it has also been observed that legal communities create networks that reduce transaction costs between agents, and their value increases as more agents adopt them.[2] Therefore, one important step of the standardisation process is to find a common language that can help to create a harmonisation of concepts. For all these reasons, the use of standard documents is strongly supported in day-to-day business life.

Examples of this trend for standardisation can be found in most of the functions of a company (i.e., information technology, engineering, production, procurement, finance and, of course, legal matters). In the accounting area, for example, companies belonging to an international group, albeit based in different countries, are requested to adopt either international or local accounting principles. When analysing the standardisation of accounting principles, various legislative solutions have been established in order to supersede the differences existing between countries' legislations. To give an example, in Italy, a legislation intervention occurred so that companies that issue listed securities, and even financial institutions, are required to adopt International Financing Reporting Standards (IFRS) like companies belonging to international groups. Thus, in the field of accounting principles, the standardisation process took place by legislative intervention. Nevertheless, standardisation in the legal field is more challenging since it is more difficult to supersede local differences. As for the contractual area, this massive legislative intervention is ongoing. A lot of work has been done within the EU regarding the harmonisation process and further work is under discussion. In the Green Paper[3] on the conversion of the Rome Convention of 1980, the need for the harmonisation of international private law is described and seen as one of the ways to avoid a possible lack of uniformity and certainty that may create a disruption and unjustified advantage to the involved parties.

---

[2] Legrand defines legal culture as 'the framework of intangibles within which interpretative community operates, which has normative force for this community [...] and which, over the longue duree, determines the identity of a community as community': P. Legrand, *Fragment on Law-as Culture* (W. E. J. Tjeen Willink, Schhordijk Institute, 1999).

[3] Commission of the European Communities, *Green Paper on the conversion of the Rome Convention of 1980 on the law applicable to contractual obligations into a Community instrument and its modernisation*, COM (2002) 654 final.

The importance of harmonisation has been recognised at the Community level,[4] but there is still discussion regarding the extent of such harmonisation. In any case, notwithstanding the legislative discussion, in day-to-day business the use of standard documentation is widespread; however, standardisation in the legal field is not as easy as it is in other functions or areas of companies (such as finance). The difficulties lie in the historical differences existing between legal systems and, moreover, in the legal field, the harmonisation of documents does not mean the automatic harmonisation of concepts.

Another important reason as to why the use of standard documentation is strongly supported in a corporation is related to the stakeholder of these contracts. We have to consider that day-to-day contractual negotiations take place in many cases between commercial or technical people and without a lawyer being present. It is easy to understand how standard documents are very helpful in these situations. This reason, combined with a lack of sufficient time when discussing contracts, has allowed the further development of standard documents.

Now that we have defined and analysed the reasons as to why standardisation has become so important in day-to-day business life, we should then focus on which problems are related to the standardisation processes in the legal field.

Standardisation in the legal field encounters obstacles in the historical differences existing between legal systems. As we have observed, common structures originate from common law systems. These standard documents have been transplanted into other environments not pertaining to the original common law systems. Therefore, the use of common contracts developed in common law countries by 'different law' countries raises a variety of problems related to the legal theory of the transplant. We need, then, to focus our analysis on the transplanting problems related to the use of common law drafted contracts and also to the meaning that those contracts have in their country of origin.

2   Standard contractual structures, their impact on national legislations and the expectations of the parties

The transplant of standard instruments developed in common law countries into other specific legal systems can create problems related

---

[4] For a further analysis of the status of the Europeanisation of contract law, see C. Twigg–Flesner, *The Europeanization of Contract Law* (Routledge-Cavendish, 2008).

to the enforceability and validity of standard contractual clauses with respect to local legislation requirements. In order to carry out a proper evaluation activity, lawyers need to spend time and pay sufficient attention to the intended use of the clause they have decided to use and to the specific situation they are facing. These characteristics are seldom at our disposal in typical hectic working days. Standard draft contracts and, in particular, 'boilerplate' clauses represent a good summary of the best practice developed in day-to-day business life.

Boilerplate clauses, in fact, are the result of best practises developed with respect to the allocation of typical risk policies, as are present in contracts. In this respect and according to this point of view, the use of standard documents is useful as a basis for discussion in our daily work in this respect. Nevertheless, a critical assessment of these clauses must be done before using them, in order for them to remain viable instruments. Through some practical examples, implementation problems can be more easily understood.

Before analysing these practical examples, it is important to underline the role that contracts play in the company. Contracts are, in fact, the instruments that define roles, identify responsibilities and contain the expectations of the parties as a result of their contractual relationship. Contracts are considered to be an exchange of promises whereby the parties identify their common understanding of what their expectations are with respect to the transaction. Contracts are the principal instrument by which companies communicate with each other. Monateri defines the contract as the most important example of globalisation within the legal system.[5] The length or the complexity of contractual dispositions can dramatically change depending on whether the common law approach or the civil law approach is used.

In fact, one of the main differences between the common law approach and the civil law approach to contracts was correctly expressed in the definition given by Monateri, who qualifies Anglo-American contracts as 'tough' contracts ('contratto rude') and European continental contracts as dewy contracts ('contratto rugiadoso'). Common law contracts have been characterised by the principle of certainty and predictability.[6]

---

[5] P. G. Monateri, 'Lex Mercatoria e competizione fra ordinamenti', *Rivista di Sociologia del Diritto*, 2, 3 (2005), 229–240.

[6] G. Cordero-Moss, 'International Contracts between Common Law and Civil Law: Is Non-state Law to be Preferred? The Difficulty of Interpreting Legal Standards such as Good Faith', *Global Jurist (Advances)*, 7 (2007), 1.

Effects of this principle can be found in the extremely detailed definition of the duty and rights of the parties ('tough contracts' in Monateri's definition). Monateri deems that 'tough contracts' are the result of a market battle, and the contract can be defined as a 'temporary truce' between the parties.[7] For that reason, in the common law approach, everything referring to the parties' relation (duties, onus, etc.) is defined inside the contract with little possibility for the judge to intervene. On the contrary, civil law systems can rely on the definition contained in the civil or commercial codes whereby the substance and fundamental structure of the different types of contracts are clearly identified. For that reason, in Continental Europe, traditional contracts were less detailed than in the common law countries. In any case, the technique used in the common law system clearly prevailed in day-to-day business use even in the civil law countries, so that currently it is almost impossible to even draft contracts without having in mind the common law system structure.

After having clarified the importance of contracts for the company's life and the substantial differences existing between the common and civil law approaches, the practical effect caused by having an enforceability problem of specific contractual clauses becomes quite clear.

The first characteristic of a contract is to reflect the expectation of the parties and consequently their risk allocation. Therefore, the first negative impact of the unenforceability of contractual clauses will be on the expectations of the parties; parties will not be able to rely on a correct assessment of their expectations and will not have an efficient allocation of the economic (but also technical) risks connected to the transaction.

We can then start our analysis of specific boilerplate clauses in order to analyse the practical effect of what was discussed above.

One of the most frequently used clauses is the one related to transfer of title whereby INCOTERMS are often used as a reference. Transfer of title is one of the most important contractual clauses, considering its impact on revenue recognition. Generally accepted accounting principles (GAAP), in fact, state strict rules in order to assess if and how revenues can be recognised, and these rules are referred to in the occurrence of a transfer of title. It is easy to understand how the problem related to the transfer of the title of the goods plays an essential role in the overall economic risk assessment of a contract and how a wrong allocation of this risk can create a disruption caused by a discrepancy between the contractual instrument used and the expectation of the parties. In order

---

[7] Monateri, 'Lex Mercatoria e competizione fra ordinamenti'.

to have correct revenue recognition, transfer of title must be clearly identified and defined under the contract. If contractual clauses do not support the transfer of title in a proper manner, we may face severe problems. In day-to-day business, parties normally rely on INCOTERMS in order to define transfer of title. From a legal perspective, this is not a correct way of proceeding, as these rules are not applicable to the transfer of the title of the goods. INCOTERMS play an important role in the harmonisation and creation of a common basis of discussion in order to set up a way to define transportation and responsibilities connected with transportation. Nevertheless, rules defined in these conditions cannot be taken as a definition of rules applicable to transfer of title. If the parties want to achieve a clear transfer of title ruling, they must refer to the applicable legislation. INCOTERMS rule transportation and delivery but not transfer of title. Therefore, transfer of title must be treated in the contract in a proper autonomous way so that when and how goods become the property of the other party are clearly defined. This is one of the examples of a disruption with important economic effects caused by a negative or incorrect legal assessment during the negotiation phase. In the above-mentioned case, in fact, if the parties do not have a proper and clearly identified clause in the contract as to how to transfer the title, they can face problems in the realisation of their revenues.

Another important boilerplate clause is the one related to the termination for breach of contract. The effect of the termination under most civil law and common law jurisdictions is different. Common law will, in most cases, expect a damage recovery from a breach of contract, whereby the civil law may experience the intervention of a specific performance awarded by the judge. As Oliver Wendell Holmes stated in 1881: 'The only universal consequence of a legally binding promise is that the law makes the promisor pay damages if the promised act does not come to pass.'[8] Consequences on the expectations of the parties can be very different when considering these general principles of law. What will happen from a risk point of view if one of the parties does not consider the risk of specific performance as an actual risk? Specific performance can be expensive with respect to payment of damages (i.e., needing to reorganise the production in order to achieve the order of performance). Payment of damages can be less expensive. Let us then imagine the following scenario to help and clarify: a contract is entered into between A and B. A, which is expecting performance from B, is a

[8] O. W. Holmes, *The Common Law* (Little Brown, 1881), p. 301.

civil law-oriented party and B is a common law-oriented party. The contract, drafted in a common law style, contains an exclusion clause, whereby all remedies other than those referred to in the contract are excluded. The contract is governed by Italian law. If B did not identify the specific performance as an occurrence, once this happens it will face severe economic impact. In fact, under Italian law, termination remedies are defined by the law and there are serious doubts as to whether these remedies can be excluded by the parties. In this case, then, the parties may face enforceability problems with respect to their exclusion clause and one of the parties may be forced to execute the contract as a consequence of an award in that sense.

The above exclusion clauses underscore an important tendency existing in the drafting of an international standard contract that aims to eliminate any influence from local legislation by inserting specific exclusion clauses under the contract. The expectation of the parties is to create a barrier from the real world – the state legislation must not affect the contractual relationship, but can the parties actually avoid any influence from the 'real world?' It is not always possible to create a completely 'untouchable' contract. Considering the above-mentioned exclusion clause as an example, Article 1462 of the Italian Civil Code does not allow the parties to exclude remedies related to the nullity or validity of a contract. Another important boilerplate clause on exclusion of remedy is the one related to the exclusion of any increase in price. The expectation of the parties is to define a general waiver of the possibility to request an increase of price due to unforeseeable events in order to avoid, for example, any claim for extra costs or any possibility of requesting a price increase due to inflation of the costs of raw materials (these types of clauses are normally defined as 'hardship clauses' in the common law system).

It is the important impact on the profitability of a contract that is easy to understand. An increase in the cost of raw materials and the postponement of the execution of the contract are fundamental issues connected with the worldwide economic crisis. The possibility of excluding these types of remedies is still under discussion under Italian law. In particular, much discussion has taken place regarding whether the exclusion of these remedies is allowed on a specific type of contract, namely 'appalto' (construction contracts). What happens if exclusion clauses are not enforceable once the case is in front of an Italian court? Can these clauses be considered as a 'styled clause' and thus consequently have no effect, or are those clauses null and void and therefore we have to assume the nullity of the entire contract? In any case, this matter of unclear interpretation is of paramount economic impact.

This issue is unclear from a doctrine point of view. From a practical perspective, it is an economic risk. What would happen in the event that the contractor applies for a price revision notwithstanding a contrary contractual disposition and the judge follows its position?

The solution is to insert at the end of any clause a borderline statement with the following wording – 'to the extent permitted by applicable law'. This can be a good knowledge-management solution once we have experience that a clause can become null, but from the allocation of a risk point of view, the problem was not treated and the risk was not allocated. Therefore, as a consequence, the expectations of the parties have not been met! However, if we have solved the legal problem connected with the nullity of a contract, from a risk management point of view, the expected effects of the clause cannot be met and therefore the parties cannot rely on the solution they identified at the beginning of the contractual negotiations. It is important to duly note that a proper allocation of risks from an economic point of view takes into consideration only the company and not the discussed legal solution.

As we showed at the beginning of this chapter, the aim of the standardisation is to create common principles, but we also observed that this activity is not so easily accomplished in the legal field considering all the differences between legal systems. Indirect and mostly consequential damages are a good example of the problem related to the definition of common principles.

Damages are one of the most 'important' legal ghosts existing in the field of contract law, due to their potential economic and financial impact. It is then easy to understand that a correct allocation of risk with respect to damages is of the utmost importance for the profitability of the entire contract. The expectation of the parties is doubled with respect to damages remedies: on one side, there is the expectation of one party that wants to be indemnified for all damages arising from the contract and caused by the other party; and, on the other side, there is the expectation of the other party to limit its liability. Therefore, the trigger point in the discussion of these clauses is the damages and what type of damages can be identified with regard to the responsibilities. Under the general name of damages we find, in standard clauses on limitation of liability, reference to the words 'indirect and consequential damages'. But what types of damages are identified by the words 'consequential' and 'indirect' damages? Problems connected to the lack of uniformity in the definition of common principles arise with respect to these definitions.

Italian law, as well as law in other civil law countries, does not utilise the word 'consequential'. Therefore, if a clause drafted in a common law environment is transplanted in Italy and literally translated, what should the consequences be from a legal point of view? To thoroughly understand this question, the definition of 'consequential losses' under common law systems must be clarified. My research in the common law area had been promptly driven in the right direction by a good friend, the Queen's Counsel: the question is not to look for a definition of 'consequential damages' but to understand on which of the limbs of the famous *Hadley* v. *Baxendale* decision the damages fall. I then fully understood why, in the last few years, in the common law system, especially in England and Wales, the reason why the clause related to indirect and consequential losses suffered an important drafting alteration. It is primarily related to the deep debate on the distinction between the first and the second limbs of the *Hadley* v. *Baxendale* decision.[9]

A little history on the debate can be helpful to understand the historical background we are discussing. Since the time of the *Victoria Laundry*,[10] the standard clauses on exclusion of consequential losses had been drafted without further explanation or definition as to what kind of losses were part of the definition of consequential losses. After some important cases in the last decade,[11] a standard clause on exclusion or limitation of consequential losses would be drafted by including a list of the possible damages that could occur (e.g., loss of profit, loss of use and loss of revenues). This was done in order to avoid a general reference to indirect and consequential damages, as had been done in the past. In fact, before these milestone cases, we had clauses drafted in a way that did not provide for a specific list of indirect and consequential losses, thus providing only general references to indirect and consequential damages. After the intervention of the judges, reliable clauses on indirect and consequential damages have been drafted by making a list of different types of damages (e.g., loss of profit, loss of use and loss of revenues). Italian law does not contemplate the wording 'consequential losses'

---

[9] *Hadley* v. *Baxendale* (1854) EWHC Exch J70.
[10] *Victoria Laundry Ltd* v. *Newman Industries Ltd* [1949] 1 All ER 997, [1949] 2 KB 528, CA.
[11] Among the most representatives cases on this debate are: *Hotel Services Ltd* v. *Hilton International Hotels (UK) Ltd* [1997] EWCA Civ 1822; and *British Sugar Plc* v. *Nei Power Projects Ltd* (1997) 87 Build LR 42, CA.

because it defines two categories of damages related to *lucrum cessan* and '*danno emergente*'. As in the common law system, loss of profit and loss of use can be interpreted as falling into one category or the other by virtue of the application of the general principles existing on damages.

For that reason, due to the lack of uniformity in the interpretation of the word 'consequential', we had to figure out a practical solution that helped the day-to-day business community to supersede the uncertainty in the legal field. The evolution of indirect and consequential damages is very important for various reasons. First, it underscores the implied practical effects after some important cases failed in front of the court. Secondly, it also helped us to understand that transplanting clauses from other legal systems does not imply that the clauses are interpreted in accordance with the interpretation made in their country of origin.

We started our analysis by considering that standard contracts have been modelled on the common law system. We now have to consider the evolution given by solutions defined by day-to-day practices that do not strictly pertain to the common law system. The interpreter must pay more attention in order to verify the content and the extent of the clauses analysed, and therefore the interpreter must also consider their meaning in the respective country of origin.

To some extent, standard contracts are no longer strictly referred to in the common law system, as they have been manipulated in such a way that the origin has been obscured. We can refer to the Hayek[12] theory in order to understand this principle. Hayek stated that the law (as opposed to legislation, which is based on authority) drives the selection of the most efficient rules for all the community! This is the same process that occurs in the discussion related to international contracts where, at the end, the parties need to find out a common basis for discussion in an economically efficient way.

3   The in-house lawyer perspective

Therefore, given all of the above, from an in-house lawyer's perspective, and in addition to the standard contract models, we have to consider that the evolution of the drafting of the international contract was influenced by another important instrument related to the internal regulations of companies. Internal regulations provide rules and direction on some

---

[12] F. A. von Hayek, *Law, Legislation and Liberty, Vol. I, Rules and Order* (University of Chicago Press, 1973).

important issues related to risk allocation (e.g., best practice in the drafting of contractual clauses). Most of the time, this *corpus iuris* is a good mixture between common practice and the law, whereby the benchmark is often given by the law of the parent company.[13] For this reason, in-house lawyers need to face and deal with their own internal regulations in their analysis of the contractual relationship. Sometimes a risk can be the difficulty in finding the line between the company's internal regulations and the applicable state law, especially if the former is very detailed and strict. Internal regulations can then be considered as another important factor that influences the evolution of the drafting of international standard contracts.

After having considered the origins and the practical impact of the standardisation of international contracts, we can conclude that multiple factors influence the day-to-day business discussion over contracts. One of the most important driving factors that we have analysed is the reduction of the influence of local legislation. In fact, it has been observed that drafters of international contracts aim to reduce, as much as possible, the interpretation and 'uncertainty' relating to applicable contract law and to the interpretation in the litigation phase.[14] The drafters' strong desire is the achievement of self-management: the parties want to decide and govern their own rules with respect to the contract they are drafting.

Conversely, we can observe that contractual clauses are drafted in a specific manner in order to allocate the risks related to specific trans-actions and normally should come both from experience (a sort of distillation of best practices) and from the interpretation of the law. For that reason, considering that standardisation provides help in creat-ing a common base of discussion between the parties and makes it possible to work on the differences, it is important to conclude that there are differences between legal systems and that those differences can create an unexpected situation if questions are raised in front of a court or in an arbitration. In addition, to ignore differences and to believe that it is possible to create a neutral legal system is a chimera and cannot be considered a correct allocation of the risks. It is of the utmost

---

[13] It is in fact likely to find a *corpus iuris* influenced by the common law in companies belonging to or owned by a company from a common law system, even though the business may be carried out in non-common law countries.

[14] M. Fontaine and F. De Ly, *La redazione dei contratti internazionali*, Italian translation by Renzo Maria Morresi (Giuffrè Editore, 2006), pp. 806–820.

importance for an in-house lawyer to know that differences exist between legal systems and also to understand the reason why clauses have been drafted in a specific manner. Only with this awareness will in-house lawyers be able to correctly allocate the expectations of their stakeholders.

We can then easily understand how the contract regulation effectively becomes a truce between different factors such as internal regulations, standard documents and the requirements of the stakeholders. The role of the in-house lawyer is to define and analyse, with respect to the expectations of the parties, if and how the instruments at the lawyer's disposal are the right ones.

The scope of an in-house lawyer's role is to best allocate the risk relating to the transaction by combining the need for the internal procedures of the company and the law applicable to the specific situation. The use of standard documents can be a helpful instrument in day-to-day business if used with a critical assessment during contract negotiations.

This critical allocation of the risk must follow a defined process: the first step is to understand the expectation of the parties (what we are intending to allocate); then it is necessary to verify the enforceability of the proposed instruments (by answering the following question: are the clauses that we are using enforceable under the applicable law?); and the last step is to verify that the correct instrument to be used. Without a critical assessment of the proposed standard contract, no positive risk allocation can be done.

PART 2

Methodological challenges

~

Introduction to Part 2

Part 1 showed that international contracts are often written on the basis of common law-inspired models and do not regard the applicable law as a guide to the drafting. Before turning to how the various national laws may affect the interpretation and application of an international contract (which will be the subject of Part 3), some methodological questions must be addressed. The circumstance that international contracts are drafted without taking into particular consideration the requirements and assumptions of any particular contract law may seem hard to reconcile with the necessity of interpreting and applying international contracts in accordance with a particular law.

Taking contract practice as a starting point, the observer could be tempted to question whether an international contract shall be subject to a law that was not considered during the drafting. However, when seeking solutions that adequately cater to the peculiarities of international contract drafting, it is necessary to bear in mind their feasibility and effectiveness. Does the drafting constitute a sufficiently clear basis for selecting the governing law? Are harmonised sources available on a transnational level and capable of fully regulating the interpretation and application of contracts, thus making national contract laws redundant?

In Chapter 3, Giuditta Cordero-Moss analyses the implications that the style of contract drafting may have when choosing the governing law. Chapter 3 verifies to what extent generally acknowledged rules, trade usages or transnational restatements of principles may contribute to overcoming the tension between the style of the contract and the law governing it. Gerhard Dannemann reports in Chapter 4 how German courts have been coping with the methodological challenges of contracts modelled on a foreign legal tradition. In Chapter 5, Edward T. Canuel analyses how common law courts interpret and apply the contractual mechanism of exculpatory clauses. He finds that these clauses have varying legal effects even within the same legal family, thus showing that it is not always appropriate to expect that the wording of the contract will be applied equally irrespective of the governing law. If the same wording may have different legal effects within the same legal family, even larger discrepancies may be expected when the involved legal traditions belong to different families. Jean-Sylvestre Bergé observes in Chapter 6 that the circulation of legal models is a phenomenon occurring on different levels and shows that the system of the EU forces acceptance of legal concepts belonging to different legal traditions.

3

Does the use of common law contract models give rise to a tacit choice of law or to a harmonised, transnational interpretation?

GIUDITTA CORDERO-MOSS

Before turning to how the various national laws may affect the interpretation and application of an international contract (which will be the subject of Part 3 of this book), some methodological questions must be addressed. Should an international contract be governed by a national law different from the one that inspired its drafting? Should an international contract be governed by a national law at all? Rather, should not an international contract be subject to a harmonised, transnational law? The thesis of this chapter is that the applicable law should be chosen according to the general conflict rules, even though this would lead to a situation where the contract is governed by a law different from the law that inspired it. Furthermore, the contract is ultimately subject to a state law, even though the underlying transaction is international. These two aspects are dealt with separately in Sections 1 and 2 below.

1 Does the drafting style imply a choice of the applicable law?

The first question regards the choice of the applicable law. An international contract is potentially governed by the laws of at least two different countries, those with which the legal relationship has a connection: these could be the countries where the parties have their respective place of business, the country where the contract is to be performed or other countries with which the contract had other connections.

A judge who has to decide a question arising out of an international contract first of all has to find out which law governs. To do so, the judge will look at the private international law of his or her own country. As is known, private international law, also called conflict of laws or choice-of-law rules, is a branch of the national law of every single legal system, which means that each private international law might contain its own peculiar rules to identify which country's substantive law governs the contract. This might lead to a considerable lack of harmony in the field of international contracts, because the identity of the law governing the contract might change according to which private international law is applied, i.e., according to which country the proceeding was started in. To avoid this undesirable result, many rules of private international law have been made uniform by international convention or supranational instruments.

The most relevant supranational instrument in the area that is of interest here is the EU Regulation 593 of 2008, known as 'Rome I', which is the successor of the Rome Convention of 1980 on the Law Applicable to Contractual Obligations, binding the members of the European Community. The Rome I Regulation is the private international law in the area of contracts that prevails across the whole EU, with the exception of Denmark, in respect of which the Rome Convention still applies.

In the field of commercial contracts, the most important connection that determines the governing law is the choice made by the parties, so-called party autonomy. In the Rome I Regulation, party autonomy is regulated in Article 3. If the contract contains a choice-of-law clause or if the parties have afterwards specified which law shall regulate their relationship, the contract will have to be interpreted in accordance with that law and will have to be subject to the rules of that law. If the parties have not chosen the governing law, this will be determined by other conflict rules, based on various connecting factors – in Article 4 of the Rome I Regulation, the connecting factor is the seat of the party making the characteristic performance.

The question that will be examined below is: how explicitly do the parties have to choose the governing law? If the contract contains a choice-of-law clause determining that the contract is to be governed by a civilian law, for example, Norwegian law, the choice is expressed clearly. However, if the contract is written on the basis of a common law model and contains some clauses that do not make any sense under Norwegian law but have a clear effect under the original law, could the parties be deemed to have made a tacit choice of the original law for that particular part of the contract? The Rome I Regulation permits different parts of the contract to be subject to the law of a different country, and this could theoretically be an example of this principle of severability.

The question of tacit choice of law would become even clearer if the contract did not contain any choice of law at all, so that it would be quite legitimate to scrutinise whether the parties meant to subject the whole contract (as opposed to only part of it) to the system of origin of the contract model. Could the parties be deemed to have made an implied choice of law in favour of the original law under which the model was developed, rather than being deemed not to have made any choice (the latter alternative would lead to the application of the law determined by the other applicable conflict rules, i.e., the seat of the party making the characteristic performance)?

As specified in Article 12 of the Rome I Regulation, the applicable law governs the interpretation and application of the contract. This extends to filling any gaps in the contract with rules of the applicable law, as well as correcting any clauses that might be contrary to mandatory rules of the governing law. Therefore, if the applicable law belongs to a civilian system, the common law-inspired contract will be fully governed by the chosen civilian law.

1.1   Tacit choice of law

The wording of Article 3 of the Rome I Regulation[1] makes it clear that, to be considered valid, a tacit choice of law has to appear as an actual choice made by the parties, even if not made expressly. Among other things, this means that the theory of the hypothetical choice of law, which was to be found prior to the Rome Convention in, for example, German private international law, is no longer applicable.[2] It is therefore not sufficient to argue that the parties (or reasonable persons under the same conditions as the parties) would have made a certain choice of law had they considered the question. A hypothetical choice of law may be a reasonable solution to the question of the governing law, but it is not allowed under the wording and the spirit of Article 3, which requires evidence that the parties have actually considered the question and have made a real choice in favour of a specific law. This actual choice of law does not need to be expressed in words and it is sufficient that it is clear from the terms of the contract or other circumstances. However, implying a choice

---

[1] 'The choice must be made expressly or clearly demonstrated by the terms of the contract or the circumstances of the case.'

[2] See M. Giuliano and P. Lagarde, *Report on the Convention on the Law Applicable to Contractual Obligations*, OJ C 282, 31.10.1980, comment to Article 3, para. 3 ('Giuliano-Lagarde Report'); and U. Magnus, *Staudingers Kommentar zum Bürgerlichen Gesetzbuch mit Einführungsgesetz und Nebegesetzen*, Einleitung zu Art 27ff EGBGB, Article 27–33 EGBGB, etc. (Sellier, 2002), Article 27, notes 60ff. with further references.

of law actually made by the parties from the circumstances is quite different from determining what would be a reasonable choice under those circumstances.

Among the examples of tacit choice made in the Giuliano-Lagarde Report to the Rome Convention is the case of a specific contract form that is known for having been written under a specific governing law, such as the Lloyd's policy of marine insurance developed under English law.[3] By applying this contract form, the parties may be deemed to have tacitly chosen English law. The Rome I Regulation has not brought any modifications to the principles of the Rome Convention in regard of tacit choice of law. Therefore, the observations made by the Giuliano-Lagarde Report under the Rome Convention, are also relevant to the Rome I Regulation.

The case of an identifiable contract form knowingly written under a certain law is quite different from the case assumed here of a contract inspired by a more generalised way of drafting agreements. The practice of general commercial contracts such as agency, distribution, sale, commercial cooperation, etc., finds its inspiration in a plurality of sources such as international standards, international commercial publications, research databases, experience from previous transactions in a variety of countries, etc. The final contract may be based on a patchwork of all these sources. This means, first, that the model upon which the contract is based may be difficult or impossible to determine. Secondly, even the legal system(s) under which the model was developed cannot be identified clearly. While it is clear that these contracts are inspired by common law, it is not usually at all justified to automatically assume that the original legal system is the English system, rather than the US system, the Australian system or any other system of common law. Even if they belong to the same legal family, there may be considerable differences between the contract laws of, for example, England and the US.[4] If the state law under which the specific contract was developed is not identifiable or if there is no international usage to subject that specific model to a specific law, the interpreter is left without rules on the interpretation of contracts, on contractual remedies, on duties between the parties, etc., that can be applied to the contract. A generic reference to the common law tradition would not be of much help.

---

[3] Giuliano-Lagarde Report.
[4] On the different legal effects a contract may have under English law and under US law, see Chapter 5 of this book by Edward Canuel.

A specific state law as a system of origin is not usually identifiable in the commercial contracts drafted as described above, and this would be sufficient to exclude the possibility that an actual choice of law is demonstrated with reasonable certainty, as the Rome I Regulation requires. In addition, the identification of a system of origin for the contract is usually impossible when international contracts are negotiated by lawyers coming from different legal systems (none of which necessarily belongs to the common law family) and on the basis of their own respective international experience and documentation. Even if it is assumed that the first draft presented by one party was developed under a specific legal system (which is not always the usual practice), the origin of that draft is not necessarily known to the other party and is generally lost during the negotiations, after each of the parties has added to and modified the clauses of the first drafts in several rounds. The final text that comes out of this process can hardly be said to permit, with reasonable certainty, the implication that the parties actually wanted to choose for their contract the law under which the first draft was originally developed (if any).

Therefore, the simple fact that the contract is written in English and follows the common law drafting technique is not sufficient to identify, with any certainty, the law under which the contract was developed. It would be totally arbitrary to assume that the parties intended English law to govern the contract, as the most representative or well-known law within that legal family. In addition, trying to apply a minimum denominator common to a majority of common law systems would be not only very vague but against the rule of Article 3 of the Rome I Regulation, which assumes a clear choice of the law of a specific state.

1.2   Closest connection

If the parties have not chosen the applicable law, the connecting factor will be, according to the first and second paragraphs in Article 4 of the Rome I Regulation, the seat of the party making the characteristic performance. The third paragraph in Article 4 provides for an exception: 'Where it is clear from all the circumstances of the case that the contract is manifestly more closely connected with a country other than that indicated in paragraphs 1 or 2, the law of that other country shall apply.' Does the circumstance whereby the contract was inspired by the common law create a connection with another country that is manifestly closer than the one based on the general conflict rule?

First of all, reference must be made to the reasoning made above in respect of the possibility of a tacit choice of law: as long as no specific state law can be identified as the system of origin of the contract, no connection with a specific country may be assumed.

Furthermore, such a connection would be irrelevant in identifying the closest connection. The wording of Article 3, specifying that the closer connection must be 'manifest', is meant to show that the exception should be applied restrictively, as recitals 20 and 21 in the preamble of the Rome I Regulation also underline. Neither the language of a contract nor the style of drafting is mentioned among the elements that would create such a connection to override the connecting factor based on the general conflict rule. That the escape clause of the closest connection shall be used restrictively is confirmed by the history of the provision. Its predecessor, Article 4 of the Rome Convention, had a different structure that gave a prominent role to the formula of the closest connection. The first paragraph of Article 4 contained a wording that provided for a flexible approach as to which circumstances may be considered in order to determine the applicable law, and the second paragraph provided a presumption that gave more objectivity: the closest connection was presumed to be with the country of residence or main place of business of the party making the characteristic performance. The interpretation of this second paragraph has not been uniform: some courts have considered it a weak presumption and have applied the fifth paragraph of Article 4[5] to rebut it whenever the circumstances of the case showed a closer connection with another country. On the contrary, other courts have considered the presumption of Article 4(2) to be strong and have disregarded other circumstances of the case unless there are exceptional situations. This latter interpretation corresponds better to the spirit of Article 4, which inserted the presumption to ensure predictability in the application of the criterion of the closest connection.[6] If, as a

---

[5] '[. . .] the presumptions in paragraphs 2, 3 and 4 shall be disregarded if it appears from the circumstances as a whole that the contract is more closely connected with another country.'

[6] Giuliano-Lagarde Report, comment to Article 4, para. 3. For further references to problems of interpretation that arose out of the relationship between the second and the fifth paragraphs of Article 4, see the Green Paper on the Rome Convention, *Green Paper on the conversion of the Rome Convention of 1980 on the law applicable to contractual obligations into a Community instrument and its modernisation,* 14.1.2003, COM (2002) 654 final. For a more extensive development of the reasoning made in the text here, see also G. Cordero-Moss, *International Commercial Law,* 2nd edn, Publications Series of the Institute of Private Law No. 185 (University of Oslo, 2010), pp. 323ff.

general rule, any other factors were allowed to be evaluated (such as the language of the contract or its legal style), the choice of law would be deprived of this predictability. The strength of the presumption became even clearer when the Rome Convention was transformed into the Rome I Regulation. The previous approach of a flexible connecting factor (closest connection, in Article 4(1)) which is clarified by a presumption (of the habitual residence or main place of business of the party making the characteristic performance, in Article 4(2)) has been changed into a series of fixed rules (all based on the connecting factor of the characteristic debtor's habitual residence or main place of business) with a residual flexible connecting factor (closest connection) to be used in the event that the party making the characteristic performance cannot be identified or as an escape.

In conclusion, the legal style in which the contract is written does not seem to be a relevant criterion in assessing with which country the contract has its closest connection.

1.3   Conclusion

From the foregoing, it seems possible to conclude that the drafting style, legal technique and language of a contract as such are not sufficient bases for a tacit choice of law or as a circumstance showing close connection capable of prevailing over other connecting factors. The governing law will be chosen on the basis of the connecting factor generally applicable to contracts, without regard to the drafting style of the contract.

2   Is a uniform interpretation of international contracts that is independent from the applicable law possible?

Since international contracts are written in a style that does not depend on the applicable law, it is legitimate to enquire whether they may be interpreted according to principles that are also not affected by the applicable law, i.e., transnational principles. In this respect, it is necessary to distinguish between contract clauses that regulate specific matters without any impact on aspects of general contract law and contract clauses that have an impact on principles and general contract law rules. The former may easily be subject to uniform interpretation, as long as this may be founded on applicable transnational sources. The latter will be affected by the principles, rules and legal traditions of the applicable law.

2.1   Transnational sources

A variety of instruments seeks to achieve harmonisation in the area of international commercial contracts:

(i) binding instruments – such as the 1980 United Nations (Vienna) Convention on Contracts for the International Sale of Goods ('CISG') creating a uniform law for the aspects of sale contracts that it regulates;

(ii) instruments issued by international bodies but without binding effect, either as models to be adopted by the legislature, such as the 1985 UNCITRAL Model Law on International Commercial Arbitration as revised in 2006, or as instruments to be adopted by the parties, such as the UNCITRAL Arbitration Rules, issued in 1976 and revised in 2010;

(iii) instruments issued by private organisations such as the International Chamber of Commerce and without binding effect unless the parties to the contract adopt them – such as the International Commercial Terms ('INCOTERMS') or the Uniform Customs and Practice for Documentary Credits ('UCP 600'); and

(iv) restatements of principles of general contract law issued by international organisations, branch associations or academic groups – such as the UNIDROIT Principles of International Commercial Contracts ('UPICC')[7] and the Principles of European Contract Law ('PECL')[8] – or endorsed by competent authorities, such as the Common Frame of Reference ('CFR') currently planned in the EU, and for the moment only at the stage of a draft proposed by a group of scholars, known as the Draft Common Frame of Reference ('DCFR').[9]

Sources without a binding effect but with an authority based on their persuasiveness and their representativeness are generally referred to as soft law. As opposed to the other above-mentioned types of instruments

---

[7] *UNIDROIT Principles of International Commercial Contracts* (International Institute for the Unification of Private Law, 2004).

[8] O. Lando and H. Beale (eds.), *Principles of European Contract Law*, Parts 1 and 2 (Kluwer Law International, 2002); and O. Lando and H. Beale (eds.), *Principles of European Contract Law*, Part 3 (Kluwer Law International, 2003).

[9] Study Group on a European Civil Code/Research Group on EC Private Law (eds.), *Principles, Definitions and Model Rules of European Private Law – Draft Common Frame of Reference (DCFR)* (Sellier, 2009).

that may be defined as soft law, the CISG is a binding convention; nevertheless, in addition to its direct binding effect, it is sometimes referred to as having an authoritative effect that goes beyond its territorial and substantive scope of application and makes it one of the most important sources of soft law for general contract law. Together with two other illustrious instruments, the already-mentioned UPICC and PECL, it is sometimes referred to as the 'Troika', a body of transnational law particularly apt to govern commercial contracts.[10]

Both the CISG in its original binding function and some instruments of soft law, such as those mentioned above and issued by the UNCITRAL and ICC, have a specific scope of application. The CISG applies to certain aspects of the contract of sale; the model law and the Arbitration Rules apply to the procedural aspects of arbitration; INCOTERMS apply to the passage of risk from seller to buyer and other specific obligations between the parties; and the UCP 600 apply to the mechanism of documentary credits. None of these instruments have the goal of regulating all contract law aspects of the relationship between the parties, such as the validity of the contracts, their interpretation or all remedies for breach of contract. None of these sources create structural problems and all of them may successfully achieve harmonisation within their respective scope of application. They usually integrate the governing law by specifying details that lie within an area that may freely be regulated by the parties. If any of these sources reflects a trade usage, it will be applicable even without the need of reference by the parties. If any of these sources has been ratified or adopted by the legislature, it will govern that particular area of the law.

Characteristic of the restatements of general contract law is, conversely, the goal to act as the law that governs all aspects of the legal relationship between the parties and thus replaces the state governing law in its totality.

2.2 Does transnational law have the force of law?

The goal of replacing the governing law creates, first of all, a challenge in terms of private international law. If the restatements of general contract law or other sources of soft law are to replace the governing law, they will

---

[10] See, for example, O. Lando, 'CISG and its Followers: A Proposal to Adopt Some International Principles of Contract Law', *American Journal of Comparative Law*, 53 (2005), 379–401, 379ff.

not be subject to any mandatory rules of the otherwise applicable law, with the exception of overriding mandatory rules. On the contrary, if these instruments are incorporated into the contract and become contract terms, they remain subject to any mandatory rules of the applicable law, are interpreted according to the governing law's underlying principles and are integrated by the governing law's default rules. The wording of Article 1.4 of the UPICC seems to suggest the latter alternative: 'Nothing in these Principles shall restrict the application of mandatory rules, whether of national, international or supranational origin, which are applicable in accordance with the relevant rules of private international law.' Also, the Rome I Regulation excludes the possibility that the parties may select sets of rules that are not state laws (with an exception for possible future European instruments of contract law).[11] This was the conclusion of a long process started with the Commission's Green Paper on the conversion of the Rome Convention.[12] A draft issued during the process gave the parties a certain room for choosing a non-state body of law to govern the contract.[13] The opposition to this opening was such that the final text of the Regulation excluded this possibility and specified in the preamble (recital 13) that nothing prevents the parties from *incorporating* transnational instruments of soft law into the contract. However, as a consequence of such incorporation, transnational instruments are given the status of a term of contract, not of governing law.

While private international law prevents the parties from choosing transnational law to govern their contract when disputes are decided by courts of law, there is often greater flexibility in disputes that are submitted to arbitration. The UNCITRAL Model Law on International Commercial Arbitration, for example, which has been adopted more or less literally in over fifty countries, provides in Article 28(1) that the arbitral tribunal shall apply the 'rules of law' chosen by the parties. This terminology, as opposed to the word 'law' used in Article 28(2) to cover the eventuality that the parties have not made a choice, is often interpreted to be an opening to transnational law.

Yet, the fact that the parties, in the frame of arbitration, may choose to replace the governing law with transnational sources is not sufficient to ensure a harmonisation of the general contract law. First of all, there may

---

[11] Council Regulation No. 593/2008, Article 3.

[12] *Green Paper on the conversion of the Rome Convention of 1980.*

[13] *Proposal for a Regulation of the European Parliament and the Council on the law applicable to contractual obligations (Rome I), COM (2005) 650 final.*

be gaps in the transnational sources, so that ultimately the application of a state law may be necessary.[14] Furthermore, as will be seen below, certain principles of general contract law are deeply rooted in the legal tradition of the interpreter and harmonisation will not be achieved in full until there is a centralised court that establishes a uniform legal tradition. An instrument with the task of harmonising different legal traditions must be precise and leave little to the judge's discretion, otherwise the harmonised rules are applied differently by the different countries' courts.[15]

2.3   Does transnational law exclude the applicable law?

Transnational sources of soft law may complement the applicable law, but are not able to replace it. The interaction between these sources and the governing law may prejudice the desired harmonising effect.

2.3.1   Specific contract regulations

One example of specific contract regulations may be INCOTERMS. The interpretation of the terms of delivery contained therein is undoubtedly harmonised, and everybody who reads a contract saying, for example, that delivery shall be made 'FOB Rotterdam according to INCOTERMS 2000' knows that the goods have to be loaded and cleared for export by the seller on the ship nominated by the buyer at the named port, that the buyer must take delivery on board of the ship, that the risk of damage to the goods passes from the seller to the buyer when the goods are loaded, etc. If INCOTERMS were the only source applicable to the contract, there would be no rules on the validity of the contract, on the effects that

---

[14] Both the UPICC and the PECL shall be interpreted autonomously; see, respectively, Articles 1.5 and 1:106. However, should it still be impossible to fill a gap, the governing law shall be applied. It is expressly provided for in the second paragraph of Article 1:106 of the PECL, and implied by the UPICC, whose model clause recommends the use of state law as a supplement; see the official commentary to the UPICC, published by UNIDROIT in 2004 at www.unidroit.org/english/principles/contracts/principles2004/integralversionprinciples2004-e.pdf, comment No. 4 to Article 1.6, last accessed 15 March 2010.

[15] H. Eidenmüller et al., 'The Common Frame of Reference for European Private Law – Policy Choices and Codification Problems', Oxford Journal of Legal Studies, 28 (2008), 659–708, criticising the DCFR for not being sufficiently precise. The DCFR was presented by two academic groups in the framework of the Joint Network on European Private Law with the aim of contributing to the development of a European law of contracts, and was largely based on the PECL. See also R. Schulze (ed.), CFR and Existing EC Contract Law, 2nd revised edn (Sellier, 2009).

the sale has for third parties who are creditors, etc. Obviously,
INCOTERMS do not have the goal of being the only applicable source
of law, because they do not regulate these aspects of the contract.
Therefore, they need to be integrated with an applicable law. This may
have an impact not only on the areas that are not regulated by
INCOTERMS, but even within their scope of application. Suppose that
goods were destroyed after the risk passed to the buyer. According to
INCOTERMS, the buyer is obliged to pay the price. Suppose that the
applicable law is of a state that has ratified the CISG and that therefore
the sales agreement is also regulated by the CISG. Article 66 of the CISG
provides that the buyer is not obliged to pay the price even if the damage
occurred after the risk passed, as long as the damage was due to the
seller's act or omission. Thus, the CISG interacts with INCOTERMS in
such a way that it modifies their application. Hence, INCOTERMS
ensure harmonisation of the rules within their scope of application to a
large extent, but not completely.

2.3.2   General contract regulations

Other clauses that often appear in international contracts are even more
difficult to interpret uniformly, because they may require the involvement of general principles that are deeply rooted in the interpreter's legal
tradition. Many contracts attempt to achieve harmonisation by inserting
clauses aimed at rendering the contract self-sufficient, with the precise
purpose of excluding interference by external elements, including the
applicable law. According to the logic underlying this drafting style, if the
contract is to be interpreted and applied exclusively on the basis of its
words, it will be interpreted and applied equally, irrespective of any legal
tradition. In many situations, the intent of the parties is successful:
contracts are written in a detailed and comprehensive manner, and
they mainly regulate matters that are within the scope of the parties'
contract freedom. By this combination, and if the contract is sufficiently
clear, there is often no room for interference by the applicable law.
Therefore, the interpretation and application of the clauses will not be
affected by the differing legal traditions or by the application of transnational sources.

Under some circumstances, however, a literal application of the
clauses may challenge some fundamental principles of the applicable
law, including, first of all, the principle of good faith (some examples will
be made below). How are the clauses to be interpreted in these situations?
On the basis of their wording, which may possibly conflict with the

principle of good faith in the governing law? Or on the basis of the principle of good faith, thus disregarding the words of the contract? And how exactly is the content of the principle of good faith to be determined?[16] As the chapters in Part 3 of this book will show, different legal systems have different approaches.[17] This chapter will deal with transnational law's ability to achieve harmonisation in these situations.

The clauses discussed here are frequently part of international commercial contracts, irrespective of the type of contract. Not only are they generally expected to be an integral part of contract drafting, they are also immediately recognised and thus very seldom discussed during the negotiations. The drafting of these clauses is often considered to be a mere 'copy and paste' exercise. They are often referred to as 'boilerplate', standard language with a general applicability that follows automatically and does not require particular attention. The following are examples of the most typical clauses:

Entire agreement The Contract contains the entire contract and understanding between the parties hereto and supersedes all prior negotiations, representations, undertakings and agreements on any subject matter of the Contract.

No waiver Failure by a party to exercise a right or remedy that it has under this contract does not constitute a waiver thereof.

No oral amendments No amendment or variation to this Agreement shall take effect unless it is in writing, signed by authorised representatives of each of the Parties.

Severability If a provision of this Agreement is or becomes illegal, invalid or unenforceable, that shall not affect the validity or enforceability of any other provision of this Agreement.

Conditions/fundamental terms The obligations regulated in Section [xx] are fundamental and any breach thereof shall amount to a

---

[16] On the various roles that the principle of good faith may have in contract law, see H. Beale, 'General Clauses and Specific Rules in the Principles of European Contract Law: The "Good Faith" Clause', in S. Grundmann and D. Mazeaud (eds.), *General Clauses and Standards in European Contract Law* (Kluwer Law International, 2006), pp. 205–218, 207ff.

[17] For a thorough analysis of the different approaches to good faith in the various legal systems of Europe, see R. Zimmermann and S. Whittaker, *Good Faith in European Contract Law* (Cambridge University Press, 2000). See also G. Cordero-Moss, 'International Contracts between Common Law and Civil Law: Is Non-State Law to be Preferred? The Difficulty of Interpreting Legal Standards such as Good Faith', *Global Jurist (Advances)*, 7 (2007), Article 3, 1–38.

fundamental breach of this contract [*Alternative:* [Time] is of the essence].

Sole remedy [Liquidated damages paid in accordance with the foregoing provision] shall be the Buyer's sole remedy for any delay in delivery for which the Seller is responsible under this Agreement.

Subject to contract This document does not represent a binding agreement between the parties and neither party shall be under any liability to the other party in case of failure to enter into the final agreement.

Through these clauses, the parties attempt to exhaustively regulate the contract's interpretation (entire agreement) and validity (severability), the exercise of remedies for breach of contract (no waiver, conditions, sole remedy), and the legal effects of future conduct (no oral amendments, subject to contract). At the same time, these clauses attempt to exclude any rules that the applicable law may impose on these aspects.

This drafting style has the same approach that inspired the original common law models: *caveat emptor.*[18] A commercial contract between professionals, often written by expert lawyers, is expected to reflect careful evaluations made by each of the parties of its respective interests. The parties are assumed to be able to assess the relevant risks and to make provisions for them. The negotiations are expected to be carried out in a way that adequately takes care of each of the parties' positions, and the final text of the contract is deemed to reflect this. The contract is deemed to have been written accurately, so that each party may use the contractual regulation to objectively quantify its risk and, for example, insure against it. Contracts may also be assigned to third parties, for example, as collateral for other obligations or in the frame of other transactions. Contracts must therefore contain all elements according to which they will be interpreted, and interpretation must be made objectively and on the basis of the contract's wording. Under these circumstances, a literal and thus predictable application of the contract is perceived as the only fair application of contracts. It would be unfair to draw on external elements in addition to the wording of the contract, such as the conduct or silence of one of the parties that may have created expectations in the other party at some stage during the negotiations or even after the contract was signed. How can a contract circulate and be used as a

---

[18] This formula was pronounced by Lord Mansfield in *Stuart* v. *Wilkins*, I Dougl. 18, 99 Eng. Rep. 15 (1778) and has since been used to characterise the approach of English contract law, whereby each party has to take care of its own interests.

basis for calculating an insurance premium, granting a financing or be assigned to a third party if its implementation depends on elements that are not visible from the contract itself?

Sometimes, however, a literal application of the clauses may lead to results that may seem unjustified or not proportional to the interests of the other party. The following cases may serve as illustrations:

Entire agreement   What happens if the parties have, on a previous occasion, agreed on certain specifications for certain products, but have not incorporated those specifications into the present contract? Can the contract be interpreted in light of the previously agreed specifications, in spite of the Entire Agreement clause?

No waiver   Assume that the contract gives one party the right to terminate in case of delay in the delivery. What happens if the delivery is late, but the party does not terminate until, after a considerable time, the market changes and the contract is no longer profitable? The real reason for the termination is not the delay, but the change in the market. May the old delay be invoked as a ground for termination or is there a principle preventing it, in spite of the no waiver clause?

No oral amendments   What happens if the parties agree on an oral amendment and afterwards one party invokes the NOA clause to refuse performance (for example, because it is no longer interested in the contract after the market has changed)?

Severability   Some contract laws provide that the invalidity of certain contract terms renders the whole contract invalid. This conflicts with the clause. Moreover, a literal interpretation of the clause may lead to an unbalanced contract, if the provision that becomes invalid or unenforceable has significance for the interests of only one of the parties.

Conditions, essential terms   Assume that the contract defines delay in delivery as a fundamental breach; there is a delay, but it does not have any consequences for the other (innocent) party. What happens if the innocent party terminates the contract because the market has changed and the contract is no longer profitable? Can the clause on fundamental breach be invoked, even if the real reason for the termination is not the delay, but the change in the market?

Sole remedy   Assume that the contract defined the payment of a certain amount as the sole remedy in case of breach. What happens if the non-defaulting party is able to prove that the breach has caused a considerably larger damage than the agreed amount?

Subject to contract   Assume that the parties entered into a Letter of
Intent specifying that failure to reach a final agreement will not expose
any of the parties to liability. What happens if one party never really
intended to enter into a final agreement and used the negotiations only
to prevent the other party from entering into a contract with a third
party?

The drafting style of commercial contracts attempts to exclude any
interference from external elements and to create a self-sufficient system
detached from the governing law. The assumption is that if the parties
had wanted to restrict or qualify the application of the contract provisions, they would have written the restrictions or the qualifications in the
contract. Rules of interpretation of the governing law, principles of good
faith and other mandatory rules would interfere with the contract and
create uncertainty. Part 3 of this book will show that often contracts do
not succeed in creating a self-sufficient system detached from the governing law. This means that two contracts with exactly the same wording
might have different legal effects, depending upon the governing law.
This is sometimes considered to be confusing and undesirable. Would
transnational law be a suitable alternative to the various state laws and
reinstate uniformity for international contracts?

2.4   Does transnational law provide a uniform standard?

The UPICC and the PECL are the most systematic restatements of
transnational principles of contract law, and therefore they will be used
as a basis for the analysis in this chapter. Both restatements contain a
general clause on good faith in, respectively, Articles 1.7 and 1.201,
requiring each party to act in accordance with good faith and fair dealing
in international trade. They also contain numerous provisions[19] that
apply the general principle of good faith to specific situations.

In other words, the general principle of good faith is, in these restatements, an overriding principle that functions as a corrective action to the

---

[19] Comment No. 1 to Article 1.7 (last accessed 15 March 2010) mentions the following
provisions: Articles 1.8, 1.9(2); 2.1.4(2)(b), 2.1.15, 2.1.16, 2.1.18 and 2.1.20; 2.2.4(2), 2.2.5
(2), 2.2.7 and 2.2.10; 3.5, 3.8 and 3.10; 4.1(2), 4.2(2), 4.6 and 4.8; 5.1.2 and 5.1.3; 5.2.5; 6.1.3,
6.1.5, 6.1.16(2) and 6.1.17(1); 6.2.3(3)(4); 7.1.2, 7.1.6 and 7.1.7; 7.2.2(b)(c); 7.4.8 and 7.4.13;
9.1.3, 9.1.4 and 9.1.10(1). The PECL also have numerous specific rules applying the principle
of good faith, for example, in Articles 1:202; 2:102, 2:104, 2:105, 2:106, 2:202 and 2:301; 4:103,
4:106, 4:109 and 4:110; 5:102; 6:102; 8: 109; 9:101, 9:102 and 9:509.

mechanisms regulated in the contract whenever a literal application leads to results that seem too harsh on one of the parties. In order to apply this principle, the interpreter shall look beyond the wording of the contract. An accurate implementation of the contract may be considered to be against the principle of good faith if it amounts to an abuse of right. An abuse of right is defined by the official commentary to Article 1.7 of the UPICC as follows: 'It is characterised by a party's malicious behaviour which occurs for instance when a party exercises a right merely to damage the other party or for a purpose other than the one for which it had been granted, or when the exercise of a right is disproportionate to the originally intended result.'[20] Under the drafting style described above, if the parties had granted a certain contractual remedy for a certain purpose and not for another, they should have spelled it out in the contract. If they had intended to exclude some results from the possible consequences of exercising a certain right, they should have regulated that expressly. How can this be reconciled with the discretion that the UPICC give to the interpreter?

An example is Article 2.1.15(3) of the UPICC,[21] providing liability for the party that has started negotiations without serious intentions to eventually enter into the contract. The official comment to this provision reads: 'One particular instance of negotiating in bad faith which is expressly indicated in paragraph (3) of this Article is that where a party enters into negotiations or continues to negotiate without any intention of concluding an agreement with the other party.' Would this prevail over the subject to contract clause mentioned above, which has the purpose of exempting the parties from any liability in the event that they do not reach the final agreement?[22] According to the language of the clause, the exemption is absolute and is not affected by the reasons for starting or breaking off the negotiations. However, according to Article 1.7(2) of the UPICC, the parties may not derogate from the general principle of good faith.

In short, it is evident that the clauses described above are affected by the principle of good faith contained in the restatements. The principle of good faith in the UPICC and in the PECL overrides the language of the

---

[20] Comment No. 2 to Article 1.7 (last accessed 15 March 2010).

[21] The corresponding provision in the PECL is Article 2.301.

[22] For a more extensive analysis of the function and effects of Letters of Intent, particularly from the point of view of the common law–civil law tension, see G. Cordero-Moss, 'The Function of Letters of Intent and their Recognition in Modern Legal Systems', in R. Schulze (ed.), *New Features in Contract Law* (Sellier, 2007), pp. 139–159.

contract. The next question is then: are the restatements so precise that they can provide a basis for uniform interpretation?

In the commentary to Article 1.7, the UPICC affirm that the standard of good faith must always be understood as 'good faith in international trade' and that no reference should be made to any standard that has been developed under any state law.[23] This approach is in line with the requirement of autonomous interpretation of the UPICC contained in Article 1.6 thereof: the UPICC are an instrument with an international character, and it would not serve the purpose of becoming a uniform law if the courts of every state interpreted them each in a different way, in light of their own legal culture. However, while the requirement of autonomous interpretation of the UPICC and the corresponding requirement in Article 1:106 of the PECL are understandable in light of the ambitions of harmonising the law of contracts, they do not contribute towards creating clarity in respect of the content of good faith as a standard, as will be seen below.

Legal standards, or general clauses, are, per definition, in need of a specification of their content that depends to a large extent on the interpreter's discretion. When the general clause belongs to a state system, the interpreter's discretion is restricted or guided by principles and values underlying that particular system – for example, in the constitution, in other legislation or in society.[24] How would the interpreter evaluate the wording of the contract, which seems to provide for and permit the very conduct sanctioned by the principle of good faith? An interpreter belonging to a tradition where there is no general principle of good faith might tend to consider that the clear wording of the contract indicates that the parties had considered all eventualities, taken provision for them and accepted the consequences, and that therefore the articles of the UPICC and the PECL are not applicable. An interpreter belonging to a legal tradition with a strong general principle of good faith may consider that the consequences of a literal application of the contract must be mitigated if they disrupt the balance of interests between the parties. To the former interpreter, fairness or good faith

---

[23] Comment No. 3 to Article 1.7 (last accessed 15 March 2010).

[24] For an analysis of the application of general clauses, with particular but not exclusive reference to the German system, see P. Schlechtriem, 'The Functions of General Clauses, Exemplified by Regarding Germanic Laws and Dutch Law', in Grundmann and Mazeaud (eds.), *General Clauses and Standards in European Contract Law*, pp. 41–55, 49ff.

interpretation consists in an accurate interpretation of the contract. To the latter, it consists in intervening and reinstating a balance between the parties.

Where does the interpreter of transnational sources look for guidance?

In an international setting, it is natural to look for inspiration and guidance to the body of rules regulating international contracts and emanating from non-authoritative and non-state sources, the so-called *lex mercatoria*.

The most important of the sources that are usually considered to constitute the *lex mercatoria* (generally recognised principles, trade usages, contract practice and, according to some authors, international conventions) seem to give no specific criteria upon which a notion of good faith and fair dealing may be shaped, as will be seen immediately below.

There is no generally recognised uniform notion of good faith and fair dealing that might be valid for all types of contracts on an international level, and there is hardly a notion that is generally recognised for one single type of contract either.[25] There is no evidence of trade usages in respect of how the standard of good faith (if any) is applied in practice.[26] Among the most authoritative sources mentioned for the principle of good faith in international trade[27] are the UPICC and the PECL; however, these rely on the existence of this principle in international trade in order to determine its precise scope. In a rather circular logic, the principle of good faith is based on the restatements, and the restatements are based on the principle of good faith. There are few principles in respect of good faith and fair dealing that may be considered common to civil law and common law systems, and, even among civil law systems, there are considerable differences.[28]

---

[25] For a detailed analysis, see G. Cordero-Moss, 'Consumer Protection Except for Good Commercial Practice: A Satisfactory Regime for Commercial Contracts?', in Schulze (ed.), *CFR and Existing EC Contract Law*, pp. 78–84.

[26] On the establishment of uncodified usage and the *lex mercatoria*, see R. Goode, 'Usage and its Reception in Transnational Commercial Law', *International and Comparative Law Quarterly*, 46 (1997), 1–36.

[27] See, for example, the recognised digest of principles of the transnational law published by K. P. Berger, Trans-lex.org, commenting on Article 1.1, at www.trans-lex.org/output. php?docid=901000&legis_principle_ref=1, last accessed 13 March 2010. For a detailed analysis of the various sources mentioned in this digest, see Cordero-Moss, 'Consumer Protection Except for Good Commercial Practice', pp. 80–84.

[28] See Zimmermann and Whittaker, *Good Faith in European Contract Law*. See also Cordero-Moss, 'International Contracts between Common Law and Civil Law'.

Even focusing on the common core that underlies the different legal techniques of the various systems[29] may be of little help. Piecemeal solutions in English law[30] in certain areas make it possible to reach results comparable to the general principle of good faith in other systems. To what extent this may be useful in substantiating a general clause on good faith in international trade is uncertain. Although English law may, by applying its own remedies or techniques, achieve results in part similar to those that the principle of good faith may make it possible to achieve in some of the other systems, it also makes it possible to avoid these results by clear language in the contract. Many clauses used in commercial contracts were developed precisely with the aim of avoiding those results.

Contract practice is generally drafted on the assumption that the contracts shall be interpreted literally and without influence from principles such as good faith. As a consequence of the broad adoption of this contractual practice, the regulations between the parties move further and further away from the assumption of a good faith and fair dealing standard, even in countries where the legal system does recognise an important role to good faith.

The instrument that is generally considered as a high expression of the *lex mercatoria*, the CISG, has willingly omitted including good faith as a duty between the parties, which renders the very existence of this criterion in the transnational context dubious. The CISG is silent on the question of good faith as a duty between the parties, in spite of repeated requests during the drafting phase to expressly mention that the parties have to perform the contract according to good faith. During the drafting of the convention, specific proposals on good faith were presented in the precontractual phase, as well as general proposals dealing with the requirement of good faith. The specific proposals relating to precontractual liability were rejected and the generic proposals on good faith were incorporated in Article 7 in such a way that the principle of good faith is

---

[29] Modern comparative studies showed that the common law/civil law divide is much more complex than is traditionally believed. Thus, under certain circumstances common law reaches the same results that would be reached under civil law on the basis of the good faith principle. On the other hand, civilian law has a much less unitary approach to good faith than is traditionally assumed. See Zimmermann and Whittaker, *Good Faith in European Contract Law*, p. 678: despite the observation that the principle of good faith is relevant to all or most of the doctrines of modern laws of contract, the authors conclude that each system draws a different line between certainty and justice.

[30] The expression is taken from a famous observation made by Judge Brimham LJ in *Interfoto Picture Library Ltd* v. *Stiletto Visual Programmes Ltd* [1988] 2 WLR 615.

not directed at regulating the parties' conduct in the contract, but at the contracting state's interpretation of the convention.[31] The main arguments against the inclusion of good faith as a duty of the parties were that the concept was too vague to have specific legal effects, and that it would be redundant if mention thereof had only the character of a moral exhortation. Therefore, the CISG does not contribute to the determination of a standard of good faith for international contracts.

The theory of transnational law (also traditionally referred to as *lex mercatoria*) has received strong support in certain academic circles, but has been met with scepticism by legal practice.[32] The main reasons for this scepticism are that it is quite demanding to determine what the exact content of the *lex* is, that the principles that can be determined as being part of the *lex* are mainly quite vague and therefore cannot be used to decide specific disputes of a legal-technical character,[33] and that the content of the *lex* is quite fragmentary, leaving many areas of the law uncovered.

Some of these negative aspects may be remedied by the restatements, systematisations and standardisation of the *lex* that have been produced in recent years, such as the UPICC and the PECL. However, subjecting a contract to regulation by commercial practices or generally acknowledged principles or restatements thereof would leave too much room for discretion, thus representing an uncertain ground for the solution of potential disputes. The theory of the *lex mercatoria* seems to be based on the assumption that the parties desire a flexible system in which the interpreter (judge or arbitrator) can adapt to their needs. On the contrary, practitioners emphasise that they desire a predictable legal system

---

[31] For an extensive evaluation of this matter, as well as references to literature and to the legislative history in this respect, see A. Kritzer, *Pre-Contract Formation*, editorial remark on the internet database of the Institute of International Commercial Law of the Pace University School of Law, www.cisg.law.pace.edu/cisg/biblio/kritzer1.html, pp. 2ff. (last accessed 15 March 2010), also featuring extensive references to the Minority Opinion of M. Bonell, who was representing Italy under the legislative works. According to Bonell, an extensive interpretation of the CISG would justify application of both the concepts of pre-contractual liability and good faith. See also R. Goode, H. Kronke, E. McKendrick and J. Wool, *Transnational Commercial Law – Text, Cases and Materials* (Oxford University Press, 2007), pp. 279ff.

[32] As Lord Mustill incisively put it twenty years ago: 'the commercial man is a conspicuous absentee from the writings on the lex mercatoria', in Mustill LJ, 'The New Lex Mercatoria: The First Twenty-Five Years', *Arbitration International* 4, 2 (1987), 86–119, 86. The same may be affirmed today.

[33] In the words of Mustill LJ, these principles are 'so general that they are useless': 'The New Lex Mercatoria', 92.

that can be objectively applied by the interpreter; the task of adapting the contract to the specific needs of the case is the task of the contract drafters, not the interpreter.[34]

UNIDROIT has taken a measure that is to be commended for contributing to the development of a body of case law that may enhance a harmonised interpretation and thus predictability of the UPICC: following the example of CLOUT, a system established by UNCITRAL for the collection and dissemination of court decisions and arbitral awards relating to UNCITRAL instruments, UNIDROIT has established UNILEX,[35] a database collecting case law and a bibliography on the UPICC and the CISG. In 1992, UNILEX started collecting and publishing, inter alia, arbitral awards that contain references to the UPICC. Making available the case law that (if at all published) otherwise would be scattered among the publications issued by different arbitral institutions all over the world is a valuable step promoting the development of a uniform body of law. When the number of the collected decisions becomes significant and their level of detail is such that they can be used to determine the specific scope of general clauses such as the principle of good faith, the UPICC will be in a position to contribute to the harmonisation of general contract law.

To test the ability of the UPICC to harmonise contract law with the help of UNILEX, it is interesting to examine the case law collected in respect of Article 2.1.17 of the UPICC. This Article recognises the abovementioned Entire Agreement clauses, according to which the document signed by the parties contains the whole agreement and may not be supplemented by evidence of prior statements or agreements. However, the UPICC provision specifies that prior statements or agreements may be used to interpret the contract. This is one of the applications of the general principle of good faith; however, it is unclear how far the principle of good faith goes in overriding the clause inserted by the parties. If prior statements and agreements may be used to interpret the contract, does this mean that more terms may be added to the contract because, for example, the parties have discussed certain specifications at length during the negotiations and this has created in one of the parties the reasonable expectation that they would be implied in the

---

[34] For an interesting analysis of this aspect, see W. Grosheide, 'The Duty to Deal Fairly in Commercial Contracts', in Grundmann and Mazeaud, *General Clauses and Standards in European Contract Law*, pp. 197–204, 201.

[35] www.unilex.info.

contract? Article 1.8 of the UPICC would seem to indicate that this would be the preferred approach under the UPICC. According to this provision, a party may not act in a way inconsistent with reasonable expectations that it has created in the other party. According to this logic, the detailed discussion during the phase of negotiations of certain characteristics for the products may create the reasonable expectation that those specifications have become part of the agreement even if they were not written into the contract; their subsequent exclusion on the basis of the Entire Agreement clause may be deemed to be against good faith.

UNILEX contains two decisions on Article 2.1.17: the ICC award No. 9117 of 1998 and an English Court of Appeal decision.

In the ICC award, the arbitral tribunal emphasises that an Entire Agreement clause is to be considered as typical in a commercial contract and says that 'there can be no doubt for any party engaged in international trade that the clauses mean, and must mean, what they say'.[36] The contract also contained a no oral amendments clause, which is recognised in Article 2.1.18 of the UPICC, a provision containing the same restrictions as Article 2.1.17 regarding conduct that has created expectations in the other party. The arbitral tribunal said that 'the explicit integration clause and the written modification clause, as contained in the Contract, operate as a bar against the assumption that a certain behaviour or practice could reach the level of becoming legally binding between the Parties'. Thus, according to this award, the principle of good faith contained in Articles 1.7 and 1.8 of the UPICC and specified in Articles 2.1.17 and 2.1.18 does not affect a literal application of the contract's language. This approach seems to be consistent with the ideology underlying the drafting style of international contracts, as described above. Consequently, it considerably restricts the applicability of the principles underlying the UPICC.

The other decision mentioned in UNILEX under Article 2.1.17 is by the English Court of Appeal.[37] There Mummery LJ stated that, under English law, extrinsic evidence could be used to ascertain the meaning of a term contained in a written contract. On the contrary, extrinsic evidence could not be used to ascertain the content of the contract.[38] Lady Justice Arden considered this distinction too conservative and argued for

---

[36] The award may be found at www.unilex.info/dynasite.cfm?dssid=2377&dsmid=13621&x=1 (last accessed 12 March 2010), clicking on 'full text'. The paragraphs are not numbered.

[37] *Proforce Recruit Ltd* v. *The Rugby Group Ltd* [2006] EWCA Civ 69.   [38] *Ibid.*, at 41.

a larger use of extrinsic evidence, referring to the UPICC in support of her view.[39]

UNILEX, in summary, shows two decisions on Article 2.1.17 of the UPICC: an arbitral award advocating the primacy of the contract's language and an English Court of Appeal decision assuming in an *obiter dictum* that the UPICC provide for the primacy of the principle of good faith (in this case, the real intention of the parties).

Evidently, this is not sufficient to give guidance as to how to solve the conflict between the contract's language and the principle of good faith.

Regarding the development of the PECL, it is interesting to observe that they are central in the ongoing work on a European contract law. In 2004,[40] the European Commission entrusted a joint network on European private law with the preparation of a proposal for a CFR. The CFR is intended to be a toolbox for the Community legislator: it could be used as a set of non-binding guidelines by lawmakers at the Community level as a common source of inspiration, or for reference in the lawmaking process. The Study Group on a European Civil Code and the Research Group on the Existing EC Private Law jointly used the PECL as a basis for a DCFR that was finalised at the end of 2008.[41] The DCFR is currently subject to debate, both by politicians[42] and scholars.[43] Depending on the development of this process, the PECL may become the basis of a European body of rules that eventually may be subject to interpretation or application by the European Court of Justice. In such a case, over time, a coherent body of case law would be formed and the content of the principle of good faith would be easier to determine.

3   Conclusion

Although international contracts are often drafted according to a relatively recognisable style that may be deemed to be loosely inspired by the common law, each contract will be subject to a specific state law, and the

---

[39] *Ibid.*, at 57.

[40] Communication, *European contract law and the revision of the acquis: the way forward*, COM (2004) 651 final.

[41] Study Group on a European Civil Code/Research Group on EC Private Law (eds.) *Principles, Definitions and Model Rules*.

[42] Discussion on the topic of the CFR in the Council of the European Union, initiated by the Presidency on 28 July 2008, 8286/08JUSTCIV 68 CONSOM 39.

[43] Eidenmüller *et al.*, 'The Common Frame of Reference'; N. Jansen and R. Zimmermann, '"A European Civil Code in All But Name": Discussing the Nature and Purposes of the Draft Common Frame of Reference' (2010) 69 CLJ, 98–112.

governing law will be identified without having regard to the style in which the contract is written.

Only where the drafting style clearly can be taken as a conscious choice made by the parties to apply a specific state law will it be deemed to be a tacit choice of law. Where the parties may not be assumed to have made an actual choice, the applicable law will be chosen according to the connecting factor of the conflicts rule for contracts. This may lead to applying a civilian law to a contract that was inspired by the common law.

The challenges that may arise may not be overcome by assuming that international contracts are subject to transnational rules permitting a uniform interpretation and application, thus avoiding the peculiarities of the various legal traditions. Transnational sources of soft law have proven to be extremely useful when they have a specific scope of application and can be used to integrate the parties' contract and the governing law on determined, technical matters. However, their capacity to also replace the governing law in respect of the general contract law is more doubtful.

First of all, transnational law does not have the force of law necessary to be considered by a court as applicable law. An arbitral tribunal may have the power to apply transnational sources instead of the governing law, but often this would lead to new difficulties, because these sources are not sufficiently precise to allow a uniform interpretation. Moreover, no coherent case law is developed as long as there is no centralised tribunal that applies these sources. A uniform application of transnational law assumes a common understanding of the underlying principles. For the moment, this is lacking: while commercial practice seems to adopt an approach close to that of the common law in drafting contracts that aspire to be self-sufficient and objectively interpreted, the restatements of principles seem to follow the civil law tradition and attach great importance to considerations of equitable justice. However, they also insist on detaching these criteria from the legislative, judicial and doctrinal tradition of specific legal systems in favour of an autonomous interpretation based on international standards. In turn, not many sources are available to establish the meaning of good faith and fair dealing as a standard in international trade.

In conclusion, international contracts may end up being subject to a state law that is not fully compatible with the principles underlying some of the clauses written by the parties. Part 3 of this book will illustrate some of the conflicts that may arise and how these will be dealt with in various jurisdictions.

4

Common law-based contracts under German law

GERHARD DANNEMANN[*]

1 Introduction

Courts must sometimes apply German law to a contract in spite of the fact that its terms are based on common law contract models. Problems may arise from such a mismatch between applicable law and contract terms. Their solutions straddle the borderline between substantive law, i.e., rules that tell us whether there is a contract and which rights and obligations arise under such a contract, and private international law, i.e., rules that tell us which country's law applies.

Normally, if a contract has been formulated with a particular contract law in mind (for example, English law), private international law rules will point to the application of that law. Within the EU, this question is governed by the Rome I Regulation, which provides:[1]

> Article 3 Freedom of choice
> 1. A contract shall be governed by the law chosen by the parties. The choice shall be made expressly or clearly demonstrated by the terms of the contract or the circumstances of the case. By their choice the parties can select the law applicable to the whole or to part only of the contract.

If parties have given any thought to the question of which law should be applicable, they will normally choose the same law that they have used as a model. If the contract contains no choice-of-law clause, obvious reliance on one particular legal system in the formulation of a contract can sometimes be seen as demonstrating a choice by the terms of the contract.

[*] I am grateful to Arne Gutsche for having edited the footnotes and for further helpful comments.
[1] Regulation (EC) No 593/2008 of the European Parliament and of the Council of 17 June 2008, on the law applicable to contractual obligations (Rome I), OJ 2008 No. L 177, p. 6.

Nevertheless, there are a variety of situations which can lead to a contract being subjected to a legal system which is different from the one on which its terms are based.

First, parties can consciously model their contract on one system and then expressly choose to subject the contract to another system's law. Some might argue that this should trigger the professional liability of any legal practitioner involved, but this will nonetheless happen in practice. Sometimes, there is a trade practice of using formulations based on a particular legal system. Contracts for carriage by sea are a case in point. English law has long dominated global sea trade. Parties who are not based in England may wish to borrow from English law but would rather have any dispute brought before courts in a different country, using the contract law of that other country. A variant of this situation is a partial choice of law, by which two or more different laws apply to one and the same contract. This is rarely helpful, but is expressly permitted under Article 3(1) of the Rome I Regulation.

Secondly, parties may make an express choice of one legal system without being aware that the terms of the contract are based on a different law. Parties may simply copy a contract which they have used on a previous occasion, without realising that this contract is based on a particular legal system, and add a clause which chooses the law at their seat of business in the belief that this is generally more advantageous for their position. The present author once acted as counsel in an arbitration case in which a German main contractor had insisted on a German choice of law for a contract with an English sub-contractor. The staff of the German company had copied the contract terms from another agreement, possibly their contract with the client, and this contract was obviously based on common law. Moreover, parties may simply have negotiated clauses in the order in which they are listed in the contract. Because choice-of-law clauses will usually figure at the end, parties may thus have negotiated all details of a contract in terms which are based on one law before they even begin to discuss which law should apply to this contract. Practitioners could easily avoid this unfortunate situation by reversing the usual order and placing choice of law (and jurisdiction) clauses at the beginning.

Thirdly, even where parties have agreed on a choice-of-law clause that points to the law on which the contract is based, the contract can nevertheless end up being governed by a different law. If the case is brought before an English court and neither party invokes the foreign choice-of-law clause, English courts will normally simply apply English law. German courts, on the other hand, must apply a chosen foreign law regardless of any party relying on that choice. However, German courts conveniently construct a tacit fresh choice of law, namely of German law, in the situation where both parties argue before the court on the basis of German law,[2] even if they have failed to realise that the contract is subjected to a different legal regime. Alternatively, parties may have chosen the law on which the contract is modelled, but this choice is not valid. This will rarely happen in commercial contracts for goods or services, but can occur in areas where the choice of law is limited or excluded. Inheritance, family, employment and consumer law can serve as examples, but even in mutually commercial situations one cannot always be certain that a choice will succeed in contracts relating to company law, banking law, cartel law, competition law, etc.

Fourthly, parties may have wasted no thoughts on the applicable law, and other connecting factors, which point to a different law, prove to be more relevant than the use of a particular law as model.

2   Likely problems

What problems are likely to arise if a contract which is modelled on one legal system is subjected to the law of a different legal system? Such contracts suffer a loss of context – of both mandatory rules and fallback provisions. They may presume the existence of legal institutions which are unknown to other legal systems. They may have been written around problems which do not exist in the law which governs the contract. Worse, they may have failed to write around problems which do exist in the applicable law and may for this reason malfunction or become void.

Looking at an English–German context, it is arguably more dangerous to have a German law-based contract governed by English law than vice versa. For a German-style contract under English law, the main pitfalls are as follows.

Under the doctrine of consideration, amendments which benefit one party only may be void,[3] and offers which appear to be binding for a certain amount of time are not binding at all. As neither is a problem

---

[2] See, e.g., BGH 12.12.1990, NJW 1991, 1292, where the court left open whether the contract was initially governed by English law.

[3] See *Williams* v. *Roffey Bros & Nichols (Contractors) Ltd* [1991] 1 QB 1, where, however, the Court of Appeal held the 'practical benefit' of having performance completed in time to be sufficient consideration.

under German law, a German law-based contract will make no effort to write around such problems by offering some consideration or by using a deed.

German law has no doctrine of privity. German contracts make frequent use of third parties acquiring rights under a contract between two other parties. This is now possible under English law, but only if clearly provided in the contract.[4] German contracts do not need to be specific on this point.

Penalty provisions are void under English law, whereas they are valid under German law.[5] German contracts will generally make no attempt to shift penalty provisions into the safer waters of liquidated damages.

English contract law is generally more concerned with certainty and expects parties to write their contracts around deficiencies in English law. In *The Aliakmon*, copper coil was damaged on board the defendant's ship at a time when the risk, but not the property, had passed to the claimant.[6] The claimant could not recover its loss because it did not own the copper coil at the time when it was damaged. The owner of the copper coil could not recover because, due to the passing of risk, it had suffered no financial loss. Should judges try to avoid this unintended and entirely undeserved escape from liability? Not according to the House of Lords. Lord Brandon held that there was no *lacuna* in English law and this was just a case of poor contract drafting.[7] In consequence, if a clever solicitor can write around a problem in English contract law, this is not a problem with which an English judge should be overly concerned. However, this chapter deals with contracts which frequently have not been written by clever solicitors, because clever solicitors would rarely combine a German-style contract with an English choice-of-law clause. Little sympathy should therefore be expected from the English judiciary for these cases.

Moreover – and this is a related point – the traditionally more literal interpretation under English contract law leaves less room for judges to bridge the gap between the applicable English law and the 'model' of German law.[8]

---

[4] Section 1 of the Contracts (Rights of Third Parties) Act 1999.

[5] §341 of the Bürgerliches Gesetzbuch (German Civil Code, BGB).

[6] *Leigh & Sillivan Ltd* v. *Aliakmon Shipping Co. Ltd* [1986] AC 785.

[7] *Ibid*. See also *Surrey County Council* v. *Bredero Homes Ltd* [1993] 1 WLR 1361.

[8] Some of this gap has been bridged by *Investors Compensation Scheme Ltd* v. *West Bromwich Building Society (No. 1)* [1998] 1 WLR 896, where Lord Hoffmann held that 'the law does not require judges to attribute to the parties an intention which they plainly could not have had'.

Such problems which German law-based contracts may experience under English law can serve as a contrast foil for the main topic of this chapter, which is concerned with the reverse situation. What can go wrong if German law applies to contracts which are based on common law?

There are fortunately few if any pitfalls which would make an entire contract void. To a certain degree, English-style contracts travel more easily because they typically attempt to combine all rules into one agreement, to a level of detail which will frequently astonish German lawyers. They would, for instance, not specify in a contract what should happen if a contractual time period ends on a public holiday, because that is set out in the German Civil Code (§193 BGB). However, even though English contracts tend to contain an extensive set of rules which expressly cater for a multitude of situations, there are nevertheless several dangers.

English-style contracts are written with common law remedies in mind. They ignore the fact that specific performance is the primary remedy in German law and that a party who wants to rely on a different remedy will normally have to do something to convert the primary claim for performance into a secondary claim for, say, damages or restitution, such as issuing a warning in case of delay[9] or making time of the essence (§323 BGB).[10] Even a very detailed common law-style contract may thus fail to alert a party who wishes to rely on its remedies that these essential steps must be taken.

English-style contracts are also written against the background of default strict liability for contractual promises. Under German law, mere failure by a party to provide what is owed under the contract will, as a default rule, not in itself attract liability, as the party must additionally be responsible for this

---

[9] §286 BGB Delay by the obligor

  (1) If, after notice from the obligee to perform, such notice having been given after performance became due, the obligor fails to perform, that notice puts him in default.
  The English translation of this and of the following provisions has been taken from Geoffrey Thomas and Gerhard Dannemann, German Civil Code – Bürgerliches Gesetzbuch. Bilingual edition of the provisions amended by the Law of Obligations Reform Act, German Law Archive (2002), www.iuscomp.org/gla/statutes/BGB.htm.

[10] §323 BGB Termination for non-performance or for performance not in accordance with the contract

  (1) If under a synallagmatic contract the obligor fails to effect performance when due or to perform in accordance with the contract, the obligee may terminate the contract, if he has fixed, to no avail, an additional period of time for performance.

failure under §280 BGB. So, if a party should be strictly liable under the contract, this must be made clear.[11]

More interventionist statutes apply, in particular relating to the use of standard terms (§§305–310 BGB). Contracts modelled on English contract law will do nothing to make their provisions conform to German law controls of standard terms in commercial contracts, with the result that some clauses may be void.

More interventionist German judges will interpret English-style contracts. The combination of nitty-gritty detail regulation in English contracts (which would primarily call for a literal interpretation) meets purposive interpretation and occasionally social engineering on the basis of good faith designed for German contracts, which generally leave much more open to interpretation.

Arbiters may be less interventionist, but they are frequently not as familiar with German law as German judges. In most situations where German law applies to a common law contract, one of the parties is German, and a 'neutral', i.e., a non-German arbiter, is appointed. It is easier to find an expert in English law who is not a British citizen (who might, for example, carry an Australian, Canadian, Irish or New Zealand passport) than it is to find an expert in German law who is not a German citizen.

3   Court practice

Cases in which courts have had to deal with English-style contracts governed by German law are numerous, but not easily accessible. Scholarly writing in Germany may have underestimated the scale of those contracts and the scope of associated problems. The largest commentary on the German Civil Code and its Introductory Act, *J. von Staudingers Kommentar zum Bürgerlichen Gesetzbuch*, presently consists of more than 100 parts which together fill perhaps three metres of library shelves. This commentary devotes exactly one sentence to our topic, from which we learn that this is a matter of contractual interpretation.[12]

---

[11]   *§280 BGB Compensation for breach of duty*

(1) If the obligor fails to comply with a duty arising under the obligation, the obligee may claim compensation for the loss resulting from this breach. This does not apply if the obligor is not responsible for the failure.

For an example of where a common law-based clause was clear enough to attract strict liability under German law, see BGH 28.09.1978, BGHZ 72, 174 (discussed below).

[12]   *J. von Staudingers Kommentar zum Bürgerlichen Gesetzbuch mit Einführungsgesetz und Nebengesetzen*, 13th edn (Sellier, 2002), Article 32 EGBGB No. 30 (U. Magnus).

The leading work on international contracts by Reithmann and Martiny consists of 3,529 sections, of which exactly one – No. 254 – addresses our problem, and also considers this as an issue of interpretation.[13] There is the odd article which explores the same topic,[14] but apparently not in the same depth as achieved outside Germany.[15] There also appears to be no larger German contribution or monograph on this issue.[16]

Database searches yield some results, but are unlikely to provide a comprehensive overview. There are no obvious search categories which would reveal cases of common law-based contracts governed by German law. Moreover, sometimes courts may not even have been aware that a contract they were struggling to come to terms with under German law was so unruly because it was modelled on a common law legal system.

The cases which the present author has managed to identify come from four categories: shipping, financial securities, brokerage and works contracts.

3.1   Shipping contracts, exclusion and penalty clauses

Some shipping cases reveal that the issue of German law applying to English-style contracts is older than the German Civil Code. There are several late nineteenth-century cases decided by what was then Germany's highest court, the Reichsgericht (Imperial Court), which concern contracts for carriage of goods by sea or other charterparties with English-style contract terms, or at least some English-style clauses.

The oldest such case may be a decision of 16 July 1883, in which the Reichsgericht had to interpret a very long-winded clause in which the carrier attempted to exclude any liability, and this long clause included,

---

[13]   C. Reithmann and D. Martiny (eds.), *Internationales Vertragsrecht*, 6th edn (Dr. Otto Schmidt Verlag, 2004), at No. 254 (Martiny).

[14]   G. Weick, 'Zur Auslegung von internationalen juristischen Texten', in G. Köbler, M. Heinze and J. Schapp (eds.), *Geschichtliche Rechtswissenschaft, Freundesgabe für Alfred Söllner zum 60. Geburtstag am 5.2.1990* (Giessener rechtswissenschafliche Abhandlungen, 1990), pp. 607–628, at pp. 619–627 (discussing mainly a case of a common law-inspired FIDIC (civil engineering) contract being subjected to Libyan law).

[15]   G. Cordero-Moss, 'International Contracts between Common Law and Civil Law: Is Non-state Law to Be Preferred? The Difficulty of Interpreting Legal Standards such as Good Faith', *Global Jurist (Advances)*, 7, 1 (2007), Article 3.

[16]   Scholarly writing can be found on the more general question of how law which is not applicable according to conflict rules may nevertheless have a bearing on a case, the most recent monograph being G. Dannemann, *Die ungewollte Diskriminierung in der internationalen Rechtsanwendung. Zur Anwendung, Berücksichtigung und Anpassung von Normen aus unterschiedlichen Rechtsordnungen* (Mohr Siebeck, 2004).

inter alia, the expressions 'Peril of Navigation excepted' and 'Freight earned, ship lost or not lost'.[17] The contract, which was between two German parties, was subjected to the law in force at Bremen. The goods were placed on board and, while the boat was still in port and both the captain and the first officer were away overnight, the boat was flooded and the goods damaged. Was that a case of '[p]eril of navigation excepted'? And was this clause to be interpreted in the meaning of the applicable law of Bremen or of English law, on which this clause was obviously based?

In this decision, the Reichsgericht demonstrates a rather ambivalent approach towards interpretation. On the one hand, the judges firmly reject that they should in any way be bound by English law notions when applying German law:

> Apart from the fact that one would have to sacrifice any independent legal development, it would amount to an unjustified imposition if one were to expect him [the carrier] to accept words being used in a particular meaning only because this meaning has repeatedly been applauded by English judges.[18]

On the other hand, the same judgment also holds that, when interpreting the bill of lading, it is 'naturally useful to draw on opinions of English judges for help and suggestions'.[19] Ultimately, the Reichsgericht quotes two English judgments to show that they come to the same conclusion as English judges would have – namely, that perils of navigation do not require the ship to be in motion.[20]

Fourteen years later, the Reichsgericht adopted the approach which has prevailed ever since.[21] At issue was an indemnity clause, which might have been considered to be a penalty clause, which in turn would have been void under English law. The Reichsgericht held that the contract had to be interpreted according to the true intention of the parties

---

[17]   RG 16.6.1883, RGZ 11, 100.

[18]   *Ibid.*, at 105; all translations are mine unless indicated otherwise. The German original reads: 'es ist, ganz abgesehen davon, daß man bei anderen Grundsätzen auf eine selbständige Rechtsentwicklung überhaupt verzichtet, eine nicht berechtigte Zumutung, daß er [der Verfrachter] die Worte in einem bestimmten Sinne bloß deshalb gelten lassen müsse, weil dieser wiederholt den Beifall englischer Richter gehabt habe.'

[19]   *Ibid.* The German original reads: 'selbstverständlich die Verwertung der Meinungen englischer Richter als Förderungs- und Anregungsmittel durchaus nützlich.'

[20]   *Ibid.*, at 107; *Good* v. *London Steam Ship Owners Mutual Protection Association* (1870–71) LR 6 CP 563; *Hayn Roman & Co* v. *Culliford* (1877–78) LR 3 CPD 410.

[21]   RG 22.5.1897, RGZ 39, 65.

without clinging to the words used, as was then required under §278 of the Commercial Code and is now generally required for all contracts under §133 BGB. The court explained:

> This sentence in particular requires English legal notions to be used for establishing the meaning and scope of the individual clauses of the charter party. The appeal judge has overlooked that the form used in the present case is based throughout on an understanding of carriage of goods by sea which is particular to English law. If this was merely a translation of a contract which reveals German legal thinking and German legal views, the choice of language would matter little. But this is obviously not the case. Apart from the clause in question, which is particular to English business transactions, the contract also contains in its other parts provisions which are generally common in English charterparties, which are expressed in certain forms, reflecting a long tradition, and which in English business and jurisprudence are associated with a certain meaning, which most certainly cannot always be derived from the mere wording. This applies, for example, to the well-known exception clause:

> 'The Act of God, peril of the sea, fire, barratry of the Master and Crew etc. etc. excepted.'

> and this cesser of liability clause:

> 'For the freight . . . the Captain is to hold himself to the Cargo . . . and not to the Shippers. . . . whose responsibility shall cease whenever the Cargo is put on board.'

> Any attempt to understand the meaning of these clauses by merely translating them into the German language is futile. One rather has to assume that, if parties use such terms which are generally established in English shipping practice, they wish to associate with these clauses the same meaning which these clauses are understood to have in England.[22]

---

[22] *Ibid.*, at 67–8. The German original reads: 'Gerade dieser Satz aber nötigt dazu, für die Ermittelung der Bedeutung und Tragweite der einzelnen Klauseln der Chartepartie auf englische Rechtsauffassungen zurückzugehen. Der Berufungsrichter verkennt, daß das hier benutzte Formular durchweg von der dem englischen Rechte eigentümlichen Auffassung des Seefrachtgeschäftes getragen ist. Handelte es sich bloß um die Übersetzung eines von deutschen Rechtsgedanken und deutscher Rechtsauffassung zeugenden Kontraktes, so würde auf die Wahl der Sprache allerdings kein Gewicht zu legen sein. Das ist aber offensichtlich nicht der Fall. Denn außer der hier in Rede stehenden, dem englischen Geschäftsverkehre eigentümlichen Klausel enthält der Vertrag auch in seinen anderen Teilen Bestimmungen, die in englischen Charterpartien allgemein üblich sind, die in einer gewissen seit langer Zeit herkömmlichen Form ausgedrückt werden, und mit denen man in England im Geschäftsverkehre und in der

With this judgment, the Reichsgericht found the appropriate reconciliation between conflict of law rules, which require courts to respect an express choice of German law, and contract terms, which are obviously based on English law. Under the applicable German contract law, contracts are to be interpreted without clinging to the literal meaning of words used; parties who consciously use English contract terms want these clauses to have the same meaning as they would under English law.

However, the same case sees the Reichsgericht struggle with one problem. Penalty clauses are void under English law, while liquidated damages clauses are permitted – what about an English-style indemnity clause on the borderline between penalty clauses and liquidated damages, to which German law applies? The Reichsgericht notes that in England, 'courts are leaning against penalties', but believes that the sum fixed is reasonable and in effect liquidated damages rather than a penalty.[23] But what if this had been a prohibited penalty clause under English law?

German law does not prohibit penalty clauses. On the contrary, §580 HGB contains something rather similar to a penalty clause for contracts for carriage of goods by sea if the freighter repudiates the contract before the journey starts. In this case, the carrier can claim half the agreed-upon rate without having to prove any loss. And because English law enters the case only through the minds of the parties, i.e., as a tool for explaining what the parties wanted to achieve with the contract, the only route by which a German court could have held the penalty clause to have no effect is also through the minds of the parties. The court would have to

---

Rechtspflege einen bestimmten, keineswegs immer schon aus dem bloßen Wortlaute abzuleitenden Sinn verknüpft. So die bekannte exception clause:

> "The Act of God, peril of the sea, fire, barratry of the Master and Crew etc. etc. excepted."

und dieser cesser of liability clause:

> "For the freight . . . the Captain is to hold himself to the Cargo . . ., and not to the Shippers, . . . whose responsibility shall cease whenever the Cargo is put on board."

Es kann nicht angehen, den Sinn dieser Klauseln einfach durch eine Übersetzung ins Deutsche ermitteln zu wollen. Vielmehr muß angenommen werden, daß, wenn sich die Parteien derartiger, im englischen Seefrachtverkehre allgemein eingebürgerter Wendungen bedienen, sie damit auch den Sinn verbinden wollen, der diesen Klauseln in England beigemessen wird.'

[23] *Ibid.*, at 69.

argue that the parties did not intend this clause to have any effect because it would be void under English law, and that it was included in the contract for decoration rather than for any effect. Such an argument would be very difficult to maintain.

Yet nearly 100 years later, in 1991, the Bundesgerichtshof (Federal Court of Justice), Germany's highest court in civil and criminal matters, still fails to give any explanation as to how a penalty clause, valid under the applicable German law, could become void just because it has been modelled on English contract law. This was a case of repudiation of a contract for carriage of goods by sea, where an English indemnity clause met the fallback penalty provision of §580 HGB. All connecting factors in the contract pointed to Germany, except that the contract was based on a GENCON form, which in turn was inspired by English law. The clause read as follows:

> Indemnity for non-performance of this Charterparty, proved damages, not exceeding estimated amount of freight.

It is difficult to see how this provision could be mistaken for a penalty clause. All it does is to place a contractual cap on ordinary damages for breach of contract. Be that as it may, the Bundesgerichtshof sensed danger, and this is how the court found its way out of this situation:

> When interpreting the contract, one cannot ignore the fact that neither the parties nor the agent used for formulating the agreement have any close connections to the Anglo-Saxon legal family. There is therefore no particular reason to assume that the contracting parties wanted to understand this clause, which is used in the same form in German language standard contracts ... and which then is doubtlessly valid, in the English sense. It is in particular the fact that the validity of indemnity clauses has been doubtful in England for decades, but that it nevertheless continues to be used in German shipping circles in knowledge of this fact, which indicates that those who employ this clause are not guided by an Anglo-Saxon under-standing, at least if both parties to the contract are German merchants.[24]

---

[24] BGH 2.12.1991, NJW-RR 1992, 423, at para. 25. The German original reads: 'Bei der Auslegung des Vertrages kann nicht außer acht bleiben, daß er weder nach den Parteien noch nach der Person des bei der Formulierung der Abmachungen eingeschalteten Maklers nähere Beziehungen zum angelsächsischen Rechtskreis hat. Deswegen besteht kein besonderer Anlaß für die Annahme, daß die Vertragschließenden die Klausel, welche in gleicher Form auch in deutschsprachigen Vertragsformularen verwendet wird (...) und dann unzweifelhaft wirksam, ist in englischem Sinn haben verstehen wollen. Gerade der Umstand, daß die Rechtsgeltung der Indemnity-Klausel in England seit Jahrzehnten zweifelhaft ist, sie aber gleichwohl in deutschen Schiffahrtskreisen in Kenntnis dieser Tatsache weiterverwendet wird, spricht dafür, daß die Verwender sich

First, one can note that the Bundesgerichtshof backtracks a little. If a clause agreed between German-based parties looks no different from a normal German clause, English law is not relevant for interpretation. This raises difficult questions of how to interpret a common law-based contract which, as most such contracts would, contains a mixture of clauses which look very English and others which could easily figure in a German-style contract.

Secondly, if the parties to the contract had indeed been influenced by English legal thinking, this seems to imply that a clause which is valid under the applicable German law would be construed as invalid by way of interpretation if the parties to this contract had been influenced by English legal thinking and if such a clause had been void under English law. This is very difficult to reconcile with either German conflict of law rules or with substantive rules on the interpretation of contracts.

This decision by the BGH's Second Senate for Civil Matters is also not easily squared with a previous decision by the same Senate from 1978,[25] which was probably overlooked in the 1991 judgment. The 1978 case concerned a cargo which included, inter alia, seventy vats of bicarbonate of soda, which were declared as such to the Lebanese custom authorities. The declaration had failed to mention, however, that ammunition was buried within the bicarbonate of soda. The ship was seized and fines were imposed. The shippers claimed that they were entirely innocent and had no knowledge of the ammunition. The carriers nevertheless held the shippers liable under the following clause in the bill of lading:

> The Carrier has the right to have the value estimated or to have the contents, measurement or weight verified by experts and if the particulars furnished by the Shipper turn out to be incorrect the Carrier is entitled to charge double the freight which should have been charged had the cargo been correctly described, together with the cost of checking.

Under English law, this clause would in all likelihood be construed as an invalid penalty clause. However, this was again a case of an English-style contract being subjected to German law. In this case, the court did not even mention the fact that English law is hostile towards penalty clauses. The court instead discussed, as a matter of German law, whether a penalty clause can be stipulated in such a way that no fault is required for the clause to operate, as the present clause simply turned on the issue

---

jedenfalls dann nicht vom angelsächsischen Rechtsverständnis leiten lassen, wenn beide Vertragsteile deutsche Kaufleute sind.'
[25] BGH 28.09.1978, BGHZ 72, 174.

of whether the information was correct. The court held that this was possible without violating good faith and upheld the clause.

In summary, we have one judgment by the Federal Court of Justice which upholds an English-style penalty clause and one which expresses serious concerns about enforcing an English-style 'penalty clause' which in fact is no penalty clause at all.

3.2   Financial securities and good faith

The next group of cases concerns financial securities. Two German judgments relate to English-style 'standby letters of credit' which were governed by German law.[26] There is no full equivalent to standby letters of credit in German civil or commercial law, but parties are naturally free to create new types of contracts or import them from abroad. Furthermore, as 'standby letters of credit' somewhat resemble a 'Bürgschaft aufs erste Anfordern' (German demand guarantee), there could be no serious problem with enforcing such contracts. Both judgments use purposive interpretation when deciding between a literal interpretation as proposed by the claimant and a literal interpretation as proposed by the defendants. English courts would probably just do the same. In both cases, purposive interpretation confirmed what the courts rightly thought to be the correct literal interpretation.

The only aspect which is particularly interesting in the present context is the fact that the headnote for one of the judgments states that 'abuse of law' can be raised as a defence under §242 BGB, the famous provision on good faith,[27] against a claim based on a poorly worded standby letter of credit. The judgment by the Oberlandesgericht (Court of Appeal) at Frankfurt clarifies that this is argued only as a safeguard, presumably in case the Bundesgerichtshof should disagree with the court's literal and purposive interpretation. It is nevertheless a clear sign that German courts would be willing to argue good faith against the wording of an English-style contract governed by German law.

---

[26] BGH 26.04.1994, NJW 1994, 2018; OLG Frankfurt 18.3.1997, WM 1997, 1893. No mention is made in the judgments of the Uniform Customs and Practice for Documentary Credits (UCP) or the Uniform Rules for Demand Guarantees (URDG), both developed by the International Chamber of Commerce. The 1995 UN Convention on Independent Guarantees and Stand-By Letters of Credit or an earlier draft of it might also have been available as model.

[27] *§242 BGB Performance in good faith*
  The obligor must perform in a manner consistent with good faith taking into account accepted practice.

3.3 Brokerage and good faith

There is an interesting recent case in brokerage which confirms this suspicion. In 2005, the Bundesgerichtshof had to decide a case in which a company instructed a broker to find a buyer for the company's business, against payment of 10 per cent of the purchase price received by the company.[28] The broker found a buyer, but the business was neither sold as such, nor by the company. Instead, the buyer simply bought all shares from the shareholders and paid the price directly to them without bothering about the commission. The broker sued the company and also both shareholders for 10 per cent commission on the deal. The defendants relied on the wording of the contract. This was written in the English language, using English legal terminology, and its wording did indeed not cover this situation. The Appeal Court had therefore rejected the claim, but the Bundesgerichtshof held that this situation was covered by the economic purpose of the transaction, relied on good faith and allowed the claim. If we apply *The Aliakmon* principles, there was no gap to be bridged, as this was just a case of poor contract drafting. But, of course, the contract was governed by German law and interpreted in the German fashion. The Bundesgerichtshof held that the particular way in which the business was sold was covered by the economic purpose of the agency agreement, which would therefore be interpreted as covering the present situation. Invariably, reference was also made to good faith. It should also be mentioned that English courts have bridged some of this gap by occasionally overriding the literal meaning of contractual provisions on the ground that this flouts common business sense.[29]

3.4 Construction contracts, warnings and fault

The present author also has first-hand experience of a contract for works which was modelled on English law but subjected to German law by way of an express choice-of-law clause. The party which the author represented was a UK company involved as a sub-contractor in a very large construction project in which the other party was the main contractor.

---

[28] BGH 21.12.2005, NJW-RR 2006, 496.

[29] *Investors Compensation Scheme Ltd v. West Bromwich Building Society (No. 1)* [1998] 1 WLR 896, per Lord Hoffmann. An all-too-literal interpretation can also be overcome through estoppel by convention; see *Amalgamated Investment & Property Co. Ltd v. Texas Commerce International Bank Ltd* [1982] QB 84. I am grateful to Edwin Peel for having pointed this out to me.

The factual issues concerned conformity to the specifications of both the sub-contractor's and the main contractor's work. Legal issues between the sub-contractor and the main contractor included:

- which of two different sets of specifications the parties had agreed to;
- acceptance of the work;
- the availability of remedies for delay and for defects;
- the scope and validity of a clause which limited any damages payable by the sub-contractor to 25 per cent of the contract price; and
- the validity of a 'penalty clause' whereby, in case of delay, the sub-contractor was to pay 5 per cent of the contract price.

The case was eventually settled. This is often a very sensible solution. In that case, though, legal uncertainty played a dominant role amongst the incentives. This legal uncertainty was aggravated by a divergence between the law on which a contract is modelled and the law which applied to this contract.

On the facts of this case, German law requires that 'warnings' be issued in order to trigger a claim for damages for delay under §286 of the BGB,[30] and a similar step must be taken by the client in order to switch from a performance-based claim for repair of defects in works contracts to a claim for damages. Additionally, while there is strict liability for performance if this is possible, some remedies require the defaulting party to be responsible for non-performance. It is possible to agree otherwise, i.e., that no warning is necessary and that liability is strict, but English-style contracts do not normally include clauses on warnings being unnecessary and will frequently not say anything on whether fault or responsibility is required to trigger remedies. Thus, this opened up a number of additional legal questions which would not have arisen for either a common law-style contract under English law or a German-style contract under German law.

3.5   Control of standard terms and exclusion clauses

It may well be a coincidence that none of the cases discussed above turned on the control of standard terms. German law subjects standard contract terms, even for business-to-business transactions, to a general unfairness test,[31] which goes beyond what is provided for English law in the Unfair Contract Terms Act 1977. This might result in a situation

---

[30] See above, note 9.
[31] §§305–310 of the BGB. See in particular:

where parts of an English-style contract will not be upheld by German courts on the ground that those clauses are not on all fours with the requirement of good faith.[32] For example, a clause which seeks to exclude liability without making an exception for gross negligence is likely to be void.[33] Exceptions have in the past been allowed if such an exclusion is supported by business usage, as in the shipbuilding industry.[34] In other situations, however, standard terms may not even generally exclude the user's liability for simple negligence, as, for example, in one case which concerned a contract for storage, probably because the fate of the goods is almost completely in the hands of the party who provides storage.[35] Similarly, standard clauses which seek to cap liability to a certain amount will also be held void if they fail to make an exception for gross negligence.[36]

English law does not normally distinguish between simple and gross negligence, so that contract terms based on English law are unlikely to make the necessary exceptions. Standard contract term control could thus eliminate various clauses from common law-based contracts and replace them with German background law.[37]

4   Conclusions

The approach taken by the Reichsgericht in 1897, namely to see English-style clauses in contracts governed by German law as a matter

§307 BGB Review of subject-matter
  (1) Provisions in standard business terms are invalid if, contrary to the requirement of good faith, they place the contractual partner of the user at an unreasonable disadvantage. An unreasonable disadvantage may also result from the fact that the provision is not clear and comprehensible.
  (2) In case of doubt, an unreasonable disadvantage is assumed if a provision
      1. cannot be reconciled with essential basic principles of the statutory rule from which it deviates, or
      2. restricts essential rights or duties resulting from the nature of the contract in such a manner that there is a risk that the purpose of the contract will not be achieved.

[32] See Cordero-Moss, 'International Contracts between Common Law and Civil Law'.
[33] See, e.g., BGH 19.09.2007, BGHZ 174, 1 (sale of used cars).
[34] BGH 3.3.1988, NJW 1988, 1785; U/B/H §309 No. 7 at 43.
[35] BGH 19.2.1998, NJW-RR 1998, 1426.
[36] OLG Düsseldorf 29.11.1990, VersR 1991, 240 (parcel delivery).
[37] See J. R. Maxeiner, 'Standard-Terms Contracting in the Global Electronic Age: European Alternatives', *Yale Journal of International Law*, 28, 1 (2003), 141–156, on likely surprises which the German legislation can cause to common law-oriented contract lawyers.

of contractual interpretation, will usually make sense.[38] If parties use English-style clauses, they will often have done so with English law in mind. It will therefore be usually right to translate these clauses into a German-law meaning by using English law as a tool of understanding. But this approach may be less obvious when all connecting points (such as the domicile, place of business or nationality of the parties and the place of performance) are German and can become problematic if parties did not have English law in mind, such as when they simply plagiarised English-style contracts without realising what they were buying into. This may explain those German judgments which appear more reluctant to opt for the 'English interpretation of German contracts' approach, including both the 1883 judgment of the Reichsgericht and the 1991 judgment of the Bundesgerichtshof which have been discussed above.[39] Using the will of such parties as an entrance gate for English legal thinking can be just as artificial as the numerous terms which English courts have implied into the contracts of entirely unsuspecting parties.[40]

Penalty clauses demonstrate another limit of the prevailing approach which imports notions of English law in order to explain what parties had in mind. It is difficult to argue that clauses which are valid under the applicable law should be void because they would be under the law from which parties have copied the clause. German courts have occasionally flirted with the idea of striking down penalty clauses on this ground. If they ever were to hold such clauses void, they would go beyond inter-pretation in substantive law and would have created a new conflicts rule to the effect that English law applies to English-style penalty clauses in a contract which otherwise is governed by German law. Splitting the applicable law to a contract will, however, generally cause more problems than it solves.

We have seen that some problems may arise if English-style contracts are subjected to the stricter control exercised by German statutes and courts. A case in point is the control of standard terms under §§305–310 BGB, which has frequently been used to invalidate contract clauses even in commercial contracts. Exclusion clauses which are not specifically adapted to these provisions run the danger of being invalid. More interventionist German judges might also interpret contracts against their wording on the ground of good faith where English judges would

---

[38] RG 22.5.1897, RGZ 39, 65; BGH 2.12.1991, NJW-RR 1992, 423.
[39] RG 16.6.1883, RGZ 11, 100.
[40] As, for instance, in the famous case of *Taylor* v. *Caldwell* (1863) 3 B&S 826.

have let the literal meaning prevail. It should be added, though, that the present author has not found any evidence of exaggerated interventionism when German judges have applied German law to common law-based contracts.

We have furthermore noticed that common law-style contracts to which German law applies may be unnecessarily demanding on judges, arbiters and counsels, who may find it difficult to place English-style contracts within a German law context. First, they may simply overlook the foreign element in a contract and for this reason struggle with problems of interpretation. Secondly, even where the foreign element is noticed, they may find it difficult to cope with this particular exercise in conflicts and comparative law.

We have noticed that a loss of legal context occurs whenever a common law-style contract is governed by German law or vice versa. In consequence, some remedies might not be available. This will frequently counteract the main potential advantage of using English-style clauses in contracts governed by German law, namely that such clauses are internationally more recognisable and that they may in particular correspond to contract terms under which one of the parties is bound under a contract with a third party. In the vast majority of cases, however, this is likely to create a mere illusion of certainty and uniformity. If, for instance, a main contractor copies terms from its contract with a client to which English law applies and transplants these clauses to its contract with a sub-contractor to which German law applies, this seeming uniformity is illusionary indeed. This will not exclude the typical risk which a middleman tries to eliminate by using identical contract terms – namely being liable towards the client for a failure of a sub-contractor without being able to resort to the sub-contractor. The sub-contractor may indeed not be liable towards the main contractor, because, for example, responsibility for this failure is required in order for the sub-contractor to be liable under German law, whereas the main contractor may be strictly liable to the client under the English law contract.

The main disadvantage of using common law-style contracts within German law is the legal uncertainty which this creates. Some legal systems cope better with uncertainty than with results which are perceived as unfair, and the German legal system is certainly a case in point. However, the same cannot be said about English contract law, which seems to be preoccupied with legal certainty almost more than with anything else. If certainty is a priority, using common law models in a German legal environment is perhaps not a recipe for disaster, but definitely not a wise choice.

5

Comparing exculpatory clauses under Anglo-American law: testing total legal convergence

EDWARD T. CANUEL

Commercial transactions are increasingly global in scope, spanning jurisdictions and indeed legal families and traditions. Within the comparative law framework, globalisation elevates the prominence and relevance of legal convergence through legal transplants, as attempts have been made under private law regimes to achieve certain minimal levels of contractual standardisation.[1] Legal convergence theory, a currently popular yet controversial comparative law concept, holds that different legal systems may apply different technicalities, but in the end arrive at similar results. In essence, significant distinctions between legal systems are frequently only on the surface.[2]

Testing the validity of total convergence theory, this chapter examines specific, commercially important contractual provisions known in the Anglo-American legal family as 'exculpatory clauses'. Section 1 of this

---

[1] Note that calls in European private law for systemic legal integration and harmonisation, and the possibility of a single European civil law, have dominated substantial legal scholarship. F. Nicola, 'Book Review: The Enforceability of Promises in European Contract Law (ed. by James Gordley)', *Harvard International Law Journal*, 44 (2003), 597, 605; A. Hartkamp and M. Hesselink (eds.), *Towards a European Civil Code* (Kluwer Law International, 1998); M. Hesselink, *The New European Private Law: Essays on the Future of Private Law* (Kluwer Law International, 2002); P. Legrand, 'Against a European Civil Code', *Modern Law Review*, 60 (1997), 44.

[2] See U. Mattei, L. Antoniolli and A. Rossato, 'Abstract: Comparative Law and Economics' (1999), 505, 508, available at http://encyclo.findlaw.com/0560book.pdf (last accessed 28 May 2010) (convergence refers to 'the phenomenon of similar solutions reached by different legal systems from different points of departure'). For a critical view of total legal convergence, see G. Cordero-Moss, *Anglo-American Contract Models and Norwegian or other Civilian Governing Law*, Publications Series of the Institute of Private Law No. 169 (University of Oslo, 2007).

chapter explores the weight and necessity of the comparative legal method. It also further sets the groundwork for this by introducing legal convergence within the context of exculpatory clauses. Section 2 reviews how exculpatory clauses are treated in the US legal context, analyses the legal theory of unconscionability and examines the divergent treatment such clauses receive in different US jurisdictions. While convergence scholarship often involves the comparison of legal concepts between different legal families, this section explores the use of exculpatory clauses within a single legal family, the common law legal tradition. Accordingly, Section 3 utilises a comparative approach, reviewing the use of exculpatory clauses in the context of an important commercial industry, tow and towage, under Anglo-American law. The chapter concludes by surmising that total convergence is problematic.

1   Introducing the comparative legal method: the first step in evaluating total legal convergence

Chinese philosopher Lao Tzu's foresight holds true to comparative law when he wrote that 'a journey of a thousand miles begins with a single step'.[3] Comparisons can be made in a variety of different ways or steps. A method of untangling the convergence-theory web involves the comparative legal *method*, a valuable tool with impact both for scholars and practitioners. Comparative law allows us to venture beyond a simple, mechanical application of given rules.[4] Rather, the comparative approach teaches the analysis of legal problems on a more flexible level, a process where legal concepts can be compared, evaluated and reflected upon.[5]

In such a sense, comparative law scholars may discern legal patterns transcending individual legal systems, discover a certain system's unique attributes, find new alternatives to previously accepted, traditional legal rules or reveal unintended domestic similarities.[6] Comparative study also

---

[3] Lao Tzu, 'Tao Te Ching', in Emily Morrison Beck (ed.), *Bartlett's Familiar Quotations* (Little, Brown and Company, 1980), p. 65.

[4] R. Sacco, 'Legal Formants: A Dynamic Approach to Comparative Law', *American Journal of Commercial Law*, 39 (1991), 1–34, 343–402; R. Sacco, 'One Hundred Years of Comparative Law', *Tulane Law Review*, 75 (2001), 1159–1176; see also C. A. Rogers, 'Review Essay: Gulliver's Troubled Travels, or the Conundrum of Comparative Law', *George Washington Law Review*, 67 (1998), 149–190, 157.

[5] K. Schadbach, 'The Benefits of Comparative Law: A Continental European View', *Boston University International Law Journal*, 16 (1998), 331–422, 415.

[6] D. A. Farber, 'Book Review: The Hermeneutic Tourist: Statutory Interpretation in Comparative Perspective', *Cornell Law Review*, 81 (1996), 513–529, 515.

reveals how different laws handling the same problem actually function in practice. Through this approach, a comparison necessarily assumes two or more sectors, laws or periods of time, which are analysed with the purpose of discovering differences and similarities.

While a detailed comparison of the common and civil law systems is beyond the scope of this chapter, any comparative law piece must distinguish essential systemic characteristics from these widely held legal traditions. Under the civil law tradition, courts interpret and apply written laws, which include codes, statutes and decrees.[7] The civil law system presents the law-giving role to the legislator, who crafts a code that controls the judiciary's acts, while the civilian judges must identify the proper existing rule and apply it to the facts of the subject case.[8] Alternatively, the common law family is composed of organic law, with judges reliant upon *stare decisis*.[9] The importance civil law courts place on *stare decisis* is less well settled: the value given to precedents in the civil law context is a source of dissention among legal scholars.[10]

---

[7] See P. G. Stein, 'Relationships among Roman Law, Common Law and Modern Civil Law: Roman Law, Common Law and Civil Law', *Tulane Law Review*, 66 (1992), 1591–1603, 1595–1596; J. L. Freisen, 'When Common Law Courts Interpret Civil Codes', *Wisconsin International Law Journal*, 15 (1996), 1, 7; J. Dainow, 'The Civil Law and the Common Law: Some Points of Comparison' *American Journal of Comparative Law*, 15 (1967), 419–435, 424.

[8] See R. B. Cappalli, 'Open Forum: At the Point of Decision: The Common Law's Advantage over the Civil Law', *Temple International and Comparative Law Journal*, 12 (1998), 87, 96–97. See, generally, Shumei Lu, 'Gap Filling and Freedom of Contract' (2000) (Athens: Master's Thesis, University of Georgia), available at http://digitalcommons.law.uga.edu (last accessed 20 June 2008).

[9] See Cappalli, 'Open Forum', 92; M. Sellers, 'The Doctrine of Precedent in the United States of America', *American Journal of Comparative Law*, 54 (2006), 67–88, 86; see also *Auto Equity Sales* v. *Superior Court of Santa Clara County*, 369 P.2d 937 (1962), 939–940 ('the doctrine of stare decisis requires all tribunals of inferior jurisdiction to follow the precedents of courts of superior jurisdiction, to accept the law as declared by superior courts, and not to attempt to overrule their decisions').

[10] See Freisen, 'When Common Law Courts Interpret Civil Codes', 8 (stating that existing judicial decisions are not formally binding legal sources). See also J. H. Merryman, *The Civil Law Tradition* (Little, Brown and Company, 1985), pp. 46, 60; R. David and J. E. C. Brierly, *Major Legal Systems in the World Today* (Stevens and Sons Publishing, 1985), pp. 136–137. But see W. Ewald, 'What's So Special about American Law?', *Oklahoma City University Law Review*, 26 (2001), 1083–1115, 1088 (civilian courts do not embrace the same necessity for precedents as in the common law system; civil law courts may in practice follow precedent to avoid the chance of a reversal, causing the subject court embarrassment and possibly adversely affecting the subject judge's promotional chances); C. Pejovic, 'Civil Law and Common Law: Two Different Paths Leading to the Same Goal', *Victoria University of Wellington Law Review*, 32 (2001), 817–842, 821, No. 8 at

Comparativists also note key distinguishing traits *within* the civil law family, as demonstrated by reviewing the Scandinavian legal traditions.[11] Compared to other civil law traditions, Scandinavian regimes lack a systematic codification of the law of obligations and significantly elevate equitable justice over individual autonomy.[12]

1.1 Legal convergence theory: discussion points

Modern comparative law research focuses on finding underlying similarities across legal families. A clear trend is to highlight the fact that perceived divergent outcomes based on systemic differences may be overemphasised. Looking deeper, disparate legal systems may apply different technicalities, but in the end lead to similar results. This is convergence theory.

Convergence theory may be evaluated through the lens of a certain form of exemption provision,[13] an exculpatory clause. Given the great importance of legal convergence in both scholarship and practice,[14] this chapter will additionally address the related topic of legal technicalities, showing that they may have a deeper significance than expected. This chapter will not focus on comparisons across legal families, but across states belonging to *one* family: the Anglo-American family. Ultimately, total convergence within a single legal family cannot be presumed, which

---

www.upf.pf/IMG/doc/16Pejovic.doc (last accessed 28 May 2010). See also M. A. Glendon *et al.*, *Comparative Legal Traditions* (West Publishing, 1994), p. 208.

[11] For a basic overview of the various Scandinavian legal systems, see M. Bogdan, *Comparative Law* (Kluwer Law International, 1994); K. Zweigert and H. Kötz, *Introduction to Comparative Law* (Oxford University Press, 1998). See also Pejovic, 'Civil Law and Common Law', 818 ('the term "civil law" has two meanings: in its narrow meaning it designates the law related to the areas covered by the civil codes, while the broader meaning of civil law relates to the legal systems based on codes as contrasted to the common law system').

[12] G. Cordero-Moss, 'International Contracts between Common Law and Civil Law: Is Non-state Law to be Preferred? The Difficulty of Interpreting Legal Standards such as Good Faith', *Global Jurist (Advances)*, 7 (2007), 1, 14. Unlike other countries inspired by Germanic law, Norway founded its contract interpretation on the Act on Formation of Contracts of 1918 and has not codified its obligations law. See *ibid.*, 13, referring to J. Hov, 'Avtaleslutning og ugyldighet', in *Kontratsrett I* (Papinian, 2002), pp. 60, 167–168.

[13] 'A contractual provision relieving a party from liability resulting from a negligent or wrongful act': Bryan A. Garner (ed.), *Black's Law Dictionary* (West Publishing, 1999).

[14] See L. Nottage, 'Comment on Civil Law and Common Law: Two Different Paths Leading to the Same Goal', *Victoria University of Wellington Law Review*, 32 (2001), 843–851, 848.

further suggests that it is even more difficult to assume total convergence across many families.[15] Investigating convergence theory, a review of exemption clauses in the US and its different jurisdictions, illustrates a lack of total convergence. Additionally, through comparing the US regime to that of its common law cousin, England, a lack of complete convergence is revealed.

Exemption clauses relieving liability from negligent acts, also known as exculpatory provisions, will be reviewed under a comparative framework. These important contract provisions are found in many standardised agreements used in daily commerce. To evaluate possible convergence within the American legal regime, one must understand how the exemption clauses are evaluated under US law. This involves reviewing the limitations of the clauses' use based upon unconscionability and public policy, also revealing tensions regarding the boundaries of American contractual freedom.[16]

Cases from different US state and federal jurisdictions will be compared. Understanding US law sets the stage for comparing the American and English legal regimes by analysing exemption clauses in a specific area of admiralty law – towage. The result will reveal that total convergence has not occurred in one legal family and will raise doubts as to whether such convergence could spread *across* legal families.

---

[15] See, generally, G. Cordero-Moss, 'Commercial Contracts between Consumer Protection and Trade Usages: Some Observations on the Importance of State Contract Law', in R. Schulze (ed.), *Common Frame of Reference and Existing EC Contract Law* (Sellier, 2008), p. 65. See also J. H. Merryman, 'On the Convergence (and Divergence) of the Civil Law and the Common Law', in *The Loneliness of the Comparative Lawyer and other Essays in Foreign and Comparative Law* (Kluwer Law International, 1999), pp. 17, 27.

[16] Under the common law, freedom of contract is often held to be prime. Parties are free to enter into mutually beneficial economic exchanges. Absent public policy exceptions, courts will not inquire into the bargain's wisdom. The words and terms used in the contracting parties' agreement will otherwise have control, as parties will live with the benefits and burdens of their bargain. See *Baltimore & Ohio Sw. Ry. Co.* v. *Voigt*, 176 U.S. 498, 505 (1900). Compare this to the principles of good faith, which are held to be central under the civil law. See Garner (ed.), *Black's Law Dictionary*, p. 693 (good faith is 'an intangible and abstract quality with no technical meaning or statutory definition, and it encompasses, among other things, an honest belief, the absence of malice and the absence of design to defraud or to seek an unconscionable advantage'); A. D. Mitchell, 'Good Faith in WTO Dispute Settlement', *Melbourne Journal of International Law*, 7 (2006), 339–373 (in a civil law context, good faith is 'a principle of fair and open dealing'). For an interesting discussion of good faith and freedom of contract in the comparative law context, see Cordero-Moss, 'International Contracts between Common Law and Civil Law', 12.

Legal technicalities will also be examined, reviewing the breadth of their significance. Contracts may be shaped for the purpose of meeting specific requirements of one legal system, as evidenced in the admiralty context. Legal systems may have different technicalities, rules or requirements: writing a valid contract in one system means complying with these technicalities. Another system may demand different technicalities in order to have a contract validated in its jurisdiction. Contracts will thus be written differently to obtain the same result in different systems. If these contracts migrate into each different legal system, any potential convergence could be annulled.

2   Exculpatory clauses: background, interaction with contractual theories and duties

The starting point for analysis begins with the exculpatory clause itself, related to the exemption clause. An exemption clause is a 'contractual provision providing that a party will not be liable for damages for which that party would otherwise have ordinarily been liable'.[17] American courts often specify exemption clauses excluding negligence as exculpatory clauses. Such a clause is defined as a 'contractual provision relieving a party from liability resulting from a negligent or wrongful act'. In fact, Corbin labels the term 'exemption clauses' as 'the British terminology for exculpatory clauses'.[18] Clauses exempting liability from negligence are found in many standard business contracts, often involving essential commercial activities. Such contracts serve important purposes, attempting to streamline efficiencies in business transactions that are crucial to the daily conduct of business.[19] Simplifying standard transactions, non-negotiated boilerplate contracts may reduce transaction costs, saving drafters time and expense.[20]

---

[17] K. Bruett, 'Can Wisconsin Businesses Safely Rely upon Exculpatory Contracts to Limit their Liability?', *Marquette Law Review*, 81 (1998), 1081, referring to Garner (ed.), *Black's Law Dictionary*, p. 566 (the term 'exculpatory clause' is defined as '[a] contract clause which releases one of the parties from liability for his or her wrongful acts').

[18] A. L. Corbin, *Corbin on Contracts*, 15 vols., Joseph Perillo (ed.), (Matthew Bender and Company, 2002), vol. vii, Section 29.7, p. 401.

[19] See, generally, *Arrowhead School Dist. No. 75, Park County v. Klyap*, 79 P.3d 250 (2003).

[20] See E. A. Farnsworth, *Farnsworth on Contracts*, 3 vols. (Aspen Publishers, 1998), vol. ii, Section 4.26, p. 533; James P. Nehf, 'Writing Contracts in the Client's Interest', *South Carolina Law Review*, 51 (1999), 153.

To understand the possibility of convergence within the American legal system's disparate legal jurisdictions, in light of exculpatory clauses, the method employed by courts must be discussed. US courts evaluate the clauses, particularly within the context of boilerplate contracts, by considering issues and factors such as unconscionability, adequate disclosure, relative bargaining power and public policy.[21]

2.1   The role of unconscionability

Unconscionability is an amorphous term.[22] It has been defined in *Williams* v. *Walker-Thomas Furniture, Co.* as an 'absence of meaningful choice on the part of one of the parties together with contract terms which are unreasonably favorable to the other party'.[23] The concept is also embedded in the Uniform Commercial Code ('UCC' or 'Code') at §2–302.[24] Unconscionability moved outside the UCC and migrated into the general law of contracts.[25] This contractual theory is primarily applied to consumer transactions, with courts stating that businesses are expected to guard against their own commercial dealings to a larger extent than consumers.[26] In the commercial context, courts tend to limit the doctrine's use to contracts involving small businesses that appear to be differentiated by implication from larger corporations by courts.[27]

---

[21] Farnsworth, *Farnsworth on Contracts*, vol. ii, Section 5.2, pp. 12, 14.

[22] Farnsworth laments that 'Nowhere under the Code's many definitions is there one of *unconscionability*. That the term is incapable of precise definition is a source of both strength and weakness' (emphasis in original): Farnsworth, *Farnsworth on Contracts*, vol. i, Section 4.28, p. 555. See also Corbin, *Corbin on Contracts*, vol. vii, Section 29.3, p. 377 ('Unconscionability is one of the most amorphous terms in the law of contracts').

[23] *Williams* v. *Walker-Thomas Furniture, Co.*, 350 F.2d 445, 449 (D.C. Cir. 1965) (unconscionability is the 'absence of meaningful choice on the part of one of the parties together with contract terms which are unreasonably favorable to the other party'); *A&M Produce Co.* v. *FMC Corp.*, 135 Cal. App. 3d 473 (1982) (unconscionability is defined as 'a flexible doctrine designed to allow courts to directly consider numerous factors which may adulterate the contractual process').

See also, Farnsworth, *Farnsworth on Contracts*, vol. i, Section 4.28, p. 555; *NEC Technologies, Inc.* v. *Nelson*, 478 S.E.2d, 771–772 (1996).

[24] The Code, which effectively merged equity doctrine into law, is a uniform act promulgated to harmonise the law of the sale of goods and other transactions. For a detailed treatment of §2–302 of the UCC (Unconscionable Contract or Clause), see Corbin, *Corbin on Contracts*, vol. vii, Section 29.3, pp. 383–387. See also §2–719(3) of the UCC.

[25] Corbin, *Corbin on Contracts*, vol. vii, Section 29.3, pp. 382–383.

[26] *Ibid.* See also Farnsworth, *Farnsworth on Contracts*, vol. i, Section 4.28, pp. 562–563.

[27] See, e.g., *De Valk Lincoln Mercury* v. *Ford Motor Co.*, 811 F.2d 326 (Seventh Cir. 1987); *Stirlen* v. *supercuts, Inc.*, 60 Cal. Rptr. 2d 138 (Ct. App. 1997).

A further divide was raised in *NEC Technologies, Inc.* v. *Nelson*, where the court analysed unconscionability in terms of both procedure and substance.[28] Procedural unconscionability focuses on the contract-making process, with courts looking to factors including the parties' business acumen, experience, bargaining power, the contract language's comprehensibility and the 'oppressiveness' of the terms.[29] Concerning substantive unconscionability, courts focus on issues such as the contractual terms' commercial reasonableness, the purpose and effect of the terms, parties' risk allocation and other public policy concerns.

The impact of unconscionability in practice is controversial, as Corbin writes:

> Most claims of unconscionability fail. The mere fact that there is a lack of equivalence between the performances of the parties does not even get close to the establishment of unconscionability. A harsh result alone is an insufficient ground for a finding of unconscionability. Superior bargaining power is not in itself a ground for striking down a resultant contract as unconscionable.[30]

Further, as Farnsworth discusses:

> On the whole, judges have been cautious in applying the doctrine of unconscionability, recognising that the parties often must make their contract quickly, that their bargaining power will rarely be equal, and that courts are ill-equipped to deal with problems of unequal distribution of wealth in society.[31]

2.2 Assent, duty to read

Courts will also seek to ensure parties assented to exculpatory clauses. The common law 'duty to read' has been one measure to recognise assent. Under that duty, a party who executes an instrument manifests assent to it and later cannot complain that it neither read nor understood the agreement.[32] The same rule applies even without a signature if the acceptance of a document purporting to be a contract implies assent to its

---

[28] *NEC Technologies, Inc.* v. *Nelson*, 478 S.E. 2d, 771–772 (1996).

[29] *Ibid.* See also Farnsworth, vol. i, Section 4.28, p. 557 ('fashionable' to brand 'an absence of meaningful choice' as procedural unconscionability); Corbin, *Corbin on Contracts*, vol. vii, Section 29.4, pp. 387–389 (holding that elements of both procedural and substantive unconscionability are frequently present).

[30] Corbin, *Corbin on Contracts*, vol. vii, Section 29.7, pp. 392–393.

[31] Farnsworth, *Farnsworth on Contracts*, vol. i, Section 4.28, p. 559.

[32] A. L. Corbin, *Corbin on Contracts*, vol. vii, Section 29.8, pp. 402–403.

terms (such as bills of lading or insurance policies).[33] There are many qualifications to this duty indicating that there was actually no assent to the contractual terms, including: (i) the document was illegible; (ii) the terms were not sufficiently called to the attention of a party; and (iii) misrepresentation of the document's contents.[34] Nevertheless, there is also case law *subverting* the established duty-to-read proposition when dealing with form contracts on three grounds: (i) no true assent existed to a particular term; (ii) public policy dictates that a particular term be removed, even if there was assent, because it contravenes public policy; or (iii) the term is unconscionable.[35] Courts may now incorporate all three elements in such 'modified' duty-to-read analysis.[36]

At first blush, unconscionability suggests that common and civil law can converge. In this specific context, common law courts may apply the law in a way resembling that usually found in the civil law context. That context is grounded on good-faith principles and approaches, meaning a flexible application of principles and general clauses of fair and open dealing.[37] Nevertheless, the diversity of decisions within the US reveals that outcomes may not be the same, again doubting consistent convergence in practice.

One such example is *Weaver* v. *American Oil Co.*, 276 NE2d 144 (1971), an Indiana Supreme Court case, which involved a lease from an oil company to a gas station operator. The station owner signed the lease without reading it. The lease provided that he would indemnify the oil company, acting as lessor, for damages caused by the lessor's negligence: the clause rather broadly excluded liability.[38] The court did

---

[33] See *ibid.*, p. 403.   [34] See *ibid*, pp. 404–415.

[35] *Weaver* v. *American Oil Co.*, 276 NE2d 144 (1971).

[36] See, generally, Corbin, *Corbin on Contracts*, vol. vii, Section 29.10, pp. 415–424.

[37] See L. A. DiMatteo, 'An International Contract Law Formula: The Informality of International Business Transactions Plus the Internationalisation of Contract Law Equals Unexpected Contractual Liability', *Syracuse Journal of International Law and Commerce*, 23 (1997), 67–111, 85–86, referring to Dennis Campbell (ed.), *Legal Aspects of Doing Business in Western Europe* (Kluwer, 1983), pp. 295, 218 ('Civil law states tend to use a more expansive approach to the good faith obligation applying it to both contract formation and performance. Common law states prefer a more narrow good faith duty applicable only to contract performance'). See also Cordero-Moss, 'Commercial Contracts between Consumer Protection and Trade Usages', 65, 68; Cordero-Moss, 'International Contracts between Common Law and Civil Law', 12.

[38] 'Lessor, its agents and employees shall not be liable for any loss, damage, injuries, or other casualty of whatsoever kind or by whomsoever caused to the person or property of anyone (including Lessee) on or off the premises, arising out of or resulting from Lessee's use, possession or operation thereof, or from defects in the premises whether apparent or

not find true assent, and held public policy violations and contractual unconscionability.

Finding an unequal power relationship between the oil company and the gas station owner, the court raised its view of an evolving freedom of contract. First, the court cited Justice Frankfurter's dissent in the landmark Supreme Court case, *U.S. v. Bethlehem Steel*, 315 U.S. 289, 312 (1942):

> Fraud and physical duress are not the only grounds upon which courts refuse to enforce contracts. The law is not so primitive that it sanctions every injustice except brute force and downright fraud. More specifically, the courts generally refuse to lend themselves to the enforcement of a 'bargain' in which one party has unjustly taken advantage of the economic necessities of the other.
>
> The traditional contract is the result of free bargaining of parties who are brought together by the play of the market, and who meet each other on a footing of approximate economic equality. In such a society there is no danger that freedom of contract will be a threat to the social order as a whole. But in present-day commercial life the standardized mass contract has appeared. It is used primarily by enterprises with strong bargaining power and position. The weaker party, in need of the good or services, is frequently not in a position to shop around for better terms, either because the author of the standard contract has a monopoly (natural or artificial) or because all competitors use the same clauses.[39]

Reflecting upon Justice Franfurter's dissent, the *American Oil* court held that:

> When a party can show that the contract, which is sought to be enforced, was in fact an unconscionable one, due to a prodigious amount of bargaining power on behalf of the stronger party, which is used to the stronger party's advantage and is unknown to the lesser party, causing a great hardship and risk on the lesser party, the contract provision, or the contract as a whole, if the provision is not separable, should not be enforceable on the grounds that the provision is contrary to public policy.

---

hidden, or from the installation existence, use, maintenance, condition, repair, alteration, removal or replacement of any equipment thereon, whether due in whole or in part to negligent acts or omissions of Lessor, its agents or employees; and Lessee for himself, his heirs, executors, administrators, successors and assigns, hereby agrees to indemnify and hold Lessor, its agents and employees, harmless from and against all claims, demands, liabilities, suits or actions (including all reasonable expenses and attorneys' fees incurred by or imposed on the Lessor in connection therewith) for such loss, damage, injury or other casualty. Lessee also agrees to pay all reasonable expenses and attorneys' fees incurred by Lessor in the event that Lessee shall default under the provisions of this paragraph.' *Weaver v. American Oil Co.*, 276 NE2d, 144, 145 (1971).

[39] *Ibid.*, 146.

> The party seeking to enforce such a contract has the burden of showing that the provisions were explained to the other party and came to his knowledge and there was in fact a real and voluntary meeting of the minds and not merely an objective meeting.[40]

The court thus found the contract to be unconscionable. The objective assent which stems from a duty to read cannot bind a contracting party to clauses which are unfair, unless the provisions are brought to the obligated party's attention and explained. The rationale is that an informed, voluntary consent must be required as such provisions impose a greater risk to a weaker party in the midst of a power relationship with a much stronger contracting partner.[41]

Other jurisdictions take a markedly different approach, particularly in the commercial context. Take, for instance, the recent US Federal District Court of Minnesota case, *Hormel Foods Corporation* v. *Chr. Hansen, Inc.*, 2001 WL 1636490 (D.Minn.) (no page numbers available online). In that case, Hormel, the international food producer, alleged that Hansen sold it dry mustard spice which, unfortunately, also contained pieces of rubber. Hansen, in turn, contracted with the firm Montana Specialty Mills to produce the mustard. Hormel was not pleased with such a distasteful, unsavoury situation: customers do not appreciate rubber-enhanced Dijon. A lawsuit followed and parties with any possible link to this troublesome spice were included in that action. After Hormel sued Hansen, Hansen joined Montana to the suit, who in turn sued the manufacturers of a rubber conveyor belt identified as the contamination source.

Investigating the underlying agreement and its implications on third-party suppliers, the court held that an exculpatory clause would be enforced where there is 'no vast disparity in the bargaining power between the parties and the intention to do so is expressed in clear and unequivocal language'.[42] The exculpatory clause was extremely broad and did not specifically refer to acts of negligence. It held that:

> Hansen shall indemnify and hold Montana harmless from 'any liability of whatsoever nature or kind' derived from Hansen's use of the spice blend.[43]

---

[40] *Ibid.*, 147–148.
[41] See *Kansas City Power & Light Company* v. *United Telephone Company of Kansas, Inc.* 458 F.2d 177 (1972).
[42] *Hormel Foods Corporation* v. *Chr. Hansen, Inc.*, 2001 WL 1636490 (D.Minn.) (no page numbers available online).
[43] *Ibid.*

Even with such broad wording not specifically indicating negligence, the court upheld the clause, focusing on the fact that the contracting parties should have known what they were bargaining into.

Similarly, the *Pinnacle Computer* v. *Ameritech Publishing, Inc.*, 642 N.E.2d 1011 (1995) court in the US Federal District Court of Appeals in Indiana distinguished itself from its *American Oil* brethren. In that case, a yellow pages advertiser brought suit against a publisher for breach of contract when the advertiser's display ad was mistakenly omitted from the correct section of the yellow pages.[44] The appellate court found that the contracting parties mutually assented to an enforceable exculpatory provision.

The *Pinnacle* court distinguished the case before it from *American Oil*, while the court's decision closely analysed the *American Oil* facts. There, the gas station businessman was a man with only one-and-a-half year's worth of high school education and was told to sign, without any explanation, the oil company's standard lease drawn up by the company's attorneys.[45] The exculpatory clause was in fine print and contained no title heading. The *Pinnacle* facts were different. In *Pinnacle*, the plaintiff, a business owner, had a higher level of education. He was a president of a company engaged in a fairly technical career: the sale, repair and installation of computer-related equipment.[46] Although he alleged that the clause was not explained to him prior to signing the contract, the court found that he had the ability, unlike the *American Oil* gas station owner, to read and understand the clause's significance. Further, the clause was printed in a manner designed to emphasise its most crucial provisions. As the court said: 'Nothing in the designated matters in this case demonstrates that Ameritech's contract was one that no sensible person not under delusion, duress or in distress would make, and that no honest and fair person would accept.'[47]

Thus, there is a tension among jurisdictions regarding enforceability of contracts in a commercial setting: the referenced cases cut across jurisdictions and revealed different outcomes within one nation's legal system.[48] In general, a contracting party may exempt another party

---

[44] *Pinnacle Computer* v. *Ameritech Publishing, Inc*, 642 N.E.2d 1011, 1012 (1995).
[45] See *ibid.*, 1017.   [46] See *ibid.*
[47] *Pinnacle Computer* v. *Ameritech Publishing, Inc*, 642 N.E.2d, 1011, 1017 (1995).
[48] See *Continental Airlines* v. *GoodyearTire & Rubber Co.*, 819 F.2d 1519, 1527 (9th Cir. 1987) (the court held that invoking the unconscionability doctrine in a matter involving 'two large, legally sophisticated companies' made 'little sense'); *K&C Westinghouse Elec. Corp.*, 263 A.2d, p. 390 (PA. 1970).

from liability resulting from ordinary negligence. Note, however, that courts do not enforce agreements to exempt parties from liability 'if the liability results from that party's own gross negligence, recklessness or intentional misconduct'.[49] Nevertheless, the general enforceability rule does not apply to certain agreements, including when a party released from liability renders a public service and the agreement relates to that service.[50] In such instances, courts consider a variety of factors, including whether the activity is suitable for public regulation, whether there is a decisive unequal bargaining power and whether the clause is part of a standardised contract.[51] Although there are several cases involving exemption-from-negligence provisions based upon public policy, courts tend to tightly limit such provisions to very specific situations.[52]

While US courts may agree that an exculpatory provision cannot be enforced if the words do not clearly express an intention to exclude liability, they clearly disagree on exculpatory clause *construction*. Several cases express that a liability exemption is not interpreted from liability of harm negligently caused and require that the provision *expressly intended* to include the actor's negligence.[53] Other courts acknowledge that the intention to exclude liability for negligence may be made clear without specifically using the word 'negligence'.[54] Such an example was found in the *Hormel* case, where the liability based on negligence was not specifically exempted. Yet again, American law takes different perspectives when handling these clauses.

In a comparative sense, US jurisdictions do not share unanimity as to interpreting exculpatory clauses. A specific area of admiralty law, tug and towing, further demonstrates how Anglo-American family members have comparatively divergent views on exculpatory clauses.

---

[49] Corbin, *Corbin on Contracts*, vol. xv, Section 85.18, p. 455.   [50] *Ibid.*, pp. 455–456.

[51] *Brooks* v. *Timberline Tours, Inc.*, 127 F.3d, p. 1273 (10th Cir. 1997).

[52] See, e.g., *Pittsburgh, C.C. & St. L. Ry.* v. *Kinney*, 115 N.E. 505 (Ohio 1916); *Tunkl* v. *Regents of University of California*, 383 P.2d , 442, 445–446 (Cal. 1963); *Harris* v. *National Evaluation Sys.*, 719 F. supp. 1081 (N.D. Ga. 1989).

[53] See, e.g., *Eller* v. *NationsBank of Texas, N.A.*, 975 S.W.2d 803 (Texas Ct. App. 1998); *Freddi-Gail, Inc.* v. *Royal Holding Corp.*, 34 N.J. super. 142, 133 (1955); *J.A. Jones Constr. Co.* v. *City of Dover*, 372 A.2d, 540 (Del super. Ct. 1977).

[54] See, e.g., *Lexington Ins. Co.* v. *Tires Into Recycled Energy & supplies, Inc.*, 522 S.E., 2d 798 (1999); *Basin Oil Co.* v. *Baash-Ross Tool Co.*, 271 P.2d 122 (1954).

3   Testing convergence within the Anglo-American family: towage contracts and exculpatory clauses

In practice, exculpatory provisions are involved in contracts contending with significant commercial interests. Such is the case with towage,[55] which plays a strong, vibrant role in global transport, and holds an important place in the American economy. Towage-service contracts are often complex, reflecting the substantial hazards and enormous potential liabilities involved in providing towage services. The towage contract is the parties' agreement that the tug will 'skillfully and carefully move the towed object and deliver it in good condition to the agreed destination'.[56] In American towage law, a tower may, with limitations, contract to exculpate itself from liability for its own negligence.

3.1   The development of US law: Bisso and beyond

The current US law of towage and exculpatory clauses developed from the seminal US Supreme Court case, *Bisso* v. *Inland Waterways Corp.*, 349 U.S. 85 (1955), and its progeny.[57] That case involved a contract to tow an oil barge on the Mississippi River. Due to the tug's negligent towage, the barge collided with a bridge pier and sank.[58] Sued by the barge owners, the defendants invoked two clauses contained in the towage agreement.[59]

---

[55] A. L. Parks and E. V. Cattell, Jr. (eds.), *The Law of Tug, Tow and Pilotage* (Schiffer Publishing, 1994), p. 18 ('Towing is the employment of one vessel to expedite the voyage of another when nothing more is required than accelerating of its progress'). See also B. L. Feingerts and M. S. Stein, 'Exculpatory Provisions in Towage Contracts', *Tulane Law Review*, 49 (1975), 392; The American Waterways Operators at www.american-waterways.com/about_industry/index.html (last accessed 11 January 2010) (the towage industry adds $5 billion a year to the US economy).

[56] J. C. Sweeney, 'Collisions Involving Tugs and Tows', *Tulane Law Review*, 70 (1995), 581, 591–592.

[57] For a spirited discussion of *Bisso* involving preeminent admiralty scholars and practitioners, see 'Panel Discussion of Collision, Towage, Salvage, and Limitation of Liability (March 18, 1999)', *Tulane Maritime Law Journal*, 24 (1999), 405.

[58] *Bisso* v. *Inland Waterways Corp.*, 349 U.S., 85, 86 (1955).

[59] *Ibid.* The clauses held that:

(4) The movement contemplated will be done at the sole risk of the 'craft to be towed' and its cargo, and neither the boats and/or any other equipment used in said service nor the owner, charterer or hirer thereof shall be liable for any loss or damage to the 'craft to be towed' or its cargo nor for any damage done by the 'craft to be towed,' however occurring.

The masters and crews and employees of all boats and/or other equipment assisting the 'craft to be towed' shall, in the performance of said service, become

The court refused to enforce the clauses, with the majority citing public policy reasons. First, the court found the pressing need to discourage negligence, which could be achieved by making wrongdoers pay damages.[60] Secondly, it sought to protect those needing towed goods or towage services from being overreached by other actors (including possible monopolies) who were empowered to drive 'hard bargains'.[61] Thus, *Bisso* prohibits exculpatory language that relieves a tug from all liability for negligent towage.

Justice Frankfurter wrote a blistering twenty-two-page dissent. Among other things, he argued that the clauses should be enforceable on policy grounds. He did not find any evidence of unequal bargaining power.[62] He found no basis that the tug industry was so concentrated in ownership that tug owners had the ability, as monopolists, to dictate terms.[63] He also attacked the majority decision, alarmed by the court's use of judicial interpretation and concerned that the majority undermined contractual freedom principles.[64]

The number of exceptions and limitations to the *Bisso* holding, and the clever ways around that holding, show how the common law evolves. For example, the Supreme Court again addressed negligent towage in *Boston Metals Co.* v. *The Winding Gulf*, 349 U.S. 122 (1955), a case decided the same day as *Bisso*. *Boston Metals* involved a collision between an obsolete destroyer towed to a scrapping yard and a third vessel. The destroyer sank and the third vessel was damaged. The contract between the tug company and the destroyer's owners provided that: (i) the tug master and crew became the servants of the tow; and (ii) the tow owner would indemnify the tug company against all damage.[65] The tug was guilty of negligent navigation. The Supreme Court held that *Bisso* controlled and ignored the contract language specifying that the master and crew of the tug company would become servants of the tow. Public policy could not be circumvented by stipulating that the tug's employees would be considered the agents of the tow in order to shield the tug from liability.[66]

Dixilyn Drilling Corp. v. *Crescent Towing & Salvage Co.*, 372 U.S. 697 (1963) involved a contract where a tow would indemnify the tower

---

and be the servants of the 'craft to be towed' regardless of whether the 'craft to be towed' assists in the service in any way and irrespective of whether they be aboard the 'craft to be towed' or in command thereof. *Ibid.*, 120.

[60] *Ibid.*, 91.   [61] *Ibid.*   [62] *Bisso* v. *Inland Waterways Corp.*, 349 U.S., 85, 116 (1955).
[63] *Ibid.*   [64] *Bisso* v. *Inland Waterways Corp.*, 349 U.S., 85, 100 (1955).
[65] Sweeney, 'Collisions Involving Tugs and Tows', 593–594.
[66] Parks and Cattell, Jr. (eds.), *The Law of Tug, Tow and Pilotage*, pp. 70–71.

against third-party claims based on the tower's negligence. Further, the tow would provide the tower with the benefit of the tow's insurance. In a brief opinion, the Supreme Court, citing *Bisso*, overturned the Fifth Circuit decision which had upheld the clause. The Supreme Court suggested in *dicta* that the clause violated public policy given that the provision released the tower from all liability for its negligence.[67]

The *Bisso* court and subsequent decisions made it clear that the Supreme Court would not permit exculpatory language relieving tugs from all liability stemming from negligent towage. Comparing US, English and Canadian admiralty law on this issue reveals contrasts and opposing views *within* the Anglo-American family.

3.2   The common law family comparison: English law

English law recognises the validity of exculpatory clauses in towage contracts. The central case is *The President Van Buren* (1924) 19 Ll. L. Rep. 185. In this case, the tug owner was the Port of London Authority, a statutory authority controlling docks and wharves. Any vessel using the Authority's docks was required to employ its tugs: the Authority effectively had a monopoly over tug services.[68] Included in the conditions for the use of the tugs was a clause that tug masters and crew were to be servants of the towed vessel, and were thus effectively subject to the vessel's orders and control.[69] The vessel would also indemnify the Authority for any damage to its property or for other loss caused by the towed vessel.

The relevant exemption provision was as follows:

> The masters and crew of the tugs and transport men shall cease to be under the control of the port authority during and for all purposes connected with the towage or transport and shall become subject in all things to the orders and control of the master or person in charge of the vessel or craft towed or transported and are the servants of the owner or owners thereof who hereby undertake to pay for any damage caused to any of the port authority's property or premises and to bear, satisfy and indemnify the port authority against liability for all claims for loss of life or injury to person or loss or damage by collision or otherwise to the vessel or to or by the vessel or craft towed or to or by any cargo or other thing on board the same or to or by any vessel cargo or property of any other

---

[67] *Ibid.*

[68] See also Feingerts and Stein, 'Exculpatory Provisions in Towage Contracts', 404.

[69] *The President Van Buren* (1924) 19 Ll. L. Rep. 185, 186–187.

person or persons or to the tug or tugs supplied, whether such damage loss or injury arise or be occasioned by any accident or by any omission, breach of duty mismanagement, negligence or default of any of such masters, crew or men or any servant of the authority or any other person or from or by any defect or imperfection in the tug or tugs supplied.[70]

While a towage was in progress, a collision occurred between the tug and the steamship, resulting in damage to both vessels. In the Authority's suit against the steamship owners, the owners counterclaimed for their damages. They alleged that the exculpatory provision was void due to it being against public policy. The court disagreed. Reaching a very different decision from *Bisso*, the *Van Buren* court held that the clause was *not* against public policy and granted full damages against the steamship owners. In a decision heavily laden with economic and free-dom of contract discussions, the court held that the terms of the towage agreement were not against public policy despite the Authority's monopoly.[71]

Just how far apart were the judicial positions in both *Bisso* and *Van Buren*? One must consider that the *Bisso* court majority invalidated the exculpatory provision, largely motivated by public policy. The *Bisso* court was very concerned that a monopolistic tendency would cause overreaching. In a sense, freedom of contract was subordinated to a perceived important public concern. Even Justice Frankfurter's stinging dissent did not suggest that the clause should be upheld if a monopolistic situation existed. Rather, he found no evidence before the court that the tug owner could exercise any degree of monopolistic compulsion.

The English judge deciding *The President Van Buren*, Mr Justice Hill, clearly indicated in his opinion the divergent Anglo-American views of these clauses in the towage context, stating:

> On the first point as to whether the agreement is valid and not void as against public policy, I think the answer on this matter is that which I have already expressed, namely, that the English law, in my view, very fortunately regards business men as capable of knowing their own busi-ness and of making contracts for themselves and is very unwilling to limit the power of capable people to make what bargains they like.
>
> I can conceive no principle of public policy which should lead the Courts to say: 'We ought to step in and say "This or that contract ought not to be made by competent people," when the people making it are competent people. It is said that the Port of London Authority is a

---

[70] *Ibid.*
[71] Feingerts and Stein, 'Exculpatory Provisions in Towage Contracts', 392, 404.

monopoly. It is said that everybody has a right to the use of the tugs on equal terms, but here, it is said, you cannot employ any other tugs than the Port of London Authority's tugs. There it is.

If you do not like these terms and if they are too onerous, nobody forces you to use the Port of London Authority's docks. I do not like to enlarge upon it because it seems to me to be so clear that, if you are talking of public policy, the highest interest of public policy is that the law should not interfere with the transactions of business men when it can help it'.[72]

This demonstrates a complete divergence in results between the US and English legal systems.[73] In addition, it demonstrates a divergence in how freedom of contract is interpreted, at least in this specific issue, between both countries. In the *Van Buren* decision, where monopolistic tendencies widely existed, the English court upheld an exculpatory clause without hesitation. This strong belief in permitting such clauses within towage agreements in the UK can also be found today when reviewing the Unfair Contract Terms Act 1977.[74] This Act regulates agreements by restricting the operation and legality of many contract terms.[75] It creates obligation in contract and tort. Nevertheless, the provisions of this Act generally do not apply to any towage contract, unless the tow owner is dealing as a consumer, which is generally not the case. In those limited instances where the owner is acting in such function, the Act prohibits exemption clauses for the tug's negligence if the clauses are unreasonable.

The US Supreme Court dealt with opposing English and US legal perspectives on exculpatory clauses within the towing context in *The Bremen* v. *Zapata Off-Shore Co*, 407 U.S. 1 (1972). Zapata, an American corporation, entered into a contract with the Bremen's owner, Unterweser, a German corporation.[76] Unterweser would tow Zapata's oil rig from the US to Italy.[77] While towed in international

---

[72] *The President Van Buren* (1924) 19 Ll. L. Rep. 185, 187.

[73] Note that Canada follows its Commonwealth cousin, England, by similarly upholding towage exculpatory clauses. See *Mitsubishi Canada Ltd* v. *Rivtow Straights Ltd* (12 May 1977, sup. Ct. British Columbia) cited in Parks and Cattell, Jr. (eds.), *The Law of Tug, Tow and Pilotage*, p. 117.

[74] See, generally, Unfair Contract Terms Act 1977 (1977 c. 50) at www.opsi.gov.uk/ RevisedStatutes/Acts/ukpga/1977/cukpga_19770050_fn_1 (last accessed 10 January 2010).

[75] See S. Rainey, *The Law of Tug and Tow (and Allied Contracts)* (LLP, 2002), pp. 19–20.

[76] *The Bremen* v. *Zapata Off-Shore Co.*, 407 U.S. 1, 2 (1972); see also M. Mousa Karayanni, 'The Public Policy Exception to the Enforcement of Forum Selection Clauses', *Duquesne Law Review*, 34 (1996), 1009, 1016.

[77] *The Bremen* v. *Zapata Off-Shore Co*, 407 U.S. 1, 2 (1972).

waters, a storm damaged the rig and Zapata filed an admiralty suit in the US alleging negligent towage and breach of contract.[78] The contract's forum selection clause held that disputes were to be settled at the London Court of Justice.[79] The court recognised the forum selection clause. Since the agreement provided for adjudication in an English court and contained an exculpatory clause, the result was to permit the tower to reap the benefit from an invalid *Bisso* clause.[80] The court distinguished the case from *Bisso* where the towage took place strictly in American waters.[81]

Perhaps playwright George Bernard Shaw and Winston Churchill were quite correct when they claimed that 'England and America are two countries divided by a common language'.[82] As we have seen, perhaps that observation could be extended, as England and America are two countries divided by a common legal tradition.

3.3   The role of legal technicalities

In order to be enforced, contracts will be drafted to meet a legal system's specific requirements. Another system may demand different technicalities to have a contract validated in its jurisdiction. Contracts will thus be written differently in order to obtain the same results in different systems. As such, contracts moving beyond jurisdictions can produce different results. Comparing cases that limit, if not circumvent, the *Bisso* holding demonstrates the significance of legal technicalities.

Through insurance, creative lawyers achieved what *Bisso* denied – devising a strategy to shift liability to the tow insurers. But how did this shift occur? Since *Bisso*, bargaining on the cost of liability insurance replaced the effort to draft exculpatory clauses exposing the towed vessel to the consequences of tugboat negligence. The towed vessel owner has a choice. First, it can rely on the tug's insurers at an additional cost for towage.[83] Alternatively, it can rely on its own insurer at a reduced towage

---

[78] See *ibid.*, 3–4.

[79] 'Any dispute arising [between the parties] must be treated before the London Court of Justice': *The Bremen v. Zapata Off-Shore Co*, 407 U.S. 1, 2 (1972).

[80] See *ibid.*, 15–16.

[81] *Ibid. The Bremen* is a classic forum selection clause case and, in that respect, was later overruled at the federal level by statute. See 28 U.S.C., Section 1404(a). See also *Stewart Organization, Inc. v. Ricoh Corp.*, 487 U. S. 22 (1988).

[82] This popular quotation may be found at www.quotationspage.com/quote/897.html (last accessed 10 January 2010).

[83] See Sweeney, 'Collisions Involving Tugs and Tows', 596.

cost.[84] If the towed vessel owner opts for its own insurer, the owner will name the tugboat company as an additional insured, for which the vessel owner may be required to pay an added premium.[85]

When damage occurs to the barge (or cargo) as a result of the tug's negligence, the tug is protected under the insurance covering the damaged property. As these insurers have waived subrogation against the tug, once they have paid the loss, they have no right of recovery against the tug.[86] The tug owner remains liable in case the insurers fail to pay, for example, if the insurers became insolvent after issuing the policy. The tug remains responsible to the tow to the extent that there is an uninsured retention or deduction actually paid by the tow.[87] Within the post-*Bisso* insurance context, economics and cost-shifting are held to be of high importance.

In *Fluor Western, Inc.* v. *G & H Offshore Towing Co.*, 447 F.2d 35 (5th Cir. 1971), the court held that a cross-insurance scheme could be applied in the towage context without violating the *Bisso* rule.[88] The case involved an action by an underwriter who insured cargo lost when, due to the tug's negligence, a barge sank. At issue were clauses in two separate agreements. The first contract, between the cargo interest and the tug, stated that the cargo interest would provide insurance for the full value of the cargo and would waive subrogation rights against the tug. In the second contract, the policy specified that the insurance company would waive its subrogation rights against the barge owners and towers. The plaintiff insurance company contended that such contractual provisions essentially absolved the towage contractors of responsibility for negligence. Therefore, these clauses should presumably have been void against public policy, as set out in *Bisso*.

The Fifth Circuit viewed circumstances quite differently. The court disagreed with the plaintiff's argument and held that the parties' arrangement did *not* violate *Bisso*, providing three key reasons. First, the cargo owner did not waive any rights it had against any party responsible for loss.[89] As such, if the insurance company had not covered

---

[84] See *ibid*.

[85] See *ibid*. Given such circumstances, the towed vessel owner should obtain a waiver of subrogation against the tugboat company and the tugs used in the tow. See *ibid*. See also Parks and Cattell, Jr. (eds.), *The Law of Tug, Tow and Pilotage*, p. 117.

[86] See *ibid*., pp. 78–81. [87] See *ibid*., pp. 86–87.

[88] Sweeney, 'Collisions Involving Tugs and Tows', 596.

[89] *Fluor Western, Inc.* v. *G & H Offshore Towing Co.*, 447 F.2d 35, 39–40 (5th Cir. 1971); Feingerts and Stein, 'Exculpatory Provisions in Towage Contracts', pp. 392, 397.

the losses, the cargo owner had the right to sue the tower.[90] Secondly, the transport agreement itself contained no waiver of rights: the actual waiver of subrogation was between the cargo owner and the underwriter in a *separate* contract.[91] Finally, and key to *Bisso*, there was no inequality of bargaining position and public policy did not require any specific party to pay insurance premiums.[92]

Judicial approval of the liability insurance shift with waiver of subrogation was cemented under *Twenty Grand Offshore, Inc.* v. *West India Carriers, Inc.*, 492 F.2d 679 (5th Cir. 1974). The question there concerned the validity of towage contract provisions requiring both the tug owner and tow owner to do two things: (i) to fully insure their respective vessels; and (ii) to obtain in each of their insurance policies both a waiver of subrogation as to the other party and a designation of the other party as an additional insured.[93]

The tugboat crew was negligent and the towed barge ran aground. The barge owner breached its obligations under the towage contract, as: (i) it did not name the tugboat as an additional insured; and (ii) it failed to obtain the waiver of subrogation.[94] The District Court judgment was reversed by the Fifth Circuit, which held in favour of the barge owner. The court held that the *Bisso* doctrine was not:

> so encompassing that in instances of fair dealing, with no anti-competitive forces at work, the parties to a towing contract cannot agree to include an insurance clause and thereby reduce the towing rate while not affecting the rights of the tug and barge *inter se*.[95]

The question then became the amount of the towed vessel's damage covered by insurance. The tugboat company was found liable for damages *not* covered by insurance due to the tugboat's negligence.[96] However, the towed vessel would be responsible for the portion of its damages that should have been covered by its own insurance.

---

[90] *Ibid.*   [91] *Ibid.*   [92] *Ibid.*

[93] Under the agreement, each party was to 'fully insure its vessel, to effect a waiver of subrogation, and to name the other party as an additional insured'. *Twenty Grand Offshore, Inc.* v. *West India Carriers, Inc.*, 492 F.2d 679, 680 (5th Cir. 1974). See also Parks and Cattell, Jr. (eds.), *The Law of Tug, Tow and Pilotage*, pp. 78–79.

[94] *Twenty Grand Offshore, Inc.* v. *West India Carriers, Inc.*, 492 F.2d 679, 680 (5th Cir. 1974). See also Sweeney, 'Collisions Involving Tugs and Tows', 581, 596.

[95] See *Twenty Grand Offshore, Inc.* v. *West India Carriers, Inc.*, 492 F.2d 679, 683 (5th Cir. 1974).

[96] See *ibid.*, 679, 683. See also Sweeney, 'Collisions Involving Tugs and Tows', 581, 596.

Again, there is no uniform, uncontested US judicial resolution on this matter. As demonstrated in a discussion of liability-exempting clauses in cases of negligence, US jurisdictions do not always speak with one voice. Take for instance, the Third Circuit in *PPG Industries* v. *Ashland Oil Co.,* 592 F.2d 138 (3rd Cir. 1978). In this case, the United States Court of Appeals for the Third Circuit held that benefit-of-insurance agreements waiving rights of subrogation are incompatible with *Bisso's* bar of contract provisions shifting responsibility for a tower's negligence. Finding that benefit-of-insurance arrangements were simply an indirect attempt at exculpation for negligence, the *PPG Industries* court was 'unpersuaded by [Fifth Circuit] cases tending to place a different focus on this issue'.

Through this comparative approach, the possibility of total legal convergence is called into question. Contract practice adapts and evolves to meet the technicalities of the applicable law. As demonstrated through a review of the various cases, sophisticated contracts, clauses and mechanisms are developed by lawyers to meet the requirements of the applicable law and will be interpreted in light of those requirements. If the same contract clauses are interpreted under a different law that does not have the same requirements, such provisions may not necessarily have the same effects. The foreign law may have other requisites only satisfied by employing a different clause. The difference in technicalities is not so easily annulled. Full legal convergence may be difficult to achieve when the contracts are shaped and developed on the basis of these technicalities.

4   Conclusion: a step away from total legal convergence

A journey of a thousand miles begins with a single step. That said, one must wonder what the likelihood is of a possible single, uniform step down a comparative law journey: that of legal convergence. Given the comparison of exculpatory clauses under American and, indeed, Anglo-American law, one must seriously question the possibility, in practice, of full legal convergence.

A comparison of American law revealed divergences among different courts. *American Oil* demonstrated that courts may wield principles of unconscionability and public policy to invalidate an exculpatory clause in the commercial context. Then again, courts may uphold the clauses. The *Hormel* and *Pinnacle Computer* courts did just that. Some jurisdictions require the specific word 'negligence' in a clause seeking to limit liability from negligence, while others do not.

These diverse holdings illustrate the practical tensions when exploring legal families, particularly when testing the possibility of legal convergence. Decisions from a broad sampling of different American regions, venues and jurisdictions have been analysed. Cases were discussed from states such as Indiana and Minnesota, cases from the Fifth and Third Federal Circuits. One must question whether divergent economic or social traditions played a role in different court approaches, a further factor questioning the possibility of total legal convergence.

When discussing towage contracts, the different approaches under the US, English and Canadian systems also illustrate a marked split within one legal family. For example, *Bisso* mandates that liability from negligence cannot be excluded from a contract. The *President Van Buren* case allows such liability under English law. These cases also demonstrate, on this specific issue, how freedom of contract is interpreted differently. The *Bisso* court intervened to halt possible monopolistic tendencies, preventing the enforcement of a clause agreed to by the contracting parties. The *Van Buren* court left the contracting parties to the freedom of their bargain, despite such actual monopolistic tendencies. Indeed, there is a continuous 'tug of war' between the freedom to enter into market exchanges and the possible limits imposed on those exchanges. The *Bisso* holding is also in stark contrast to the contractual freedom perspectives found in other Supreme Court decisions, including that in *Baltimore & Ohio SW. R.R. Co.* v. *Voigt*, 176 U.S. 498, 505 (1900). There the court held that 'If there is one thing which more than another public policy requires it is that . . . contracts, when entered into freely and voluntarily, shall be held sacred, and shall be enforced by courts of justice'. Again, this demonstrates different perspectives within one legal system, let alone within one legal family.

In this journey of exploring convergence, post-*Bisso* cases do clearly reveal an important aspect of legal technicalities. These decisions demonstrate how law develops to answer socioeconomic needs or concerns, and how judicial systems and practitioners respond. The *Fluor* and *Twenty Grand* cases demonstrate an ingenious method to carve out exceptions to *Bisso*, allowing liability from negligence to be shifted to insurers.

Writing a contract in one jurisdiction may not lead to the same consequences in another. Take, for example, the Fifth Circuit decisions in *Fluor* and *Twenty Grand* – allowing liability to be shifted from negligence through insurance schemes. If a contract in that jurisdiction was brought to the Third Circuit for interpretation as in *PPG Industries*, it is doubtful whether such contractual liability-shifting would be upheld. There again we see that contracts migrating into other legal systems may annul any contemplated legal convergence.

Such is the role that exculpatory clauses play when testing total legal convergence. The provisions challenge jurists, invoke deep debate on fundamental viewpoints of freedom of contract and provide attorneys with fodder for exasperation, if not creativity. These clauses show divergent court decisions within the American legal system – not to mention between the US and English courts. In such contexts, one must seriously question whether total legal convergence is indeed possible.

6

Circulation of common law contract models in Europe: the impact of the European Union system

JEAN-SYLVESTRE BERGÉ

1 The European Union system and circulation of common law contract models

There are several ways to assess the reception by a legal system of contract models from another legal system.

The easiest way is to examine how a national judge applies his or her law to a foreign contract model. For instance, within the area of contract law could be considered the case law of the Cour de Cassation or the appellate courts and tribunals, in terms of their ability to enforce contract models from different systems of common law.

While not strictly speaking a specialist in contract law but rather in EU and comparative law, I will suggest another line of enquiry. My aim will be to try to show that EU law and, particularly, the case law of the European Court of Justice compel national lawyers to welcome into their systems legal situations located in another Member State. Thus, European law promotes the movement of models and leads the national lawyer to handle rules of foreign systems.

2 An almost perfect example: the *Courage* case

In an attempt to illustrate my demonstration, I will rely on an almost 'perfect' example: the *Courage* ruling: ECJ, 20 September 2001, Case C-453/99.

The referral requesting a preliminary ruling originates from a dispute in England involving a brewery and a publican, who were both bound by a lease agreement and an exclusive purchasing clause. The disagreement concerned the settlement of various bills corresponding to deliveries of beer. Pursued for payment, the publican opposes the nullity of the contract under Article 81(1) and (2) EC and counterclaimed for damages. Both the defence claim and the counterclaim raised a difficulty in terms of English law.

According to the national judge (Court of Appeal – England & Wales), two obstacles arose. The first one related to the ability of a party to an illegal agreement to plead the nullity of a contract to which it had consented. The second concerned the ability of that same party to claim damages due to an abnormally high price levied against it by its co-contracting party.

In both situations, the English judge found that the defendant's participation in an illegal agreement was potentially such as to deprive him of the possibility of invoking an exception of nullity and, *a fortiori*, of the counterclaim for damages. While questioning itself on the compatibility of that solution with EU law, the Court of Appeal referred the following four questions to the Court of Justice:

1) Is Article 81 EC (ex Article 85) to be interpreted as meaning that a party to a prohibited tied house agreement may rely upon that Article to seek relief from the courts from the other contracting party?
2) If the answer to question 1) is yes, is the party claiming relief entitled to recover damages alleged to arise as a result of his or her adherence to the clause in the agreement which is prohibited under Article 81?
3) Should a rule of national law which provides that courts should not allow a person to plead and/or rely on his or her own illegal actions as a necessary step to recovery of damages be allowed as consistent with EU law?
4) If the answer to question 3) is that, in some circumstances, such a rule may be inconsistent with EU law, what circumstances should the national court take into consideration? (Para. 16)

3   The context of the case in EU law

The questions posed by the English court were in line with the broader theme of the relationship between national law and EU law.

In this case, the relationship is specifically about determining how the first two paragraphs of Article 81 EC – which lay down respectively: 1) a rule prohibiting agreements restricting competition; and 2) a principle of automatic nullity – should be implemented, especially in a basic contractual litigation.

The procedural treatment of the nullity of the contract is contrary to the rules of the economic public order (main action, exception of nullity), its nature (absolute or relative), its extent (partial or total) and its consequences (restitutions and possibly damages). Are they solely abandoned to the cautiousness of the laws and state judges of each Member State or is EU law likely to intervene in one way or another?

The answer is known. It bears the name of the 'principle of procedural autonomy' that was formulated more than twenty-five years ago by the Court of Justice.[1]

The reasoning behind this principle consists of two stages:[2]

1) in the absence of Community rules [EU law], it is up to the domestic legal order of each Member State to designate the courts that have jurisdiction and to lay down procedural rules (and, quite often, substantive rules, the border between 'procedural' and 'substantive' being somewhat blurred in the present case situation, so that the principle of 'procedural autonomy' does not exclude any reference to considerations of substantive law), designed to safeguard the rights which individuals derive from the direct effect of EU Law;

2) however, these rules must not be less favourable than those governing similar domestic actions (principle of equivalence), and, most of all, they must not render practically impossible or excessively difficult the exercise of rights conferred by the European legal order (principle of effectiveness).

In other words, when the law fails to deliver all means of its implementation, it relies on different national laws. Still, EU law does not entirely step aside. It continues to ensure compliance with its rules in the name of a double necessity of legal effectiveness and uniform application.

4   The three lessons drawn from the *Courage* case

One is allowed to draw different lessons from how EU law seeks to understand national law of contracts through the use of a framework governing the principle of procedural autonomy.

The most important lesson for our research is the third one. However, to understand it, it is necessary to introduce the two others beforehand.

---

[1] See, in particular, the first rulings on recovery of charges and taxes unlawfully collected by Member States: ECJ, 16 December 1976, *Rewe*, Case 33/76, ECR, p. 1989; ECJ, 16 December 1976, *Cornet*, Case 45/76, ECR, p. 2043.

[2] For a reminder see, e.g., the *Courage* ruling, para. 29.

5   First lesson: in contract law, the use of the principle of procedural autonomy is rather exceptional and of a subsidiary nature

Because it takes different paths from those traditionally used in national law and because it involves new protagonists that are more remote and less familiar than those we are used to at the domestic level, EU law may be perceived with an element of overstatement. Yet the caricature is not always appropriate, as suggested by the principle of procedural autonomy that, in contractual matters, plays a rather exceptional and altogether subsidiary role.

What is the importance of the phenomenon we are studying here? In the field of contract law, the European judge rarely has recourse to the principle of procedural autonomy. If one puts aside the (beautiful) purely procedural issues, in particular those relating to the definition of the position of the national judge regarding the implementation of the European rule,[3] two areas of EU law which affect contract law are mainly called upon. The first area, which we will not consider here, relates more or less to the European principle of free movement and the manner in which national regulations may be declared inapplicable in relations between individuals, including co-contractors.[4] The second area concerns us more, since it is in direct contact with the theme of this chapter: the law of free competition.

In this matter, barring any error on our part, there are only two case law manifestations of the principle of procedural autonomy, the very same ones that are the subject of this chapter. Yet, even through these two illustrations, one notes that the principle is called upon as a last resort, in a simply subsidiary manner.

As we have seen it in the (aforementioned) *Courage* case, different questions were put before the Court of Justice. For the record, the matter was whether, under EU law, a party to an illegal agreement must be granted the right to plead the nullity of the legal relationship to which it is party and, if so, whether it has the liberty, and under what conditions, to

---

[3] For an overview of solutions, see, for example, the collective work under the supervision of S. Guinchard *et al.* (eds.), *Droit processue*, 4th edn (Précis Dalloz, 2007).

[4] For a summary analysis of this very abundant question, see, in French, with numerous references cited, the analysis suggested by L. Soubelet in 'Le rôle conféré par le droit communautaire aux droits nationaux des États membres' *Chronique de droit européen*, III, Université de Paris Ouest Nanterre La Défense, *Les Petites Affiches*, 19 May 2003, No. 99, p. 6.

fill a claim for damages. Despite appearances, these two questions do not
equally concern the principle of procedural autonomy. The Court of
Justice understood it perfectly, as it takes special care to make the
division between what concerns the pure and simple principle of primacy
of EU law and what is solely delimited by it. In this regard, the Court
considered that only the second question was likely to concern the
principle of procedural autonomy.[5] Indeed, without any hesitation, the
ruling was based on several major decisions of European case law in
order to reaffirm: 1) the autonomous dimension of the European legal
order (para. 19); 2) the essential nature of competition policy regarding the functioning of the internal market (para. 20); and finally 3) the
direct effect, including relations between individuals, of Article 81(1) EC
(para. 23). Hence the conclusion, according to which:

> any individual can rely on a breach of Article 81 Section 1 of the Treaty
> before a national court even where he is a party to a contract that is liable
> to restrict or distort competition within the meaning of that provision.
>
> (Para. 24)

When primary or secondary EU law delivers the principles that guide its
implementation with sufficient strength and precision, there is no need
to have recourse to a necessarily more subtle concept of a framework
governing the procedural autonomy of the Member States. EU law is
partially self-sufficient, without necessarily having an obligation to interfere with national law.

6   Second lesson: the European framework governing the principle of procedural autonomy aims at establishing a correlation between partly autonomous and partly hierarchised legal systems

Among the different ways of approaching the relationship between EU
law (in this case competition law) and national law (in this case contract
law), the most widespread consists in opposing systems, bringing them
into conflict, so as to determine whether, within the scope of EU law,
national law is compatible or not. However, this way of understanding
the relationship between sets of rules does not allow us to grasp all of the
legal reality. There are indeed situations where the primacy of EU law

---

[5] See comments below on this point.

does not totally deprive national law of its autonomy and, conversely, where a certain autonomy of national law resists the primacy of EU law.

Consequently, the idea is not to find an antinomy but rather a correlation between systems. It is neither more nor less than finding a way to harmonise national solutions with those from EU law.

The European framework governing the principle of procedural autonomy is unquestionably one of those situations, as it has no other aim than to establish a dialogue between EU law and national law. It reflects a will to seek 'balance between the principle of "judicial subsidiarity", which implies that the procedural autonomy of national law is respected, and the principle of the primacy of EU Law, which requires that an effective judicial protection of rights resulting from EU Law is ensured'.[6]

The *Courage* decision illustrates, in its own way, this inseparable double movement of autonomy and primacy.

Regarding autonomy, the power of the Member States has been reasserted in defining the consequences on civil law grounds, attached to a violation of Article 81 EC, such as the obligation to repair the damage caused to a third party or a possible obligation to enter into a contract (an implied, but hardly questionable solution in the *Courage* ruling).

Regarding primacy, the Court of Justice takes care to clarify that the effectiveness of European competition law would be called into question:

> if it were not open to any individual to claim damages for loss caused to him by a contract or by conduct liable to restrict or distort competition. Indeed, the existence of such a right strengthens the working of the European competition rules and discourages agreements or practices, which are frequently covert, which are liable to restrict or distort competition. From that point of view, actions for damages before the national courts can make a significant contribution to the maintenance of effective competition in the EU and [. . .] there should not [. . .] be any absolute bar to such an action being brought by a party to a contract which would be held to violate the competition rules.
>
> (*Courage* ruling, paras. 26–28)

Ultimately, it is in the conciliation of contrary requirements that the intervention of EU law is emerging in a close relationship with national solutions. EU law does not entirely squash national law. On the contrary, it draws useful, sometimes necessary, tools from national law for its implementation. The situation is not that of an irreducible conflict of

---

[6] D. Simon, *Le système juridique communautaire*, 3rd edn (PUF, 2001), No. 335, p. 425.

rules. It is more likely a search for a concordance between a specialised European legal order, which is therefore incomplete, and national legal orders that have made the choice to confer primacy upon it.

7   Third lesson: the intervention of EU law leads to a rereading of national laws, which is rather nuanced and has a broad meaning

The understanding of national law conducted through the European prism with these broad guidelines may finally begin. There is no room here for snap judgments or attempts to retreat into oneself. The approach is deliberately nuanced. It also carries a broad meaning.

The analysis is unquestionably nuanced considering how, in the *Courage* case, the Court of Justice construed the rule of effectiveness contained in the European principle of procedural autonomy. The question posed by the English judge was to discover the circumstances under which EU law concedes that national law may refuse the possibility of seeking damages to a party to an illegal agreement. In the present case, the action of the publican aimed at obtaining compensation for damage suffered as a result of high tariff conditions offered by the other contracting party was determined, in accordance with national law, by his degree of liability in the conclusion of a contract considered as potentially contrary to the competition rules.[7] Yet it was precisely on the question of assessing the degree of liability that the Court of Justice was asked to give its opinion.

In order to do so, the Court proceeded in three steps. First, it started to draw all the resources from its case law so as to guide it towards the solution. For this reason, it noticed, in particular, that a certain amount of recognition has been given to the maxim according to which a litigant should not profit from his or her own unlawful conduct, where this is proven (para. 31). Secondly, the Court examined the circumstances that could be sufficient to let a national judge allow an action of the co-contracting party that is the victim of an illegal agreement. Based on the information added to the debate by the UK, it noted, for example, that a co-contracting party that is found to be in a markedly weaker position is deprived of its ability to avoid damage resulting from the

---

[7] For the presentation of this English rule and the use of the *ex turpi causa non oritur actio* adage, see, e.g., G. Samuel, *Law of Obligations and Legal Remedies*, 2nd edn (Cavendish Publishing, 2001), pp. 239ff.

illegal agreement, so it must be able to engage the liability of the other contracting party (para. 33). Finally, the Court rejected the objection according to which the reasoning conducted on the consequences in civil law of a breach of Article 81 EC would contradict the European definition of the agreement. In reality, there was no interference between the two parts of the reasoning, which were quite distinct one from another, since the first was solely part of EU law, whereas the second was more modestly delimited by the principle of procedural autonomy.

In the end, the Court found that EU law:

> does not preclude a rule of national law barring a party to a contract liable to restrict or distort competition from relying on his own unlawful actions to obtain damages where it is established that that party bears significant responsibility for the distortion of competition.

It can be seen that EU law gives, as a general guideline, indications that should enable a correct implementation of the national law of contracts. It is up to the state judge who is the European common law judge to implement them, which gives him or her substantial room for manoeuvre.

The approach of the Court of Justice is not simply nuanced; it also carries a broad meaning. Indeed, the decision does not exclusively apply to the English law of unlawful contracts. It can be transposed to all national laws of Member States and leads to understanding the comparative approach in a particular way – probably too little exploited.

Thus, for the French lawyer, the Court of Justice's ruling is an invitation to assess the adequacy of its rules faced with the European principle of procedural autonomy. Yet to notice that this ruling of the Court of Justice undoubtedly reinforces our national solutions is not the least reassuring of the lessons in these times of great European hesitation. First of all, it also has an effect on the ability of a party to an illegal contract to seek its annulment and to act, if necessary, in tort. Nothing in our civil law, as a rule, stands in the way of an action by the co-contracting party, a victim merely because it has participated in the conclusion of an unlawful legal act. The exception of indignity, formulated by the famous maxim *Nemo auditur propriam turpitudinem allegans*, has a reduced scope of application in our law. As we know, it affects only claims for restitution resulting from the nullity of the prohibited contract.[8]

---

[8] For an overall analysis, see, with numerous references cited: Ph. le Tourneau, *Juris-Classeur Civil, App. Articles 1131 to 1133* (LexisNexis).

But there is more. Should we stick only to the restitutions field, it is striking to notice how our national law is willing to adhere to the analysis used by the Court of Justice in an entirely different legal environment. Indeed, the expression *Nemo auditur* has a somewhat misleading nature.[9] It willingly gives way to the Roman maxim *In pari causa turpitudinis, cessat repetitio* and its variants, which allow us to explain why, when the illegality is unequal between the parties to the contract, the claim for restitution is sometimes available only to the least guilty of them.

Is this not the same reasoning as that implemented by the Court of Justice in the context of English law? In these two totally different situations, it ultimately comes down to ensuring that legal action is not totally closed to the party which, far from having orchestrated the illegal agreement, is the one suffering from its consequences. Clearly, the meaning of the Court of Justice's analysis exceeds the scope of one single state law. On the contrary, it intends to enable us to hold a dialogue between different national legal systems. This is perfectly normal when it comes to participating in a European construction (albeit modestly and by small steps), a process which necessarily requires the finding of renewed forms of community or unity of rights.

8   Conclusion

The *Courage* case helps us to think about the other way through which EU law promotes the movement of national models in Europe and their comparison.

Comparative law is no longer only concerned with comparing national laws. There is also an international dimension to the comparison and, as far as we are concerned, a European one.

The European framework modifies the comparative method. Comparing laws has become a triangular process: a contract model, which has been designed according to the rules of one particular national system, is taken into account in another one, because a third one, the EU system, requires such a circulation.

The search for a proper implementation of EU law in each Member State fosters interactions between national laws.

---

[9] See, in particular, on this discussed question, *ibid.*, No. 121ff.

PART 3

The applicable law's effects on boilerplate clauses

~

Introduction to Part 3

Today, international commercial contracts are, with only a few exceptions, drafted on the basis of common law models. As Part 1 of this book showed, these models are only to a limited extent adapted to meet the requirements of the contract law that will govern them. As seen in Part 2, the simple adoption of a contract model inspired by common law may not be deemed to be a tacit choice of common law to govern the contract (particularly because common law is not a defined system). Part 2 also showed the difficulty of harmonising general contract law on an international level. Thus, contracts often present clauses and terminology that are not tailored to, or even not compatible with, the applicable law.

This drafting practice creates a need for coordinating the legal concepts upon which the contract is based, with the legal concepts that the governing law imposes on the contract.

There are various examples of clauses that are obviously inspired by a common law system and do not have a corresponding provision in the chosen law, if the law chosen by the parties to govern the contract belongs to a civilian system. For example, in a contract subject to a civilian law and with an exclusive jurisdiction clause in favour of the courts in a civilian country, a clause regulating the use of equitable remedies such as estoppels would not make sense. These are a phenomenon of common law and do not exist in civilian laws.

There are, however, examples where the poor coordination between the common law contract model and the civilian governing law is less evident. The function of the ubiquitous clauses of representations and warranties, for example, is primarily connected to the common law distinction between precontractual representations on the one hand and terms of the contract on the other hand, a distinction that does not exist, at least not with the same legal effects, in many civilian systems.

While it may be possible to dismiss the clause in the former example as an irrelevant regulation allowed because the parties did not notice its incongruity, the interpretation of the latter example requires more consideration: representations and warranties are a contractual regulation of the information exchanged between the parties, a matter which is subject to the specific rules and principles of many civil law systems. Does such a clause mean that the parties intended to add the contractual regulation to the rules and principles of the governing law? Or does it mean that the parties wanted to regulate the matter as set forth in the contract instead of following the governing law's rules and principles? And, if so, are the parties allowed to depart from the governing law's rules and principles?

Contract laws generally do not contain many mandatory rules, apart from areas relating to the protection of the weaker contractual party or other areas of regulatory concern, which are generally not relevant to the questions that may arise out of commercial contracts and boilerplate clauses. Therefore, most of the results that the parties wanted to achieve will be compatible with the governing law. However, in exceptional situations, particularly where the contractual mechanism is abused for speculative purposes, the governing law might put a stop to the full implementation of the parties' will. When this happens, a common law contract model subject to a civilian governing law might be interpreted in a different way from the one envisaged by the original drafters.

The drafting style may be deemed to be an expression of the parties' will to exhaustively regulate their legal relationship in the contract. A document that sets forth a very extensive regulation, that specifies, in every detail, all the consequences of various situations that may arise during the life of the contract, that contains clauses with long lists of information exchanged between the parties, and that also contains a clause specifying that the contract document is to be deemed the exhaustive regulation of the relationship between the parties seems clearly to indicate that the parties wanted their contract to regulate all aspects of their relationship and intended to exclude any addition from outside the contract.

As is well known, most civilian doctrines of interpretation do not operate with the maxim *inclusio unius est exclusio alterius*, which is at the root of the assumption of exhaustiveness. Traditionally, if the circumstances so require, a civilian judge will not refrain from extending, by analogy or otherwise, the scope of the written contract. An antithetic interpretation, according to which anything that the parties have not expressly regulated in the contract may not be deemed to have been intended to be part of the contract, is not usual in the civilian tradition. Should the contract contain a choice-of-law clause in favour of a civilian governing law (and even more so if the governing law was determined on the basis of other conflict rules), this might seem to contradict the intention by the parties to have the contract interpreted as if it were exhaustive. How can this contradiction be overcome?

It seems that within international commercial transactions, the use of this drafting style is so widespread that it may, to a certain extent, be considered to be an acknowledged contract practice. This may render it more likely that the parties have desired to limit, to whatever extent possible, any interference from outside the contract by taking the regulation of most of the conceivable details into their own hands. The size of and degree of detail in the contract regulation make it evident that this is the intention, and it may be inferred even if the contract was looked upon individually. When the majority of international commercial contracts adopt this style, it is even easier to conclude that the parties were aware of the habit of giving an exhaustive character to the contract and that they wanted to adhere to this contract practice.

However, this exhaustiveness-intention by the parties does not give them more power to regulate their relationship than they already have under the freedom of contract that the governing law grants them.

While the parties may, by adopting a certain detailed and extensive style, avoid creative additions to the contract that the interpreter may be tempted to make under the applicable doctrine of interpretation, they cannot go further than regulating their interests in a way that is permitted under the governing law, i.e., they cannot use the drafting style as a tool to avoid interference by the governing law and obtain results that would violate mandatory rules or fundamental principles of the governing law.

In other words, fundamental principles of the governing law, such as good faith in the performance of the contract and the prohibition of abuse of a right, may still correct and limit the contractual regulation. However, the only purpose of applying these rules would be to prevent a violation of these mandatory rules. These principles should not correct and limit the contract if the only purpose is to integrate the contractual regulation in order to obtain a better result, a more balanced contract or a fairer distribution between the parties. This latter integration of the contract regulation, which might be permissible under certain civilian systems, is excluded by the exhaustive character of the contract.[1]

The following chapters will examine the interaction between the contract and the governing law from the point of view of English law and of laws representing the main sub-families of the civil law: the Germanic, Romanistic, Scandinavian and East European families. Thus, in Chapter 7, the analysis will be made under English law by Edwin Peel; in Chapter 8, under German law by Ulrich Magnus; in Chapter 9, under French law by Xavier Lagarde; in Chapter 10, under Italian law by Giorgio De Nova; in Chapter 11, under Danish law by Peter Møgelvang-Hansen; in Chapter 12, under Finnish law by Gustaf Möller; in Chapter 13, under Norwegian law by Viggo Hagstrøm; in Chapter 14, under Swedish law by Lars Gorton; in Chapter 15, under Hungarian law by Attila Menyhárd; and in Chapter 16, under Russian law by Ivan S. Zykin.

As the next chapters will show in detail, it does not seem possible to fulfil the ambition of creating a fully self-sufficient contract that is completely isolated from the governing law. Interestingly, a full isolation is not even possible in respect of English law, which has indirectly provided the basis for the comprehensive drafting style and the connected desire of an exhaustive contract regulation. Drafters are advised to consider the effects of the contract under the governing law and not to rely on the pure text that they have signed.

1   Clauses analysed in Part 3

To ensure consistency in the analysis carried out in various chapters, the authors were given a list of clauses containing examples of contractual regulations particularly apt to create coordination problems with the governing law. The list was based on the material examined in the research project upon which this book is based, which included contracts actually seen in the practice of the project's participants as well as standard contracts issued by companies, branch organisations or international organisations. As should be expected for boilerplates, the

---

[1] That commercial contracts should be interpreted objectively on the basis of their wording is even recognised in legal systems that traditionally give significant importance to the necessity of obtaining a fair decision, thus allowing for relatively free interpretations on the basis of the purpose of the contract, of good faith principles, etc. In the past few years, the Norwegian Supreme Court has repeatedly affirmed that commercial contracts should be interpreted objectively, so as to respect the parties' interest in predictability (Rt. 1994 s. 581, Rt. 2000 s. 806, Rt. 2002 s. 1155, Rt. 2003 s. 1132).

wording of each clause on the list varies very little from source to source. Therefore, the clauses listed below may be seen as examples of typical boilerplates.

The authors were also given a list of cases that may help illustrating the need for coordination with the governing law. Both are reproduced below.

1.1   Entire agreement

The Contract contains the entire contract and understanding between the parties hereto and supersedes all prior negotiations, representations, undertakings and agreements on any subject matter of the Contract.

1.2   No waiver

Failure by a party to exercise a right or remedy that it has under this Contract does not constitute a waiver thereof.

1.3   No oral amendments

No amendment or variation to this Agreement shall take effect unless it is in writing, signed by authorised representatives of each of the Parties.

1.4   Severability

If a provision of this Agreement is or becomes illegal, invalid or unenforceable, that shall not affect the validity or enforceability of any other provision of this Agreement.

1.5   Conditions/essential terms

The obligations regulated in Section 13 are fundamental and any breach thereof shall amount to a fundamental breach of this contract [*alternative*: Time is of the essence].

1.6   Sole remedy

[Liquidated damages paid in accordance with the foregoing provision] shall be the Buyer's sole remedy for any delay in delivery for which the Seller is responsible under this Agreement.

1.7   Subject to contract

This document does not represent a binding agreement between the parties and neither party shall be under any liability to the other party in case of failure to enter into the final agreement.

1.8   Material adverse change

Conditions precedent to Closing

Since the date of [the Agreement], there has not been any Material Adverse Change in the condition (financial or otherwise), business, assets, liabilities or results of operations of [the Party and its Subsidiaries taken as a whole].

'Material Adverse Change' means any result, occurrence, condition, fact, change, violation, event or effect that, individually or in the aggregate with any such other results, occurrences, conditions, facts, changes, violations, events or effects, is materially adverse to:

(1) the financial condition, business, assets, liabilities or results of operations of the Company and its Subsidiaries, taken as a whole,

(2) the ability of the Company to perform its obligations under this Agreement, or

(3) the ability of the Company to consummate the Merger; provided, however, that in no event shall any of the following constitute a Company Material Adverse Change:

   (1) any change or effect resulting from changes in general economic, regulatory or political conditions, conditions in the United States or worldwide capital markets;

   (2) any change or effect that affects the oil and gas exploration and development industry generally (including changes in commodity prices, general market prices and regulatory changes affecting the oil and gas industry generally);

   (3) any effect, change, event, occurrence or circumstance relating to fluctuations in the value of currencies;

   (4) the outbreak or escalation of hostilities involving the United States, the declaration by the United States of a national emergency or war or the occurrence of any other calamity or crisis, including acts of terrorism;

      [. . .]

      (14) any of the matters referred to in Schedule . . .

1.9   Liquidated damages

If, due to the fault of the Seller, the goods have not been delivered at dates according to the delivery schedule as provided in this Agreement, the

Seller shall be obliged to pay to the buyer liquidated damages for such delayed delivery at the following rates:

(1) For each complete week, the liquidated damages shall be 0.5% of the value of the goods delayed.

(2) The total amount of the above mentioned liquidated damages will not exceed 25% of the Price for the delayed goods.

(3) The payment of liquidated damages shall not release the Seller from its obligation to continuously deliver the goods.

1.10   Indemnity

(1) 30.1 Contractor shall indemnify Company Group from and against any claim concerning personal injury to or loss of life of any employee of Contractor Group, and loss of or damage to any property of Contractor Group, and arising out of or in connection with the Work or caused by the Contract Object in its lifetime. This applies regardless of any form of liability, whether strict or by negligence, in whatever form, on the part of Company Group.

Contractor shall, as far as practicable, ensure that other companies in Contractor Group waive their right to make any claim against Company Group when such claims are covered by Contractor's obligation to indemnify under the provisions of this Art. 30.1.

(2) 30.3 Until the issue of the Acceptance Certificate, Contractor shall indemnify Company Group from costs resulting from the requirements of public authorities in connection with the removal of wrecks, or pollution from vessels or other floating devices provided by Contractor Group for use in connection with the Work, and claims arising out of loss or damage suffered by anyone other than Contractor Group and Company Group in connection with the Work or caused by the Contract Object, even if the loss or damage is the result of any form of liability, whether strict or by negligence in whatever form by Company Group.

Contractor's liability for loss or damage arising out of each accident shall be limited to NOK 5 million. This does not apply to Contractor's liability for loss or damage for each accident covered by insurances provided in accordance with Art. 31.2.a) and b), where Contractor's liability extends to the sum recovered under the insurance for the loss or damage.

Company shall indemnify Contractor Group from and against claims mentioned in the first paragraph above, to the extent that they exceed the limitations of liability mentioned above, regardless of any form of liability, whether strict or by negligence, in whatever form, on the part of Contractor Group.

After issue of the Acceptance Certificate, Company shall indemnify Contractor Group from and against any claims of the kind mentioned in the first paragraph above, regardless of any form of liability, whether strict or by negligence, in whatever form, on the part of Contractor Group.

1.11   Representations and warranties

Each Party represents and warrants to and for the benefit of the other Party as follows:

(1) It is a company duly incorporated and validly existing under the laws of ... (in respect of the Seller) and of ... (in respect of the Buyer), is a separate legal entity capable of suing and being sued and has the power and authority to own its assets and conduct the business which it conducts and/or proposes to conduct;

(2) Each Party has the power to enter into and exercise its rights and to perform and comply with its obligations under this Agreement;

(3) Its entry into, exercise of its rights under and/or performance of, or compliance with, its obligations under this Agreement do not and will not violate or exceed any power granted or restriction imposed by any law or regulation to which it is subject or any document defining its constitution and do not and will not violate any agreement to which it is a party or which is binding on it or its assets;

(4) All actions, conditions and things required by the laws of ... to be taken, fulfilled and done in order to enable it lawfully to enter into, exercise its rights under and perform and comply with its obligations under this Agreement, to ensure that those obligations are valid, legally binding and enforceable and to make this Agreement admissible in evidence in the courts of ... or before an arbitral tribunal, have been taken, fulfilled and done;

(5) Its obligations under this Agreement are valid, binding and enforceable;

(6) ...

(7) ...

(40) ...

1.12   Hardship

(1) Where the performance of a contract becomes more onerous for one of the parties, that party is nevertheless bound to perform its obligations subject to the following provisions on hardship.

(2) There is hardship where the occurrence of events fundamentally alters the equilibrium of the contract either because the cost of a party's performance has increased or because the value of the performance a party receives has diminished, and

(a) the event was beyond its reasonable control and was one which it could not reasonably have been expected to have taken into account at the time of the conclusion of the contract; and that

(b) the event or its consequences could not reasonably be avoided or overcome.

If such hardship occurs the parties are bound, within a reasonable time of the invocation of this Clause, to negotiate alternative contractual terms which reasonably allow for the consequences of the event.

Alternative regulations

Alternative I

Where paragraph 2 of this Clause applies, but where alternative contractual terms which reasonably allow for the consequences of the event are not agreed by the other party to the contract as provided in that paragraph, the party invoking this Clause is entitled to termination of the contract.

Alternative II

Where paragraph 2 of this Clause applies, but where alternative contractual terms are not agreed upon, the contract remains in force in accordance with its original terms.

Alternative III

Where paragraph 2 of this Clause applies, but where alternative contractual terms are not agreed upon, the party invoking this Clause may bring the issue of revision before the arbitral forum, if any, provided for in the contract, or otherwise before the competent courts.

1.13   Force majeure

Alternative I

The Supplier shall not be liable for delay in performing or for failure to perform its obligations if the delay or failure results from any of the following: (i) Acts of God, (ii) outbreak of hostilities, riot, civil disturbance, acts of terrorism, (iii) the act of any government or authority (including refusal or revocation of any licence or consent), (iv) fire, explosion, flood, fog or bad weather, (v) power failure, failure of telecommunications lines, failure or breakdown of plant, machinery or vehicles, (vi) default of suppliers or sub-contractors, (vii) theft, malicious damage, strike, lock-out or industrial action of any kind, and (viii) any cause or circumstance whatsoever beyond the Supplier's reasonable control.

Alternative II

(1) Unless otherwise agreed in the contract between the parties expressly or impliedly, where a party to a contract fails to perform one or more

of its contractual duties, the consequences set out in paragraphs 4 to 9 of this Clause will follow if and to the extent that that party proves:

(a) that its failure to perform was caused by an impediment beyond its reasonable control; and

(b) that it could not reasonably have been expected to have taken the occurrence of the impediment into account at the time of the conclusion of the contract; and

(c) that it could not reasonably have avoided or overcome the effects of the impediment.

(2) Where a contracting party fails to perform one or more of its contractual duties because of default by a third party whom it has engaged to perform the whole or part of the contract, the consequences set out in paragraphs 4 to 9 of this Clause will only apply to the contracting party:

(a) if and to the extent that the contracting party establishes the requirements set out in paragraph 1 of this Clause; and

(b) if and to the extent that the contracting party proves that the same requirements apply to the third party.

(3) In the absence of proof to the contrary and unless otherwise agreed in the contract between the parties expressly or impliedly, a party invoking this Clause shall be presumed to have established the conditions described in paragraph 1 [a] and [b] of this Clause in case of the occurrence of one or more of the following impediments:

(a) war (whether declared or not), armed conflict or the serious threat of same (including but not limited to hostile attack, blockade, military embargo), hostilities, invasion, act of a foreign enemy, extensive military mobilisation;

(b) civil war, riot, rebellion and revolution, military or usurped power, insurrection, civil commotion or disorder, mob violence, act of civil disobedience;

(c) act of terrorism, sabotage or piracy;

(d) act of authority whether lawful or unlawful, compliance with any law or governmental order, rule, regulation or direction, curfew restriction, expropriation, compulsory acquisition, seizure of works, requisition, nationalisation;

(e) act of God, plague, epidemic, natural disaster such as but not limited to violent storm, cyclone, typhoon, hurricane, tornado, blizzard, earthquake, volcanic activity, landslide, tidal wave, tsunami, flood, damage or destruction by lightning, drought;

(f) explosion, fire, destruction of machines, equipment, factories and of any kind of installation, prolonged break-down of transport, telecommunication or electric current;

(g) general labour disturbance such as but not limited to boycott, strike and lock-out, go-slow, occupation of factories and premises.

(4) A party successfully invoking this Clause is, subject to paragraph 6 below, relieved from its duty to perform its obligations under the

contract from the time at which the impediment causes the failure to perform if notice thereof is given without delay or, if notice thereof is not given without delay, from the time at which notice thereof reaches the other party.

(5) A party successfully invoking this Clause is, subject to paragraph 6 below, relieved from any liability in damages or any other contractual remedy for breach of contract from the time indicated in paragraph 4.

(6) Where the effect of the impediment or event invoked is temporary, the consequences set out under paragraphs 4 and 5 above shall apply only insofar, to the extent that and as long as the impediment or the listed event invoked impedes performance by the party invoking this Clause of its contractual duties. Where this paragraph applies, the party invoking this Clause is under an obligation to notify the other party as soon as the impediment or listed event ceases to impede performance of its contractual duties.

(7) A party invoking this Clause is under an obligation to take all reasonable means to limit the effect of the impediment or event invoked upon performance of its contractual duties.

(8) Where the duration of the impediment invoked under paragraph 1 of this Clause or of the listed event invoked under paragraph 3 of this Clause has the effect of substantially depriving either or both of the contracting parties of what they were reasonably entitled to expect under the contract, either party has the right to terminate the contract by notification within a reasonable period to the other party.

(9) Where paragraph 8 above applies and where either contracting party has, by reason of anything done by another contracting party in the performance of the contract, derived a benefit before the termination of the contract, the party deriving such a benefit shall be under a duty to pay to the other party a sum of money equivalent to the value of such benefit.

2   Cases illustrating the need for coordination with the applicable law

A literal interpretation of the contract may lead to a result conflicting with mandatory rules or principles of the applicable law. In particular, there may be difficulties in coordinating the contract with the applicable law in three different respects.

2.1   Clauses aiming at fully detaching the contract from the applicable law

If the clause aims at fully detaching the contract from the applicable law, there may be a conflict with mandatory rules or principles of the applicable law – such as the duty to cooperate loyally, to interpret the contract in good faith and to exercise remedies in good faith.

This may be relevant in particular to the following clauses:

Entire agreement   What happens if the parties have, on a previous occasion, agreed on certain specifications for certain products, but have not incorporated those specifications into the present contract? Can the contract be interpreted in light of the previously agreed specifications, in spite of the entire agreement clause?

No waiver   Assume that the contract gives one party the right to terminate in case of delay in the delivery. What happens if the delivery is late, but the party does not terminate until, after a considerable time, the market changes and the contract is no longer profitable? The real reason for the termination is not the delay but the change in the market. May the old delay be invoked as a ground for termination or is there a principle preventing it, in spite of the no waiver clause?

No oral amendments   What happens if the parties agree on an oral amendment and afterwards one party invokes the no oral amendments clause to refuse performance (for example, because it is no longer interested in the contract after the market has changed)?

Severability   Some contract laws provide that the invalidity of certain contract terms renders the whole contract invalid. This conflicts with the clause. Moreover, a literal interpretation of the clause may lead to an unbalanced contract if the provision that becomes invalid or unenforceable has significance for the interests of only one of the parties.

Conditions, fundamental breach   Assume that the contract defines delay in delivery as a fundamental breach and that there is a delay, but it does not have any consequences for the other (innocent) party. What happens if the innocent party terminates the contract because the market has changed and the contract is no longer profitable? Can the clause on fundamental breach be invoked, even if the real reason for the termination is not the delay but the change in the market?

Sole remedy   Assume that the contract defined the payment of a certain amount as the sole remedy in case of breach. What happens if the non-defaulting party is able to prove that the breach has caused a considerably larger damage than the agreed amount?

Subject to contract   Assume that the parties entered into a letter of intent specifying that failure to reach a final agreement will not expose any of the parties to liability. What happens if one party never really intended to enter into a final agreement and used the negotiations merely to prevent the other party from entering into a contract with a third party?

Material adverse change   What happens if one party invokes this clause to avoid a deal that it has lost interest in? The real reason for invoking the clause is not a change in external circumstances but in the party's own evaluation thereof.

2.2   Clauses using a terminology with legal effects not known to the applicable law

Some clauses regulate remedies for breach of contract and reimbursement of damages by using a terminology with specific legal effects under English law. This may interfere with regulations contained in the applicable law.

This may be relevant in particular to the following clauses:

Liquidated damages   Some legal systems permit the parties to agree on contractual penalties; these may be cumulated with reimbursement of damages. Does the use of the English terminology 'liquidated damages' prevent this?

Indemnity   Some contracts use the term 'indemnity' to designate a guaranteed payment. Does the use of the English terminology, which assumes damage actually has occurred, prevent the guaranteed payment when no actual damage has occurred?

2.3   Clauses regulating matters already regulated in the applicable law

Some clauses regulate matters that are already regulated in the applicable law. How do these two regulations interact with each other: do they integrate each other or do they exclude each other?

This may be relevant in particular to the following clauses:

Representations and warranties   In some systems, the parties are under a duty to inform the other party of material matters that may have an impact on the other party's assessment of its interests under the contract. If the list of representations and warranties left out one such matter, is the party nevertheless obliged to disclose it to the other party? Or did the other party waive the legal protection that it has under the applicable law when it agreed to a detailed list of representations and warranties? Is the latter to be interpreted as being exhaustive or is it to be integrated by the information duties under the governing law?

Hardship   In some systems, the law regulates the consequences of supervening, external events that make the performance excessively onerous for one party. If the parties regulate the matter in their contract, does it mean that the contract regulation will be the only applicable regulation or will it be integrated by the applicable law?

Force majeure   Many *force majeure* clauses describe *force majeure* events as events beyond the control of the parties that may not be foreseen or reasonably overcome. Is this definition applied equally independently of the applicable law? In particular, what is deemed to be beyond the control of one party: is it sufficient to prove that a party has been diligent and has acted in good faith?

7

The common law tradition: application of boilerplate clauses under English law

EDWIN PEEL

1 Introduction

The majority of this chapter is taken up with an analysis of how English law regulates the types of clause that are the principal focus of this book. Before that analysis can be undertaken, it is necessary to make a few preliminary observations about the general approach of the courts to the policing of 'boilerplate' clauses.

1.1 Content

Freedom of contract remains the core principle at the heart of the English law of contract. The content of a contract remains almost entirely in the hands of the parties to it. There are few 'default' provisions which will be included in the absence of any express agreement of the parties. Prominent examples are the terms implied by statute in contracts for the sale of goods that the goods will comply with any description, or sample, and will be of 'satisfactory quality' and 'fit for purpose'.[1] Such terms will often be excluded by the contrary agreement of the parties, so that it is ultimately the intention of the parties which prevails.[2] In some instances, the parties may be quite happy to rely on the minimal content supplied by the operation of law, e.g., some building contracts, particularly in the residential context, may be entirely oral, or at the very least will remain informal and contain no more than the express obligation of the employer to pay the price and the implied obligation of the

---

[1] Sale of Goods Act 1979, Sections 13–15.
[2] Though such exclusions are themselves regulated by statute under the Unfair Contract Terms Act 1977, Section 6.

contractor to carry out the work with reasonable skill and care.[3] In other instances, the parties will wish to avail themselves of the opportunity to alter the content of the contract to provide additional protection for their interests. This of course can involve transaction costs, but one way to reduce those costs is to employ 'standard forms' for contracts of a recurring nature. If one continues with the example of building contracts, such standard forms are commonplace, with variations in the model depending upon the nature of the work undertaken.[4]

The use of standard forms has given rise to an obvious tension in the English law of contract. At the risk of oversimplification, it is a tension borne of two rather different 'types' of standard form.[5] As Lord Diplock put it in *A Schroeder Music Publishing Co* v. *Macaulay*:[6]

> Standard forms of contracts are of two kinds. The first, of very ancient origin, are those which set out the terms upon which mercantile transactions of common occurrence are to be carried out. Examples are bills of lading, charterparties, policies of insurance, contracts of sale in the commodity markets. The standard clauses in these contracts have been settled over the years by negotiation by representatives of the commercial interests involved and have been widely adopted because experience has shown that they facilitate the conduct of trade. Contracts of these kinds affect not only the actual parties to them but also others who may have a commercial interest in the transactions to which they relate, as buyers or sellers, charterers or ship owners, insurers or bankers. If fairness or reasonableness were relevant to their enforceability the fact that they are widely used by parties whose bargaining power is fairly matched would raise a strong presumption that their terms are fair and reasonable.
>
> The same presumption, however, does not apply to the other kind of standard form of contract. This is of comparatively modern origin. It is the result of the concentration of particular kinds of business in relatively few hands. The ticket cases in the 19th century provide what are probably the first examples. The terms of this kind of standard form of contract have not been the subject of negotiation between the parties to it, or approved by any organisation representing the interests of the weaker party. They have been dictated by that party whose bargaining power, either exercised

---

[3] Supply of Goods and Services Act 1982, Section 13.

[4] See the Joint Contracts Tribunal (JCT) series.

[5] See, generally, O. Prausnitz, *The Standardisation of Commercial Contracts* (Sweet & Maxwell, 1937); D. Yates and A. J. Hawkins, *Standard Business Contracts* (Sweet & Maxwell, 1986), C. M. Schmitthoff, 'The Unification or Harmonisation of Law by Means of Standard Contracts and General Conditions', *International & Comparative Law Quarterly*, 17 (1968), 551.

[6] [1974] 1 WLR 1308 at 1316. See also *R W Green Ltd* v. *Cade Bros Farms* [1978] 1 Lloyd's Rep. 602 at 607.

alone or in conjunction with others providing similar goods or services, enables him to say: 'If you want these goods or services at all, these are the only terms on which they are obtainable. Take it or leave it.'

The principal focus of this book is on 'commercial transactions'. It may often be the case that, in such transactions, it is standard forms of the first type which will have been employed, but that will not always be the case.[7] It will be seen, in the analysis of particular clauses, that the tension between these two 'types' of form is evident in the approach of English law.[8]

Our concern is not just with standard *forms*, but with particular *clauses*. The term 'boilerplate' is understood to be derived from the metal plates on which syndicated or ready-to-print copy was supplied to newspapers. The point of such plates was that they could not be modified before printing, hence the borrowing of the term to refer to clauses in a contract which are not intended to be the subject of any negotiation. In fact, in the commercial transactions which are the principal focus of this book, a 'boilerplate' clause may well be the subject of negotiation, and perhaps of modification, in the particular contract at hand. The clause is 'boilerplate' or 'standard form' in the sense that one party (or possibly both) requires a clause of that *type*, but there is still room for negotiation as to its precise content. For example, a seller may require some limit on its potential liability but be required to negotiate what that limit should be, or a buyer may wish to have predetermined the level of damages payable for the seller's breach but be required to negotiate what that level should be.[9] Where the clause in question has been the subject not only of historical negotiation (standard forms of the first type), but also of negotiation in the particular contract before the courts, the grounds for intervention will have narrowed yet further. Put simply, the content of a contract is for the parties to determine for themselves, but a factor which the courts may take into account is whether it is *both* parties who have so determined and not just one of them.

---

[7] This is reflected most obviously in Section 3 of the Unfair Contract Terms Act 1977, which applies the test of reasonableness to exemption clauses in commercial contracts which have been entered into on the basis of one party's 'written standard terms of business'.

[8] For criticism of the decision in *Schroeder* in particular and the courts' ability to regulate anti-competitive practices via the medium of individual cases in general, see M. J. Trebilcock, 'The Doctrine of Inequality of Bargaining Power', *University of Toronto L.J.*, 26 (1976), 359.

[9] An apparent shift to a broader test of 'unconscionability' in the regulation of liquidated damages would seem to have expanded the room for negotiation: see Section 2.7 of this chapter.

One method of taking this into account which can be applied generally
and is mentioned here, rather than by reference to any of the particular
clauses which are analysed below, is incorporation, i.e., determining
whether the parties have agreed, or must be taken to have agreed, to
the particular clause in question. The English courts have left themselves
very little room for manoeuvre when it comes to terms set out in a
document which is intended to have contractual effect and which is
signed by the party to be bound.[10] Beyond that, incorporation is determined by reasonable notice, a concept which, by its very nature,
affords the courts a degree of flexibility. In particular, the courts have
employed the principle that the more 'onerous or unusual' the clause in
question, the more explicit the steps which must have been taken to have
reasonably brought it to the notice of the party to be bound.[11] However, it
is important to stress that, at least in its orthodox form, the concern of
the courts is with clauses which are *unusual*, not with those which are
simply *unreasonable*.[12] The limit of the common law tradition in this
regard is that the courts may ask whether the parties have agreed to a
particular bargain, not whether they should be held to the bargain to
which they have agreed.[13]

1.2   Interpretation

If it is for the parties to determine the content of their contract in the
first instance, it is nonetheless a legitimate question for the courts to
ask: what exactly is it that they have determined? This is a question of
interpretation. The English law of contract has a long history of
interpretation being employed to curb the worst abuses of standard
forms or boilerplate clauses. The prime example is the application of

[10] *L'Estrange* v. *F Graucob Ltd* [1934] 2 KB 394. For criticism, see *McCutcheon* v. *David MacBrayne Ltd* [1964] 1 WLR 125 at 133; cf. J. R. Spencer, 'Signature, Consent and the Rule in *L'Estrange v Graucob*' [1973] CLJ 104.
[11] *J Spurling Ltd* v. *Bradshaw* [1956] 1 WLR 46; *Thornton* v. *Shoe Lane Parking Ltd* [1971] 2 QB 163; *Interfoto Picture Library Ltd* v. *Stiletto Visual Programmes Ltd* [1989] QB 433.
[12] This has been queried: 'The balance of authority is that the courts have no power to declare terms void because they are unreasonable. This is perhaps the nub of the matter: unable to declare a clause void because it is unreasonable, the courts are now declaring it unincorporated because it is unusual. A discredited rule of public policy has been reinstated as a rule based on an inference from the intention of parties: the plaintiff is only deemed to know of and assent to terms that are usual.' M. Clarke, 'Notice of Contractual Terms' [1976] CLJ 51 at 70.
[13] This is a matter for legislation: see text to note 22.

the principle of *contra proferentem*, in both of its forms: first, that 'in case of doubt, wording is to be construed against the party who proposed it for inclusion in the contract'[14] (applicable to boilerplate clauses generally) and, secondly, that 'wording in a contract is to be construed against a party who seeks to rely on it in order to diminish or exclude his basic obligation, or any common law duty which arises apart from contract'[15] (applicable to exemption clauses).[16] More generally, 'the fact that a particular construction leads to a very unreasonable result must be a relevant consideration. The more unreasonable the result, the more unlikely it is that the parties can have intended it, and if they do intend it the more necessary it is that they shall make that intention abundantly clear'.[17]

This latter passage of Lord Reid highlights both the way in which interpretation can operate as a control against boilerplate clauses[18] and its limits. If the parties have made their intention sufficiently clear, there is no room for the 'indirect' control of unreasonableness via interpretation. It is when these limits have been reached that the courts have, on some occasions, felt it necessary to go beyond interpretation.[19] It is precisely at this point that they have been found to have overreached themselves so far as the common law is concerned.[20] The supervision of the fairness of

---

[14] *Youell* v. *Bland Welch & Co Ltd* [1992] 2 Lloyd's Rep. 127 at 134.

[15] *Ibid*. See, to similar effect, the comments of Staughton LJ in *Pera Shipping Corp.* v. *Petroship SA* [1984] 2 Lloyd's Rep. 363 at 365.

[16] See, generally, E. Peel, 'Whither *Contra Proferentem*', in A. Burrows and E. Peel (eds.), *Contract Terms* (Oxford University Press, 2007).

[17] *Wickman Ltd* v. *Schuler AG* [1974] AC 235 at 251. See, more recently, *Horwood* v. *Land of Leather Ltd* [2010] EWHC 546 (Comm).

[18] In *Schuler* itself, a clause by reference to which one of the parties claimed an entitlement to terminate for breach of 'condition'.

[19] Most notably in the form of the doctrine of 'fundamental breach' promoted by Lord Denning to control unreasonable exemption clauses: *Karsales (Harrow) Ltd* v. *Wallis* [1956] 1 WLR 936; *Harbutts 'Plasticine' Ltd* v. *Wayne Tank Co Ltd* [1970] 1 QB 447.

[20] In *Photo Production Ltd* v. *Securicor Transport Ltd* [1980] AC 827, the House of Lords finally laid to rest the doctrine of fundamental breach and reasserted that whether a clause excluded or limited liability even for a serious or 'fundamental breach' was purely a matter of construction. It is reported that, shortly after this decision, Lord Denning addressed an after-dinner audience in Oxford along the following lines: 'I am told by Lord Diplock that I may no longer hold that an exemption clause is unenforceable because the breach is a fundamental one. It is a matter of construction. Let me tell you, ladies and gentleman, I know how to construe.' For recent examples of what this probably means in practice, see: *Internet Broadcasting Corporation Ltd* v. *MAR LLC* [2009] EWHC 84 (Ch), [2009] 2 Lloyd's Rep. 295; *A Turtle Offshore SA* v. *Superior Trading Inc* [2008] EWHC 3034 (Admlty), [2009] 1 Lloyd's Rep. 177.

the bargain is, to the extent that it is subject to supervision at all,[21] a matter for legislation.[22]

1.3   Good faith

This is a very brief excursus into good faith. Some will say that is the only type of excursus possible when it comes to English law. The rather obvious, but nonetheless important, point to make at the outset is that the English law of contract does not exclude consideration of 'good faith'. Indeed, it is just such a consideration that forms the basis of much of the law. Thus, one party will not be held to a contract which he entered into on the basis of a sufficiently important mistake in circumstances where that mistake was known to, or ought to have been known to, the other party,[23] all the more so if the mistake was induced by something said by the other party which was not true.[24] Similarly, one party will not be held to a contract which was obtained in circumstances where his consent was obtained by some form of illegitimate pressure,[25] or by taking advantage of a relationship of trust and confidence with that other party or a third party.[26] Other examples could be given. They show that, to the extent that there is any difference between English law and the law of other legal systems, it is a difference of degree. The point is well put by Bingham LJ:[27]

> In many civil law systems, and perhaps in most legal systems outside the common law world, the law of obligations recognises and enforces an overriding principle that in making and carrying out contracts parties should act in good faith. This does not simply mean that they should not deceive each other, a principle which any legal system must recognise; its effect is perhaps most aptly conveyed by such metaphorical colloquialisms as 'playing fair,' 'coming clean' or 'putting one's cards face upwards on the table.' It is in essence a principle of fair and open dealing . . . English law has, characteristically, committed itself to no such overriding

---

[21] Few of the legislative controls concern themselves solely, if at all, with the 'substantive' fairness of the bargain.

[22] For example, in the context of exemption clauses, the Unfair Contract Terms Act 1977. See also the Unfair Terms in Consumer Contracts Regulations 1999 (SI 1999/2083), as amended by the Unfair Terms in Consumer Contracts (Amendment) Regulations 2001 (SI 2001/1186); and the Consumer Credit Act 1974 (as amended by the Consumer Credit Act 2006).

[23] So-called cases of unilateral mistake: G. H. Treitel and E. Peel, *The Law of Contract*, 12th edn (Sweet & Maxwell, 2007), paras. 8–033ff (referred to as *Treitel* hereafter).

[24] Misrepresentation: *ibid.*, Chapter 9.   [25] Duress: *ibid.*, paras. 10–002ff.

[26] Undue influence: *ibid.*, paras. 10–008ff.

[27] *Interfoto Picture Library Ltd* v. *Stiletto Visual Programmes Ltd* [1989] QB 433 at 439.

principle but has developed piecemeal solutions in response to demonstrated problems of unfairness.

It is often the case that in 'demonstrated problems of unfairness', English
law reaches the same, or a similar, solution on a 'piecemeal' basis as that
reached by other legal systems through the application of an 'overriding
principle' of good faith.[28] This observation might be borne in mind when
considering instances of potential unfairness in the context of the particular clauses which are analysed in the remainder of this chapter. One
further general observation that may be made is that the courts have very
largely confined themselves to demonstrated problems of what is sometimes referred to as 'procedural' unfairness, i.e., unfairness in the bargaining process, rather than with 'substantive' unfairness i.e., unfairness
in the bargain itself: 'Under English law there is no general duty to
negotiate in good faith, but there are plenty of other ways of dealing
with particular problems of unacceptable conduct occurring *in the course
of negotiations* without unduly hampering the ability of the parties to
negotiate their own bargains without the intervention of the courts.'[29]

1.4   Conclusion and methodology

This brief preliminary has sought to establish several broad propositions.
The first is that freedom of contract lies at the heart of the common law
tradition. It is entirely consistent with that freedom for the courts, nonetheless, to ask *whether* the parties had agreed on a particular clause
(incorporation) and, if they had, *what* exactly it is that they had agreed
(interpretation). One does not need to be a legal realist[30] to acknowledge
that in answering these questions, the courts have room to take account
of considerations of fairness, reasonableness or good faith. This is hardly
surprising since such considerations are not unknown to English law,
albeit they are largely confined to the supervision of the bargaining
process rather than the bargain itself. It has therefore been suggested

---

[28] For a helpful survey, see R. Zimmermann and S. Whittaker (eds.), *Good Faith in
European Contract Law* (Cambridge University Press, 2000). One notable example
where the difference in degree seems capable of producing different solutions is the
unwillingness of the English courts to recognise as enforceable an agreement to negotiate
in good faith: E. Peel, 'Agreements to Negotiate in Good Faith', in A. Burrows and
E. Peel, *Contract Formation and Parties* (Oxford University Press, 2010), Chapter 2.
[29] *Cobbe* v. *Yeoman's Row Management Ltd* [2006] EWCA Civ 1139, [2006] 1 WLR 2964 at
[4], per Mummery LJ (emphasis added).
[30] And the author of *Treitel* is no legal realist.

that the difference between the approach of English law and that of other legal systems is one of degree. Differences in degree can matter, of course. Writing extra-judicially, Lord Steyn has observed that 'there is not a world of difference between the objective requirement of good faith and the reasonable expectations of parties',[31] but in English law there is *a* difference and it might be thought to be exemplified by the approach taken to the clauses about to be considered.

In approaching the analysis of particular clauses, I have adopted the illuminating technique employed by Giuditta Cordero-Moss in the last of the workshops around which this book is based of asking two very specific questions: (i) what is the legal background for the development of the clause in question, or, to put it another way, what would happen as a matter of English law if the clause was not there?; (ii) will such a clause be applied without restriction in situations where the result may be unexpected or unfair? I have eliminated from any specific consideration two types of clause – the severability provision and the 'material adverse change' provision. This is in part because of the confines of space, but is in part also a reflection of the fact that there is little, if any, direct judicial consideration of such clauses.

2   The clauses

2.1   Entire agreement[32]

As a matter of English law, it is necessary to draw a distinction between entire agreement clauses in two senses: the narrow and the wide. The sample clause which has been put forward for consideration states as follows:

> The Contract contains the entire contract and understanding between the parties hereto and supersedes all prior negotiations, representations, undertakings and agreements on any subject matter of the Contract.

The sample clause is an example of an entire agreement clause in the narrow sense. It is this narrow sense which will be considered first, but some consideration will also be given to the wider sense, if only to confirm the approach of the English courts to such clauses generally.

---

[31] (1997) 113 LQR 433 at 439. This is a theme about which his Lordship has also written judicially: *First Energy (UK) Ltd* v. *Hungarian International Bank Ltd* [1993] 2 Lloyd's Rep. 194 at 196.

[32] G. McMeel, *The Construction of Contracts: Interpretation, Implication and Rectification* (Oxford University Press, 2007), Chapter 24.

If one starts by asking what would happen if this clause was not included in a contract governed by English law, the answer is, arguably, nothing very different because of the parol evidence rule. This states that evidence cannot be admitted (or, even if admitted, cannot be used) to add to, vary or contradict a written instrument.[33] Thus, where a contract has been reduced to writing, neither party can rely on extrinsic evidence of terms alleged to have been agreed, i.e., on evidence not contained in the document itself.

One difficulty with the rule is that when a contract is reduced to writing, there is only a presumption that the writing was intended to include all the terms of the contract and this presumption is rebuttable, such that the parties may adduce evidence to show that the written document was not intended to set out all the terms on which the parties had actually agreed. It has been argued that this turns the parol evidence rule (as applied to contracts) into 'no more than a circular statement'.[34] The circularity argument goes thus: if the rule applies only where the written document is intended to contain *all* the terms of the contract, evidence of other terms would be useless even if admitted (since they would not form part of the contract), while the rule never prevents a party from relying on evidence of terms which *were* intended to be part of the contract. There is much force in this view.[35]

The primary purpose of the parol evidence rule is to promote certainty, but this may be at the expense of justice if it results in the rejection of evidence of other terms that were actually agreed and relied upon by one party. By contrast, the reception of such evidence may cause injustice to the other party, if he or she reasonably believed that the document drawn up by the parties formed an exclusive record of the contract. Where the evidence is rejected because the party relying on it cannot overcome the presumption which seems to arise from the fact that the document *looks* like a complete contract, the greater injustice would appear to lie in the exclusion of the evidence, for the presumption

---

[33] *Jacobs v. Batavia & General Plantations Trust Ltd* [1924] 1 Ch 287 at 295; *Rabin v. Gerson Berger Association Ltd* [1986] 1 WLR 526 at 531, 537; *The Nile Rhapsody* [1992] 2 Lloyd's Rep. 349 at 407, affirmed [1994] 1 Lloyd's Rep. 382; *Orion Insurance Co v. Sphere Drake Insurance Plc* [1992] 1 Lloyd's Rep. 239 at 273.

[34] Law Commission Report on *The Parol Evidence Rule* (Law Com. No. 154), para. 2.7; G. Marston, 'The Parol Evidence Rule: The Law Commission Speaks' [1986] CLJ 192; cf. Beldam LJ in *Youell v. Bland Welch & Co Ltd* [1992] 2 Lloyd's Rep. 127 at 140 – 'the rule, if rule it be'.

[35] For an argument that it is, nonetheless, more than mere circularity, see *Treitel*, para. 6–013.

seems to be based on the nature and form of the document, rather than on any actual belief of the party relying on it, that it formed an exclusive record of the contract.

It is in this context that one may consider the role and effect of an entire agreement clause of the type set out above. It is essentially intended to operate as an express incorporation of the parol evidence rule[36] and in that sense it is a clause which aims at detaching the contract from the need to have English law as the governing law.[37] If anything, it aims at even greater certainty than the parol evidence rule, since one does not need to ask whether the document *looks* like it was intended as an exclusive record of the contract; one has the express agreement of the parties to that effect. Because it amounts to an express incorporation of the parol evidence rule, its interpretation and enforcement is subject to the same dilemma referred to in relation to the rule itself. For example, the Law Commission has said: 'it may have a strong persuasive effect but if it were proved that, notwithstanding the clause, the parties actually intended some additional term to be of contractual effect, the court would give effect to that term.'[38] There are surprisingly few reported cases on the interpretation and effect of entire agreement clauses, but one of those few decisions supports this view. In *Cheverny Consulting Ltd* v. *Whitehead Mann Ltd*,[39] the court was required to consider claims for payment under a consultancy agreement which contained the following clause:

> This Agreement constitutes the entire agreement between the parties to it with respect to its subject matter and shall have effect to the exclusion of any other memorandum agreement or understanding of any kind between the parties preceding the date of this Agreement and touching and concerning its subject matter.

Crucially, the court had made a finding of fact that the main agreement had been accompanied by an unsigned side-letter which was, the entire agreement clause apart, intended to take effect contemporaneously with

---

[36] Though it has also been said that it operates 'to denude what would otherwise constitute a collateral warranty of legal effect': *Inntrepreneur Pub Co Ltd* v. *East Crown Ltd* [2000] 2 Lloyd's Rep. 611 at 614; *Ravennavi SpA* v. *New Century Shipbuilding Co Ltd* [2006] EWHC 733 (Comm), [2006] 2 Lloyd's Rep. 280, [2007] EWCA Civ 58, [2007] 2 Lloyd's Rep. 24.

[37] It is suggested that the practice of including such clauses probably originated in the US: H. Beale, *Chitty on Contracts*, 30th edn (Sweet & Maxwell, 2008), 12–104, No. 435. See Uniform Commercial Code, para. 2–202.

[38] Law Com. 154, 1986, Cmnd. 9700, para. 2.15.   [39] [2005] EWHC 2431.

the main agreement.[40] In those circumstances, it was held that the entire agreement clause failed to exclude the side-letter for two reasons, though the judge placed greater emphasis on the second: first, 'This Agreement' was not further defined. As the judge held, if the side-letter had been stapled to the back of the main agreement, 'This Agreement' would have included the side-letter and the judge saw no reason to reach a different conclusion when it was supplied *along with* the main agreement; secondly, the clause only excluded 'any other memorandum agreement . . . *preceding* the date of the Agreement'. The judge found that the main agreement and the side-letter were 'devised for execution on the same occasion'.[41]

It should be noted that the decision in *Cheverny* is one which is reached solely on the basis of interpretation and is therefore a good example of the general observation made above that the courts can, via the orthodoxy of interpretation, avoid unreasonable results. It is noticeable that since this decision, the 'standard form' of an entire agreement clause does seem to have been altered to try and meet the objections raised by the judge, i.e., by giving a more explicit definition to 'This Agreement' or 'This Contract'[42] and dropping any reference to 'preceding' or 'prior' statements or representations. Would such a clause, leaving no room for an interpretative 'escape', be enforced if the court made the same finding of fact as in the *Cheverny* case that the parties had agreed to an additional term at variance with the recorded contract?[43] It seems

---

[40] The effect of the side-letter was to amend the 'trigger' for payment of additional consideration in the form of shares. In the Court of Appeal ([2006] EWCA Civ 1303), it was found that the trial judge had been wrong to rely on the evidence of one of the witnesses so as to conclude that there was an agreement on the side-letter, leaving aside the effect of the entire agreement clause. The matter was therefore remitted to the court for a further hearing, where the same result, that the entire agreement clause did not rule out the enforceability of the side-letter which was found to be binding on a proper consideration of the evidence, was reached: [2007] EWHC 3130 (Ch).

[41] The same might be said of the sample clause used – what does 'This Contract' mean? And does the clause only rule out 'prior' representation, etc?

[42] E.g., 'This Agreement, including the Schedules hereto, and the other Project documents referred to herein . . .'.

[43] In effect, this question was considered in the second trial in the *Cheverny* case, when Rattee J asked what the result would be if the entire agreement clause had deprived the side-letter of any contractual effect. He found that the parties had dealt with each other in a manner consistent with the side-letter, which gave rise to an estoppel by convention (see *Amalgamated Investment & Property Co Ltd (In Liquidation)* v. *Texas Commerce International Bank Ltd* (1982) QB 84) such that the defendant was estopped from denying that it was bound by the terms of the side-letter.

never to have been argued that an entire agreement clause might be caught by the provisions of the Unfair Contract Terms Act 1977. Potentially, it could be caught by the provision in Section 3(2)(b) under which one party 'cannot by reference to any contract term … claim to be entitled (i) to render a contractual performance substantially different from that which was reasonably expected of him, or (ii) in respect of the whole or any part of his contractual obligation, to render no performance at all'.[44] It may be that it has been generally accepted that entire agreement clauses seek only to define the obligations of the parties and are not the sort of 'bogus' exclusion clauses at which this provision is clearly aimed, but *ex hypothesi*, we are concerned at this stage with the situation where one party has undertaken an obligation via the additional term but seeks to avoid performance of that obligation by reference to the entire agreement clause. In this regard, it may be noted that the Office of Fair Trading has regarded entire agreement clauses as potentially unfair under the Unfair Terms in Consumer Contracts Regulations 1999.[45]

Support for the view that the English courts may not allow an appropriately drafted entire agreement clause to be relied upon if the outcome would be unfair or unjust, and that the source of control may lie in the reasonableness test imposed by the Unfair Contract Terms Act 1977, may be derived from the approach they have taken to such clauses in their wider sense. The sample clause, as drafted, only has the effect of excluding additional claims for breach of contract; it does not exclude claims for misrepresentation, i.e., claims to rescind the contract and/or claim damages on the basis that one party was induced to enter it as a result of a precontractual misrepresentation of the other.[46] To achieve this result, additional wording is usually added, of which the following is an example:

> The parties agree that these terms and conditions (together with any other terms and conditions expressly incorporated in the Contract) represent the entire agreement between the parties relating to the sale and purchase of the Equipment and that *no statement or representations*

---

[44] Section 3 as a whole only applies where one party 'deals as consumer' or on the other party's 'written standard terms of business'.

[45] OFT Bulletin 1 at 16 (though this draws no distinction between entire agreement clauses in the narrow sense and 'non-reliance clauses' which seek to avoid liability in misrepresentation, as discussed in the following text).

[46] *Thomas Witter Ltd* v. *T.B.P. Industries Ltd* [1996] 2 All ER 573; *Deepak Fertlizers and Petrochemicals Corp* v. *ICI* [1999] 1 Lloyd's Rep. 387 at 395.

made by either party have been relied upon by the other in agreeing to enter into the Contract.[47]

The particular feature of this wording is that it does not simply 'exclude' or 'limit' liability for misrepresentation. Rather, it seeks to operate on the basis that no such liability arises in the first place. This is because an essential ingredient of liability is that the claimant must have relied on the false representation of the defendant. By agreeing to the clause, the claimant acknowledges that it has not so relied. A variant on the 'non-reliance' clause is the 'no representation' clause, under which the parties acknowledge that no representations have even been made save those which are then set out in the contract itself.

Entire agreement clauses in this wider sense have become common-place such that they are now 'standard form' or 'boilerplate'. They take this form in an attempt to avoid the controls set out in Section 3 of the Misrepresentation Act 1967, which states as follows:

> If a contract contains a term which would exclude or restrict –
> (a) any liability to which a party to a contract may be subject by reason of any misrepresentation made by him before the contract was made; or
> (b) any remedy available to another party to the contract by reason of such a misrepresentation,
>
> that term shall be of no effect except in so far as it satisfies the requirement of reasonableness as stated in section 11(1) of the Unfair Contract Terms Act 1977; and it is for those claiming that the term satisfies that require-ment to show that it does.

By drafting the extended entire agreement clause on the basis of 'non-reliance' or 'no representation', the opportunity is created to argue that such clauses do not purport to 'exclude' or 'restrict' liability and are therefore not subject to the test of reasonableness.[48]

---

[47] Taken from *Watford Electronics Ltd* v. *Sanderson CFL Ltd* [2001] EWCA Civ 317, [2001] BLR 218.

[48] Of course, in commercial transactions, it is highly likely that such a clause would be found to be reasonable in any event, but the aim of the extended entire agreement clause is to avoid the uncertainty created by the very application of the test. This is particularly valuable in the context of Section 3 of the Misrepresentation 1967 since, although it was inserted in its current form by Section 8 of the Unfair Contract Terms Act 1977, it is much broader in its scope. The key controls in the 1977 Act do not apply to certain types of contract (see Sched. 1, para. 1) and, as noted above (note 44), the controls in Section 3 in particular only apply if one party deals as consumer or on the other's written standard terms of business.

The current approach of the English courts is to regard such clauses as giving rise to a contractual estoppel.[49] It has also been suggested that, as such, they cannot be subject to the test of reasonableness under Section 3 of the 1967 Act.[50] That, however, has been seen as an approach which would elevate form over substance. The point has been best expressed by Toulson J as follows:[51]

> The question is one of substance and not form. If a seller of a car said to a buyer 'I have serviced the car since it was new, it has had only one owner and the clock reading is accurate,' those statements would be representations, and they would still have that character even if the seller added the words 'but those statements are not representations on which you can rely.' *Cremdean Properties Ltd v Nash* [1977] EGLR 80, which Mr Nash cited, is authority for the principle that a party cannot by a carefully chosen form of wording circumvent the statutory controls on exclusion of liability for a representation which has on proper analysis been made.
>
> If, however, the seller of the car said 'The clock reading is 20,000 miles, but I have no knowledge whether the reading is true or false,' the position would be different, because the qualifying words could not fairly be regarded as an attempt to exclude liability for a false representation arising from the first half of the sentence.

[49] 'I can see no reason in principle why it should not be possible for parties to an agreement to give up any right to assert that they were induced to enter into it by misrepresentation, provided that they make their intention clear, or why a clause of that kind, if properly drafted, should not give rise to a contractual estoppel of the kind recognised in *Colchester Borough Council v. Smith*': *Peekay Intermark Ltd v. ANZ Banking Group Ltd* [2006] EWCA Civ 386, [2006] 2 Lloyd's Rep. 511 at [56]. See also *Bottin v. Venson* [2006] EWHC 3112 (Ch); *Donegal International v. Republic of Zambia* [2007] EWHC 197 (Comm), [2007] 1 Lloyd's Rep. 397; *JP Morgan Chase Bank v. Springwell Navigation Corporation* [2010] EWCA Civ 1221; *Foodco UK Ltd v. Henry Boot Developments Ltd* [2010] EWHC 358 (Ch); *Titan Wheels Ltd v. RBS* [2010] EWHC 211 (Comm); and *Raiffeisen Zentralbank Osterreich AG v. RBS* [2010] EWHC 1392. Alternatively, such a clause may give rise to an estoppel by representation: *Grimstead v. McGarrigan* [1999] All ER (D) 1163; *Watford Electronics Ltd v. Sanderson CFL Ltd* [2001] EWCA Civ 317, [2001] BLR 218 at [39]–[40]; *Quest 4 Finance Ltd v. Maxfield* [2007] EWHC 2313 (QB), (2007) 2 CLC 706. The submission in *FoodCo UK LLP v. Henry Boot Developments Ltd* that contractual estoppel is limited to 'no representation' clauses and estoppel by representation is limited to 'non-reliance' clauses was dismissed out of hand.

[50] See *Watford Electronics Ltd v. Sanderson CFL Ltd* [2001] EWCA Civ 317, [2001] BLR 218 at [41], where Chadwick LJ described such a contention as 'bizarre'.

[51] *IFE Fund SA v. Goldman Sachs International* [2006] EWHC 2887 (Comm), [2007] 1 Lloyd's Rep. 264 at [69] (the Court of Appeal – [2007] EWCA Civ 811, [2007] 2 Lloyd's Rep. 449 – did not deal expressly with this particular issue). See also *Raiffeisen*, above note 49 at [314]–[315].

Thus, if a seller has clearly, as a matter of fact, made a representation and intended it to be relied upon, his or her attempt to rely upon a clause which says that he or she has not made the representation, or it has not been relied upon, will be treated as an attempt to exclude or restrict a liability which would otherwise have accrued.[52] If, however, there is doubt as to whether a representation was made or was intended to be relied upon, a clause of the type in question will be seen as having legitimately determined the scope of the obligations of the seller and will not be subject to the test of reasonableness.[53] This now seems to represent the approach of the English courts.[54] There is a parallel here with the approach which, it is suggested above, may be taken with respect to entire agreement clauses in the narrow sense.[55] In both senses, the clause may be drafted in such a way as to ensure that there can be no claim in the first place (in a narrow sense, for breach of contract; in a wider sense, for misrepresentation). But if relied upon when, but for the clause in question, the court is of the view that a claim would have arisen, reliance on the clause may be struck down as unreasonable using the tests available in Section 3 of the Unfair Contract Terms Act 1977, and Section 3 of the Misrepresentation Act 1977, respectively. The limit of this test so far as Section 3 of the 1977 Act is concerned is that it only applies where one party deals as a consumer, or on the other party's written standard terms of business. Of course, if such a clause is included in, and relied upon, in the context of a commercial contract, there will be a strong argument to be made that it should be regarded as reasonable. The aim in this part has not been to determine precisely *when* such clauses should be regarded as unenforceable because they are unreasonable, but merely to establish that there is scope for such an argument as a matter of English law.

---

[52] See *Trident Turboprop (Dublin) Ltd* v. *First Flight Couriers Ltd* [2009] EWHC 1686 (Comm), [2008] 2 Lloyd's Rep. 581 and the 'but for' test employed by Aikens J (at [48]). On appeal ([2009] EWCA Civ 290, (2009) 3 WLR 861), there was no further consideration of the scope of Section 3 in this sense.

[53] In the *Goldman Sachs* case itself, the 'no representation' clause relied upon was held to fall into the latter category and was not therefore subject to the reasonableness test in Section 3. Cf. *JP Morgan Chase Bank* v. *Springwell Navigation Corporation* [2010] EWCA 1221.

[54] In addition to the cases already cited, see *Thomas Witter* v. *TBP Industries* [1996] 2 All ER 573; *Government of Zanzibar* v. *British Aerospace (Lancaster House) Ltd* [2000] 1 WLR 2333; *Peart Stevenson Associates Ltd* v. *Holland* [2007] EWHC 1868 (QB), [2007] 2 CLC 706; contrast *Wm. Sindall Plc* v. *Cambridgeshire C.C.* [1994] 1 WLR 1016 at 1034E.

[55] See text to note 45.

2.2   No waiver

A no waiver clause may take various forms. The sample clause used for the purposes of this book states as follows:

> Failure by a party to exercise a right or remedy that it has under this contract does not constitute a waiver thereof.

One hesitates to ask the question of what would happen if the clause was not there. An assessment of English law relating to 'waiver' is not really something to be attempted within the understandable confines of the space herein, if only because the word 'waiver' is often used both by the courts and contract drafters to refer to several quite different principles or doctrines.[56] In the context of a no waiver clause, one may be concerned with a waiving of any breach of the contract or a waiving of the rights to which such a breach may give rise. Thus, there may be 'waiver by election', i.e., the breach may have entitled the innocent party to elect either to terminate the contract or affirm it. He or she must make his or her election and if he or she chooses to affirm the contract, he or she has waived by election the right to terminate. There may also be 'total waiver', i.e., the innocent party waives the breach itself so that he or she may not even sue for damages.

Whichever type of waiver one is referring to, it will not be made out unless there is a 'clear and unequivocal representation' from the innocent party by words or conduct, e.g., in the context of waiver by election, that he or she elects to affirm the contract rather than terminate. Therefore, the right to terminate is not lost by *mere* failure to exercise it: such failure is not normally a sufficiently clear indication that the right will not be exercised.[57] But where, as a matter of business, it is reasonable to expect the injured party to act promptly, unreasonable delay in exercising the right to terminate may give rise to the inference that the contract has been affirmed.[58] The aim of a no waiver clause is to influence the inferences which may be drawn from a delay or failure to exercise the right.

In the last of the workshops, it was reported that there had been virtually no judicial consideration of how such a clause might fare. It was possible to point to *State Securities Plc* v. *Initial Industry*,[59] in which a no waiver clause prevented any affirmation being implied from the acceptance of payments due under the contract. According to the High

---

[56] See further, *Treitel*, paras. 18–075ff.
[57] See *The Scaptrade* [1981] 2 Lloyd's Rep. 425 at 430 (affirmed [1983] 2 AC 694, without reference to this point).
[58] *Ibid.* at 430; *The Laconia* [1977] AC 850 at 872.   [59] [2004] All ER (D) 317 (Jan).

Court, 'it appears that there is no general principle of (English) law that one cannot restrict the operation of the doctrine of waiver by contract'. It was suggested that while that statement of principle may be correct, the point could nevertheless be reached where a court would be persuaded of the clear and unequivocal representation necessary for affirmation, not-withstanding the existence of such a clause.

This was not a bold prediction, but it has been fulfilled by the decision of the Court of Appeal in *Tele2 International Card Co v. Post Office Ltd.*[60] It provides an ideal test case.[61] In short, under a contract for the supply of prepaid phonecards, Tele2 had, by 24 December 2003, failed to provide a parent-company letter of guarantee and was therefore in 'material breach', giving the Post Office the right to terminate.[62] The Post Office did not exercise that right until a year later and in the meantime continued with the performance of the contract (under which phonecards were supplied for sale to Post Office customers).[63] The defence of the Post Office to the argument that it had, by its conduct, elected to affirm the contract and could not now terminate rested on the following Clause 16:

> In no event shall any delay, neglect or forbearance on the part of any party in enforcing (in whole or in part) any provision of this Agreement be or be deemed to be a waiver thereof or a waiver of any other provision or shall in any way prejudice any right of that party under this Agreement.

That defence failed, for the following reasons given by Aikens LJ:[64]

> In short, Clause 16 cannot prevent the fact of an election to abandon the right to terminate from existing: either it does or it does not. This

---

[60] [2009] EWCA Civ 9.

[61] Perhaps inevitably after so little judicial consideration, the decision in *Tele2* was quickly followed by a further decision in *CDV Software Entertainment AG v. Gamecock Media Europe Ltd* [2009] EWHC 2965. It does not appear to add anything to what is said by Aikens LJ in the *Tele 2* case.

[62] The obligation to provide the guarantee was an annual one, i.e., it had to be provided in each December to cover the following year. One suspects that this is why there was no submission by the Post Office that Tele2 was guilty of a continuing breach on the strength of which the contract could be terminated even after an earlier affirmation.

[63] It may be noted that no point was taken that the Post Office's real motivation for wishing to terminate the contract was dissatisfaction with the performance of Tele2 rather than the failure to provide the guarantee. If a party has the right to terminate, it is no bar to its exercise that the innocent party has some ulterior motive, including the wish to escape from a bad bargain: *Arcos Ltd v. Ronaasen Ltd* [1933] AC 470 (where the contract was terminated for breach of 'condition'). Where, however, the task is to establish whether the innocent party has the right to terminate at all (on the grounds of a 'substantial failure to perform'), some account may be taken of any ulterior motive: see *Treitel*, para. 18–033 and the cases discussed therein.

[64] At [56].

conclusion is reinforced, I think, by the terms of Clause 16 itself. Although it stipulates that 'in no event shall any delay, neglect or forbearance' on the part of any party in enforcing a provision of the Agreement '. . . be or be deemed to be a waiver' of the provision or '. . . shall in any way prejudice any right of that party under this Agreement,' it does not deal at all with the issue of election of whether or not to exercise a contractual right. The general law demands that a party which has a contractual right to terminate a contract must elect whether or not to do so. This clause does not attempt to say that the doctrine of election shall not apply – *even assuming that any contractual provision could exclude the operation of the doctrine.*

This passage exhibits the same two-pronged approach noted in relation to entire agreement clauses. First, there is an element of interpretation, in the sense that Aikens LJ leaves open the possibility that a differently worded clause might meet with greater success, e.g., one which deals explicitly with election by reserving the right to terminate notwithstanding continued performance. Nonetheless, one suspects that it would still fall foul of the words highlighted in italics,[65] i.e., even an appropriately drafted clause would have to give way to broader considerations of fairness if, in the assessment of the court, one party had, by its conduct, evinced an intention to affirm the contract.[66] This conclusion may be reached on the basis that such conduct amounted to a waiver itself of the protection of the no waiver clause.

2.3   *No oral amendments*

The sample clause states as follows:

> No amendment or variation to this Agreement shall take effect unless it is in writing, signed by authorised representatives of each of the Parties.

It is another clause which is surprisingly short on direct consideration by the English courts. If it was not there, then, assuming the contract is not one which is required to be in writing under the general law (e.g., contracts for the sale of land[67] or contracts of guarantee),[68] the parties

---

[65] Which may be contrasted with the statement of principle in the *State Securities* case above.

[66] *Quaere* if that conduct is accompanied by express and continuous reservations of the right to terminate?

[67] Law of Property (Miscellaneous Provisions) Act 1989, Section 2. See *Treitel*, para. 5–008.

[68] Statute of Frauds 1677, Section 4. See *Treitel*, paras. 5–010ff.

would be free to amend or vary their agreement in writing or orally, but of course variations made orally may be harder to prove than those put in writing. Any question of 'authorisation' would be one for the law of agency.

In *World Online Telecom Ltd* v. *I-Way Ltd*,[69] the Court of Appeal considered it sufficiently *arguable* that a no oral amendments provision could, itself, be overridden by an oral variation that it should dismiss an application for summary judgment which depended on a finding that the provision was conclusive.[70] This further observation of Schiemann LJ might be noted:[71]

> I have been impressed by the submission that the purpose of a clause such as clause 21 is not to prevent the recognition of oral variations, but rather, casual and unfounded allegations of such variations being made . . . [I]f in cases such as the present we allow something going to trial, precisely that is allowed against which the parties may be regarded as having sought to safeguard themselves.

Schiemann LJ may have been 'impressed', but he still allowed the claim of an overriding oral variation to go to trial. The dilemma here is not dissimilar to that with entire agreement clauses above. An entire agreement clause may make complete sense if it rules out claims of additional terms based on what has been referred to as 'a threshing through the undergrowth' of the parties' contractual negotiations,[72] but the courts feel uneasy if it is relied upon to prevent the enforcement of what appears to have been an otherwise valid and enforceable agreement of the parties. Similarly, if the evidence, in the absence of a no oral amendments clause, indicates that the parties plainly intended a variation of the contract, may the clause be relied upon by one of them to resile from that agreement? For any legal system which allows some room for the will theory, the dilemma is acute: which manifestation of the parties' intention is to be preferred – their initial intention that there should be *no* oral variation or their later intention that the contract *has been* orally varied? Clearly, the courts are unwilling to rule out the latter.

---

[69] [2002] EWCA Civ 413.

[70] See also *Westbrook Resources Ltd* v. *Global Metallurgical Inc* [2009] EWCA Civ 310, [2009] 2 Lloyd's Rep. 224 at [13], per Moore-Bick LJ: 'there is no reason why the contract, including the clause requiring variations to be in writing, could not have been varied orally.'

[71] At [9].   [72] *Inntrepreneur Pub Co Ltd* v. *East Crown Ltd* [2000] 2 Lloyd's Rep. 611 at [7].

2.4　Conditions

By conferring on a term the status of a 'condition', the intention of the parties is to predetermine that any breach of the term in question will confer on the innocent party the right to terminate the contract. As a matter of general law, the innocent party may terminate the contract if there has been what may be referred to as a 'repudiatory breach', which will occur in two situations: where the term breached is regarded as a 'condition' or where the term is not a condition, but the effect of the breach is sufficiently serious that termination is justified. There are also some terms where it is thought that their breach could never justify anything more than damages and such terms are, for these purposes, referred to as 'warranties'. The end result of all of this is a tripartite classification of the terms of the contract into the following:

Conditions:　a term of the contract, any breach of which will entitle the innocent party to terminate, regardless of how serious the effect of the breach actually is.

Warranties:　a term of the contract, any breach of which will only sound in damages (though there is room to argue that even a sufficiently serious breach of warranty could give rise to the right to terminate and, on this basis, there are really only two categories: conditions and all other terms).[73]

Innominate terms:　as the name rather suggests, these are terms which are regarded as neither conditions nor warranties; if the effects of the breach of an innominate term are sufficiently serious, the innocent party will have a right to terminate; otherwise, he or she will have only his or her right to damages.

The condition/warranty distinction has the obvious advantage of certainty; a party who can point to a breach of condition can terminate the contract safe in the knowledge that he or she has the right to do so. A party who terminates for what he or she thinks is a sufficiently serious breach of an innominate term is at the risk of a later finding by the court that the breach was not sufficiently serious and it is the innocent party's termination which was unlawful, putting him or her in the position where he or she is guilty of a repudiatory breach and liable in damages.

---

[73] See, further, *Treitel*, para. 18–048; cf. *Koompahtoo Local Aboriginal Land Council* v. *Sanpine Pty Ltd* [2007] HCA 61 (13 December 2007) at 109, per Kirby J.

The courts may find for themselves that a term is a condition if it is regarded as sufficiently important[74] and they may be directed to so classify a term by legislation.[75] But what is most helpful to the parties and most conducive to certainty is that they may *expressly* stipulate that a term is a condition. The sample clause employs the following language:

> The obligations regulated in Section 13 are fundamental and any breach thereof shall amount to a fundamental breach of this contract.

In fact, such language is rarely likely to be employed, if only because the term 'fundamental breach' has a specific and rather checkered history in English law (mainly in relation to the enforceability of exclusion clauses),[76] to the extent that its use is rather disapproved of. If one thinks about other forms of wording, one could be forgiven for thinking that one should simply say which of the terms of the contract are to be regarded as 'conditions'. But use of the word 'condition' alone may not work. For example, in *Wickman Ltd* v. *Schuler AG*,[77] under a distribution contract, the distributor was required to visit six named customers per week. This was described as a 'condition', but the supplier was held to be not entitled to terminate for its breach – it was said that the parties could not reasonably have intended it to be a condition in the strict sense.[78] Once again, one sees the control over potential unfairness which may be maintained through interpretation; indeed, *Schuler* is the case in which one finds the *dictum* of Lord Reid referred to above that the more unreasonable the result, the more unlikely it is that the parties can have intended it.

But what if the parties have employed language that leaves no room for interpretative control? What is the scope for potential unfairness and is there any control over it beyond interpretation? The fact that breach of a condition leads to the right to terminate may not, in itself, promote unfairness, since the parties may include express provisions allowing

---

[74] This is usually the case with precise time clauses in commercial contracts, e.g., the type of time clauses seen in cif and fob contracts such as the giving of notice of readiness to load: *Bunge Corp* v. *Tradax Export SA* [1981] 1 WLR 711.

[75] E.g., the implied terms in contracts for the sale of goods that the goods will comply with description or sample and will be of satisfactory quality or fit for purpose are implied as conditions: Sale of Goods Act 1979, Sections 13–15. But note that the right to terminate may be qualified by the provisions of Section 15A, discussed further below.

[76] See notes 19 and 20 above.   [77] [1974] AC 235.

[78] To put this decision into some sort of context, it should be noted that the contract as a whole was not well drafted and there have been very few reported decisions to similar effect when the parties have chosen to employ the language of 'condition'.

for termination if one of a number of 'triggers' is met, one of which may be a breach falling short of a breach of condition[79] (such provisions may be referred to as an express contractual power to terminate to distinguish them from a breach of condition, which gives rise to a right to terminate under the general law). If there is any room for unfairness in this regard, it is that where the right to terminate is based on a breach of 'condition', one of the parties may have been taken by surprise,[80] but as we have seen in the *Schuler* case, this is precisely where there is a role for interpretation.[81]

Perhaps greater potential for unfairness lies in the fact that while a breach of condition and a breach which triggers a contractual power to terminate can both give rise to termination, the former also amounts to a 'repudiatory breach', whereas the latter does not, unless the breach in question also happens to be sufficiently serious to amount to a repudiatory breach.[82] The principal practical consequence of this lies in any associated claim for damages. Where a contract has been terminated for a

---

[79] Other triggers may not involve any *breach* at all but only certain *events*, such as the appointment of a receiver.

[80] It may also be noted that certain phrases have, in effect, acquired the status of a code which is accepted by the courts as indicating designation as a condition, e.g., terms stating that time shall be 'of the essence' expressly convert the relevant time stipulation into a condition. The potential for surprise may provide the basis for a challenge that the term in question is 'unfair' under the Unfair Terms in Consumer Contracts Regulations 1999 (SI 1999/2083).

[81] There is also room for interpretative control where termination is based on a contractual power: in *Rice* v. *Great Yarmouth BC*, unreported, 30 June 2000, CA, a four-year contract for gardening/grounds service contained the following clause: 'If the contractor commits a breach of any of its obligations under the Contract, the Council may, without prejudice to any accrued rights or remedies under the Contract, terminate the Contractor's employment under the Contract by notice in writing having immediate effect.' It was held that the parties could not have meant to confer the right to terminate for literally *any* breach and what they must have meant was for any repudiatory breach. On this basis the clause added nothing to the parties' rights under the general law. The decision is somewhat controversial: S. Whittaker, 'Termination Clauses', in Burrows and Peel, *Contract Terms*, Chapter 13. It is precisely to avoid the sort of decision reached in *Rice* that the parties often stipulate that the breach must have been more than just *a* breach, e.g., a 'material breach' (on which see *Dalkia Utilities Services Plc* v. *Celtech International Ltd* [2006] EWHC 63, [2006] 1 Lloyd's Rep. 599 at [92]).

[82] Since this elusive distinction between the two modes of termination is one which can escape even those familiar with English law (see the difficulties faced by the terminating party in the following: *Dalkia Utilities* v. *Celtech* [2006] EWHC 63, [2006] 1 Lloyd's Rep. 599; *Stocznia Gdynia SA* v. *Gearbulk Holdings* [2010] QB 27, [2009] EWCA Civ 75; *Shell Egypt West Manzala GmbH* v. *Dana Gas Egypt Ltd* [2010] EWHC 465 (Comm)), there is a rather obvious potential for problems to emerge if the types of clause on which they are based are made subject to a different governing law.

repudiatory breach, including a breach of condition, damages may be claimed in full for the 'loss of bargain', i.e., to put the claimant in the same position as if the remaining obligations under the contract had been performed. Where a contract has been terminated under a contractual power and the trigger for that termination is a non-repudiatory breach, damages may only be awarded for the loss which flows from that particular breach and not for the loss of the contract as a whole. It has been suggested elsewhere in this chapter that, in many instances, English law is capable of reaching a 'fair' result in the face of the otherwise unreasonable consequences of a boilerplate clause, but this may be one instance where that view cannot be advanced. The point may be illustrated by one leading case.

In *Lombard North Central* v. *Butterworth*,[83] computer equipment was provided under a hire-purchase agreement which contained the following standard terms:

> The Lessee agrees . . .
>
> 2(a) to pay to the lessor: (i) punctually and without previous demand the rentals set out in Part 3 of the Schedule together with Value Added Tax thereon punctual payment of each which shall be of the essence of these Leases . . .
>
> 5. In the event that (a) the Lessee shall (i) make default in the due and punctual payment of any of the rentals or any sum of money payable to the Lessor hereunder or any part thereof . . . then upon the happening of such event . . . the Lessor's consent to the Lessee's possession of the Goods shall determine forthwith without any notice being given by the Lessor, and the Lessor may terminate this Lease either by notice in writing or by taking possession of the Goods . . .
>
> 6. (Upon termination) (a) the Lessee shall pay . . . to the Lessor: (i) all arrears of rentals; and (ii) all further rentals which would . . . have fallen due to the end of the fixed period of this Lease less a discount thereon for accelerated payment at the rate of 5 per cent per annum . . .

The lessee defaulted in the payment of one instalment of £584.05, the contract was terminated and the equipment repossessed. The principal issue was whether the lessor's claim for payment of the sum due under Clause 6 amounted to a penalty and was therefore unenforceable.[84] If the contract could only have been terminated under the express contractual power provided by Clause 5, then the only claim for damages at large was for the loss flowing from the failure to pay the instalment, i.e., £584.05.[85] If the contract could be terminated for a repudiatory breach, then

---

[83] [1987] 1 All ER 267.   [84] For the law on penalties generally, see Section 2.7 below.
[85] As in *Financings Ltd* v. *Baldock* [1963] 2 QB 104, with which the *Lombard* decision is usually contrasted.

damages at large would represent the full 'loss of bargain', i.e., the remaining instalments due (£8,264.31), less a discount in the interest element because of accelerated receipt (£1,221.49) and the proceeds from the resale of the equipment (£172.85),[86] making for a total of £6,869.97. Since, under Clause 2, punctual payment had been made 'of the essence', the hirer was guilty of a breach of condition and the higher sum was recoverable as damages at large, which meant that the figure produced by Clause 6 could not be regarded as a penalty.[87]

In the context of this book, two observations may be made. First, the enforceability of Clause 6 was very much dependent on the inclusion of Clause 2, and its interpretation and effect as a matter of English law. The result could be quite different if both clauses are divorced from the governing law on the basis of which they have been drafted. Secondly, the decision in *Lombard* was reached by the Court of Appeal with evident reluctance, but on this occasion it was considered unavoidable in order to ensure consistency in the underlying governing law; in particular, allowing the parties to stipulate expressly which of the terms of the contract were to be regarded as conditions with the consequence that any breach thereof would be regarded as a repudiatory breach.[88]

2.5   Sole remedy

The sample clause included for consideration states as follows:

> [Liquidated damages paid in accordance with the foregoing provision] shall be the Buyer's sole remedy for any delay in delivery for which the Seller is responsible under this Agreement.

---

[86] Given that over £8,000 was still due in payments for the equipment, it is a little surprising that the resale figure was not challenged as a failure to mitigate.

[87] See, to similar effect, the decision in *BNP Paribas* v. *Wockhardt EU Operations (Swiss) AG* [2009] EWHC 3116 (Comm). Since that involved an attack on the closing out provisions in the ISDA Master Agreement, one cannot underestimate the commercial significance of the decision that those provisions do not amount to a penalty and are therefore enforceable.

[88] It has been noted above that there may be a basis for intervention under the 1999 Regulations (note 80), but those Regulations are of course confined to consumer contracts. Similarly, for agreements which are regulated under the Consumer Credit Act 1974, the hirer can avoid the worst rigours of the decision in *Lombard* by exercising his or her right to terminate (Section 99) subject to payment of a maximum of one-half of the total price of the goods or such lower sum as the court may order (Section 100). In the context of termination under an express contractual power, there may be scope to grant equitable relief from forfeiture: *On Demand Information Plc* v. *Michael Gerson (Finance) Plc* [2002] UKHL 13, [2003] 1 AC 368; *Treitel*, para. 18–063.

In the absence of such a clause, the parties would have the full range of the remedies available under the general law. The guiding principle in the assessment of a sole remedy clause was laid down by Lord Diplock in *Gilbert-Ash (Northern) Ltd* v. *Modern Engineeering (Bristol) Ltd*:[89]

> It is, of course, open to parties to a contract . . . to exclude by express agreement a remedy for its breach which would otherwise arise by operation of law . . . But in construing such a contract one starts with the presumption that neither party intends to abandon any remedies for its breach arising by operation of law, and clear express words must be used in order to rebut this presumption.

Following on from the discussion of termination above, as a recent example, one might refer to the *Dalkia Utilities* case,[90] in which one of the issues was whether the parties had agreed to limit themselves to the remedies set out in a self-contained contractual regime for termination. The relevant clause in this regard stated as follows:

> 15.7 The consequences of termination set out in this clause represent the full extent of the parties' respective rights and remedies arising out of any termination save for those rights remedies and liabilities which arise prior to termination.

Based on the *Gilbert-Ash* principle, this was interpreted to refer only to 'termination' pursuant to the express contractual power set out in the contract, so that the parties retained all the rights and remedies which attached to a termination for repudiatory breach.[91] As the judge said:[92]

> Clause 15.7 does not seem to me sufficiently clear, as it would need to be, to exclude the parties' common law right to accept a repudiatory breach of contract (e.g., an outright refusal to perform) as discharging the innocent party from further liability and to claim damages for the loss of the contract.

The *Gilbert-Ash* principle is yet another instance of interpretative control; since the starting point is that the parties should be entitled to whatever remedies the general law would award to them, they will only be deprived of those remedies if their intention in this regard is sufficiently manifest. It is with the *Gilbert-Ash* principle in mind that the sample clause appears to have been worded and one is inclined to think

[89] [1974] AC 689.   [90] See above, note 81.
[91] For the differences between the two modes of termination, see text to note 82.
[92] At [21].

that it would work as a matter of interpretation. What then of controls beyond interpretation as a means of avoiding an unjust outcome?

As a matter of the common law, with few exceptions,[93] the parties are as free to determine the availability and extent of remedies as they are to determine their primary obligations. One notable exception is the rule against penalties, which is discussed below.[94] It should also be noted that a term which seeks to exclude remedies rather than liability still qualifies as an exclusion clause for the purposes of the statutory controls on the use of such clauses in the Unfair Contract Terms Act 1977.[95] So, in consumer contracts or commercial contracts made on one party's written standard terms,[96] such a clause will be unenforceable if it fails the test of reasonableness.[97]

2.6   Subject to contract

The sample clause put up for consideration states as follows:

> This document does not represent a binding agreement between the parties and neither party shall be under any liability to the other party in case of failure to enter into the final agreement.

This may be regarded as a long-form subject to contract provision, since the phrase 'subject to contract'[98] has itself come to bear an acknowledged meaning. In the absence of such a clause, the question of whether the parties had reached a binding and enforceable agreement would turn on the general law under which it may not be binding because it is 'incomplete', i.e., the parties have failed to reach agreement on matters of

---

[93] E.g., where fraud is involved: *Treitel*, para. 7–040; *HIH Casualty & General Insurance* v. *Chase Manhattan Bank* [2003] UKHL 6, [2003] 2 Lloyd's Rep. 61; *S Pearson & Son Ltd* v. *Dublin Corp* [1907] AC 351 at 353, 362.

[94] Section 2.7.

[95] By virtue of Section 13(1)(b): 'To the extent that this Part of this Act prevents the exclusion or restriction of any liability it also prevents . . . (b) excluding or restricting any right or remedy in respect of the liability, or subjecting a person to any prejudice in consequence of his pursuing any such right or remedy.' It is beyond the confines of this chapter to consider the scope and effect of the provisions of the 1977 Act, but they are one of the principal controls over the abuse of certain types of boilerplate clause. See, generally, *Treitel*, paras. 7–049ff.

[96] Section 3(1).

[97] Sole remedy clauses may also be challenged as unfair under the 1999 Regulations: see above, note 80.

[98] Or its equivalent, e.g., 'subject to details' in the context of shipping: *The Nissos Samos* [1985] 1 Lloyd's Rep. 378 at 385; *The Junior K* [1988] 2 Lloyd's Rep. 583.

sufficient importance that the court is able to conclude that the parties did not intend to be bound. But if the agreement is complete, or appears to be, the presumption will be that the parties intended to be bound. The inclusion of a 'subject to contract' provision is meant to negate the intention to be bound even if the agreement is 'complete', at least until the parties have taken some further formal step, such as the execution of a final agreement or the 'exchange' of contracts.[99]

Reliance on a subject to contract clause by sellers of land to threaten to withdraw at the last minute in order to extract a higher price[100] has been described by one judge as a 'social and moral blot on the law'.[101] There are also other instances where, at the very least, a sense of unease can be felt about the impunity with which one party may go back on what is otherwise a concluded agreement. In a few cases, the courts have been able to find that 'subject to contract' did not really mean, or no longer meant, to negate contractual intention.

A good example of the first category of case is *Alpenstow* v. *Regalian Properties*.[102] The parties entered into an agreement under which the claimants agreed that if, following the grant of planning permission which the defendants had helped them to secure, they wished to dispose of the land in question, they would serve a notice on the defendants of their willingness to sell a 51 per cent interest in the freehold or pay the defendants £500,000. The defendants agreed to accept the notice within twenty-eight days after its service 'subject to contract'. The letters in which this agreement was set out went on to provide a detailed timetable for submission, approval and exchange of contracts and completion; in particular, the defendants were under a duty to approve the draft contract, subject only to reasonable amendments. In these circumstances, the words 'subject to contract' were held not to negate contractual intention, but to mean that the parties had not yet settled all the details of the transaction, i.e., this was one of those cases where they went to the issue of *agreement* and not *intention*. It should be noted that, although the *Alpenstow* case was referred to above as a good example, counsel's endeavours in the case had been unable to unearth any earlier authority. That is a fair reflection of the strength of the presumption as to the meaning of 'subject to contract' and the need for a 'very strong and

---

[99] *Winn* v. *Bull* (1877) 7 ChD 29; *Eccles* v. *Bryant & Pollock* [1948] Ch 93.
[100] A phenomenon known as 'gazumping'.
[101] *Cohen* v. *Nessdale* [1981] 3 All ER 118 at 128 (decision affirmed [1982] 2 All ER 97).
[102] [1985] 1 WLR 721.

exceptional context'[103] in which to rebut it. One might nevertheless add to this category the auction sale where the words 'subject to contract' were typed on one of the contractual documents by clerical error[104] or the notice exercising an option to purchase land which was expressed to be 'subject to contract'.[105] In both cases, those words were regarded as meaningless and there was found to be a clear intention to be bound. One might say that these decisions are examples of a 'purposive' interpretation and now that the courts seem more purposive[106] than they might have been in the past,[107] there may be greater scope to reach similar decisions in cases where the 'background'[108] would allow for it. This might be supported, indirectly, by cases where a similarly purposive approach has led to a finding that the parties did not intend to be bound, notwithstanding the absence of the words 'subject to contract'.[109]

The second category of case, where 'subject to contract' is expunged by implication rather than through formal exchange, includes cases where the courts have overlooked certain technical slips in the process of

---

[103] *Ibid.* at 730.

[104] *Munton* v. *GLC* [1976] 1 WLR 649. The intention of parties to an agreement for the sale of land by auction is to enter into a binding contract as soon as the bidder's offer is accepted by the fall of the auctioneer's hammer: *Treitel*, para. 2–008.

[105] *Westway Homes* v. *Moore* (1991) 63 P & CR 480.

[106] The 'literal' approach was never entirely literal and nor is the 'purposive' approach entirely purposive: *Charter Reinsurance Co Ltd* v. *Fagan* [1997] AC 313 at 326, 350; *Petromec Inc* v. *Petroleo Brasileiro SA Petrobras* [2005] EWCA Civ 891, [2006] 1 Lloyd's Rep. 121 at [23]. See also *Prenn* v. *Simmonds* [1971] 1 WLR 1382 and the observation of Lord Wilberforce (at 1384) that: 'there is no need to appeal here to any modern, anti-literal, tendencies, for Lord Blackburn's well-known judgment in *River Wear Commissioners* v. *Adamson* (1877) 2 App Cas 743, 763 provides ample warrant for a liberal approach.'

[107] As a consequence of Lord Hoffmann's 're-statement' of the principles of interpretation in *Investors Compensation Scheme Ltd* v. *West Bromwich Building Society* [1998] 1 WLR 896 at 912–913 (it might, strictly speaking, have to be said that they apply here only by analogy, since the question to be decided is whether there *was* a contract between the parties). And see now *Chartbrook Ltd* v. *Persimmon Homes Ltd* [2009] UKHL 38, (2009) 1 AC 1101. Not all agree with purposiveness: see, e.g., Sir C. Staughton, 'How Do Courts Interpret Commercial Contracts?' [1999] CLJ 303 and a number of Court of Appeal decisions referred to therein.

[108] Or the 'matrix of fact' as some may still prefer to call it.

[109] *Pateman* v. *Pay* (1974) 263 EG 467. It has to be said that there are equally few of these cases. The fact that the test of contractual intention is an objective one (in *Pateman*, there was a finding of sharp practice on the party who sought to claim that the agreement was binding) will usually mean that the parties *are bound* in the absence of an express qualification that their agreement is 'subject to contract': *Tweddell* v. *Henderson* [1975] 1 WLR 1496; *Storer* v. *Manchester CC* [1974] 1 WLR 1403 at 1408.

exchange itself[110] and those where the evidence supports the finding of a subsequent agreement to remove the effect of the words 'subject to contract'. In *Sherbrooke v. Dipple*,[111] the Court of Appeal adopted and applied the words of Brightman J in *Tevanan v. Norman Brett (Builders) Ltd*[112] that: 'parties could get rid of the qualification of "subject to contract" only if they both expressly agreed that it should be expunged *or if such an agreement was to be necessarily implied.*'[113] The position was perhaps best summed up by Bridge LJ in the unreported case of *Credit Suisse White Weld Ltd v. Davis and Morris*:[114]

> The common understanding of all who are familiar with conveyancing practice is that when a negotiation for the sale and purchase of land is being conducted with a stipulation introduced by either party that it shall be subject to contract, neither party will assume any binding contractual obligation until the formal written contracts have been exchanged.
>
> Of course, that common understanding can be displaced, and it is perfectly possible for the parties to such a negotiation to manifest an intention to assume contractual obligations at some other time and in some other way: but in order that the common understanding shall be thus displaced, the intention to be contractually bound at some other time and in some other way must be clearly and unambiguously manifested.

The same approach is taken in contracts generally, as opposed to those involved in conveyancing practice. See, for example, the view of Lord Walker in the very recent decision of the Supreme Court in *RTS Flexible Systems Ltd v. Molkerei Allois Müller GmbH & Co KG (UK Production)*:[115]

> Whether in such a case the parties agreed to enter into a binding contract, waiving reliance on the 'subject to [written] contract' term or under-standing will again depend upon all the circumstances of the case, although the cases show that the court will not lightly so hold.

In the *Müller* case itself, work had begun on the supply and installation of automated packaging under a letter of intent. When the four-week term of that letter of intent had expired and work continued, the question was whether it did so under contract. The principal argument against the existence of a contract was that the parties negotiated on the basis that it

---

[110] E.g., *Harrison v. Battye* [1975] 1 WLR 58.   [111] (1980) 255 EG 1203.
[112] (1972) 223 EG 1945.   [113] Emphasis added.   [114] Unreported, 20 December 1977.
[115] [2010] UKSC 14, [2010] 1 WLR 753 at [56]. The Supreme Court is the successor to the House of Lords and has been sitting since late 2009.

would be governed by Müller's standard terms (the MF\1 Form of Contract), Clause 48.1 of which stated: 'This Contract may be executed in any number of counterparts provided that it shall not become effective until each party has executed a counterpart and exchanged it with the other.' Nonetheless, the Supreme Court found that this was a case where the parties had waived reliance on 'subject to contract', particularly because they had reached agreement on all the terms that were essential and work had been carried out. The language in which this conclusion is expressed is worthy of note:[116]

> The clear inference is that the parties had agreed to waive the subject to contract clause, viz Clause 48. Any other conclusion makes no commercial sense. RTS could surely not have refused to perform the contract as varied pending a formal contract being signed and exchanged. Nobody suggested that it could and, of course, it did not. If one applies the standard of the reasonable, honest businessman suggested by Steyn LJ, we conclude that, whether he was an RTS man or a Müller man, he would have concluded that the parties intended that the work should be carried out for the agreed price on the agreed terms, including the terms as varied by the agreement of 25 August, without the necessity for a formal written agreement, which had been overtaken by events.

One should be wary of drawing too much by way of a conclusion from this decision. As Lord Walker noted, the court will not lightly hold that the parties waived reliance on 'subject to contract' and each case will depend on its own facts.[117] He also noted that: 'The moral of the story is to agree first and to start work later.'[118] Nonetheless, one observation might be made. A reference is made in the passage to Lord Steyn[119] and the standard of the reasonable honest businessman. It is Lord Steyn, as noted above, who has said that 'there is not a world of difference between the objective requirement of good faith and the reasonable expectations of parties'.[120] Is this then, in some sense, the doctrine of good faith at work in English law? If it is, it is invoked only in the same limited sense as has been seen with interpretation; in this context, one asks whether the parties really meant 'subject to contract' in the strict sense (cases in the first category, such as *Alpenstow*) or whether they still intended to be 'subject to contract' (cases in the second category, such as *Müller*).

---

[116] At [86], per Lord Walker.   [117] At [54].   [118] At [1].
[119] In this context as Steyn LJ in *G Percy Trentham Ltd* v. *Archital Luxfer Ltd* [1993] 1 Lloyd's Rep. 25 at 27.
[120] See text to note 31.

That there is no room for a full-blown application of good faith would seem to be borne out by the unjust, or potentially unjust, results which can flow when the parties intended to and remained 'subject to contract'. Some of this potential stems from the fact that, despite the arguments of some to the contrary,[121] it seems that the effect of 'subject to contract' in English law is not just to negate the intention to be bound *in contract*, but to negate any form of liability at all.

A good illustration in this regard is *Regalian Properties Plc v. London Docklands Development Corporation.*[122] The parties were negotiating for a licence to develop land for housing. These negotiations were at all times described as 'subject to contract'. The contract envisaged by the parties was delayed because of the Development Corporation's request for further designs by new architects, which led to the claimant incurring very considerable expenditure. An increase in the value of the land led to the Corporation's refusal to go ahead at the price originally agreed upon, and the negotiations then came to an end. Regalian sought recovery of the approximately £3 million which they had paid to professional firms in respect of the proposed development, not in contract, but by way of a *quantum meruit*. They failed for two reasons: (1) the work done had not benefited the Development Corporation; and (2) they had, in any event, taken the risk that because the negotiations remained subject to contract, they would not result in a contract. The first reason is perfectly valid. There can be no *quantum meruit* where the expenditure incurred has not benefited the claimant; the second is a little more arguable if it means that even if a benefit had been conferred on the development corporation, there could be no claim for unjust enrichment.[123]

There may now be further room for argument here, after the decision of the House of Lords in *Yeoman's Row Management Ltd v. Cobbe.*[124] A developer and the owner of a block of flats reached an agreement 'in principle' that if the developer succeeded in securing planning permission to demolish the flats and build six new terraced houses, the owner would sell the flats to the developer for an upfront price of £12 million

[121] I have made my own attempt in *The Blundell Lectures* 2007, 'Pre-contractual liability in property law – a contradiction in terms?'.

[122] [1995] 1 WLR 212. Cf. *William Lacey (Hounslow) Ltd v. Davis* [1957] 1 WLR 932.

[123] To some extent, the additional wording in the sample clause above is intended to produce the same 'over-inclusive' effect given to 'subject to contract' in English law, in its references to '*any* liability'. At least as a matter of English law, it is wording that is likely to succeed.

[124] [2008] UKHL 55, [2008] 1 WLR 1752.

and a half-share of any surplus of the proceeds of sale in excess of £24 million. After permission was granted, the owner resiled from the agreement and sought better terms, which the developer refused. The House of Lords reversed the decision of the lower courts and refused the developer a proprietary remedy, on the basis that the developer had taken the risk involved in an unenforceable agreement in principle.[125] They did, however, award the developer a personal remedy in the form of a *quantum meruit* to cover his expenses and a fee for his services assessed at a rate appropriate for an experienced developer.[126] What is not explained is why the same reasoning which ruled out the proprietary claims did not also rule out the personal claim, namely that the developer had taken the risk that there would not be an enforceable contract so that he might not be 'paid' at all. As we have just seen with the *Regalian* case, that has been the approach of the courts in cases where work has been done 'subject to contract' and, in its discussion of the proprietary claims, the House of Lords had seemed to assimilate the reasoning in other subject to contract cases[127] with those applicable to the incomplete and unenforceable agreements in *Cobbe*.

2.7   Liquidated damages

The sample clause states as follows:

> If, due to the fault of the Seller, the goods have not been delivered at dates according to the delivery schedule as provided in this Agreement, the Seller shall be obliged to pay to the buyer liquidated damages for such delayed delivery at the following rates:
> i) For each complete week, the liquidated damages shall be 0.5% of the value of the goods delayed.

---

[125] Even if the agreement had been complete, it was unenforceable for want of writing under the Law of Property (Miscellaneous Provisions) Act 1989, Section 2.

[126] In addition to possible claims based on estoppel or unjust enrichment, the parties may try to protect themselves from the wasted expenditure and loss of opportunity that may result from the breakdown of negotiations which are 'subject to contract' by entering into collateral contracts such as an agreement to negotiate ('lock-in agreements'). Here, it has to be said, English law has set itself against any enforceable standard of good faith, with the result that such agreements are unenforceable: *Walford* v. *Miles* 1992] 2 AC 128. See, generally, E. Peel, 'Agreements to Negotiate in Good Faith', in Burrows and Peel, *Contract Formation*, Chapter 2. However, the parties may create an enforceable 'lock out', i.e., an agreement not to negotiate with any other party for a defined period of time: *Pitt* v. *PHH Asset Management Ltd* [1993] 1 WLR 327; cf. *Tye* v. *House* [1997] 2 EGLR 171.

[127] Most notably, *A-G of Hong Kong* v. *Humphreys Estate* [1987] 1 AC 114.

ii) The total amount of the above mentioned liquidated damages will not exceed 25% of the Price for the delayed goods.

iii) The payment of liquidated damages shall not release the Seller from its obligation to continuously deliver the goods.

Such clauses are among the most commonplace in Anglo-American contract models. Without them, of course, damages would be assessed at large in accordance with the general law. Quite what that would amount to in any case will often be very uncertain and often more litigation costs are incurred disputing questions of quantum than of liability. Therefore, it is self-evident that a liquidated damages clause is intended to remove some of this uncertainty.

The approach of English law to liquidated damages clauses is somewhat anomalous. With one possible exception,[128] they are the only type of clause in which the courts, in the exercise of their common law powers, exercise a specific supervisory role over enforceability, i.e., a role going beyond that which would apply to any other contract term, such as defects in formation (incorporation) or questions of interpretation. It does not seem to fit easily with an attachment to freedom of contract, even in the attenuated form in which it exists in an age of consumer welfarism, for the courts to reserve a power to impose limits on what the parties have agreed they will pay to each other in the event of a breach of contract. This explains why the parties have always been given a significant degree of latitude in the assessment of whether they have attempted a 'genuine pre-estimate of loss'.[129] If anything, the current trend is for an even greater degree of latitude. The courts have regularly observed that,

---

[128] In this regard, note the observation of Lord Diplock in *A. Schroeder Music Publishing Co. Ltd* v. *Macaulay* [1974] 1 WLR 1308 at 1313: 'Under the influence of Bentham and of laissez-faire the courts in the 19th century abandoned the practice of applying the public policy against unconscionable bargains to contracts generally, as they had formerly done to any contract considered to be usurious; but the policy survived in its application to penalty clauses and to relief against forfeiture and also to the special category of contracts in restraint of trade. If one looks at the reasoning of 19th-century judges in cases about contracts in restraint of trade one finds lip service paid to current economic theories, but if one looks at what they said in the light of what they did, one finds that they struck down a bargain if they thought it was unconscionable as between the parties to it and upheld it if they thought that it was not.' Restrictive covenants are not the subject of consideration in this chapter; relief against forfeiture is, on one view, just the equitable counterpart of the rule against penalties (see *Treitel*, para. 20–141).

[129] The proof of the pudding is in the eating of course. In the case of *Alfred McAlpine Capital Projects Ltd* v. *Tilebox Ltd* [2005] EWHC 281 (TCC), [2005] Build. LR 271 at [48], Jackson J noted that in only four cases out of the many that had been brought by that time had a clause been struck down as a penalty.

in commercial contracts where the parties are of equal bargaining power, the presumption must be that the parties themselves regarded the sum stipulated or the sanction laid out as a genuine estimate of the loss to be incurred as a consequence of the breach in question.[130] They have also stressed the broad nature of the enquiry to be made in assessing a clause under the penalty rule. In *Murray* v. *Leisureplay Plc*,[131] Buxton LJ referred to a 'broad' and 'cautious' approach which emphasises that the test for a penalty is one of extravagance or unconscionability:[132]

> that (the sum stipulated) exceeds the likely amount of contractual damages ... does not render the terms penal unless the party seeking to avoid the terms can demonstrate that they meet the test of extravagance ... I regard that as a comparatively broad and simple question, that will not normally call for detailed analysis of the contractual background.

Nevertheless, it remains the case that the English courts may, and still occasionally do, strike down a liquidated damages clause as contrary to the rule against penalties.[133] The only instance in which I have come across a stated preference for a governing law other than English law on the basis that the parties' agreement is *more* likely to be upheld under that other law has occurred in the context of liquidated damages.[134]

---

[130] See, e.g., *Philips Hong Kong Ltd* v. *Attorney-General of Hong Kong* (1993) 61 Build. LR 41; *Alfred McAlpine Capital Projects Ltd* v. *Tilebox Ltd* [2005] EWHC 281 (TCC), [2005] Build. LR 271 at [48], per Jackson J: 'Because the rule about penalties is an anomaly within the law of contract, the courts are predisposed, where possible, to uphold contractual terms which fix the level of damages for breach. This predisposition is even stronger in the case of commercial contracts freely entered into between parties of comparable bargaining power.'

[131] [2005] EWCA Civ 963, [2005] IRLR 946.

[132] At [110]. Cf. *The General Trading Co (Holdings) Ltd* v. *Richmond Corporation Ltd* [2008] EWHC 1479 (Comm), [2008] 2 Lloyd's Rep. 475 at [133]. There are some who see the prevention of unconscionability as the best explanation for that rule: M. Chen-Wishart, 'Controlling the Power to Agree Damages', in P. Birks (ed.), *Wrongs and Remedies in the Twenty-First Century* (Clarendon Press, 1996).

[133] See, most recently, *Lansat Shipping Co Ltd* v. *Glencore Grain BV* [2009] EWCA Civ 855, [2009] 2 Lloyd's Rep. 688.

[134] In this regard, the decision of Colman J in *Lordsvale Finance Plc* v. *Bank of Zambia* [1996] QB 752 is of particular note. In a syndicated loan, he upheld a provision which applied an additional interest rate of 1 per cent p.a. for the period from the date of any default until payment. He took into account that syndicated loans almost invariably provide for enhanced rates of default interest to apply and that they are not struck down as penalties under New York law, which is the principal alternative governing law for such loans. The commercial implications for international banking in London, had he decided otherwise, are self-evident.

This is a view which may understate the significance of another aspect of the rule against penalties. The rule only applies *at all* to sanctions imposed for a *breach* by the payor. It does not apply to sums payable 'upon the happening of a specified event other than a breach of a contractual duty owed by the contemplated payor to the contemplated payee'.[135] The drafting possibilities to which this may give rise can be demonstrated by reference to a recent decision of the English courts concerned with another form of standard provision, in the shape of a 'take or pay' clause.

In *M&J Polymers Ltd* v. *Imerys Minerals Ltd*,[136] the relevant provisions in a supply contract were as follows:

> 5.3. During the term of this Agreement, the Buyer will order the following minimum quantities of Products:
> 5.5. Take or pay: The Buyers collectively will pay for the minimum quantities of Products as indicated in this Article at 5.3 ... even if they together have not ordered the indicated quantities during the relevant monthly period.

The first issue for the court to resolve was whether Clause 5.5 was subject to the rule against penalties. On this issue, the view of Burton J was that he could 'not see how a payment obligation can arise under Article 5.5 in a case *other than* where there has been a breach of the obligation to order under Clause 5.3. If the goods are in fact ordered, then they will be delivered, and the price will be due quite irrespective of Article 5.3 or 5.5'.[137] Nevertheless, he went on to decide that the clause was not a penalty, adopting the 'broad' approach referred to above.[138] The point to be stressed is that it seems that it would have been a relatively easy matter to have drafted the contract such that no breach would have been involved. This could have been achieved if the buyer had simply agreed

---

[135] *Export Credit Guarantee Department* v. *Universal Oil Products Co* [1983] 1 WLR 399, per Lord Roskill. Cf. *Alder* v. *Moore* [1961] 2 QB 57; *Jervis* v. *Harris* [1996] Ch 195; *Office of Fair Trading* v. *Abbey National Plc & Others* [2008] EWHC 875 (Comm), [2008] EWHC 2325 (Comm).

[136] [2008] EWHC 344, [2008] 1 Lloyd's Rep. 541.

[137] He distinguished the earlier case of *Euro London Appointments* v. *Claessens International* [2006] EWCA Civ 385, [2006] 2 Lloyds Rep. 436, where the right to a refund was lost if invoices remained unpaid for seven days or more. The fact that there was also an obligation to pay the invoices within seven days was only a coincidence; two quite separate periods could have been set for the obligation to pay and the entitlement to the refund.

[138] See text to note 132; cf. *Tullett Prebon Group Ltd* v. *Ghaleb El-Hajjali* [2008] EWHC 1924 (QB), (2008) IRLR 760.

to the minimum payment required and the supplier agreed to deliver product up to the limit represented by that payment, at the time and in the quantities ordered by the buyer. If the buyer did not then order up to the amount for which he had paid, or agreed to pay, he would not be in breach but would still have to pay, and the rule against penalties could not apply. If the buyer wanted even more product than the minimum, this could be covered by an agreement to deliver in excess, if the product is available, to be paid for *pro rata*.

Similarly, in the sample clause the same result could be achieved by redrafting it so that there is no obligation on the seller to deliver by a particular date. Instead the parties could fix the price by reference to that date, but agree that the price would reduce by 0.5 per cent for each week beyond that date when the goods were in fact delivered. Once again, one encounters here a question of interpretation, but one which can be manipulated by the parties to avoid the intervention of the courts. The ease with which a liquidated damages clause can be converted into a price variation clause and be made potentially immune from the rule against penalties provides another test case for the adherence of English law to freedom of contract when set against the prospect of an unjust result.[139]

In this regard, one might finish by considering the decision of the Court of Appeal in *Interfoto Picture Library Ltd* v. *Stiletto Visual Programmes Ltd*,[140] a case already cited for the views expressed therein by Bingham LJ on the role of fairness or good faith.[141] As part of their business, the defendants ordered some photographic transparencies from the claimants, which were sent round with a delivery note containing nine printed conditions in four columns on one sheet of A4 paper. Amongst the conditions was one which stated that the defendants had to return the transparencies within fourteen days and, if they failed to do so, there would be a holding fee of £5 per day per transparency. The defendants overlooked that they had not returned the transparencies and, by the time they did so, the holding fee amounted to £3,800. The court was clearly troubled by the prospect that the fee should be enforceable, but was able to avoid its application by recourse to the rule of incorporation noted above – that additional steps are necessary in order to have given sufficient notice of an unusual clause. It was found that a holding fee as such was quite common, but the amount to be paid was usually in the

---

[139] For some, it simply exposes the anomaly of the rule against penalties and leads to the view that it should be abolished.
[140] [1989] QB 433.   [141] See the text following note 27.

region of £3.50 per week per transparency; therefore, a holding fee clause was not a clause of an unusual type, but a holding fee for this amount was. On the face of it, the decision is consistent with the 'orthodox' position referred to in the first part of this chapter – the court acknowledged the parties' freedom of contract, but found that they had not both agreed to the holding fee. The motivation for the decision was nonetheless fairness,[142] but what would the position have been if the terms and conditions had been set out in a document which had been signed by the defendants? It seems that there would have been no room to deny incorporation,[143] but equally there would have been no room to apply the rule against penalties because the holding fee did not involve any breach; it was just another form of price variation clause. One suspects that it is with this prospect in mind that Bingham LJ observed that he did 'not wish to be taken as deciding that (the) condition was not challengeable as a *disguised* penalty clause'.[144] This residual attachment to a notion of good faith, or fairness, is occasionally detected,[145] but is often achieved indirectly by recourse to supposedly orthodox doctrines such as incorporation.

2.8   Indemnity

The sample clause states as follows:

> 30.1 Contractor shall indemnify Company Group from and against any claim concerning:
> a) personal injury to or loss of life of any employee of Contractor Group, and
> b) loss of or damage to any property of Contractor Group,
> and arising out of or in connection with the Work or caused by the Contract Object in its lifetime. This applies regardless of any form of liability, whether strict or by negligence, in whatever form, on the part of Company Group.
>   Contractor shall, as far as practicable, ensure that other companies in Contractor Group waive their right to make any claim against Company

---

[142] Bingham LJ noted (at 445) that the rule of incorporation employed by the courts 'may yield a result not very different from the civil law principle of good faith, at any rate so far as the formation of the contract is concerned'.

[143] See text to note 10.   [144] At 445–446.

[145] See also Bingham LJ in *Timeload Ltd* v. *British Telecommunications Plc* [1995] EMLR 459 when granting an interlocutory injunction to restrain the termination of a contract on notice.

Group when such claims are covered by Contractor's obligation to indemnify under the provisions of this Art. 30.1.

30.3 Until the issue of the Acceptance Certificate, Contractor shall indemnify Company Group from:

a) costs resulting from the requirements of public authorities in connection with the removal of wrecks, or pollution from vessels or other floating devices provided by Contractor Group for use in connection with the Work, and

b) claims arising out of loss or damage suffered by anyone other than Contractor Group and Company Group in connection with the Work or caused by the Contract Object,

even if the loss or damage is the result of any form of liability, whether strict or by negligence in whatever form by Company Group.

Contractor's liability for loss or damage arising out of each accident shall be limited to NOK 5 million. This does not apply to Contractor's liability for loss or damage for each accident covered by insurances provided in accordance with Art. 31.2.a) and b), where Contractor's liability extends to the sum recovered under the insurance for the loss or damage.

Company shall indemnify Contractor Group from and against claims mentioned in the first paragraph above, to the extent that they exceed the limitations of liability mentioned above, regardless of any form of liability, whether strict or by negligence, in whatever form, on the part of Contractor Group.

After issue of the Acceptance Certificate, Company shall indemnify Contractor Group from and against any claims of the kind mentioned in the first paragraph above, regardless of any form of liability, whether strict or by negligence, in whatever form, on the part of Contractor Group.

An 'indemnity' may take a number of forms[146] and in English law models, it is becoming increasingly common to find an 'indemnity' given against the consequences of the breach of a contract between the indemnifier and the indemnified.[147] In its more 'traditional' form and in the form appearing in the sample clause, an indemnity is given against

---

[146] See R. Zakrzewski, 'The Nature of a Claim on an Indemnity', *Journal of Contract Law*, 22 (2006), 54.

[147] Where the principal controversy is whether such an indemnity against 'loss' excludes remoteness and mitigation: see *Treitel*, para. 21–004; *Royscot Commercial Leasing Ltd* v. *Ismail* (1993) *The Independent*, 17 May; *The Eurus* [1996] 2 Lloyd's Rep. 408, affirmed [1998] 1 Lloyd's Rep. 351; *Jervis* v. *Harris* [1996] Ch 195; *Maple Leaf Marco Volatility Master Fund* v. *Rouvroy* [2009] EWHC 257 (Comm), [2009] 1 Lloyd's Rep. 475 at [259]; *ENE Kos* v. *Petroleo Brasileiro SA (Petrobas)* [2009] EWHC 1843 (Comm), [2010] 1 Lloyd's Rep. 87 at [34].

claims brought against the indemnified by third parties. Such an indemnity may be available as a matter of the general law even in the absence of express agreement between the parties, now regulated mainly by the Civil Liability (Contribution) Act 1978.[148] It is only available if the party which has been successfully sued by the third-party claimant can establish that another party is liable for the 'same damage'.[149] Thus, in the context of the first part of the sample clause, if there was no such clause and a member of the Company Group was sued by an employee of the Contractor, it would be necessary for the Company Group member to establish that the Contractor was, or would also have been, liable for the same injury before it could claim any contribution or indemnity under the Act. The point about a contractual indemnity is, of course, that it turns simply on the agreement of the parties and not on the need for any prior joint liability.

Indemnity clauses of this type are subject to the same sort of controls applied to exclusion clauses, i.e., they are subject to the principle of *contra proferentem* in their interpretation and, in some cases, they are also subject to the controls set out in the Unfair Contract Terms Act 1977.

A good example of the application of *contra proferentem* is provided by *EE Caledonia Ltd* v. *Orbit Valve Co Europe Plc.*[150] Caledonia (or Occidental Petroleum (Caledonia) Ltd at the relevant time) was the owner and operator of the Piper Alpha oil rig when it exploded in the North Sea in 1988. Orbit Valve was an engineering company who supplied a service engineer to work on the rig who was killed in the explosion. A claim was made against Caledonia by the family of the engineer and settled out of court, Caledonia admitting that it was guilty both of negligence and breach of health and safety regulations. Caledonia claimed an indemnity against Orbit Valve under one of the clauses of the service contract, the material parts of which were as follows:

> Each party hereto shall indemnify . . . the other . . . from and against any claim, demand, cause of action, loss, expense or liability arising by reason of the death of any employee . . . of the indemnifying party, resulting from . . . the performance of this (contract).

[148] See, generally, W. V. H. Rogers, *Winfield & Jolowicz on Tort* 18th edn (Sweet & Maxwell., 2006), paras. 21–24ff.

[149] Civil Liability (Contribution) Act 1978, Section 1; *Royal Brompton Hospital NHS Trust* v. *Watkins Gray International (UK)* [2002] UKHL 14, [2002] 1 WLR 1397.

[150] [1995] 1 All ER 174. See also *Casson* v. *Ostley PJ Ltd* [2001] EWCA Civ 1013, [2003] BLR 147.

Caledonia was unable to rely on the indemnity clause because it failed to satisfy what are sometimes referred to as the *Canada Steamship* rules.[151] These rules can be summarised as follows:

1. If the clause expressly refers to negligence, or words synonymous with negligence, it will be interpreted to cover claims based on the defendant's negligence.
2. If there is no reference to negligence but the wording used is wide enough to cover liability for negligence, it will cover claims based on the defendant's negligence but not if the defendant might have incurred some other form of liability 'not so remote or fanciful' as to be discounted. If there is another potential form of liability, the clause will be presumed to cover this and not the defendant's negligence.[152]

The indemnity in the *Caledonia* case failed because although it used general words wide enough to cover negligence, there were other forms of liability of which Caledonia could have been guilty, not the least of which was the breach of statutory duty which they had admitted under the health and safety regulations. It is with these rules and their application in the *Caledonia* case in mind that the sample clause above is probably worded, especially the express references to 'negligence'.

As far as the Unfair Contract Terms Act 1977 is concerned, the relevant provision is Section 4, which states that an indemnity must satisfy the test of reasonableness, but only if the indemnifier 'deals as consumer'.[153] If the indemnifier is acting in the course of business, the Act has no application. However, the English courts have been astute to ensure that a clause which is worded as an indemnity clause does not have the effect of operating as an exclusion clause. This is well illustrated by comparing two cases.

---

[151] After *Canada SS Lines Ltd* v. *The King* [1952] AC 192 at 208.

[152] This rule applies equally to indemnity clauses (see *Smith* v. *South Wales Switchgear Ltd* [1978] 1 WLR 165) and to clauses which seek to exclude liability. Where liability is only limited, general words will suffice to cover claims in negligence even though some other form of liability may have been incurred: the rules 'cannot be applied in their full rigour to limitation clauses' – *George Mitchell (Chesterhall) Ltd* v. *Finney Lock Seeds Ltd* [1983] 2 AC 803 at 814. It should be noted that the 'rules' are not rules as such; rather, they act as guidelines and the overall aim is to construe the relevant clause to find the meaning intended by the parties; the court may therefore find that the parties did intend to exclude liability for negligence even if, strictly speaking, the clause did not satisfy the rules: *HIH Casualty & General Insurance Ltd* v. *Chase Manhattan Bank* [2003] UKHL 6, [2003] 2 Lloyd's Rep. 61.

[153] As defined by Section 12.

In *Thompson* v. *T Lohan (Plant Hire) Ltd*,[154] under a contract of hire, Lohan provided an excavator and a driver, subject to standard terms and conditions. The excavator was driven negligently with the result that the claimant's husband was killed. The claimant sued Lohan as the employer of the driver and Lohan claimed an indemnity from the hirer under Clause 8 of the terms and conditions, which stated:

> 8 ... drivers ... shall for all purposes in connection with their employment in the working of the plant be regarded as the servants or agents of the Hirer ... who alone shall be responsible for all claims arising in connection with the operation of the plant by the said drivers ...

Although not strictly speaking an indemnity clause, such a provision has the same effect and was treated as an indemnity clause for the purposes of the Unfair Contract Terms Act.[155] Section 4 did not apply because the hirer hired the plant in the course of his business and was not dealing as a consumer.

In the case of *Phillips Products* v. *Hyland*,[156] precisely the same clause was under consideration, but the facts differed in one significant respect. The hirer was also the claimant in that the effect of the driver's negligence was not to injure a third party but to damage the hirer's property. The hirer could sue the owner for the negligence of his employee, but the owner then sought an indemnity from the hirer. The effect of Clause 8 in such a case is that no claim will be brought at all.[157] Since the liability in question was negligence liability, the clause was therefore treated as an attempt to exclude liability for negligently inflicted property damage. Section 2 of the Unfair Contract Terms Act applied and, unlike Section 4, it was not necessary for the indemnifier to be dealing as a consumer. The reasonableness test applied and the clause was found to be unreasonable and unenforceable. It is a rather good illustration of the principle that the courts will look at the substance of a clause and not merely at its form.[158]

---

[154] [1987] 1 WLR 649.

[155] The standard terms did contain an express indemnity in the following terms: '13 ... During the continuance of the hire period, the Hirer shall ... fully and completely indemnify the Owner in respect of all claims by any person whatsoever for injury to person or property caused by or in connection with or arising out of the use of the plant.' It could not be relied upon because it failed the *Canada Steamship* rules.

[156] [1987] 1 WLR 659.

[157] Unless one can find a lawyer whose powers of persuasion extend to persuading a client to sue himself or herself.

[158] 'There is no mystique about "exclusion" or "restriction" clauses. To decide whether a person "excludes" liability by reference to a contract term, you look at the effect of the term. You look at its substance': per Slade LJ in *Phillips Products* v. *Hyland* at 666. Cf.

If one applies all of this to the relevant parts of the sample clause above, it passes the *Canada Steamship* rules with flying colours (though could one get the other party to agree to such a clause?),[159] but it may not be effective if the company group tried to use it as a means of excluding its own liability to the contractor (as opposed to other members in the contractor group), since then it would be vulnerable to the reasoning in the *Phillips* case.

2.9 Representations and warranties

The sample clause states as follows:

Each Party represents and warrants to and for the benefit of the other Party as follows:

(1) It is a company duly incorporated and validly existing under the laws of . . . (in respect of the Seller) and of . . . (in respect of the Buyer), is a separate legal entity capable of suing and being sued and has the power and authority to own its assets and conduct the business which it conducts and/or proposes to conduct;

(2) Each Party has the power to enter into and exercise its rights and perform and comply with its obligations under this Agreement;

(3) Its entry into, exercise of its rights under and/or performance of, or compliance with, its obligations under this Agreement do not and will not violate or exceed any power granted or restriction imposed by any law or regulation to which it is subject or any document defining its constitution and do not and will not violate any agreement to which it is a party or which is binding on it or its assets;

(4) All actions, conditions and things required by the laws of . . . to be taken, fulfilled and done in order to enable it lawfully to enter into, exercise its rights under and perform and comply with its obligations under this Agreement, to ensure that those obligations are valid, legally binding and enforceable and to make this Agreement admissible in evidence in the courts of . . . or before an arbitral tribunal, have been taken, fulfilled and done;

the approach taken to the effect of 'no representation' or 'non-reliance' clauses under Section 3 of the Misrepresentation Act 1967: text to note 52.

[159] The fact that it is easy enough to satisfy the rules by including the word 'negligence' may provide the justification for their application against the criticism that they constitute a survival of the strained construction of exemption clauses adopted prior to the Unfair Contract Terms Act (N. E. Palmer, 'Negligence and Exclusion Clauses. Again' [1983] LMCLQ 557). If it is easy to use the appropriate words, the most likely reason they are not used is because the other party did not, or would not, agree to them. In that event, it should not be open to the defendant to claim that agreement was reached by reference to more general words; it is yet another instance of interpretation being approached on the basis of reasonableness or, perhaps, good faith.

(5) Its obligations under this Agreement are valid, binding and enforceable;

(6) ...

(7) ...

As the non-exhaustive nature of these representations and warranties implies, what calls for comment is less the particular representations and warranties set out[160] and more the need for, and role of, such provisions in English law. Put simply, warranties and representations about certain matters will be essential because without them, there will or may be no basis for a claim; it is a good illustration of the general observation made at the outset of this chapter that the content of a contract remains almost entirely in the hands of the parties to it. An obvious example is a warranty that the accounts of a target company give a true and fair view of the assets and liabilities of the company. Such a warranty may be implied,[161] but the parties will certainly wish to insist that it is made express.

The particular need for express representations and warranties is explained by the very limited nature of any duty of disclosure in English law. Indeed, the general rule is that a person who is about to enter into a contract is under no duty to disclose material facts known to

---

[160] Some of those set out strike one as superfluous in the sense that the common law, like the civil law one suspects, would regard the matters to which reference is made as already regulated by the general law. Clause 5 strikes one as almost nonsensical: either the party's obligations under the Agreement are valid, binding and enforceable or they are not; if they are not, what use is a warranty that they are when that warranty itself is an obligation under the contract? One is left with the impression that these sorts of provision may provide comfort, but are unlikely to have any real legal effect such that the position would be different if they were not there.

[161] It is a moot point whether, because such a clause is so routinely included, this militates *in favour* of its implication, should it be omitted, or *against*. Lord Hoffmann has recently 're-stated' the test for implied terms in *Att-Gen of Belize* v. *Belize Telecom Ltd* [2009] UKPC 10, [2009] 1 WLR 1988 at [21]: 'There is only one question: is that what the instrument, read as a whole against the relevant background, would reasonably be understood to mean?' There is a close connection here with interpretation which, as we have seen in earlier instances, has allowed for considerations of reasonableness (and perhaps good faith). But the same limit is applied here as is apparent in questions of interpretation: 'The fact that a particular implication is reasonable may be evidence that the parties would have agreed to it . . . But the courts will not imply a term in fact merely because it would be reasonable to do so; they will not . . . improve the contract which the parties have made for themselves, however desirable the improvement might be' (citing *Trollope & Colls Ltd* v. *NW Metropolitan Hospital Board* [1973] 1 WLR 601 at 609): *Treitel*, para. 6–032.

him or her but not to the other party.[162] Some of the 'exceptions' to this
general rule are not, in reality, exceptions, since they are best explained
on the basis of an implied representation. This is true, for example, of
a representation which is true when made but falsified by later events[163]
or a statement which is literally true but misleading.[164] Genuine exceptions are limited in nature, being confined either to contracts of a
particular type, e.g., contracts of insurance,[165] or to the effect of specific
legislation.[166]

So far as 'representations' are concerned, it is important to stress the
difference between representations which are made *in* the contract and
those which are made in the negotiations leading up to the contract, i.e.,
precontractual representations. Where representations are made in the
contract, they add little to the claims which are available for breach of
warranty, which are considered below. The real and additional potency
lies in the claims which may be made on the basis of precontractual
representations. If such a representation is false, the contract may be set
aside and damages may be available depending on the degree of fault of
the misrepresentor;[167] such damages aim to put the claimant in the same
position as if no misrepresentation had been made (which usually means
recovery of the price on the basis that, in the absence of misrepresentation, the claimant would not have done the deal). The setting out of
'representations' in the contract has led to a submission, the gist of
which is that one might, in fact, be at a disadvantage if one includes
boilerplate 'representations'. The argument is that if representations are
made in the contract they may ultimately lead to overpayment on
completion, but they are not *precontractual* representations such that
they can be said to have induced the contract in the first place, thereby
providing the remedy of rescission or damages of the type just referred

---

[162] *Norwich Union Life Ins Co Ltd* v. *Qureshi* [1999] 2 All ER (Comm) 707 at 717.

[163] *With* v. *O'Flanagan* [1936] Ch 575

[164] *Notts Patent Brick and Tile Co* v. *Butler* (1886) 16 QBD 778.

[165] 'It has been for centuries in England the law in connection with insurance of all sorts,
marine, fire, life, guarantee and every kind of policy, that, as the underwriter knows
nothing and the man who comes to him to ask him to insure knows everything, it is
the duty of the assured ... to make a full disclosure to the underwriters, without being
asked, of all the material circumstances': *Rozanes* v. *Bowen* (1928) 32 Ll. L.R. 98
at 102.

[166] For example, under certain provisions of the Financial Services and Markets Act 2000.

[167] At common law, for fraud, or negligence; under statute applying the provisions
of Section 2(1) of the Misrepresentation Act 1967. See, generally, *Treitel*, paras.
9–026–9–041.

to. It has found support from Bingham LJ,[168] but the prevailing view is that a representation can amount to both a precontractual and contractual representation, e.g., where, as is often the case, any representations made in the executed contract have also appeared in earlier drafts.[169] Indeed, when considered in conjunction with 'non-reliance' clauses which are analysed above,[170] it is clear that the parties have very considerable freedom to agree on the representations they have and have not made as the basis for the contract between them. As we have seen, it is primarily in relation to their attempts to say that they have *not* made representations that English law has some scope for intervening in the contract made.

So far as warranties are concerned, the remedies for non-fulfilment are those available for breach of contract. By contrast with damages for precontractual misrepresentation, damages for breach of warranty are awarded to put the claimant in the same position as if the warranty was true (which means recovery of any lost profit, assuming the deal was a good bargain). Whether such claims are available will, of course, depend on other boilerplate provisions such as exclusion clauses, limitation clauses and contractual time limits. Therefore, as with representations, the parties are, in this context, free to agree on the promises they have and have not made to each other. And again, it is primarily in relation to their attempts to say that they have *not* made promises that English law has some scope for intervention and is more willing to intervene in the final contract.[171] This may be borne out by the approach of the English courts to the disclosures in conjunction with which so many warranties are given.

---

[168] In *Senate Electrical* v. *STC*, unreported, 26 May 1994, he summarised the argument as follows: 'it is a manifest absurdity for the entering into the agreement to be relied upon when it is the very agreement in which the representations for the purpose of the tortious claim are said to be contained.' Though he did not, ultimately, strike out the claim, Bingham LJ did 'go almost the whole distance' with this argument.

[169] See, to this effect: *Eurovideo Bildprogramm Gmbh* v. *Pulse Entertainment Ltd* [2002] EWCA Civ 1235 at [19]. And see *MAN Nutzfahrzeuge AG and Others* v. *Freightliner Ltd and Others* [2005] EWHC 2347 (Comm), where it was not thought to be problematic that claims were advanced for misrepresentation on the basis of precontractual representations that also appeared as contractual representations in the 'representations and warranties' set out therein.

[170] Section 2.1.

[171] For a convincing thesis that no distinction should be drawn between provisions setting out the promises which have been made and those which have not, see B. Coote, *Exception Clauses* (Sweet & Maxwell, 1964).

For example, in *Infiniteland Ltd* v. *Artisan Contracting Ltd*,[172] the seller of the entire issued-share capital in three companies was said to have breached a warranty in the following terms: 'The Principal Accounts (a) give a true and fair view of the assets and liabilities of each Group Company at the Last Accounts Date and its profits for the financial period ended on that date.' As is usually the case, this warranty and others given in the share purchase agreement were qualified by disclosure in the following terms: 'The Warrantors warrant to the Purchaser that ... save as set out in the Disclosure Letter.' The seller supplied the disclosure letter and a large amount of information which, it claimed, was sufficient to disclose the error in the accounts which was said not to have given a 'true and fair view'. The trial judge had found that the level of disclosure provided had not been sufficient to avoid a claim for breach of warranty. He relied heavily on the following *dictum* in the *New Hearts* case:[173]

> Mere reference to a source of information, which is in itself a complex document, within which the diligent enquirer might find relevant information will not satisfy the requirements of a clause providing for fair disclosure with sufficient details to identify the nature and scope of the matter disclosed.

The point which was emphasised by the Court of Appeal was that this *dictum* and disclosure generally have to be seen in context, in particular, in the context of the wording of the warranty given. In the *New Hearts* case, the relevant wording was that the warranties were given 'subject to matters fairly disclosed (with sufficient details to identify the nature and scope of the matter disclosed) in the Disclosure Letter'. In *Infiniteland*, the qualification was merely 'save as set out in the Disclosure Letter' and, on the basis of that wording and the documents disclosed to the buyer's reporting accountants, the Court of Appeal held that the test was as follows:

> could it fairly be expected that reporting accountants would become aware, from an examination of the documents in the ordinary course of carrying out a due diligence exercise, that an exceptional item in the amount of £1,081,000 had been taken as a credit against cost of sales and that the effect of that was to overstate the amount of operating profits from ordinary activities by that amount ...

---

[172] [2005] EWCA Civ 758, [2006] 1 BCLC 632.
[173] *New Hearts Ltd* v. *Cosmopolitan Investments Ltd* [1997] 2 BCLC 249 at 258–259, per Lord Penrose.

It was found that that test had been satisfied. The point to be stressed in the context of this chapter is how crucial the wording of the boilerplate disclosure provision proved to be:[174] the words 'save as set out' in *Infiniteland* had the effect that the warranties given were much more heavily qualified than those given in the *New Hearts* case, based on the words 'fairly disclosed (with sufficient details to identify the nature and scope of the matter disclosed)'. It has been noted above how the courts have room for manouevre when it comes to interpretation, but this is a vivid illustration of the fact that they start with the words used in the contract.[175]

2.10   *Hardship*/force majeure

There are several examples set out in the introduction to Part 3 of hardship, or *force majeure*, clauses. The following may be thought most typical of such a provision:

> The Supplier shall not be liable for delay in performing or for failure to perform its obligations if the delay or failure results from any of the following: (i) Acts of God, (ii) outbreak of hostilities, riot, civil disturbance, acts of terrorism, (iii) the act of any government or authority (including refusal or revocation of any licence or consent), (iv) fire, explosion, flood, fog or bad weather, (v) power failure, failure of telecommunications lines, failure or breakdown of plant, machinery or vehicles, (vi) default of suppliers or sub-contractors, (vii) theft, malicious damage, strike, lock-out or industrial action of any kind, and (viii) any cause or circumstance whatsoever beyond the Supplier's reasonable control.

Without such a clause the parties are left with the doctrine of frustration.[176] Though the courts may long ago have departed from the doctrine of absolute contracts,[177] this doctrine continues to exert an influence and it is still no easy matter to persuade the courts that the parties should be

---

[174] Confirmation that everything depends on the particular wording of the warranty (or representation) and the disclosure, and on the context generally, is provided by the decision of Moore-Bick J in *Man Nutzfahrzeuge AG* v. *Freightliner Ltd* [2005] EWHC 2347.

[175] As a consequence, for the greater protection of buyers, one now often sees it stated that any warranties are qualified only by matters which are 'fully, fairly, specifically and accurately disclosed'. Before the decision in *Infiniteland*, such additional wording may have been viewed as surplusage.

[176] See, generally, *Treitel*, Chapter 19.

[177] As exemplified by *Paradine* v. *Jane* (1647) Aleyn 26.

discharged from their obligations because the contract has been frustrated. In that sense, what provisions of the type above endeavour to do is to set up a contractual regime for frustration, dependent only on what the parties have agreed upon, thereby providing the possibility of a greater degree of latitude.[178]

This may be illustrated by the leading case of *Super Servant Two*.[179] The defendants agreed to transport the claimants' drilling rig from Japan to the North Sea using, at their option, either the *Super Servant One* or the *Super Servant Two*. Shortly after the conclusion of the contract, the defendants allocated the *Super Servant Two* to transport the claimants' rig and the *Super Servant One* to the performance of another contract. Before the time set for performance of the contract with the claimants, the *Super Servant Two* sank and one of the issues for the Court of Appeal to decide was whether the contract with the claimants was frustrated. It was held that it was not frustrated because this was a case of self-induced frustration, i.e., it was not due entirely to events beyond the control of the defendants because they could have used the *Super Servant One* to fulfil the contract. This is a harsh decision and open to criticism,[180] but it is a vivid illustration of the narrow confines of frustration.

However, there was also a *force majeure* clause under which the defendants were entitled to cancel performance in the event of 'perils or danger and accidents of the sea'. The court held that, on a proper construction of this clause, the defendants were entitled to cancel provided that the sinking of the *Super Servant Two* was not attributable to any negligence on their part. Hence, a *force majeure* clause may allow for discharge in circumstances where the doctrine of frustration would not.[181] Whether a *force majeure* clause has this effect or not will, of

---

[178] See A. Berg 'The Detailed Drafting of a *Force Majeure* Clause', in E. McKendrick (ed.), *Force Majeure and Frustration of Contract*, 2nd edn (Informa Publishing, 1995).

[179] [1990] 1 Lloyd's Rep. 1.

[180] For example, the element of 'election' on the part of the defendant in preferring to fulfil the other contract with the *Super Servant One* could be eliminated if the question of which of the contracts was to be discharged was left to be determined not by the free choice of the promisor, but by a rule of law, e.g., by a rule to the effect that the various contracts should for this purpose rank in the order in which they were made. See, further, *Treitel*, para. 19–088.

[181] Another good example in this regard is that the closure of the Suez Canal was not regarded by the English courts as a frustrating event for the purpose of a number of charterparties. The crisis of 1956 produced only two reported cases in which frustration was successfully pleaded, but both cases were later overruled: *Carapanayoti & Co Ltd* v. *ET Green Ltd* [1959] 1 QB 131, overruled in the *Tsakiroglou* case [1962] AC 93; and *The Massalia* [1961] 2 QB 278, overruled in *The Eugenia* [1964] 2 QB 226. When the Canal

course, depend on its interpretation and, while it is to be construed like any other provision of the contract between the parties, one detects some influence from the doctrine of frustration itself.

A good example in this regard is *Thames Valley Power Ltd* v. *Total Gas & Power Ltd*.[182] The claimants operated a combined heat and power facility. By a contract entered into in 1995, the defendants agreed to supply the gas needed to operate the facility for a fifteen-year period. The contract contained a *force majeure* clause which referred to the parties being rendered by *force majeure* 'unable wholly or in part to carry out any of its obligations'. *Force majeure* was defined in the contract to mean 'any event or circumstances beyond the control of the party concerned resulting in the failure by that party in the fulfilment of any of its obligations under this agreement and which notwithstanding the exercise by it of reasonable diligence and foresight it was or would have been unable to prevent or overcome'.

In 2005, the defendants served notice that they would not be continuing to perform their obligations under the contract because of increases in the price of gas, a fact which had rendered it 'uneconomic' for the supply to the claimants to continue. The court held that this was not a *force majeure* event. In short, 'unable' did not extend to 'commercially impractical' in the absence of an express term to this effect. Although the judge stressed that 'each clause must be considered on its own wording and that *force majeure* clauses are not to be interpreted on the assumption that they are necessarily intended to express in words the common law doctrine of frustration', he was nonetheless influenced by earlier decisions in the context of frustration.[183] His approach was to follow that of Lord Loreburn in *Tennants Lancashire Ltd* v. *Wilson CS & Co Ltd*:[184] 'The argument that a man can be excused from performance of his contract when it becomes "commercially impossible" seems to me to be a dangerous contention which ought not to be admitted unless the parties plainly contracted to that effect.' Once again, one finds that the parties may set out their bargain for themselves and by doing so allow for

---

was closed in 1967, pleas of frustration were no more successful (e.g., *The Captain George K* [1970] 2 Lloyd's Rep. 21; *The Washington Trader* [1972] 1 Lloyd's Rep. 463). Some charterparties will now spell out the closure of the Canal as an event of *force majeure*. There was such a provision in the contract in *Super Servant Two*.

[182] [2005] EWHC 2208 (Comm), [2005] All ER (D) 155 (Sep).

[183] See, for example, *Davis Contractors Ltd* v. *Fareham Urban DC* [1956] AC 696.

[184] (1917) AC 495 at 510. It should be noted that the sellers were excused by the express terms of the contract.

a greater degree of certainty[185] than the general law, but only to the extent that they have made their intention sufficiently clear.

3   Conclusion

It is hoped that this survey of some of the leading examples of boilerplate clauses will have confirmed the introductory points with which this chapter began. English law continues to adhere to the principle of freedom of contract, particularly in the commercial context, in the sense that, a few limited exceptions apart,[186] the courts will not interfere with the bargain made between the parties. However, the courts will look closely to see precisely what is the bargain which has been reached, and it has been shown that the employment of boilerplate clauses and standard form contracts is no guarantee against the appearance of 'gaps' into which the courts can introduce notions of reasonableness, fairness and good faith, principally via the medium of interpretation. In 1978, Griffiths J noted:[187] 'Much judicial ingenuity has been expended over the last 25 years to avoid the unjust results that would flow from the literal application of unfair trading conditions.' In the years since, not much has changed. If there is one thing more than any other that may be 'lost in translation' in the employment of English law boilerplate clauses under another governing law, it may be a full appreciation of this ingenuity.

---

[185] As well as a degree of flexibility when it comes to consequences, in that a *force majeure* clause can provide for suspension or extensions of time before any final discharge of the contract.

[186] For example, from the common law, the rule against penalties; and from statute, the Unfair Contract Terms Act 1977.

[187] *Green Ltd* v. *Cade Bros.* [1978] 1 Lloyd's Rep. 602 at 609.

8

The Germanic tradition: application of boilerplate clauses under German law

ULRICH MAGNUS

1 Introduction

Germany was the world champion of exports for a few years.[1] The economic transactions leading to that result are all based on contracts which possess an international element. Many if not most of these contracts are drafted in English and use common law terminology. Some typical contract clauses stem specifically from the United States. Even between German merchants, contracts that are completely in English are not unfamiliar. However, international contracts other than sales or distribution contracts are frequently written in English, the modern *lingua franca*. This is particularly true for international construction contracts which are often based on the FIDIC (Fédération International des Ingénieurs-Conseils) contract form. It is thus not rare that German courts – and particularly arbitration tribunals – have to deal with such contracts. A specific problem that can arise in the construction of these contracts is the possible discrepancy between the common law style of the language of the contract and the applicable contract law that, in these cases, will often be German law. To exaggerate only slightly, there may be a 'clash of legal cultures'.

This specific kind of tension between the terms of a contract and a different applicable law has been the subject of some debate in Germany in recent years.[2] Nonetheless, the general phenomenon that parties act

---

[1] From 2003 until 2009, Germany was ranked first as export world champion. In 2009, China overtook Germany and gained first place.

[2] J. Gruber, 'Auslegungsprobleme bei fremdsprachigen Verträgen unter deutschem Recht' (1997) *Deutsche Zeitschrift für Wirtschafts- und Insolvenzrecht*, 353–359; O. Meyer, 'Die privatautonome Abbedingung der vorvertraglichen Abreden – Integrationsklauseln im internationalen Wirtschaftsverkehr', *Rabels Zeitschrift für ausländisches und internationales*

on a legal basis different from the applicable law has long since been well known in German private international law. It is termed 'Handeln unter falschem/fremdem Recht' (acting under wrong/foreign law).[3] With respect to contracts, it means that one or both parties used contract terms which neither originate from nor conform to the law that governs the contract. The general solution German law provides for cases of this kind is to bring into line both the intended sense of the terms by the parties and the requirements of the applicable law, mainly by way of interpretation. This will be discussed in more detail below (see Section 4). However, the main focus of this chapter will be on the various contract clauses that are being used and on their interpretation (see Section 5). There are a relatively small number of German court decisions on this issue. However, there are two preliminary aspects that must first be addressed: the general method of interpretation of contracts in Germany as opposed to the method in common law countries (Section 2) and the question of which law applies to the issue of interpretation in international contracts (Section 3).

2 General method of interpretation of contracts

Only a few words are necessary on the general method of interpretation of contracts in Germany in contrast to the common law world. The German BGB (Civil Code) addresses the interpretation of declarations and contracts in two provisions of general application (§§133 and 157). §133 of the BGB[4] stresses the principle that the true intention prevails over the literal meaning of a declaration, while §157 of the BGB[5]

Privatrecht, 72 (2008), 562–600; V. Triebel and S. Balthasar, 'Auslegung englischsprachiger Vertragstexte unter deutschem Vertragsstatut – Fallstricke der Art. 31, 32 I Nr. 1 EGBGB', *Neue Juristische Wochenschrift* (2004), 2189–2196; S. Voß, *Warranties in Unternehmenskaufverträgen – Struktur und Wirkungsweise anglo-amerikanischer Gewährleistungskataloge in Unternehmenskaufverträgen, die deutschem Recht unterliegen* (MVK, Medien-Verl. Köhler, 2002). In contrast, a recent survey of principles of the construction of contracts does not even mention the interpretation of contracts governed by German law but drafted in English; see B. Biehl, 'Grundsätze der Vertragsauslegung', *JuS* (2010), 195–200.

[3] See thereto G. Dannemann, 'Sachrechtliche Gründe für die Berücksichtigung nicht anwendbaren Rechts', in G. Hohloch, R. Frank and P. Schlechtriem (eds.), *Festschrift für Hans Stoll zum 75. Geburtstag* (Mohr Siebeck, 2001), pp. 417–436; C. Münzer, *Handeln unter falschem Recht* (Peter Lang Verlagsgruppe, 1992).

[4] 'When a declaration of intent is interpreted, it is necessary to ascertain the true intention rather than adhering to the literal meaning of the declaration.'

[5] 'Contracts are to be interpreted as required by good faith, taking customary practice into consideration.'

prescribes that the interpretation of contracts must recognise good faith and customary practice. Generally, under German law, any interpretation starts with the wording of the text of the contract and the parties' concurrent understanding of it. If this does not lead to a solution, the objective meaning in the light of the circumstances and interests of the parties is decisive.[6] In comparison to common law jurisdictions, there are still differences.[7] They concern mainly three aspects. First, courts in common law jurisdictions tend to rely on the written text of a contract more strictly than German courts do. The common law's 'parol evidence rule', which in principle allows no proof against the clear wording of a written contract, is an expression of this attitude, even though today there are many exceptions to this rule.[8] Under German law, a written contract creates only a rebuttable presumption of completeness.[9] Modifications of its content can be proved by any means.[10] Secondly, German law places greater weight on a teleological, purposive interpretation of contracts than common law does.[11] Thirdly, common law

---

[6] For the German method of interpretation of contracts, see K. Larenz and M. Wolf, *Allgemeiner Teil des Bürgerlichen Rechts*, 9th edn (Verlag C. H. Beck, 2004) §28; J. Busche, in *Münchener Kommentar zum Bürgerlichen Gesetzbuch*, vol. 1/1, 5th edn (Verlag C.H. Beck, 2006), §157, paras. 1ff.; H. Roth, in *Staudinger, Kommentar zum Bürgerlichen Gesetzbuch mit Einführungsgesetz und Nebengesetzen* (Sellier, 2003), §157, paras. 1ff.

[7] Compare also Triebel and Balthasar, 'Auslegung englischsprachiger Vertragstexte', 2191ff.; K. Zweigert and H. Kötz, *An Introduction to Comparative Law*, 3rd edn (Oxford University Press, 1998, translated by T. Weir), pp. 400ff.; further, J. Herbots, 'Interpretation of Contracts', in J. M. Smits (ed.), *Elgar Encyclopedia of Comparative Law* (Edward Elgar Publishing, 2006), pp. 325–347; S. Vogenauer, 'Auslegung von Verträgen', in J. Basedow, K. Hopt and R. Zimmermann (eds.), *Handwörterbuch des Europäischen Privatrechts*, vol. 1 (Mohr Siebeck, 2009), pp. 134ff.

[8] For English law, see K. Lewison, *The Interpretation of Contracts*, 3rd edn (Sweet & Maxwell, 2007), pp. 85ff.; for US law (with all caution against oversimplification because of the many differences among the single US states), see E. A. Farnsworth, *Farnsworth on Contracts*, 3 vols., 2nd edn (Aspen Publishers, 1998), §7.12.

[9] See BGH NJW 1980, 1680; BGH NJW 2002, 3164.

[10] See, for instance, BGHZ 20, 109; BGH NJW 1999, 1702.

[11] For England, see the so-called golden rule: 'In construing all written instruments, the grammatical and ordinary sense of the words is to be adhered to, unless that would lead to some absurdity, or some repugnance or inconsistence with the rest of the instrument, in which case the grammatical and ordinary sense of the words may be modified, so as to avoid that absurdity and inconsistency, but no further' (Lord Wensleydale in *Grey* v. *Pearson* (1857) 6 HL Cas. 61 at 106); see more recently *Jumbo King Ltd* v. *Faithful Properties Ltd* (1999) HKCFAR 279 (by Lord Hoffmann: 'If the ordinary meaning of the words makes sense in relation to the rest of the document and the factual background, then the court will give effect to the language, even though the consequences may appear

courts are more reluctant than German courts to fill gaps or even to rewrite parts of the contract.[12] These differences also affect the interpretation of contracts that are drafted in common law style but are governed by German law.

However, in my view, the national interpretation methods of construing contracts should be 'internationalised' in cases of international contracts. That means that where an international meaning of terms and phrases can be identified, this meaning should be preferred to a purely national meaning. Sets of principles like the UNIDROIT Principles of International Commercial Contracts ('UPICC'), the Principles of European Contract Law ('PECL') or the Draft Common Frame of Reference ('DCFR') may be helpful in revealing that there is an almost uniform international understanding of certain contract clauses or terms.

3 Law applicable to the interpretation of international commercial contracts

3.1   Generally applicable law

3.1.1   Applicability of the *lex contractus*

It is because of nationally differing methods of interpretation that the first aspect of interpretation of international commercial contracts is always the question of which country's law will govern the issues of interpretation. This is a matter of conflict of laws. According to the rules of private international law, the construction of a contract or one of its terms generally follows the law that governs the contract. This had

---

hard for one side or the other. The court is not privy to the negotiation of the agreement – evidence of such negotiations is inadmissible – and has no way of knowing whether a clause which appears to have an onerous effect was a quid pro quo for some other concession. Or one of the parties may simply have made a bad bargain'). See also Lewison, *The Interpretation of Contracts*, pp. 145ff. The position is very similar for the US: see Farnsworth, *Farnsworth on Contracts*, §7.12.

[12] In England, under certain conditions, the courts imply terms into a contract: see *BP Refinery (Westport) Pty Ltd* v . *Shire of Hastings* (1978) ALJR 20 (PC) (by Lord Simon of Glaisdale: 'In their [Lordships'] view, for a term to be implied, the following conditions (which may overlap) must be satisfied: (1) it must be reasonable and equitable; (2) it must be necessary to give business efficacy to the contract, so that no term will be implied if the contract is effective without it; (3) it must be so obvious that "it goes without saying"; (4) it must be capable of clear expression; (5) it must not contradict any express term of the contract'). Again, the position is very similar in US law: Farnsworth, *Farnsworth on Contracts*, §7.16.

been the standpoint of the Rome Convention on the Law Applicable to Contractual Obligations of 1980 (hereafter, the Rome Convention).[13] The same rule was incorporated into German law.[14] The now directly applicable Rome I Regulation of 2009[15] has maintained this principle.[16] It is, for instance, also enshrined in the Inter-American Convention on the Law Applicable to International Contracts of 1994.[17]

It is thus a firm principle – and not only of German and European private international law – that the interpretation of a contract will generally be governed by the *lex contractus*. However, there are some exceptions to this rule (see below, Section 3.2ff.).

3.1.2 Choice of law

The applicable contract law is primarily the law the parties have chosen.[18] Although there are some limits to such a choice,[19] these limits regularly play no marked role for international commercial contracts. The choice may be express or implied.[20] If parties base their contract on a certain law, for instance, by referring to specific institutes of that law, this will often amount to a tacit choice.[21] However, the mere use of English as the contract language does not surrender the contract to English law, as English is used in many countries.[22] In the cases this chapter is mainly

---

[13] See Article 10(1)(a) of the Rome Convention.

[14] Article 32, para. 1, No. 1 of the EGBGB (Introductory Law to the Civil Code).

[15] OJ EU L 177 of 4 July 2008, pp. 6ff., corr. OJ EU L 309 of 24 November 2009, p. 87.

[16] Article 12(1)(a) of the Rome I Regulation.

[17] Article 14(a) of the Inter-American Convention.

[18] See Article 3 of the Rome Convention, Article 27 of the EGBGB and Article 3 of the Rome I Regulation.

[19] The following limits must be taken into account: in purely domestic or inner EU transactions, the choice cannot oust the mandatory domestic or EU law (Article 3(3) of the Rome Convention, Article 27(3) of the EGBGB and Article 3(3) and (4) of the Rome I Regulation); internationally mandatory provisions (*lois de police*) can override the chosen law (Article 7 of the Rome Convention, Article 34 of the EGBGB and Article 9 of the Rome I Regulation); the *ordre public* can prohibit the application of unacceptable provisions of the chosen (foreign) law (Article 16 of the Rome Convention, Article 6 of the EGBGB and Article 21 of the Rome I Regulation).

[20] See Article 3(1), sent. 2 of the Rome Convention, Article 27(1), sent. 2 of the EGBGB and Article 3(1), sent. 2 of the Rome I Regulation.

[21] See U. Magnus, in *Staudinger, Kommentar zum Bürgerlichen Gesetzbuch mit Einführungsgesetz und Nebengesetzen*; Article 27 of the EGBGB, paras. 75ff.; D. Martiny, in *Münchener Kommentar zum Bürgerlichen Gesetzbuch*, 5th edn (2010), vol. 10; Article 3 of the Rome I Regulation, paras. 57ff.

[22] BGH NJW-RR 1990, 183; Martiny, in *Münchener Kommentar zum Bürgerlichen Gesetzbuch*, vol. 10; Article 3 of the Rome I Regulation, para. 63; Magnus, in

concerned with, the parties have expressly chosen a certain law but had drafted their contract on the basis of another law. In this case, the express choice prevails. Therefore, in principle, the interpretation rules of that law have to be applied.

3.1.3   Construction clauses

Contracts drafted in the common law style often contain a so-called construction clause, for instance, 'The terms and expressions of this contract are to be construed in accordance with English law' (or any other law). Such a clause designates at the very least the law according to which the contract has to be interpreted. If there are no indications that the parties intended to choose another law as the applicable contract law, such a construction clause is often regarded as an implied, or even express, choice of law for the whole contract, not merely for its interpretation.[23]

It will be rare that a construction clause and an accompanying choice-of-law clause will not designate the same law, but if so, any interpretation is governed by the law to which the construction clause refers.

3.1.4   Applicable law in the absence of a choice of law

In the absence of a valid choice of law by the parties, the principal rule in the EU is that the law of the country applies where the place of business of that party is located that is required to effect the characteristic performance of the contract.[24] Thus, in international sales transactions, the law at the seller's seat generally applies. In international distribution contracts, the law at the seat of the distributor generally applies.[25]

3.2   Contract interpretation under international conventions

A special case is the interpretation of a contract covered by an international convention such as the United Nations (Vienna) Convention on

---

Staudinger, Kommentar zum Bürgerlichen Gesetzbuch mit Einführungsgesetz und Nebengesetzen; Article 27 of the EGBGB, para. 85.

[23] See, for instance, OLG München IPRax 1989, 42 with note *W. Lorenz* (22) (explicit choice); LG München IPRax 1984, 318 (implied choice).

[24] See Article 4(2) of the Rome Convention, Article 28(2) of the EGBGB and Article 4(2) of the Rome I Regulation.

[25] See explicitly Article 4(1)(a) and (f) of the Rome I Regulation; for the prior law, compare Magnus, in *Staudinger, Kommentar zum Bürgerlichen Gesetzbuch mit Einführungsgesetz und Nebengesetzen*, Article 27 of the EGBGB, paras. 175ff., 286ff.; Martiny, in *Münchener Kommentar zum Bürgerlichen Gesetzbuch*, 4th edn (2006), vol. 10; Article 28 of the EGBGB, paras. 136ff., 226ff.

Contracts for the International Sale of Goods ('CISG') of 1980, which often applies to international sales transactions. This Convention is automatically applicable where the parties have their places of business in different contracting states of the CISG or where a court uses the rules of private international law that lead back to the law of a CISG contracting state.[26] Where the parties have chosen the law of a CISG state, the CISG therefore applies. This means, for instance, that where the parties have chosen German law, this choice regularly includes the CISG.[27]

In addition, the Convention covers the interpretation of contracts and their single terms, and contains its own autonomous method for the construction of contracts.[28] To that extent, the CISG supersedes any rules of (national) private international law concerning the interpretation of contracts. In the absence of a central court for the application of the CISG, only a uniform method of interpretation can preserve as uniform as possible an understanding of the Convention's provisions. However, uniformity of interpretation is not a purpose in itself, but shall secure better foreseeability and predictability and, thus, greater certainty of law. This serves the central aim of the CISG, as well as that of other uniform law conventions: to facilitate international trade and thereby promote peaceful relations between nations.[29]

First, according to Article 8 of the CISG, the intent of a party making a statement has merit if the other party knew or could not have been unaware what that intent was. Secondly, in all other cases, a statement has to be interpreted according to the understanding that a reasonable person of the same kind as the other party would have had in the same circumstances. Thirdly, all circumstances relevant for the understanding of a statement in a case have to be given due consideration. National

---

[26] See Article 1(1) of the CISG.

[27] See BGH NJW 1997, 3309 (3310); BGH NJW 1999, 1259.

[28] This is the clear majority view: see J. Honnold and H. Flechtner, *Uniform Law for International Sales under the 1980 United Nations Convention*, 4th edn (Kluwer Law International, 2009), para. 105; Magnus, in *Staudinger, Kommentar zum Bürgerlichen Gesetzbuch mit Einführungsgesetz und Nebengesetzen*; Article 8 of the CISG, para. 7; M. Schmidt-Kessel, 'Articles 8–9', in P. Schlechtriem and I. Schwenzer (eds.), *Kommentar zum Einheitlichen UN-Kaufrecht – CISG*, 5th edn (C. H. Beck, 2008), pp. 163–197, Article 8, paras. 1, 3. The autonomous method of interpreting contracts must not be mixed with the autonomous method of interpreting the CISG as such – both methods are not identical; as to the interpretation of the CISG, see Article 7 of the CISG and the commentaries to this provision.

[29] See the Preamble to the CISG.

peculiarities of interpretation such as the parol evidence rule of the common law are eliminated.[30]

Thus, if German law is applicable to an international sales transaction, this will mean that in most cases the CISG and its autonomous rules on contract interpretation have to be applied. Only if domestic German law has been chosen as the *lex causae* by clearly excluding the CISG will the 'German method' of interpretation apply to the sales contract that has to be construed.

The same principles apply to international contracts other than sales contracts.[31] Where uniform law conventions are applicable, such as the Ottawa Conventions on International Factoring or International Financial Leasing of 1988 or the many transport conventions, their interpretation rules must be respected. Only if they are inapplicable do the *lex causae* interpretation rules of the respective contract come into play.

3.3   Use of international trade terms

International contracts often incorporate terms which have an internationally standardised meaning. The most prominent example are INCOTERMS,[32] but there are many more. They are not enacted by legitimated legislators but are drafted by private organisations. Nonetheless, they are widely used and form a kind of modern *lex mercatoria*. According to the prevailing view, the *lex mercatoria* is not an autonomous body of law that applies by its own competence.[33] On the contrary, its rules are regarded as being generally subject to the control of

---

[30] See *MCC-Marble Ceramic Center, Inc.* v. *Ceramica Nuova d'Agostino, SpA*, 144 F.3d 1384 (11th Cir., 29 June 1998); cert. denied *Ceramica Nuova d'Agostino, SpA* v. *MCC-Marble Ceramic Center, Inc.*, 526 U.S. 1087 (26 April 1999); Honnold and Flechtner, *Uniform Law for International Sales*, para. 110.

[31] See generally on the interpretation of uniform law conventions: U. P. Gruber, *Methoden des Internationalen Einheitsrechts* (Mohr Siebeck, 2004); J. Kropholler, *Internationales Einheitsrecht* (J. C. B. Mohr, 1975), pp. 258ff.

[32] INCOTERMS 2000, prepared by the International Chamber of Commerce; see thereto J. Ramberg, *INCOTERMS 2000*, ICC Publication No. 620 (1999); J. Bredow and B. Seiffert, *INCOTERMS 2000* (Economica Verlag, 2000); A. Baumbach and K. Hopt (eds.), *Handelsgesetzbuch*, 34th edn (C. H. Beck, 2010). A revised version, INCOTERMS 3000, will become applicable in 2011.

[33] See, in particular, P. Mankowski, 'Überlegungen zur sach- und interessengerechten Rechtswahl für Verträge des internationalen Wirtschaftsverkehrs', *Recht der internationalen Wirtschaft* (2003) 2–14, 13; P. Mankowski, 'Stillschweigende Rechtswahl und wählbares Recht', in S. Leible (ed.), *Das Grünbuch zum Internationalen Vertragsrecht*

the mandatory provisions of the applicable national law. However, it is rather self-evident that terms like INCOTERMS should not be interpreted according to the *lex causae* of the contract. They must be understood in the sense given to them by the international community, otherwise their unifying purpose could not be achieved. Their uniform understanding serves the aim of foreseeability and predictability of law in the international arena. It is therefore necessary to interpret them in an internationally uniform way without any redress to specific national methods or rules of interpretation.[34]

3.4   Use of international standard contracts

Certain branches almost always regularly use comprehensive standard contract forms that have been developed on the basis of a specific law and that regulate, more or less, all contractual problems on the background of this specific law that, in many cases, is English common law. Such use of international standardised forms is typical, for instance, for many international insurance contracts (using the Lloyds policy), for ship sales (using the Norwegian standard form), for charter parties (using the GENCON charter form) or for international construction contracts (using the FIDIC contract form). Rarely do the parties modify the standardised content of the form or add substantial parts.

Actually, the interpretation of these standard forms is formally governed by the *lex causae* of the contract – be that as the law chosen or applicable by objective designation. However, in order to support the unifying purpose of such international standard contract forms, it is again necessary to interpret them in an 'a-national' way. Specific national interpretation methods must be left aside in the interests of a uniform understanding. Further, the terms of these standard forms must be interpreted in an internationally uniform way.

3.5   Terms specific for a certain law

Occasionally the parties of a contract use specific terms that are known only to a specific law. An example is the use of a term that specifies a legal institute that does not exist in other legal systems, for instance, the term

---

(Sellier, 2004) pp. 63–108, 100ff.; Martiny, in *Münchener Kommentar zum Bürgerlichen Gesetzbuch*; vol. 10, Article 3 of the Rome I Regulation, paras. 36ff.

[34] See, in the same sense, Baumbach and Hopt, *Handelsgesetzbuch*; INCOTERMS Einl, para. 8.

'consideration'. It is a term of art in common law countries with a specific legal meaning that, as such, is unknown in civil law countries. If used in a contract drafted in common law style but governed, for instance, by German law, the term has to be given its common law meaning unless the parties agree or it is clear from the circumstances that the term means something different.

3.6   Mid-summary

When the law applicable to the interpretation of international commercial contracts is to be determined, it is the undisputed starting point that the law should be applied that governs the contract as a whole. However, there are important exceptions to this rule:

- As far as uniform law conventions are applicable, it is necessary that contracts covered by them have to be interpreted in the way the respective convention prescribes. Generally this is an autonomous method for whose content the solution provided by the CISG can serve as a model. First, the recognisable intent behind a contract or contractual declaration is decisive. Secondly, in all other cases, the meaning from an objective viewpoint in the light of all relevant circumstances has to be taken.
- Unified international trade terms (such as INCOTERMS) that the parties incorporate into their contract must be given their international meaning and must be interpreted in an internationally acceptable way, free from national peculiarities of interpretation.
- Internationally standardised contract forms too must be interpreted in an international manner.
- Terms that are known to have acquired a precise technical meaning in a specific legal system generally have to be understood in that sense.

Both uniform trade terms and international standard contracts come close to 'objective' law for which the individual parties' intentions matter less. Their interpretation must take account of this fact.

4   'Acting under wrong law'

4.1   A well-known phenomenon

The focus of the subject of this book is on the question of which law governs the interpretation of 'normal' international contracts where none of the peculiarities discussed above is present and where the *lex contractus* and the legal background of the contract document fall apart. As already mentioned, the situation in which the applicable law and the legal background of a document differ is a well-known phenomenon of general private international law.[35] With respect to the interpretation of international contracts, this 'acting under wrong law' poses the question of whether the contract shall be interpreted in an international manner, according to the method prescribed by the applicable law or according to the method of the background law.

Mainly, in reality, the following factual situations are encountered,[36] provided always that German domestic law is the *lex contractus* and German courts are seised with the case: (1) both contract parties agree on a common law-style contract but only one of the parties originates from a common law country and is familiar with the common law background; (2) none of the parties is familiar with the common law background; (3) none of the parties, except for the representatives of both parties, are familiar with the common law background and have negotiated the contract; (4) both parties originate from a common law country.

4.2   The courts' view

The German courts generally treat these cases in the same manner.[37] The former Imperial Court (Reichsgericht)[38] held that the use of English contract clauses was an indication that the parties intended that the English understanding of the clauses should apply.[39] According to this Court, English clauses were therefore to be understood in their English sense. The Federal Court (Bundesgerichtshof) appears to distinguish now between the method of interpretation and the understanding of a certain term or formulation.[40] Concerning the method of interpretation, the Court seems to

---

[35] See, in general thereto, C. Bar and P. Mankowski, *Internationales Privatrecht*, vol. I, 2nd edn (C. H. Beck, 2003), pp. 211, 705ff.; G. Kegel and K. Schurig, *Internationales Privatrecht*, 9th edn (C. H. Beck, 2004) p. 66; S. Sonnenberger, in *Münchener Kommentar zum Bürgerlichen Gesetzbuch*; Einl. IPR, paras. 611ff.; Spellenberg, in *Münchener Kommentar zum Bürgerlichen Gesetzbuch*; Article 12 Rom I-VO, paras. 32ff.

[36] See thereto Triebel and Balthasar, 'Auslegung englischsprachiger Vertragstexte', 2190.

[37] As to the critique thereon, see Triebel and Balthasar, 'Auslegung englischsprachiger Vertragstexte', 2193ff.

[38] This court was the highest court in Germany from 1879 until 1945. Its successor is the Federal Court (Bundesgerichtshof, established in 1950).

[39] See RGZ 39, 65 (68); see also RGZ 122, 233 (235).

[40] See BGH NJW-RR 1992, 423 (425) (in that case German parties had used the GENCON Charter for a charter party. A dispute arose over whether the meaning of the term 'indemnity' in the GENCON form was to be understood in its English sense or in its

apply the law that governs the contract.[41] In all the above-mentioned factual situations, the general interpretation method would therefore be the method as prescribed by German domestic law. However, according to the Federal Court, the understanding or meaning of terms based on foreign law has generally to be that of the foreign law.[42] Like the Imperial Court, the Federal Court assumes that the parties intended to understand their contract and its terms in the sense of the foreign law. Therefore, in this Court's view, followed by the lower courts, this sense has to be accepted.[43] Only if the parties or reasonable parties had a common understanding that was different from the English meaning would this understanding prevail. In the GENCON case,[44] the Court formulated the principle that terms and clauses drafted under a foreign law should generally be given the meaning that the foreign law accords them. However, in the concrete case, the Court held that between German merchants, the German understanding of the terms 'indemnity' and 'deadweight' should prevail, because in German business circles, the indemnity clause was used in a specific sense, whereas in England, the validity of indemnity clauses was doubtful.

Largely, the German courts thus combine the interpretation method of the applicable law and the understanding of terms and clauses in accordance with the background law and apply this combination with some flexibility.[45]

4.3   Critique and solution

The approach of the Federal Court has been criticised.[46] It has been argued that, in most cases, neither the parties' intentions nor their

---

German sense). Similarly, see BGH IPRpr 1956/57 No. 55; OLG Hamburg TranspR 1993, 433 (434); OLG Hamburg RIW 1996, 68; RGZ 39, 65 (68).

[41] BGH IPRpr 1956/57 No. 55; see also OLG Frankfurt NJW-RR 1995, 36.

[42] BGH IPRpr 1956/57 No. 55 ('Die englischsprachigen Vertragsformulare, die nicht etwa Übersetzungen deutscher Texte sind, enthalten zahlreiche dem angelsächsischen Rechtsdenken angehörende Begriffe, die für jeden nach den jeweiligen Formularen geschlossenen Frachtvertrag gelten sollen, mag er im Einzelfall dem englischen oder einem anderen Recht unterstellt sein. Dies erfordert, dass derartige fremdsprachige Begriffe und Vertragsklauseln grundsätzlich nach dem Recht des Landes interpretiert werden, in dem sie entwickelt worden sind').

[43] BGH IPRpr 1956/57 No. 55.   [44] BGH NJW-RR 1992, 423.

[45] See besides the quoted decision of the BGH, for instance, OLG Köln RIW 2004, 458ff. (the interpretation of whether a 'letter of transfer' means a full assignment or a mere subrogation must take into account both the applicable law and the background law).

[46] See, in particular, Triebel and Balthasar, 'Auslegung englischsprachiger Vertragstexte', 2190ff.

interests would justify deviating from the applicable contract law, thus subjecting contract formulations or terms to another law.[47] Instead, the *lex contractus* should generally govern the interpretation of contracts drafted in a foreign language and based on foreign law. Only where both parties originate from the country according to whose law the contract was drafted should the interpretation follow that law.[48]

In my view, the statutory provision must be the starting point: the interpretation of a contract follows, in principle, the *lex contractus*.[49] A question arises of when an exception from this rule should apply so that the sense of a formulation or term should be the meaning given by another law. The answer should be based on the central principle of international (commercial) contract law: the principle of party autonomy. Where the parties, either expressly or impliedly, have made clear that their contract should be understood in a sense different from the meaning that the *lex contractus* would arrive at, then this different meaning is to be applied. Quite generally, it is possible to choose a separate *lex interpretionis* that differs from the *lex contractus*.[50] However, there must be a clear choice. Where the parties explicitly expressed this intention, for instance, by a construction clause, the answer is simple. The expressly chosen law governs the interpretation.

Problems arise with an implied choice of a separate *lex interpretionis*. In order to become no pure fiction, the implied indication must be sufficiently clear.[51] The mere use of a contract form drafted in common law style is today in itself no sufficient indication of a respective choice of this law as the *lex interpretionis*. First, since the days of the Imperial Court, English has become the *lingua franca* of international trade and business. The use of contracts drafted in English and in common law

---

[47] *Ibid.*, 2193ff. [48] *Ibid.*, 2195ff.
[49] See Article 10(1)(a) of the Rome Convention, Article 32, para. 1, No. 1 of the EGBGB and Article 12(1)(a) of the Rome I Regulation.
[50] See S. Leible, in *Anwaltkommentar BGB*, vol. 1 (Deutscher Anwaltverlag, 2005); Article 32 of the EGBGB, para. 8; Magnus, in *Staudinger, Kommentar zum Bürgerlichen Gesetzbuch mit Einführungsgesetz und Nebengesetzen*; Article 32 of the EGBGB, para. 25.
[51] A parallel can be drawn to the tacit choice of the *lex contractus*: according to Article 3(1)(2) of the Rome Convention ('demonstrated with reasonable certainty'), Article 27(1)(2) of the EGBGB ('sich mit hinreichender Sicherheit . . . ergeben') and Article 3(1)(2) of the Rome I Regulation ('clearly demonstrated'), there must be a clear indication of the parties' common intention.

style is no longer an unambiguous indication of the intention to subject the contract to legal terminology and meaning as understood in England or English common law. Secondly, the common law varies rather widely among the so-called common law jurisdictions. Again, since the days of the Imperial Court, English and US law in particular, but also other common law jurisdictions, have developed in different directions. Thirdly, the use of common law contract forms may be no rational choice of a separate *lex interpretionis* at all, but just a matter of convenience – using a contract form for lack of something better and more appropriate. Therefore, today, further circumstances or signs are necessary to show the parties' common intention that, for instance, the English or US meaning of contract formulations or terms should prevail over the *lex contractus*.

5 Discussion of specific clauses

The following section deals with a number of specific clauses that are typical for contracts drafted in common law style and discusses how they are treated by German courts. It is difficult to categorise these clauses in a convincing way. According to the structure described in the introduction to Part 3, they are divided here into three different groups: first, clauses that aim at detaching the contract from the applicable law; secondly, clauses that use terms unknown to the applicable law; and, thirdly, clauses that regulate matters already regulated in the applicable law.

5.1 Clauses aiming at fully detaching the contract from the applicable law

Certain clauses of common law-style contracts try to make the contract waterproof against any outside influence, such as oral agreements, modifications, additions, interpretation sources, etc.

5.1.1 Entire agreement clauses

An entire agreement clause as drafted in common law jurisdictions could have the following wording:

> The Contract contains the entire contract and understanding between the parties hereto and supersedes all prior negotiations, representations, undertakings and agreements on any subject matter of the Contract.

5.1.1.1 German law   Under German domestic law, entire agreement clauses or merger clauses (Vollständigkeitsklauseln or Integrationsklauseln) are not unknown.[52] They aim at fixing and concentrating the content of the contract onto the written document, excluding any external addition or modification. Not surprisingly, their precise meaning depends on their formulation. The ordinary entire agreement clause[53] is regarded as raising a rebuttable presumption that the contract document is correct and complete.[54] The clause thus moderately strengthens the presumption of general law that a written contract is the correct and complete expression of the parties' intent.[55] For this reason, entire agreement clauses are relatively rare in Germany.[56] The presumption may be rebutted by any kind of proof.[57]

If the entire agreement clause is aiming at excluding any rebuttal of the presumption, it must, in principle, expressly state that aim (for instance, 'It is irrebuttably presumed that no additional agreements have been concluded').[58] However, although the courts have not yet decided the question, it is more than doubtful whether clauses of that kind are valid under German law, because they restrict the possibility to prove the contrary. §309, No. 12 of the BGB[59] prohibits clauses which change the burden of proof to the disadvantage of the other party and §307(1) of the BGB[60] declares any standard term that disfavours the other party

---

[52] See thereto, in particular, S. Kaufmann, *Parol Evidence Rule und Merger Clauses im internationalen Einheitsrecht* (Peter Lang, 2004), pp. 197ff.; A. Lüderitz, *Auslegung von Rechtsgeschäften – Vergleichende Untersuchung anglo-amerikanischen und deutschen Rechts* (Karlsruhe, 1966), pp. 217ff.; Meyer, 'Die privatautonome Abbedingung'.

[53] See the entire agreement clause in the introduction to Part 3 of this book. In German law, such a clause would run as follows: 'Mündliche Nebenabreden bestehen nicht' (compare BGH NJW 2000, 207).

[54] BGHZ 93, 29 (33) = NJW 1985, 623; Staudinger/Schlosser (No. 21) (2006) §305b, para. 51.

[55] Kaufmann, *Parol Evidence Rule*, p. 205; Lüderitz, *Auslegung von Rechtsgeschäften*, p. 222; Meyer, 'Die privatautonome Abbedingung', 589.

[56] Meyer, 'Die privatautonome Abbedingung', 585.

[57] BGHZ 79, 281 = NJW 1981, 922; BGH NJW 1985, 623; BGH NJW 2000, 207.

[58] 'Es wird unwiderleglich vermutet, dass Nebenabreden nicht getroffen sind.'

[59] §309 of the BGB does not apply to transactions between merchants (§310(1) of the BGB).

[60] §307 of the BGB applies to transactions between merchants as well as to consumer transactions. However, the yardstick of reasonableness and good faith in §307 of the BGB corresponds in commercial transactions largely to the standard expressed in §§308 and 309 of the BGB which formally apply only to consumer transactions (see BGHZ 90, 278; BGHZ 103, 328; BGH NJW 2007, 3774). If a clause would be invalid under §§308 and 309 of the BGB, this is a *prima facie* indication that the clause should also be invalid between merchants unless reasonable grounds justify upholding it.

to an unreasonable extent and offends the principle of good faith invalid. If the entire agreement clause excludes any proof to the contrary, this is a rather drastic and unreasonable restriction of evidence, although it is not a change to the burden of proof. In the interpretation of §309, No. 12 as well as §307(1) of the BGB, it now has to be taken into account that No. 1q of Annex 1 to the Unfair Contract Terms Directive (93/13/EEC) bans any clause that is 'unduly restricting the evidence available'.[61] Both provisions must be interpreted in line with the Directive and must thus include clauses that restrict the available evidence. Therefore, irrebuttable entire agreement clauses fall under both provisions. The clearly prevailing view rightly holds an irrebuttable entire agreement clause to be invalid if used in standard contracts, irrespective of whether or not the parties are merchants.[62]

Under German law, entire agreement clauses do not regularly restrict the use of prior negotiations, conduct, etc., as a means for the interpretation of terms and clauses of the written contract.[63]

5.1.1.2 English law

The common law jurisdictions differ in their treatment of entire agreement clauses. English common law appears to ascribe such clauses with merely modestly stricter effects than German law does. It seems to be the prevailing view in England that the clause establishes a strong but not a completely irrebuttable presumption that

---

[61] In the same sense, see also H. Roth, in H. G. Bamberger and H. Roth, *Beckscher Online-Kommentar* (Beck-online, 2007) §309 No. 12, para. 2; a partly differing opinion is given in E.-M. Kieninger, in *Münchener Kommentar zum Bürgerlichen Gesetzbuch*, §309, para. 5 ('undue restriction of evidence' is relevant only for the interpretation of the general provision of §307 of the BGB, but not for §309, No. 12 of the BGB; however, this view would mean that the Directive had not been implemented correctly).

[62] Baumbach and Hopt, *Handelsgesetzbuch*, Einl vor §343, para. 9; C. Grüneberg, in *Palandt, BGB*, 69th edn (C. H. Beck, 2010), §305b, para. 5; Kaufmann, *Parol Evidence Rule*, p. 232; Kieninger, *Münchener Kommentar zum Bürgerlichen Gesetzbuch*, §305b, para. 13; S. Roloff, in H. P. Westermann, *Erman, Bürgerliches Gesetzbuch*, 12th edn (Verlag Dr. Otto Schmidt, 2008), §305b, para. 11; Schmidt, in H. G. Bamberger and H. Roth, *Bürgerliches Gesetzbuch mit Nebengesetzen*, vol. 2, 2nd edn (C. H. Beck, 2008), §305b, para. 17; W. Teske, *Schriftformklauseln in Allgemeinen Geschäftsbedingungen* (Hetmanns, 1990), p. 165; P. Ulmer, in P. Ulmer, E. Brandner and H.-D. Hensen, *AGB-Gesetz.: Kommentar zum Gesetz zur Regelung des Rechts der Allgemeinen Geschäftsbedingungen*, 9th edn (Verlag Dr. Otto Schmidt, 2001), §4, para. 39; G. von Westphalen, *Vertragsrecht und AGB Klauselwerke* (C. H. Beck, 2003), para. 37; M. Wolf, in M. Wolf, N. Horn and W. Lindacher (eds.), *AGB-Gesetz: Gesetz zur Regelung der Allgemeinen Geschäftsbedingungen*, 4th edn (1999), §9, para. S 50.

[63] BGHZ 79, 281 = NJW 1981, 922; BGH NJW 2000, 207 (208).

the contract document is the final and entire agreement of the parties.[64] It can be established in several ways that additions or modifications have been agreed upon.[65] Correspondingly, the parol evidence rule is less strictly applied in England than in the US. English common law allows many more exceptions to the rule than the laws of US states.[66]

5.1.1.3 US law   In the US, the courts of most US states regard merger clauses as establishing an almost irrebuttable presumption of the finality and completeness of the contract.[67] This corresponds to the stricter application of the parol evidence rule in the US. Moreover, a merger clause may, under certain circumstances, even exclude extrinsic evidence as a means for the interpretation of the contract.[68]

5.1.1.4 Discussion   The meaning and effects of an entire agreement clause differ less between German and English law, whereas marked differences exist between German law and the law of most US states. If, for instance, the parties have orally agreed on certain specifications for certain products but have not included the specifications in their written contract, under German law, the entire agreement clause generally does not hinder a party from proving, by all available means, that the specifications are part of the agreement. Nonetheless, this proof is a rather heavy burden. The plaintiff must prove that, despite the written contract, a valid additional agreement was reached. In particular, the plaintiff must explain and prove why the agreed addition or modification was not made part of the written contract.

---

[64] *Brikom Investments Ltd* v . *Carr and Others* [1979] 2 All ER 753; *Henderson* v. *Commercial Union Investment Management Ltd and Another* (unreported, 22 January 1998, Lexis); *1406 Pub Company Ltd* v. *Hoare and Another* (unreported, 2 March 2001, Lexis); *Ravennavi SpA* v. *New Century Shipbuilding Co. Ltd* [2007] 2 Lloyd's Rep. 24; Lewison, *The Interpretation of Contracts*, pp. 99ff.; but *contra* (irrebuttable presumption) *Inntrepreneur Pub Co. Ltd* v . *East Crown Ltd* [2000] 2 Lloyd's Rep. 611; see also Kaufmann, *Parol Evidence Rule*, p. 147 ff.; Meyer, 'Die privatautonome Abbedingung'; Lewison, *The Interpretation of Contracts*, pp. 580ff.

[65] See thereto Lewison, *The Interpretation of Contracts*, pp. 99ff.

[66] For English law, see Lewison, *The Interpretation of Contracts*, pp. 85ff.; for US law, see Farnsworth, *Farnsworth on Contracts*, §§7.2ff.

[67] See Farnsworth, *Farnsworth on Contracts*, §7.3 (pp. 225ff.: 'It is difficult to see why their effect should not be conclusive'); see further the comprehensive survey by Kaufmann, *Parol Evidence Rule*, pp. 157ff.; also Meyer, 'Die privatautonome Abbedingung', 575ff.

[68] See thereto, for instance, *767 Third Avenue LLC* v . *Orix Capital Markets, LLC*, 800 N.Y.S. 2d 357 (N.Y. Sup. Ct., 2005); see also Meyer, 'Die privatautonome Abbedingung', 575.

Under US law, it is likely that in the same situation, no proof of any addition or modification would be allowed.[69] Under English law, the many exceptions to the parol evidence rule make it probable that the oral agreement could be taken into account, for instance, on account of mistake, rectification or the like.

Thus, the German and the US understanding of the entire agreement clause would probably lead to different solutions, whereas in most cases, the German and the English understanding would not influence the final outcome. It therefore matters as to whether the clause is to be given its German or its US meaning, while the difference between the German and the English understanding can almost be neglected.

When faced with a merger clause drafted in common law style in a situation where German law is the *lex contractus*, the guiding principle should be first the explicitly and then the impliedly expressed intentions of the parties. Like the general aims of private international law, it should be the aim of the interpreter to rely on the understanding that the parties in fact intended and that is closest to them in the circumstances of the case.[70]

If in a hypothetical case both parties were German merchants who use an entire agreement clause, there is neither any need nor any reasonable justification to infer the parties' intention to apply the US meaning, unless the parties have unambiguously made clear that the US meaning should prevail or unless the contract has a close connection to a *specific* US state, so that it is reasonable for the parties and the performance of the contract to adhere to the US meaning valid in the specific US state. More or less, this is the outcome of the BGH decision of 1992 mentioned above.[71] There the Court set aside the dogma that foreign law-style contracts should be always interpreted according to the foreign law and should rely on the understanding familiar to both parties.[72]

On the contrary, if, rarely enough, German courts were assigned a case where both parties were US merchants, then it is generally justified to infer the parties' intention to interpret the merger clause in the sense familiar to both parties, despite German law being the *lex contractus*; again, unless the parties clearly agreed otherwise or the contract is closely

---

[69] It must, however, always be noted that there are differences between the single US states even with respect to the effects of a merger clause. It is therefore an oversimplification to speak of 'the US law' here.

[70] See also above in Section 4 *in fine*.   [71] BGH NJW-RR 1992, 423; see above in Section 4.

[72] BGH NJW-RR 1992, 425.

connected with Germany. However, even if the US meaning prevails, things may become more difficult, namely if both US merchants were located in US jurisdictions which give merger clauses different effects. This is certainly no reason to go back to the *lex contractus* and to interpret the merger clause according to German law. An option could be to apply the meaning that prevails among the US states, while another option would be to take the meaning of the US jurisdiction with which the contract and the parties are most closely connected. The latter option appears to be preferable, because it gives relief from the difficult task of determining the prevailing US meaning.

If, however, both parties were merchants from different non-common law countries, again, their clear agreement on the interpretation method or on the understanding of certain clauses and terms must prevail. Whether they impliedly chose the background law as a separate *lex interpretionis* depends on the circumstances. The mere use of a common law-style contract form alone should not suffice. Further circumstances should indicate a respective intention of the parties.

5.1.2   No oral amendments clauses

In common law jurisdictions, no oral amendments clauses often use the following language:

> No amendment or variation to this Agreement shall take effect unless it is in writing, signed by authorised representatives of each of the Parties.

5.1.2.1 German law   Under German law, no oral amendments clauses (Schriftformklauseln)[73] are not generally invalid even if contained in standard terms.[74] However, if their language appears to prohibit a party from relying on a different oral agreement that the parties reached afterwards, then such clauses are invalid, because they violate two central provisions on standard contract terms: they neglect the preference of individually negotiated contract terms (§305b of the BGB) and disfavour the other party in an unreasonable and inadequate way (§307 of the BGB).[75] A clause that requires writing for any modification of a contract can always be set aside by an oral agreement (provided that a clear agreement of the parties to disregard the prior form requirement can

---

[73] In German, 'Änderungen oder Ergänzungen bedürfen der Schriftform'.
[74] BGH NJW 1982, 331; BGH NJW 19985, 320ff.; BGH NJW 1986, 1809; BGH NJW 1991, 1750; BGH NJW 1995, 1488; BGH NJW 2006, 138.
[75] See the decisions cited in the preceding note.

be proved).[76] These rules apply not only to transactions with consumers, but also to those between commercial contract parties.[77]

In sum, under German law, no oral amendments clauses do not exclude the other party from relying on an oral modification or addition to the contract upon which the parties clearly agreed after they concluded the contract.

5.1.2.2 English law   Under English law, a no oral amendments clause is likely to be interpreted rather strictly so that the parties are generally bound by that clause. In conformity with the parol evidence rule, proof of an oral modification would generally be inadmissible.[78]

5.1.2.3 US law   Most US states provide that under a no oral amendments clause, a contract can generally be modified only in writing.[79] This is the solution of the Uniform Commercial Code, which has been adopted by all US jurisdictions.[80] An oral modification has, in principle, no effect except where, under certain circumstances, it is inequitable that a party invokes the clause against the other, who reasonably relied on the oral modification.

5.1.2.4 Discussion   No oral amendments clauses may lead to different solutions under German and common law, in particular US law. However, this will not always be the case. While under German law it is necessary to prove a clear agreement modifying the original writing requirement, under US law it must be shown that reliance on the form requirement would be inadequate. The final solutions will thus not always vary; however, it can be decisive whether the German or US understanding applies.

In concrete cases where the solutions vary, it must be determined which understanding should be preferred. This question must be answered in the same way as discussed before. The interpretation follows

---

[76] BGH NJW 1985, 320 (322: 'Eine Schriftlichkeitsklausel kann dadurch außer Kraft gesetzt werden, dass die Vertragschließenden deutlich den Willen zum Ausdruck bringen, die mündlich getroffene Abrede solle ungeachtet dieser Klausel gelten'); BGH NJW 1995, 1488.

[77] See BGH NJW 2006, 138 (concerning a lease between commercial parties).

[78] In *Henderson* v . *Arthur* [1907] 1 KB 10, even without a no oral amendments clause, the proof of an oral modification was rejected.

[79] See Farnsworth, *Farnsworth on Contracts*, §§7(6) and 7(6)(a).

[80] See Section 2-209(2) of the UCC.

the *lex contractus* unless there is a clear indication that the parties intended a different *lex interpretionis*. The mere use of a contract drafted in common law style, *per se*, should not be the indication. As mentioned, the German courts still apply the meaning of the foreign law unless there are sufficient indications that the parties had another intention.

5.2 Clauses that use a terminology with legal effects not known to the applicable law

The contract may use terms with legal effects that are either unknown in the applicable law or, in their technical meaning, unknown to the law that governs the contract. The *lex contractus* is then of little or no help in interpreting such terms.[81] A most obvious example of this kind could be found in the marriage contracts of Islamic couples where the parties regularly agree on a *mahr*[82] or dower, a legal institute unknown today other than in Islam-oriented countries. If German law governs the contract,[83] it is more or less necessary to go back to the law with which the parties are connected and where such legal institution is known.[84] Furthermore, it will regularly be the parties' explicit or tacit intention to understand the term in that sense.

In commercial contracts, rather than the use of completely strange terms, it is more often the case that a term or phrase also known to the *lex contractus* has acquired a different specific technical meaning in the law of the contract's language. As mentioned, 'consideration' is an example of this.[85] Another is the word 'indemnity'. In German, it is generally translated as 'Entschädigung', a neutral term equivalent to compensation. In legal English, it is generally a term of art meaning an assurance to indemnify someone against his or her liability towards the indemnifier or a third person.[86]

---

[81] See already above in Section 3.5.

[82] A sum of money the bridegroom has to pay, at least to promise to pay to the bride because of the marriage; see thereon W. Wurmnest, 'Die Mär von der *mahr* – Zur Qualifikation von Ansprüchen aus Brautgabevereinbarungen', *Rabels Zeitschrift für Ausländisches und Internationales Privatrechts*, 71 (2007), 527–558; N. Yassari, 'Die Brautgabe im iranischen Recht', *Das Standesamt* (2003), 198–201.

[83] This would be the case where, e.g., a Syrian bride and an Iraqi bridegroom who both live in Germany marry.

[84] See OLG Hamburg FamRZ 2004, 459.   [85] See above in Section 3.5.

[86] See *Jowitt's Dictionary of English Law*, vol. I, 2nd edn by J. Burke (Sweet & Maxwell, 1977), 959.

5.2.1   Indemnity clauses

Indemnity clauses as drafted in common law jurisdictions can have rather different fields of application. Their wording may therefore vary widely. Examples include the following clauses:

1) Contractor shall indemnify Company Group from and against any claim concerning:
   a) personal injury to or loss of life of any employee of Contractor Group, and
   b) loss or damage to any property of Contractor Group,
   and arising out of or in connection with the Work or caused by the Contract Object in its lifetime. This applies regardless of any form of liability, whether strict or by negligence, in whatever form, on the part of the Company Group.
2) Indemnity for non-performance of this Charter-party, proved damages, not exceeding amount of freight. (GENCON Charter 1976 No. 12)[87]
3) Termination indemnity: 12 months or legal benefit if higher.[88]

5.2.1.1 German law   In German law, indemnity clauses do not, *per se*, have a specific technical meaning. Their meaning and interpretation depends on their precise language and context. They can mean a penalty (Vertragsstrafe) as well as a liquidated damages clause (Schadenspauschalierung) or the obligation to indemnify the other party against the claims of others (Haftungsfreistellung). In commercial contracts between merchants, all these kinds of contract terms are, in principle, valid even if contained in standard contract terms.[89] However, penalty clauses are only enforceable if the penalty sum is not excessively high.[90] In addition, the clause must regularly require fault.[91] Liquidated damages clauses, in particular in standard terms, are valid if the agreed damages do not exceed the amount that could be expected in the ordinary course of events. Moreover, liquidated damages clauses must not exclude the possibility of proving that

---

[87] The GENCON Charter 1994 does not contain a similar provision.

[88] See OLG Frankfurt NJW-RR 1995, 36 (employment contract with a company director).

[89] BGH BB 1995, 1437; BGH NJW 2003, 2158; D. Coester-Waltjen, in *Staudingers Kommentar zum Bürgerlichen Gesetzbuch*, §309 No. 6, para. 28.

[90] BGH WM 1990, 1198; BGH NJW-RR 1998, 1508.

[91] See thereto Coester-Waltjen, in *Staudingers Kommentar zum Bürgerlichen Gesetzbuch*, §309, No. 6, para. 28.

the real loss was less than the agreed amount.[92] In contrast to penalty clauses, liquidated damages clauses require that, in principle, damage has occurred. On the contrary, German law does not allow the cumulation of a penalty and a damages claim for the same breach of contract. However, further losses not covered by the penalty can still be claimed.[93]

For the validity of indemnity clauses in the sense of English law, German law provides no specific requirements. If contained in standard contract terms, they must comply with the general adequacy test for such terms as laid down in §307 of the BGB.

The German court decisions that dealt with the term 'indemnity' in common law-style drafted contracts rejected a specific English meaning of the term. The Federal Court relied on the German meaning of the word because the parties were both German.[94] The OLG Frankfurt came to the same conclusion mainly because the addressee of the clause was a German employee.[95]

5.2.1.2 English law Under English law, indemnity clauses mean that the indemnifier has agreed to indemnify the other party against a liability that this party may incur either towards the indemnifier itself or towards a third party.[96] Such clauses are valid. In principle, they are to be interpreted in the same way as exemption clauses.[97] That means that they are being interpreted narrowly and, in case of any doubt or ambiguity, against the party promising the indemnity.[98]

5.2.1.3 US law In US law, indemnity clauses appear to have the same technical meaning as in English law.[99] Unless the indemnity is for an illegal act, an indemnity clause is generally valid.[100] It has to be interpreted in the same strict sense as exclusion clauses.[101]

---

[92] See §309, No. 5 of the BGB; thereon BGH NJW-RR 2003, 1056; Grüneberg, in *Palandt, BGB*, §309, para. 32; Coester-Waltjen, in *Staudingers Kommentar zum Bürgerlichen Gesetzbuch*, §309 No. 5, paras. 25ff.

[93] §340(2) of the BGB. [94] BGH NJW-RR 1992, 423.

[95] OLG Frankfurt NJW-RR 1995, 36.

[96] Lewison, *The Interpretation of Contracts*, p. 479. [97] See thereto *ibid.*, pp. 479ff.

[98] See, for instance, *White* v. *Warwick (John) & Co. Ltd* [1953] 1 WLR 1285; *Murfin* v . *United Steel Co. Ltd* [1957] 1 WLR 104; *Dairy Containers Ltd* v. *Tasman Orient Line CV* [2005] 1 WLR 215; Lewison, *The Interpretation of Contracts*, pp. 450ff.

[99] See cases such as *Jewett Publishing Co.* v. *Butler*, 34 N.E. 1087 (MA 1893); *Williams* v. *White Mountain Constr. Co.*, 749 P.2d 423 (CO 1988).

[100] See, for instance, *Atkins* v . *Johnson*, 43 Vt. 78 (1870).

[101] Farnsworth, *Farnsworth on Contracts*, §5.2 No. 17.

5.2.1.4 Discussion   Clauses containing the term 'indemnity' are particularly suited to be interpreted differently since the term translated into German (Entschädigung) is easily understood but lacks the legal connotations it carries in legal English.[102] Whether the German or the English/US meaning should prevail should again depend on the parties' express or tacit understanding. It is therefore correct that German courts have interpreted clauses using the term 'indemnity' in the sense that the parties or the addressee of the clause have most likely understood them.[103]

5.2.2   Liquidated damages clauses

A liquidated damages clause may read as follows:

> If, due to the fault of the Seller, the goods have not been delivered at dates according to the delivery schedule as provided in this Agreement, the Seller shall be obliged to pay to the buyer liquidated damages for such delayed delivery at the following rates:
>   i) For each complete week, the liquidated damages shall be 0.5% of the value of the goods delayed.
> ii) The total amount of the above mentioned liquidated damages will not exceed 25% of the price for the delayed goods.
> iii) The payment of liquidated damages shall not release the Seller from its obligation to continuously deliver the goods.

5.2.2.1 German law   As already indicated, in German law, liquidated damages clauses can be validly agreed upon between merchants even in standard form.[104] In contrast to indemnity clauses, they have a specific technical meaning. A clause is a liquidated damages clause and not a penalty clause if the agreed amount is adjusted at, and corresponds to, the damages amount which could be expected in the ordinary course of events.[105] Moreover, liquidated damages clauses even between merchants must not exclude the possibility of proving that the real loss was less than the agreed amount.[106] If the clause complies with these requirements, it would be enforceable.

---

[102] For this phenomenon see also Triebel and Balthasar, 'Auslegung englischsprachiger Vertragstexte', 2190.
[103] See BGH NJW-RR 1992, 423; OLG Frankfurt NJW-RR 1995, 36.
[104] BGHZ 67, 312; BGH NJW-RR 2000, 719.   [105] See the text of §309, No. 5 of the BGB.
[106] See §309, No. 5 of the BGB; thereon BGH NJW-RR 2003, 1056; Grüneberg, in *Palandt, BGB*, §309, para. 32; Coester-Waltjen, in *Staudingers Kommentar zum Bürgerlichen Gesetzbuch*, §309 No. 5, paras. 25ff.

5.2.2.2 English law Under English law, penalty clauses are generally invalid while liquidated damages clauses are admitted.[107] The distinction between them depends on whether the clause primarily intends to deter the other party from breaking the contract by an *in terrorem* effect (penalty) or to compensate for the loss caused by a breach (liquidated damages).[108]

5.2.2.3 US law In the US, as in England, penalty clauses are not permitted, whereas liquidated damages clauses are allowed as long as they do not clearly disregard the principle of compensation and excessively exceed the presumed loss.[109]

5.2.2.4 Discussion In both German law and the common law, the distinction between penalty clauses and liquidated damages is difficult.[110] However, while German law allows penalties to a certain extent and the common law prohibits them, the distinction and the question of whether the German or the English/US solution applies can become decisive. The answer should again depend on the parties' express or implied understanding.

5.2.3   Conclusion

Where a contract uses terms unknown to the *lex contractus*, the latter can give no guidance in their interpretation. This is at least true where it is clear from the parties' express or tacit agreement that they meant the term to be understood in its technical meaning. In this case, this technical meaning has to be accepted. However, if the parties agreed on a different meaning, that other meaning must prevail.

The same solution should apply where a term has acquired a technical meaning in the background law of the contract, even though this meaning might be unfamiliar to the *lex contractus*.

5.3   Contract clauses that regulate matters already regulated in the applicable law

Rather often, contract clauses regulate matters that the applicable law also regulates. As far as the applicable law is mandatory, it enjoys priority

---

[107] Lewison, *The Interpretation of Contracts*, p. 591 with references.

[108] See, e.g., *Lordsvale Finance Plc* v. *Bank of Zambia* [1996] QB 752.

[109] See extensively thereon Farnsworth, *Farnsworth on Contracts*, §12.18.

[110] For a comparison of the European solutions for penalty clauses, see H. Schelhaas, 'The Judicial Power to Reduce a Penalty', *Zeitschrift für Europäisches Privatrecht* (2004), 386–398.

over the contract regulations. Problems can, however, arise with respect to interpretation when the rules of the applicable law are non-mandatory. The question is always whether the contractual regulation is final and exclusive or whether it can and should be supplemented by the non-mandatory rules of the *lex contractus*. Again, this is first a matter of the applicable *lex interpretionis* and then of interpretation. Two kinds of such clauses – *force majeure* clauses and hardship clauses – will be discussed.

5.3.1 *Force majeure* clauses

A *force majeure* clause in common law style can be drafted in the following way:

> The Supplier shall not be liable for delay in performing or for failure to perform its obligations if the delay or failure results from the following: (i) Acts of God, (ii) outbreak of hostilities, riot, civil disturbance, acts of terrorism, (iii) the act of any government or authority (including refusal or revocation of any licence or consent), (iv) fire, explosion, flood, fog or bad weather, (v) power failure, failure of telecommunications lines, failure or breakdown of plant, machinery or vehicles, (vi) default of suppliers or sub-contractors, (vii) theft, malicious damage, strike, lock-out or industrial action of any kind, and (viii) any cause or circumstance whatsoever beyond the Supplier's reasonable control.

5.3.1.1 German law   The German law of obligations is still essentially based on the fault principle, though fault in any deficit of performance of the contractual obligations is presumed.[111] The debtor is thus generally not liable in a case of *force majeure*. Exemption clauses for *force majeure* are therefore less necessary than in legal systems that base their contract law, in principle, on strict liability. Nonetheless, such clauses (like the cited one) are used and they are valid. The term *force majeure* ('höhere Gewalt') is a term of art in German statutory law.[112] The courts define it as an extraordinary external event that is unavoidable.[113] The term includes not only natural events such as flooding, storm, etc., but also unavoidable acts of third persons like criminals.

---

[111] See, in particular, §§276 and 280(1)(2) of the BGB.

[112] See, for instance, §7(2) Straßenverkehrsgesetz (StVG – Road Traffic Act); §1(2) Haftpflichtgesetz (HaftPflG – Liability Act), where 'höhere Gewalt' is an excuse against strict liability.

[113] See BGH NJW 1953, 184; BGH VersR 1976, 963; BGH NJW 1988, 2733; W. Filthaut, *Haftpflichtgesetz*, 6th edn (C. H. Beck, 2010), §1, paras. 158ff.

It is rather likely that German courts, when called upon to interpret the mere formulation 'acts of God', would be confronted with the translation 'höhere Gewalt' (foreign language texts have generally to be translated).[114] And it is equally likely that the court would take the German meaning cited above unless the meaning of 'acts of God' could be inferred from the whole clause (as in the model clause cited above).[115] But without such explanation and help for interpretation, it is quite probable that the court would not even be aware that there is an interpretation problem because of the difference between 'acts of God' and 'höhere Gewalt'.

5.3.1.2 English law

Under English law, parties are, in principle, relieved from their agreed contractual duties if an unavoidable event or act occurs that renders performance of these duties impossible (discharge by frustration).[116] A *force majeure* clause of the kind quoted above would more or less merely specify this state of the law. Such a clause would therefore be valid.[117] Although the distinction is difficult to draw, *force majeure* clauses are said not to be exemption clauses[118] that must be strictly interpreted.[119] However, the so-called *ejusdem generis* principle could lead to a restriction where the listed exempting events were of the same genus (for instance, only natural events).[120] In that case, the clause would cover only comparable events. The formulation 'any cause beyond a party's control' does, however, prevent such restriction.[121] Under English law, 'acts of God' do not include anything other than natural events without any human intervention.[122] Whether the law on frustration can supplement *force majeure* clauses depends greatly on

---

[114] See §184 of the Gerichtsverfassungsgesetz (GVG – Act on the Constitution of Courts): 'The language before the court is German.'

[115] See thereto in the same sense Triebel and Balthasar, 'Auslegung englischsprachiger Vertragstexte', 2191, relying on an unpublished decision of LG Bochum (27 April 1976 – 12 O 18/76) which interpreted the German translation of 'act of God' as 'höhere Gewalt' in the sense used in Germany.

[116] See H. Beale, *Chitty on Contracts*, vol. I, 30th edn (Sweet & Maxwell, 2008), paras. 23–001ff. with extensive references.

[117] For *force majeure* clauses, see Beale, *Chitty on Contracts*, paras. 14–126ff. In *Dorset County Council* v . *Southern Felt Roofing* (1989) 48 BLR 96 (CA), the agreed risk that a party had accepted of damage caused by fire, lightning, explosion, aircraft and other aerial devices was held not to exclude liability for fire caused by negligence.

[118] See thereto Beale, *Chitty on Contracts*, para. 14–126 with references.   [119] See note 98.

[120] See on this doctrine extensively with many references Lewison, *The Interpretation of Contracts*, pp. 279ff.

[121] Beale, *Chitty on Contracts*, para. 14–127.   [122] *Ibid.*, para. 14–137.

the language of the respective clause. It is likely that in the interpretation of the above-quoted model clause, English courts would rely on the meaning given to certain terms (in particular, 'acts of God') by English case law.

5.3.1.3 US law The state of US law concerning events rendering performance impossible corresponds in principle to English law.[123] Equally, *force majeure* clauses generally confirm the existing law and are therefore valid.[124]

5.3.1.4 Discussion The question of whether *force majeure* clauses can be supplemented by national law depends on their formulation. The more detailed the clause, the less it leaves room for any supplement.

In interpreting English *force majeure* clauses, there is the danger that German courts may not be aware of differences of meaning, for instance, of terms such as 'acts of God'.

5.3.2   Hardship clauses

Hardship clauses can be encountered in the following form:

> Where the performance of a contract becomes more onerous for one of the parties, that party is nevertheless bound to perform its obligations subject to the following provisions on hardship.
>
> There is hardship where the occurrence of events fundamentally alters the equilibrium of the contract either because the cost of a party's performance has increased or because the value of the performance a party receives has diminished, and
> a) the event was beyond its reasonable control and was one which it could not reasonably have been expected to have taken into account at the time of the conclusion of the contract; and that
> b) the event or its consequences could not reasonably be avoided or overcome.

If such hardship occurs, the parties are bound, within a reasonable time of the invocation of this clause, to negotiate alternative contractual terms which reasonably allow for the consequences of the event.

5.3.2.1 German law Since the reform of the law of obligations in 2002, German statutory law acknowledges expressly that parties can request an

---

[123] See Farnsworth, *Farnsworth on Contracts*, §§9(5)ff.
[124] As to their drafting, see *ibid.*, §9(9)(a).

adjustment of the contract if circumstances that constituted the basis of the contract have fundamentally changed (Störung der Geschäfts-grundlage).[125] This regulation covers the case of hardship in the sense that performance has become more onerous.[126]

If the parties have agreed on a hardship clause, statute itself gives their agreement preference over the statutory regulation.[127]

5.3.2.2 English law Depending on their precise formulation, English law would generally regard hardship clauses as valid.[128] They prevail over the doctrine of frustration under which a party may be relieved of its obligation.

5.3.2.3 US law Similarly, in US law, hardship clauses are fully accepted.[129] They confirm and specify for the respective contract the otherwise rather vague doctrine of economic impracticability.

6 Final conclusions

In common with the general aims of private international law, it should be the aim of the interpretation of international contracts to uncover the understanding that the parties in fact intended or that is closest to them and their interests in the circumstances of the case.

Between common law and civil law jurisdictions, there are still differences in the method of interpretation of contracts and their terms. It therefore matters which law governs the interpretation issue. In principle, this is the law that governs the contract as a whole, whether this law is chosen by the parties or objectively designated. This *lex contractus* is generally also the *lex interpretionis*. However, generally, terms which are known to have acquired a precise technical meaning in a specific legal system will be understood in that sense.

In principle, national interpretation methods govern the construction of international contracts. Wherever possible, the national method should, however, be 'internationalised' where international contracts are involved. This means that where an international meaning of terms

---

[125] §313 of the BGB.   [126] Grüneberg, in *Palandt, BGB*, §275, para. 21.

[127] See §313(1) of the BGB; see also BGHZ 81, 143; BGHZ 90, 69 (74); BGH NJW 2005, 205 (206); Grüneberg, in *Palandt, BGB*, §313, para. 10.

[128] See Beale, *Chitty on Contracts*, para. 23–056.

[129] See thereto and to their drafting Farnsworth, *Farnsworth on Contracts*, §9(9)(a).

and phrases can be identified, this meaning should be preferred to a purely national meaning, unless there are clear indications that the parties agreed on a different meaning. International sets of principles, in particular the UNIDROIT Principles of International Commercial Contracts, are helpful in revealing an almost uniform international understanding of certain contract clauses or terms.

The rule that the *lex contractus* is generally the *lex interpretionis* of a contract becomes problematic when a contract is drafted in the style and on the basis of a specific law, while the *lex contractus* is another law. The law governing the contract may then differ from the law on whose background the contract was drafted. First, the parties are always free to choose explicitly a *lex interpretionis* that differs from the *lex contractus*, for instance, by using a construction clause. Secondly, the parties may also tacitly choose a separate *lex interpretionis*. Such a choice will depend on the parties' express or implied intentions. Although it is contrary to the general principle enunciated, and as a result is often modified by German courts, the mere drafting of a contract in English using common law terminology should in itself not be regarded as a tacit choice of English or US law as the *lex interpretionis*. Today, both the language and the common law terminology are too insignificant to indicate the choice of the law of a specific common law jurisdiction. Further indicative circumstances should be necessary for a tacit choice of such a law, for instance, the citizenship of and/or habitual residence of the parties in the same common law jurisdiction, and the negotiation, conclusion and performance of the contract in the same common law jurisdiction. Where such circumstances are lacking, the *lex contractus* remains the *lex interpretionis*.

There are contract situations where the interpretation of contract clauses and terms must necessarily be 'international'. This is the case with contracts to which uniform law conventions apply and, further, where the contract uses internationally unified terms (such as INCOTERMS) or where the contract is concluded according to an internationally standardised contract form. The international method of interpretation means here that courts and tribunals must strive for uniform principles of interpretation, must try to find and maintain a uniform meaning of specific contract terms and expressions, and must take into account the relevant case law of other countries.

When German courts are faced with concrete contract clauses drafted in common law style in a situation where German law is the *lex contractus,* the guiding principle should be first the explicitly and then the impliedly expressed intentions of the parties. If both parties were German merchants who use a contract drafted in common law style, there is no justification to infer their intention to apply the meaning familiar in a specific common law jurisdiction unless the parties have unambiguously made clear that this meaning should prevail, or unless the contract has a close connection to that specific common law state so that it is reasonable for the parties and the performance of the contract to adhere to the meaning valid in this state. Where, on the other hand, both parties were merchants from a common law jurisdiction, it is generally justified to infer their intention to interpret the respective clause in the sense familiar to both parties, despite German law acting as the *lex contractus*, except where the parties clearly agreed otherwise or the contract is closely connected with Germany. On the other hand, if both parties were merchants from different non-common law countries, again their clear agreement on the interpretation method or on the understanding of certain clauses and terms must prevail. Whether they impliedly chose the background law as a separate *lex interpretionis* depends on the circumstances. The mere use of a common law-style contract form alone should not suffice. Additional circumstances should be necessary to indicate that intention.

9

The Romanistic tradition: application of boilerplate clauses under French law

XAVIER LAGARDE, DAVID MÉHEUT AND JEAN-MICHEL
REVERSAC

1   Preliminary observations

Even in international matters, there is no such thing as 'lawless contracts' under French law,[1] although it is perfectly admissible in international arbitrations to provide that the arbitral tribunal shall rule in 'amiable composition', which does not require the tribunal to apply a law except for fundamental rules of due process and international public policy. However, by virtue of the principle of contractual freedom, a contract governed by French law may also refer to other norms and customs, e.g., the trade practices of the shipping industry. The general observations contained in this chapter must therefore be adapted to the specific business norms and customs that may apply to a given contract according to the field of activity involved.

These general observations should also be qualified to take into account the general approach of French judges towards contracts. The Civil Code does contain a few rules of construction in Articles 1156–1164. One should, however, point out certain qualifications regarding their exact scope and effect:

- First of all, the French Supreme Court decided that these rules of interpretation are not mandatory.[2]
  This lack of mandatory character applies to all rules of interpretation, including the rule provided by Article 1162 of the Civil Code, according

---

[1] Messageries Maritimes, Cass. Civ, 21 June 1950, RCDIP 1956.609, note Batiffol; Siret 1952.1.1 note Niboyet: 'Tout contrat international est nécessairement attaché à la loi d'un Etat.'

[2] Cass. Civ. 1, 6 March 1979, Bull I, no. 81; Cass. Com., 10 July 2001, No. 97–21.648, JCP G 2002, II, No. 10072; Cass. Civ. 1, 1 March 2005, No. 02–16.802.

to which: 'when in doubt a contract is interpreted against he who stipulated and in favour of he who contracted the obligation.'[3] This is the equivalent of the English law principle of *contra proferentem*. The rule may, however, be mandatory for certain categories of contract if there is a specific provision to that effect, as is, for instance, the case for contracts between a consumer and a professional (Article 133(2) of the Code de la consommation).

 – Moreover, construction of a contract is an issue of fact and not an issue of law. This means that no appeal to the French Supreme Court for civil matters (Cour de cassation) is permissible,[4] save in case of blatant distortion of the clear stipulations of the contract ('dénaturation de stipulations claires et précises').[5]

 – Article 1134 of the Civil Code provides that 'legally formed agreements have the force of law between the parties that made them' but immediately adds that agreements 'must be performed in good faith' (Article 1134, §3 of the Civil Code). The requirement of good faith under the Civil Code is always a source of amazement for common law lawyers and it is important to define the scope of that principle inasmuch as it can be defined.

As regards the duty to perform the contract in good faith, one can summarise it as a duty to go beyond the letter of the contract. This can essentially occur in two types of circumstances:

 • the strict application of the contract would be particularly harmful to one of the parties;
 • the strict application of the contract would not conform to the actual intention of the parties.

The effect of the principle of good faith is best illustrated by giving a few examples taken in an abundant case law:

 • a party was found in bad faith when he suddenly invoked a de jure termination clause after he had let the breach continue without reacting;[6]
 • a bank which failed to exercise its right to immediate full payment ('déchéance du terme') for six years was found to be in breach of its obligation of good faith when it then sought the payment of interest and penalties for late payment;[7]
 • a company was found to be in bad faith for preventing its distributor from applying competitive prices;[8]

---

[3] Cass. Soc. 1975, Bull. V, No. 93.
[4] Cass. sect. réunies, 2 Febuaury 1808, GAJC, 12th edn No. 159.
[5] Cass. Civ., 15 April 1872, GAJC No. 160.
[6] Cass. Civ. 1, 16 February 1999, Bull. Civ. I, No. 52.
[7] Cass. Civ. 1, 31 January 1995: Bull. Civ. I, No. 57; Defrénois 1995. 749, obs. Delebecque.
[8] Cas. Com. 24 November 1998: Bull. Civ. IV, No. 277; D. 1999. IR 9; JCP 1999. II. 10210, note Picod; *ibid*. I. 143, No. 6 s., obs. Jamin; Defrénois 1999. 371, obs. D. Mazeaud; RTD civ. 1999. 98, obs. Mestre, and 646, obs. Gautier.

- a seller who had told the buyer that he would not perform the sale was found to be in bad faith when he sought to hold the contract unenforceable as the buyer subsequently failed to comply with a suspensive condition.[9]

This could seem quite far-reaching and to be contrary to legal certainty. However, the French Supreme Court has recently ruled that if the rule of good faith allows a court to sanction the disloyal use of a contractual prerogative, it does not allow the court to affect the very substance of the rights and obligations legally agreed upon by the parties.[10]

In other words, the duty to perform in good faith is complementary to the doctrine of *pacta sunt servanda* and is by no means in contradiction to it.

Article 1135 of the same Code also provides that they 'bind not only to what is expressed, but also to all the consequences that equity, usage or law confer to an obligation in accordance with its nature'.[11]

This provision goes further than the mere compliance with the requirement of good faith in the performance of the contract. Indeed, it is not just a matter of matching the spirit of the contract against its letter. The purpose is, in an objective way, to add obligations to a contract. The two main obligations of that kind are as follows:

- A general obligation of safety ('obligation de sécurité') that is imposed on most professionals. This can be defined as an obligation to ensure that no harm is caused to the other party or his or her belongings as a result of the contract. This is often applied to contracts of transport but there is no restriction as to the scope of application of this obligation of safety.
- The duty of information and advice ('obligation d'information et de conseil'), the scope of which is also general. A professional is supposed to inform and advise the other party against the normal risks and specificities of a contract, even if that other party is a professional. However, the intensity of this duty depends on the respective knowledge and skills of the parties.

[9] Cass. Civ. 3, 23 June 2004: Bull. Civ. III, No. 132; D. 2005. 1532, note Kenfack; Contrats Concurrence Consommation 2004, No. 154, note Leveneur.
[10] Cass. Com. 10 July 2007, Bull. Civ. IV, No. 188; D. 2007. 2839, note Stoffel-Munck and note Gautier; *ibid.* AJ 1955, obs. Delpech; ibid Chron. C. Cass. 2769, obs. Salomon; *ibid.* Pan. 2972, obs. Fauvarque-Cosson; JCP 2007. II. 10154, note Houtcieff; JCP E 2007. 2394, note Mainguy; Defrénois 2007. 1454, obs. Savaux; Contrats Concurrence Consommation 2007, No. 294, note Leveneur; RLDC 2008/46, No. 2840, note Delebecque; Dr. et patr., September 2007, p. 94, obs. Stoffel-Munck; RDC 2007. 1107, obs. Aynès, and 1110, obs. D. Mazeaud; RTD Civ. 2007. 773, obs. Fages; RTD Com. 2007. 786, obs. Le Cannu and Dondero.
[11] The word 'equity' is not used in the English sense, i.e., it does not refer to any specific body of law but rather to general notions of fairness.

> The actual content of the obligation to advise or inform depends greatly on the type of contract involved and the specific circumstances of each case. For instance, in engineering contracts, the contractor will generally be expected to warn the other party of the risks associated with a particular engineering technique. The consequences of such obligations can be particularly harsh on bankers who fail to advise inexperienced borrowers or people giving a personal guarantee on the risks of the contemplated operation.[12]

For the sake of completeness, it should be noted that for certain categories of contracts, French law automatically attaches a number of obligations derived from the 'nature' of the contract. In the Civil Code, such rules are generally not mandatory. There are also mandatory rules that are generally found in specific provisions outside the general provisions of the Civil Code. Most frequently they are attached to the exercise of a specific activity, e.g., franchise, insurance, etc.

Lastly, beyond the individual clauses identified below, certain formulations often found in English wordings (e.g., fulfilment of an obligation 'to the satisfaction of X', 'best endeavours', use of the word 'reasonable') are not given the same effect under French law as they would be under English law, for instance:

- Even if there is no case law on this issue, the expression *'to the satisfaction of X'* could be interpreted by a French judge as a *condition potestative*, i.e., left to the power of the beneficiary of the obligation, in that it would leave to the latter the possibility of unilaterally deciding on the good performance of the contract. In practice, it is likely that a French judge would simply ignore this clause and would consider himself or herself competent to appreciate objectively the effect of such a clause.
- The expression 'best endeavours' under English law implies very onerous obligations and is generally opposed to 'reasonable endeavours'. Under French law, there is no uniform interpretation of the expression 'best endeavours' and it is quite likely that it would be less onerous and more uncertain than under English law. Similarly, 'reasonable endeavour' would not be used in French and would be a source of confusion.

It is therefore not advisable to simply change the choice-of-law clause of an English law-wording without having checked those points.

---

[12] E.g., Cass. Ch. Mixte, 29 June 2007, Bull No. 8, JCP 2007 II 10146, note Gouriot.

Having made these preliminary observations, one can now turn to the individual clauses envisaged in this book.

2   Entire agreement ('clause d'intégralité')

There appear to be two purposes to this clause:

- The first purpose would be replace and supersede prior agreements which may have been reached by the agreement contained in the document to which that clause refers.
- The second effect is to suggest that the agreement referred to is the exclusive source of rights and obligation between the parties.

As regards the first effect (replacement of all past agreements), such a clause is frequently used in French law and practice for this purpose and does not present any particular difficulty.

Indeed, it would be analysed as a novation of all prior agreements into a new agreement. French case law only requires that the intention to proceed to a novation be unequivocal and that it clearly results from the stipulations concluded between the parties.[13] There is little doubt that the entire agreement clause under consideration fulfils this condition.

However, it should be noted that prior agreements and documents may obviously be taken into consideration when interpreting the intention of the parties. The clause under consideration would not change that.

As regards the second purpose (the agreement becoming the exclusive source of rights and obligation between the parties), this is more problematic and, to a certain extent, this purpose of the clause is both ineffective and redundant.

It is ineffective in the sense that French case law may impose additional ancillary obligations on the parties. Thus, as explained in the preliminary observations above, French courts often impose obligations of safety as well as obligations of information and advice on professionals, whatever the clauses of the contract may be. In any event, expressly excluding such 'implied obligations' would not necessarily make a difference, since they are often considered to be public policy and, as such, cannot be contracted out.

The second purpose is also redundant as regards the main rights and obligations that have been specifically negotiated between the parties,

---

[13] Cass. Com. 31 January 1983, Bull. Civ. IV, No. 44.

since French courts are loath to add to such rights and obligations in order not to disturb the balance of the contract.[14] As a matter of fact, French courts may even ignore this purpose of the clause in case there is a gap in the conditions of implementation of any obligation (e.g., place of payment). In such a case, the judge would supply the missing stipulation by looking for the intention of the parties or by relying on established practice.

Lastly, this clause does not address the issue of amendments to the contract. This will be dealt with in Section 4 below, but it should be noted that parties could prevent an interpretation that would be based on a supposed modification of the contract by providing that any amendment should be signed and in writing.

3   No waiver

This clause is effective and (to a certain extent) redundant. Indeed, it is a general principle under French law that waiver of a right has to be specifically proven and mere inaction is not normally sufficient to establish the intent to waive a right. The clause under consideration merely incorporates this general principle of French law on waiver of a right. This means that the clause will presumably be interpreted with all the exceptions and qualifications that are applied to the principle under French law.

Thus, French courts sometimes sanction parties whose behaviour is inconsistent with their rights, essentially based on the principle of good faith imposed on all contracts by Article 1134, §3 of the Civil Code. This was, for instance, the case for a party who repeatedly tolerated the non-performance of a debtor and then, suddenly, claimed full payment.[15] The Supreme Court regularly applies this solution against banks.[16] Similarly, one can reasonably think that in the event of a clause providing for the renegotiation of the contract in case of change in circumstances, and in the event that the creditor is late in requesting its implementation (one, two years), one may invoke the behaviour of the latter to prevent him or her from relying on the clause.

---

[14] Cass. Civ. 3, 1 March 1989, RTD Civ. 1991, p. 113, obs. J. Mestre; Cass. Com., 14 October 1997, Defrénois 1998, p. 538, note Y. Dagorne-Labbe; Cass. Civ. 3, 30 May 1996, Contrats Concurrence Consommation 1996, Com. 185 obs. Leveneur.

[15] Cass. Civ. 3, 8 April 1987, P. No. 85–17596, Bull. III, No. 88; Cass. Civ. 1, 16 February 1999, P. No. 96–21997, Bull. I, No. 52.

[16] E.g., Cass. Com., 8 March 2005, P. No. 02–15783, Bull. IV No. 44.

4 No oral amendments

Such a clause is valid insofar as it contains an agreement on the form that an amendment should take. Indeed, parties can reach agreements on the issue of proof as recognised by the French Supreme Court.[17]

It is also useful insofar as, in commercial matters, there is no restriction on means of proof (Article L.110–3 of the Code of Commerce) so that a party could pretend that a written contract was amended orally.

However, it should be mentioned that it is very hard to establish that a contract was concluded orally before a French state court, as testimonies are generally not given significant weight and there is hardly any hearing of witnesses.[18] The best way to prove things in French court proceedings is still to bring written evidence, whether it be the contract itself or written documents evidencing an oral agreement. In that respect, Article 1341 of the Civil Code requires written evidence in civil matters and forbids testimonies against written documents. Even if this article is not binding in commercial matters, it is a model which is recognised by commercial judges.

The clause is also useful in that it not only forbids oral proof of a contract but also requires a signed document. In that respect, one may wonder whether a French judge would recognise the validity of a modification of contract by, say, a mere exchange of emails.

French law recognises electronic signature (Article 1316(4) of the Civil Code) and an electronic document can be considered as a written document (Article 1316(1) of the Civil Code). However, a mere email does not fulfil the requirements of reliability of Articles 1316(1) and 1316(4) and cannot be deemed to be an electronic document bearing an electronic signature that would be recognised as a 'signed written document' for the purpose of the Civil Code.

5 Severability

This clause, which purports to preserve the contract in case one of its clauses is deemed invalid, has to be considered in light of French law on the issue of severability.

---

[17] See Cass. Civ. 1, 8 November 1989, D. 1990, 369.
[18] Things are different in arbitrations where hearing of witnesses and cross-examination can usually take place.

On that issue, Articles 900 and 1172 of the Civil Code bring a distinction between onerous contracts[19] (where both parties bring consideration) and free contracts (where only one party brings consideration). This chapter shall only focus on the first category (onerous contracts).

In the case of onerous contracts, the principle is that the nullity of a stipulation results in the nullity of all others. However, this statutory solution was abandoned by case law. Indeed, the French Supreme Court now considers that the whole contract is only found void if the annulled clause was the determining and fundamental cause of the contract:[20] 'a void clause inserted in an agreement can only result in the nullity of that agreement if it constitutes an essential clause thereof.'

In these conditions and in order to avoid the uncertainty of judicial interpretation on the scope of the consequences of the nullity of one clause, it may prove useful to stipulate that the rest of the contract should be maintained notwithstanding the nullity of one clause.

However, the clause may be disregarded if the annulled clause was so fundamental that it constituted the 'cause' of the contract, i.e., the *raison d'être* of the contract. For instance, if a merchant rents material to develop a business and it is in fact impossible to develop this business, this impossibility will deprive the contract of its 'cause'.[21] Under French law, the requirement of a 'cause' of the contract is a condition of validity of any contract (Article 1131 of the Civil Code) and it cannot be contracted out even as a result of an explicit stipulation. There is often a dispute between the parties as to what constitutes the 'cause'.

In a recent case, the French Supreme Court annulled such a clause in a leasing agreement on the ground that it was contrary to the economic balance of the contract.[22]

6 Conditions

The purpose of this clause is to designate the obligations of which a breach will be considered a 'fundamental breach of the contract'.

---

[19] 'Contrats synallagmatiques'.

[20] See, for instance, Cass. Civ. 3, 24 June 1971, Bull. III No. 405; Cass. Com., 22 February 1967, Bull. III No. 67, No. 70–11730.

[21] Cass. Civ. 1, 3 July 1996, Bull. No. 286.

[22] See Cass. Com., 15 February 2000, No. 97–19.793, Bull. Civ. IV, No. 29, RLDA 2000/27, No. 1703.

The notion of 'fundamental breach of the contract' in this clause appears to be close to the notion of breach of an essential obligation under French law. This notion of essential obligation of the contract is relevant in two fields:

- The interpretation and effect of clauses limiting or excluding liability in case of breach of such obligations.[23]
- The right to unilaterally terminate the contract whereas, in principle, under French law, the termination of a contract must be requested and ordered by a court.[24]

It is probable that obligations, the breach of which is considered as a fundamental breach of contract, will be considered as a breach of an essential obligation of the contract.

Under French law, one considers as 'essential obligations' those obligations that go to the root of the bargain, i.e., for a French judge, the rights and obligations of the parties that define the economic substance of the contract.

If the parties wish to avoid the intervention of a judge in the definition of what constitutes an essential obligation of the contract, they themselves should define the obligations that are essential in the eyes of the parties and/or those that warrant a termination of the contract. One may consider that a clause such as the one in the introduction to Part 3 of this book would be interpreted by a French judge as defining the essential obligations of the contract.

One should further add that the sanctions for breach of contract other than damages are not subject to the requirement to prove a loss. In these conditions, the clause that defines fundamental/essential obligations of the contract may not be disregarded by the judge on the ground that the breach of any such obligation (e.g., the breach of a time requirement) has caused a damage.[25]

However, it should be noted that the exercise of the rights conferred by such a clause (generally unilateral termination) should be made in compliance with the duty of good faith as explained in the preliminary observations.

7   Sole remedy

A sole remedy clause would probably be viewed as a clause of limitation of liability.

---

[23] E.g., Cass. Com., 30 May 2006, Bull. No. 132.
[24] Cass. Civ. 1, 13 October 1998, Bull. I No. 300.
[25] Cass. Civ. 1, 18 November 1997, Bull. I, No. 317.

In principle, this type of clause is not prohibited.[26] However, its validity is subject to certain conditions:

- It does not deprive an essential obligation of its substance. Interestingly, in respect of the clause under consideration, a clause limiting liability of an express courier company for *late delivery* to the price gave rise to the leading authority on this issue (*Chronopost* case).[27] In that case, it was considered that timely delivery was an essential obligation of such a company and a clause limiting liability for late delivery to the price would deprive the contract of its substance. Such clauses are therefore considered unenforceable.
- The breach of the obligation was not intentional or a result of gross negligence as provided by Article 1150 of the Civil Code. For that matter, gross negligence is defined as extremely serious conduct, close to intentional breach and showing the inability of the party to perform the contractual obligation he or she had accepted.[28]

  Thus, taking the clause under consideration, if the delay was intentional or if the party in breach was grossly negligent, that party will not be able to rely on the clause.
- The damages concerned are not physical injuries.

Moreover, contracts between a professional and a consumer, the purpose or effect of whose clauses is to 'eliminate or reduce the right of compensation of the loss sustained by the non-professional or the consumer in case of breach by the professional of any of its obligations', are presumed to be illegal.

All the above exceptions result from mandatory rules.

Moreover, in case of a breach of an essential obligation of the contract, the aggrieved party could always try to seek a rescission ('résolution') of the contract in court even if that was not provided for as the 'sole remedy'.

It should also be noted that sole remedy clauses in contracts of sale may also see their scope restricted insofar as they may affect the scope of legal warranties for hidden defects ('garantie légale des vices cachés'), depending on whether the contract of sale is a for a domestic sale or for an international sale governed by the 1980 United Nations (Vienna)

---

[26] Cass. Civ. 1, 19 January 1982, D. 82, p. 457.
[27] Cass. Com., 9 July 2002, No. 99–12554; Cass. Com., 30 May 2006, No. 04–14.974, JCP E 15 June 2006, actualités 276; D. 2006, No. 38, pan. p. 2646.
[28] Cass. Com., 3 April 1990: Bull. Civ. IV, No. 108.

Convention on Contracts for the International Sale of Goods ('CISG'), which constitutes French law for international sales.

8   Subject to contract

A subject to contract clause could be quite useful under French law.

Indeed, when there is doubt as to whether a contract was concluded, judges may consider that a contract was concluded as soon as the parties agreed upon the essential elements of the contract (e.g., agreement on the subject matter and the price in the case of a sale). Thus, case law in the field of letters of intent[29] shows that French courts have a very extensive power of appreciation on the exact nature and effects of documents. French courts may consider that documents defining the objectives of a contract to be concluded but not indicating that they are preliminary documents constitute a first-frame contract even though parties are still in negotiation on the full and final contract.

Moreover, under French law, one considers that a contract is formed once so-called 'essential elements' of the contract have been agreed upon. For instance, in principle, a sale contract is deemed to be concluded once parties have agreed on the thing being sold and the price ('accord sur la chose et le prix').

However, it may be that an agreement on such first essential elements is not sufficient in the eyes of the parties and that there is not a final contract. It may also be that the parties have drafted an almost complete document but would like to have some time for reflection. In such cases, it may be desirable to indicate clearly what constitutes a contract and what constitutes a mere preparatory document.

The French Supreme Court seems to give effect to such clauses.[30] This is subject to certain qualifications. First of all, it should be noted that the words 'subject to contract' alone would probably give rise to some discussion as to what the intentions of the parties were, as this expression does not correspond to a defined category under French law. Under these conditions, it is advisable to be as precise and specific as possible in the drafting of such a clause and not simply rely on the expression 'subject to contract' to achieve that objective (all the more so as the direct translation of that expression into French would appear quite strange to a French judge).

---

[29] *Paravision International* v. *Sté Aries*, Cass. Com. 18 March 1997, No. 94–21430.
[30] Cass. Civ. 3, 2 February 1983, No. 81–12036, Bull. Civ. No. 34.

Furthermore, even if there is a sufficiently precise clause, there remains a risk that a judge would give some effect to documents presented as being non-binding. One should bear in mind that interpretation of a contract is chiefly an issue of fact and there is therefore a huge discretion of first-instance judges on any particular clause, as explained in the preliminary observations.

Thus, one may not exclude the possibility that a judge considers that a complete document signed by parties in which one would find the mention 'subject to contract' would be viewed as a contract with a *condition potestative* (a sort of arbitrary condition whereby the existence of an obligation is made dependent upon the will of the person supposed to be bound by the obligation); in such a case, the 'subject to contract' stipulation would be ignored, since a *condition potestative* is null under French law. This risk is due to the fact that some judges still have a theoretical vision of contracts and contractual negotiations. It is fair to say that this risk is decreasing under French law. For instance, in the merchant shipping field, judges understand that numerous precontractual documents may be exchanged before a contract has been reached.

In any event, the parties have an obligation to negotiate in good faith and a party may incur liability in tort (Article 1382 of the Civil Code) for having wrongly let the other party rely on his or her apparent intent to conclude the contract. Such reliance could be characterised if the parties have exchanged quasi-final documents and one of them suddenly declares that he or she does not want to sign the contract. However, such liability is limited to reliance loss and cannot cover expectation damages or loss of a chance to make profits under the contract.

9   Material adverse change

Material adverse change clauses, such as the one under consideration, are recognised by French courts. Their interpretation of the clause would generally be very close to that prevailing in common law jurisdictions. It is different from a hardship clause in that it may result in a termination of the contract as opposed to a mere renegotiation of the terms and conditions with a view to restoring the balance between the parties.

Particular attention should be paid to the drafting of the clause so that it is not considered to be a 'condition potestative' (an arbitrary condition – see above) and thus be found null. It is therefore essential that the events authorising the implementation of the clause be clearly defined and based on objective criteria that 'objectively' affect the interest of the contract. In other words, the implementation of the clause shall not be dependent upon the arbitrariness of the beneficiary of the clause and must be precise. These events should be highly unpredictable. If such events are too linked with the usual economic risks of the beneficiary, the clause will also be deemed 'potestative' and, as such, will be ignored.

10   Liquidated damages

The interpretation of a liquidated damages clause by a French judge may well surprise the parties.

To summarise the position, an English lawyer would wonder first whether it is in fact a penalty clause.[31] In such a case, the clause would be invalid. Otherwise, the clause would be applied regardless of whether the contractual damages are disconnected from the actual loss sustained.

The position is different under French law. There is no prohibition of liquidated damages (interestingly called 'clauses pénales', which literally translates as 'penalty clauses'). However, such a clause is subject to the moderating power of the judge, which is mandatory (Articles 1152 and 1226 of the Civil Code).

In these conditions, in the presence of a liquidated damages clause which is disconnected from the actual damage sustained by the victim of the breach, it is probable that a French judge: (1) systematically validates the clause; and (2) also systematically reduces the amount thereof. It seems difficult to avoid such a result.

It should also be noted that if the amount of the liquidated damages clause is manifestly too low, it may also be treated as a limitation clause (as to which, see Section 7 above).

11   Indemnity

An indemnity clause deals with the outcome of recourse actions and does not raise any difficulty, as French courts would give effect to such a clause.

Insofar as such clauses contain limitations of liability, reference should be made to the comments on the limitation clause above.

---

[31] In the sense of a provision in a contract that stipulates an excessive pecuniary charge against a defaulting party (*Webster's New World Law Dictionary*, 2010, Wiley Publishing, Inc.).

It is customary to find a mutual waiver of recourse consented by the parties in indemnity clauses. Such waivers of recourse are valid and enforceable as a matter of law when they relate to contractual liability.

They are considered as exclusions of liability and, as such, cannot be invoked in cases of gross negligence ('faute lourde') and wilful default ('dol'), in accordance with Article 1150 of the Civil Code.

It is important to stipulate whether the parties' insurers are also covered by the waiver. The victim's own insurer, subrogated in the rights of his or her insured, is normally bound by the waiver consented to by his or her insured (since he or she cannot gain more rights than the insured as a result of the subrogation). In order to preserve the insurance coverage, it is obviously necessary to get the insurer's consent to this waiver of recourse.

Regarding the liability insurer of the party liable, the position is more delicate. Indeed, under French insurance law, the victim has a direct claim against that insurer which is distinct from the claim against the party liable. In other words, failing a specific waiver of recourse as against that insurer, the victim or his or her subrogated insurer can still claim against that liability insurer.[32] In order to protect liability insurers, it is necessary to provide that the parties also waive recourse against these insurers. This stipulation is enforceable by a liability insurer under French law (it is considered as a 'stipulation pour autrui' on which a third party may rely against a party to the contract).

Obviously, the fact that the contract itself is governed by French law does not necessarily mean that there will also be recognition of direct claims against liability insurers. However, rules of conflict of laws on that point are complex and changing, and it is therefore wiser to insert specific wording to that effect.

Again, the party waiving recourse against the liability insurer of the other party must secure the prior approval of his or her own property insurer.

12 Representations and warranties

In this clause, the parties guarantee a number of elements pertaining to the validity of the contract (capacity of the parties, power of the signatories, etc.).

---

[32] Cass. Civ. 1, 20 July 1988: RCA 1988, comm. 51 and chr. 5; Cass. Civ. 1, 26 May 1993, Bull. No. 186.

Such a clause is given some effect under French law. The alleged nullity of a contract often gives rise to a discussion on the existence of a cause of nullity invoked, as well as a possible liability of one of the parties in the event of such a cause of nullity. It is a case of precontractual liability which is dealt with, in France, as liability in tort. In order to establish liability in tort, one must first establish the existence of a fault, in the sense of Article 1382 of the Civil Code, which does not systematically result from the existence of a cause of nullity. In this context, the interest of a representations and warranties clause is to confer a contractual dimension to the implicit guarantees of the precontractual period. It therefore avoids all discussion on the existence of a fault: the observation of a cause of nullity automatically constitutes a breach of contract.

Subject to these general rules, in French practice, the representations and warranties clause is mainly known in the context of share purchase agreements.

Whatever the detail of the list of representations and warranties, a purchaser may always claim that his or her consent was vitiated during the conclusion of the contract in order to seek nullity of said contract (a warranty of liability and assets is additional to the legal provisions protecting the buyer and does not prevent the latter, when his or her consent was vitiated, from invoking the nullity of the share purchase agreement, which is a legal protection that he or she has not waived).[33] Indeed, under Article 1109 of the Civil Code, 'there can be no valid consent if consent was given by mistake or if it was extorted by violence or deceived by fraud'.

In practice, nullity of the contract will only be sought on the basis of mistake or fraudulent misrepresentation and, more particularly, on the latter of these. Article 1116 of the Civil Code indeed provides that: 'fraud is one of the cases of nullity of a contract when the fraudulent manoeuvres of one party are such that it is obvious that, but for these manoeuvres, the other party would not have entered into the contract. Fraud cannot be presumed and must be proved.'

Thus, a party may always try to seek nullity of the contract if it manages to demonstrate that the other party had hidden an element that would have affected the first party's decision to enter into the contract: in other words, that it would not have entered into the contract had it known of the element.

---

[33] Cass. Com., 3 November 2004, No. 00–15725, Bull. Joly Sociétés April 2005, p. 519.

It is nevertheless preferable for the purchaser to stipulate that 'the share purchase is effected subject to the ordinary warranties, obligations and conditions of fact and of law and, notably subject to the Representations and Warranties defined hereafter' in order to avoid any useless discussion on that point.

It should be mentioned that in Anglo-Saxon practice, the term 'representations and warranties' covers the representations of the seller on the legal status of its company (the company has been validly formed, the contracts concluded by the company are in accordance with applicable law, etc.), whereas in French practice, one distinguishes between 'déclarations' (which may be translated as 'representations') on the legal status of the company and 'guaranties' (which may be translated as 'warranties') on the financial situation of the company.

This distinction is important due to the sanctions associated in practice with wrong representations and warranties on the legal status or on the financial situation of the company. In case law, a false 'déclaration' on the legal status of the company may result in the nullity of the contract even if the purchaser sustained no loss, whereas a false statement on the financial situation of the company will only give rise to damages.[34]

However, it is true that, very often, judges do not take into account these theoretical principles and focus their attention on the financial loss sustained by the purchaser or the company in order to make their decision, whatever it may be (the nullity of the contract or an award of damages).

13   Hardship

Such a clause is very important under French law as it avoids the traditional application of the theory of unforeseeability ('imprévision'). The loss of the economic balance of a contract due to unforeseen circumstances is not a cause of renegotiation of the contract. There may be future reforms of the Civil Code to recognise hardship as a cause of revision of the contract. For the time being, it is not. However, nothing prevents the parties from agreeing that the contract should be renegotiated in the event of defined circumstances.

In the way in which it is drafted, the clause suggests that the triggering event of the renegotiation is a *force majeure* event. Indeed, the clause puts an emphasis on the criteria of unforeseeability and irresistibility, which

---

[34] Cass. Com., 29 January 2008, No. 06–20.010.

are *force majeure* criteria.[35] It may therefore well be that this clause should be interpreted in light of French case law on this notion.

14   *Force majeure*

Rules relating to *force majeure* under French law are not public policy. Parties may therefore freely extend the definition of *force majeure*[36] or restrict it by a limitative list of *force majeure* cases.[37] It is also possible to stipulate the consequences of *force majeure*, notably whether and in which conditions the contract should be terminated as a result of the occurrence of a *force majeure* event, except in contracts with consumers, in which such clauses are held to be illegal.[38]

French courts will therefore give effect to such a clause on *force majeure*. They will respect the intention of the parties.

---

[35] See Cass. Ass. Plén. 14 April 2006, No. 02–11.168.
[36] Cass. Com., 8 July 1981, Bull. IV No. 312.
[37] Cass. Com., 11 October 2005, Bull. IV No. 206.
[38] E.g., Cass. Civ. 1, 10 February 1998, D. 1998, 539, note D. Mazeaud.

10

The Romanistic tradition: application of boilerplate clauses under Italian law

GIORGIO DE NOVA

1 Entire agreement clauses and no oral amendments clauses as clauses provided in alien contracts

Entire agreement clauses, also known as merger clauses as well as no oral amendments clauses, are not a usual part of traditional Italian contractual practice for two main reasons.

The first reason is that in traditional Italian practice, contracts, including those between companies, are usually short and the parties agree only on the main issues, leaving statutes to rule on the other issues: Article 1374 of the Italian Civil Code accordingly provides that 'a contract binds the parties *not only as to what is expressly provided, but also to all the consequences deriving from it by law* or, in absence, according to usage and equity' (emphasis added).

The second reason is that the problem of oral agreements made prior to or at the same time as the written agreement, or after the drawing of the document, is expressly covered by two articles of the Italian Civil Code. Article 2722 states that 'proof by witnesses is not permitted to establish stipulations which have been added or are contrary to the contents of a document, and which are claimed to have been made prior to or at the same time as the document', while Article 2723 states that 'when it is alleged that, after the drawing of a document, a stipulation has been made, in addition or contrary to its contents, the judge can admit proof by witnesses only if, in consideration of the character of the parties, the nature of the contract, and any other circumstances, it appears likely that verbal additions or modifications have occurred'.

Due to such legal limits to proof by witnesses, the Italian lawyer who drafts a contract does not see the necessity of providing clauses in the contract aimed to protect the written document.

Nevertheless, in recent years in Italy, it has become widespread practice to execute contracts written on the basis of Anglo-American models even though they are subject to Italian law. As has been stated with regard to civil law countries, 'today international commercial contracts are, with only few exceptions, drafted on the basis of common law models'.[1] These contracts, which I suggest should be called 'alien contracts',[2] aim to be complete, and they often provide entire agreement clauses and no oral amendments clauses between the so-called 'miscellaneous provisions'.

2   Entire agreement clauses and no oral amendments clauses as 'stylistic clauses'?

It has been said that 'it often happens that parties use standard form contracts containing a merger clause to which they pay no attention'.[3] The same can be said of no oral amendments clauses. This circumstance raises an issue under Italian law, because, according to Italian case law, a clause which is not based on the effective will of the parties is qualified by the courts as a 'clausola di stile' (a stylistic clause) and so is considered to be without effect.[4]

Whether a clause has been negotiated by the parties or not is a question of fact.

Assuming that an entire agreement clause and a no oral amendments clause are respondent to the effective will of the parties, the effects they can have under Italian law have to be ascertained.

3   No oral amendments clauses under Italian law

A clause which provides that no amendment or variation to the contract shall take effect unless it is in writing and signed by authorised representatives of each party shall be checked, with regard to Italian law, against the rules concerning the form and representation.

---

[1] See G. Cordero-Moss, *Anglo-American Models and Norwegian or other Civilian Governing Law*, Publications Series of the Institute of Private Law No. 169 (University of Oslo, 2007), p. 19.

[2] See G. De Nova, *Il contratto alieno*, 2nd edn (Giappichelli, 2010).

[3] See O. Lando and H. Beales, *Principles of European Contract Law* (Kluwer Law International, 2002), comment on Article 2: 105.

[4] See Italian Supreme Court, 16 November 1984; Italian Supreme Court, 15 October 1983, No. 6062; Italian Supreme Court, 12 November 1981, No. 5990.

As for the form, Article 1352 of the Italian Civil Code provides as follows: 'If the parties have agreed in writing to adopt a specified form for the future contract it is presumed that such form was intended for the validity of the contract.' If the parties are free to agree to adopt a form for a future contract, which is not required by law, there is no reason to discuss the validity of a clause which provides that a variation to a contract shall be made in writing. However, in Italian law there is discussion as to whether the agreement of the parties to adopt a specified form (e.g., the written form) can be considered as superseded in the event that afterwards the parties orally finalise the contract.

Case law is uncertain: some decisions accept that the agreement on the form can be cancelled by the conduct of the parties,[5] while other decisions require the written form to cancel the agreement on the form.[6]

As for the undersigning by an authorised representative, the clause can have effect under Italian law, because the parties can provide information on the power of the persons involved in a contract.

4   Entire agreement clauses under Italian law

As for the entire agreement clause, a clause which provides that the contract supersedes any prior agreement executed by the parties regarding the same subject matter is valid under Italian law.

Under Italian statutory law, there is no provision regulating such a clause. This clause is not customary under traditional Italian contract practice, as has been said before. However, to validate such a clause, the more general principle of novation can be applied.

On the contrary, under Italian law, a clause would not be valid which would derogate to Article 1362 of the Italian Civil Code, according to which 'that which was the common intent of the parties, not limited to the literal meaning of the words, shall be sought in interpreting the contract. In order to ascertain the common intent of the parties, the general course of their behaviour, including that subsequent to the conclusion of the contract, shall be taken into account'. It is clear that the wording 'behaviour, including that subsequent to the conclusion of the contract' also means that the behaviour prior to the conclusion is relevant for the purposes of the interpretation of the contract.

---

[5]   Italian Supreme Court, 5 October 2000, No. 13277.
[6]   Italian Supreme Court, 14 April 2000, No. 4861.

The issue of the validity of a clause aiming to bar the search of the common intent of the parties has been discussed by Italian scholars rather than in court, due to the fact that entire agreement clauses are not customary in traditional Italian contractual practice. It is very important to note that the prevailing opinion of Italian scholars is that Article 1362 of the Italian Civil Code cannot be derogated because it is an expression of the principle of good faith and it governs the activity of the judge, which is an activity based on public interest.[7]

With specific regard to an entire agreement clause, it has recently been pointed out that 'the search for the common intent of the parties holds a core position, not avoidable, in the interpretation, even if the contract is a written contract, including an Entire Agreement clause'.[8] Therefore, an entire agreement clause under Italian law cannot be interpreted as a clause derogating to Article 1362 of the Italian Civil Code, because otherwise it would be null and void. Moreover, it is a precise rule on the interpretation of a contract that 'in case of doubt, the contract or the individual clauses shall be interpreted in the sense in which they can have some effect, rather than in that according to which they would have none'.[9]

In short, under Italian law, an entire agreement clause cannot prevent the judge from interpreting the contract by examining the common intent of the parties in the light of their overall behaviour prior and subsequent to the execution of the contract. It is worthwhile noting that the same solution can be found in the UNIDROIT Principles of International Commercial Contracts 2004 at Article 2(1)(17): '*Merger clauses*. A contract in writing which contains a clause indicating that the writing completely embodies the terms on which the parties have agreed cannot be contradicted or supplemented by evidence of prior statement or agreements. *However, such statements or agreements may be used to interpret the writing* [emphasis added].'

5   Entire agreement clauses under the CISG

If the parties have chosen to apply Italian law to a contract for a sale of goods, the international conventions to which Italy is a contracting party

---

[7] See C. Grassetti, *L'interpretazione del negozio giuridico* (CEDAM, 1983), p. 258; C. Scognamiglio, 'L'interpretazione', in E. Gabrielli (ed.), *I contratti in generale*, vol. II, 2nd edn (UTET, 2006), pp. 1035–1146, 1044.
[8] See F. Mazza, 'Merger clause (o clausola di completezza)', in P. Cendon (ed.), *I contratti in generale*, vol. IV, *Clausole abusive* (UTET, 2001), pp. 725–755, 737.
[9] Article 1367 of the Italian Civil Code.

may apply. Therefore, it must be considered which effects the entire agreement clause can have with regard to the United Nations Convention on Contracts for the International Sale of Goods signed on 11 April 1980, the so-called Vienna Convention (hereafter also referred to as 'CISG').

Considering that the CISG (as provided by Article 6) can be derogated by the parties, the issue of the effects of an entire agreement clause in a contract governed by the CISG has been considered by the CISG Advisory Council in its opinion dated 23 October 2004, with the following conclusion (para. 4.6): 'Under the CISG, an Entire Agreement Clause does not generally have the effect of excluding extrinsic evidence for purposes of contract interpretation. However, the Entire Agreement Clause may prevent recourse to extrinsic evidence for this purpose if specific wording, together with all other relevant factors, make clear the parties' intent to derogate from Article 8 for purposes of contract interpretation.'

Therefore, it is necessary to check whether the specific entire agreement clause deals with contract interpretation and contains any derogation from Article 8 of the CISG, which governs the interpretation of the contract.

As for Italian law itself, according to the conclusions reached in Section 4, it can, in short, be said that: a) on the one hand, agreements, oral or written, prior to the contract are superseded by the contract, meaning that the obligations of the parties are provided by the contract, and obligations of the parties which are provided in previous agreements but not in the contract cannot be added to the obligations provided in the contract; but b) oral or written agreements, as well as the overall behaviour of the contracting parties before and after the execution of the contract, shall be considered in the interpretation of the contract.

6   Articles 2722 and 2723 of the Italian Civil Code with respect to interpreting the contract

In short, as a rule, under Articles 2722 and 2723, no oral evidence can be admitted to prove that the parties, *before* the execution of the contract, agreed orally on something which is an addition to or in contradiction with what is provided in the written contract. On the contrary, oral evidence can be admitted to prove that the parties made additions or modifications *after* the execution of the contract if it appears likely that oral additions or modifications have occurred. Regarding the last possibility, it should be considered that the no oral amendments clause bars such a possibility.

However, it must be considered that the above rules do not bar proof by witnesses aiming not to give evidence of agreements adding to or contradicting the document, but to give evidence of the meaning of the document in interpreting the written agreement. Such a distinction is stated in case law and by scholars. As for the case law, the Italian Supreme Court has decided that: 'Legal limits to the admissibility of proof by witnesses stated by Article 2722 Civil Code (which does permit the giving of evidence of added or contrary agreements, prior or simultaneous to the document) do not act when such a proof is aimed not to challenge the content of the document, but to clarify its content.'[10]

As for the scholars, the following was stated: 'quite consequent appears the exclusion of the said limits, when the proof by witnesses is aimed to clarify the content of the written agreement.'[11]

7   Entire agreement clauses and implied conditions

Some entire agreement clauses also provide that 'there are no conditions to this Agreement that are not expressed herein'.

The term 'condition' does not refer to a *condicio facti*, i.e., to a future and uncertain event on whose fulfilment the effect of the contract depends, but to the implied terms (or conditions) of the contract.

An entire agreement clause can prevent the judge from making implications regarding the terms in the contract. Of course, it cannot prevent the application of the mandatory rules of law.

---

[10] Italian Supreme Court, Section III, 16 July 2003, No. 11141.
[11] COMOGLIO, *Le prove civili* (Wolters Kluwer Italia, 1999), p. 267.

11

The Nordic tradition: application of boilerplate clauses under Danish law

PETER MØGELVANG-HANSEN

1 Danish contract law in general[1]

Denmark has no civil code but rather a variety of fragmentary statutes dealing with some special types of contract. The two central pieces of legislation in the area, *købeloven* (the Sales of Goods Act) and *aftaleloven* (the Contracts Act), date back to 1906 and 1917, respectively. New provisions protecting consumers have been added to the two Acts, but otherwise, with a few exceptions, they both look as they did when they were first enacted.[2] These old Acts are some of the finest examples of the legislative cooperation between the Nordic countries in the first half of the twentieth century.

When Denmark joined the 1980 United Nations (Vienna) Convention on Contracts for the International Sale of Goods ('CISG'),[3] the veneration for the two old Acts and the Nordic tradition was great and embodied in the fact that Denmark did not join the Convention's Part II (Formation of the Contract)[4] and that Denmark and the other Nordic countries invoked the so-called 'neighbouring country reservation'. The effect of the latter is that, according to the general rules on the conflict of

---

[1] For a general overview, see P. Møgelvang-Hansen, 'Contracts and Sales in Denmark', in B. Dahl, T. Melchior and D. Tamm (eds.), *Danish Law in a European Perspective*, 2nd edn (Thomson, 2002), pp. 237–276.

[2] An exception is the so-called General Clause that was inserted into §36 of Aftaleloven (the Contracts Act) in 1975. For more about §36, see below.

[3] See *International købelov* (International Sales of Goods Act), 733/1988.

[4] Neither did the other Nordic countries. The Danish Ministry of Justice has announced that a bill repealing the exception concerning Part II is being prepared in 2010. See www.justitsministeriet.dk/160.html.

laws,[5] the national Sales of Goods legislation applies to inter-Nordic sale contracts.[6]

The special status of the old (no longer joint) Nordic Sales of Goods Act from 1906 is also embodied in the fact that it is a general assumption in Danish legal theory and practice that, by and large, the Sales of Goods Act reflects the non-statutory, general principles of contractual obligations and thus that the rules of the Act, with a few exceptions consisting mainly of rather 'technical' rules,[7] are an important paradigm for the default rules applicable to those types of contracts that are non-statutory, for example, most service contracts and the purchase of real property.[8]

Expressed in a few words of generalisation, Danish contract law, and indeed Danish law as a whole, is characterised by a rather high degree of flexibility, informality and pragmatism. These principles are very prominent in legal theory and practice concerning the interpretation of contracts. Another characteristic feature is the relatively prominent role played by the principle of reasonableness generally (also) applied by the courts when interpreting contracts.[9]

The distinction between the interpretation of the contract and the process of filling it out with the default rules of contract law is not sharp. It is blurred by the fact that the importance of the default rules is not

[5] Denmark is a member of the European Union, but because of the Danish reservation to the EU Treaty as regards legal and home affairs, the Rome I Regulation (no. 593/2008, OJ 2008 L177/6) on the Law Applicable to Contractual Obligations does not apply in Denmark. Danish courts will continue to apply the Rome Convention, which was incorporated into Danish law by Act No. 188/1984. For more detail, see K. Hertz and J. Lookofsky, *EU-PIL. European Union Private International Law in Contract and Tort* (DJØF Publishing, 2009), pp. 75–76.

[6] See Article 94 of the CISG. Ironically enough, the other Nordic countries have passed legislation abandoning the old joint Nordic Sales of Goods Act and have adjusted their national sales law to the CISG, with the result that Denmark is now the only country where the Nordic Sales of Goods Act of 1906 is still in force.

[7] E.g., the two-year limitation period concerning non-conformity of goods: see §54 of the Sales of Goods Act. According to Danish tradition, a sharp rule to this effect must have positive statutory authority and would not be the result of judge-made law (unlike, for example, the general principle of the legal effect of failure to act – see Section 2.3).

[8] See M. Bryde Andersen and J. Lookofsky, *Lærebog i Obligationsret I* (Thomson, 2010), p. 22; and J. Lookofsky and P. Møgelvang-Hansen, 'Ny indenlandsk købelov: KBL III?', *Ugeskrift for Retsvæsen*, B (1999), 240–252, 247 (nominating the Sales of Goods Act as 'Danish Contract Law's paradigm no. 1').

[9] See J. Lookofsky, 'Desperately Seeking Subsidiarity', in *Center for International & Comparative Law Occasional Papers Vol. 1: The Annual Herbert L. Bernstein Memorial Lecture in Comparative Law. The First Six Years* (Durham, 2009), pp. 111–130, 121ff.; and B. Gomard, 'Aftalelovens §36 og erhvervskontrakter', *Erhvervsjuridisk Tidsskrift* (2008), 14–26, 25.

limited to cases where there is no basis in the contract or the circumstances surrounding it for establishing that the parties intended to regulate a particular point. Even in cases where the parties actually intended to do so but where their common intention is not clear, the court will interpret/'fill out' the contract by assuming that it implies terms leading to the solution which seems most fair, reasonable and expedient in accordance with trade usage and the general principles of contract law. In this way, the interpretation of a contract, although based on the actual situation, tends to lead to an understanding of it that complies with the general rules and principles of contract law, which are generally assumed to express what is a reasonable balancing of the parties' loyal interests in typical situations. The default rules are thus important factors influencing the application of the reasonableness principle.[10] Among the other factors serving as interpretative aids influencing the general reasonableness (or even substituting it in certain types of cases) are the notions of loyalty between contract parties, of proportionality and of abuse of rights.[11]

The correlated notions of reasonableness and flexibility are expressed in §36, the so-called general clause of the Contracts Act. The general clause was added to the Act in 1975 as a supplement to the rather precise, 'classic' rules of voidability that were not considered flexible enough to secure modern, well-balanced solutions. According to §36, the courts can wholly or partly disregard an agreement if it would be 'unreasonable or contrary to the principles of fair conduct' to uphold it. The decision can rely not only on the circumstances surrounding the formation of the contract, but also on its contents and subsequent circumstances. An even higher degree of flexibility was achieved by an amendment in 1994 to the effect that the agreement can also be amended. The general clause applies to contracts in general, but its application by the courts is a long way from being an everyday occurrence as far as commercial contracts are concerned. In areas where there is a considerable difference in bargaining power between commercial parties to a contract and in extraordinary cases, beyond what can be considered actualisation of commercial risks, where there is a need to avoid clearly unreasonable results that cannot be

---

[10] See M. Bryde Andersen, *Grundlæggende aftaleret. Aftaleretten I*, 3rd edn (Gjellerup, 2008), p. 61.

[11] See J. Ewald, *Retsmisbrug i formueretten* (Jurist- og Økonomforbundets Forlag, 2001), Chapters 6–8 and 10; L. Lynge Andersen and P. B. Madsen, *Aftaler og Mellemmænd*, 5th edn (Thomson, 2006), pp. 444–453; and Bryde Andersen and Lookofsky, *Lærebog i obligationsret I*, pp. 68–71.

met by means of interpretation or other rules or principles, the general clause serves the function of last resort, a 'safety valve'.[12]

2   Clauses aimed at fully detaching the contract from the applicable law

2.1   Entire agreement

When interpreting contracts, the courts aim at finding the common intention of the parties at the time the agreement was made, taking into account the reasonable expectations created by the contract, written and oral statements, and the behaviour of the parties, together with more pragmatic factors such as what is needed to fulfil the parties' interests in a fair and reasonable way. Information about the preceding negotiations, marketing material, previous agreements between the parties and other preceding and subsequent circumstances can be included in the basis for the decision. Whereas all kinds of facts relevant to ascertaining the intention of the parties in principle are admissible as evidence, the practical reality is often that it is hard to convince the court that the intention of the parties was in fact different from that expressed in the terms found in the parties' written contract. However, the principle of the court's freedom to assess the evidence implies that it depends on the facts of the individual case and what it would take to convince the court, and the chance that a party will be able to do so cannot be ruled out.

The entire agreement clause is, if taken literally, a far-reaching restriction of the general principles of interpretation. The purpose is to promote legal certainty in the sense that the clause, if taken literally, would exclude either party from claiming that the common intention of the parties was in fact different from what follows from the written contract. Often a claim to this effect will be unsuccessful because the written contract, e.g., due to its elaborate content, creates a strong presumption that the contract supersedes prior agreements. However, the critical point is that the entire agreement clause, if taken literally, would generally exclude a party from any attempt, including potentially successful ones, to try to convince the court that the common intention of the parties was in fact different from what can be read from the written contract. There seems to be no publicised Danish case law concerning this question. Danish courts are not likely to exclude evidence as

---

[12] See Gomard, 'Aftalelovens §36 og erhvervskontrakter', 14.

irrelevant because of the clause.[13] The general opinion in the legal doctrine is that the entire agreement clause cannot be taken literally.[14] Conversely, the clause may have the effect that it may be harder for the party in question to convince the court that the written contract does not reflect the common intention of the parties.[15]

2.2 No oral amendments

Whereas the entire agreement clause purports to rule out the relevance of facts prior to the conclusion of the contract, the no oral amendments clause concerns subsequent facts. It is the general rule of Danish law that oral agreements are as binding as written ones. Even though these oral agreements are generally harder to prove, they are nonetheless binding. In addition to the line of reasoning mentioned above (see Section 2.1) concerning the entire agreement clause, the *lex posterior* principle speaks against taking the no oral amendments clause literally in that, according to its wording, it rules out any attempt to prove the existence of a binding oral agreement that supersedes the written contract. It may, however, influence the assessment of evidence by making it harder to convince the court of the existence of an oral amendment superseding the written contract. In cases within the scope of the CISG, Article 29(2) of the Convention applies. Accordingly, a no oral amendments clause is effective, but the party in question may be precluded by his or her conduct from asserting the clause to the extent that the other party has relied on that conduct.[16] At least at the time when the CISG was adopted in Denmark, the rule in Article 29(2) did not reflect the general state of Danish contract law and was considered necessary because a contract could be amended orally, notwithstanding a no oral amendments clause.[17] There seems to be no sufficient basis for assuming that the CISG rule has in the meantime become the general rule of Danish

---

[13] E. Lego Andersen, 'Hvorledes indgår erhvervslivet aftaler?', *Erhvervsjuridisk Tidsskrift* (2008), 34–39, 37.

[14] Bryde Andersen, *Grundlæggende aftaleret*, p. 331; and M. Bryde Andersen, *Praktisk aftaleret. Aftaleretten II*, 2nd edn (Gjellerup, 2003), p. 136; Lynge Andersen and Madsen, *Aftaler og mellemmænd*, p. 401; and B. Gomard, H. V. Godsk Pedersen and A. Ørgaard, *Almindelig aftaleret*, 3rd edn (Jurist- og Økonomforbundets Forlag, 2009), p. 76.

[15] See Gomard, Godsk Pedersen and Ørgaard, *Almindelig Kontraktsret*, p. 75.

[16] Article 29(2) is found in Part III (not II) of the CISG and applies in Denmark. See text accompanying note 5.

[17] See B. Gomard and H. Rechnagel, *International Købelov* (Jurist- og Økonomforbundets Forlag, 1990), p. 96.

contract law. This also seems to be the general opinion in the legal doctrine.[18] There is no publicised case law concerning the no oral amendments clause.

2.3   No waiver

According to the general principles of the forfeit of contractual rights, by failure to act, the inactivity cannot, *per se*, have this effect. It is an additional requirement that the conduct of the inactive party has given the other party the impression that the right has been given up or that it will not be asserted, i.e., more than just inactivity is required. In practice, it depends on a rather discretionary overall evaluation whether the requirements are met.[19]

In the case of a breach of contract, a duty to give notice in different situations follows from specific statutory provisions that reflect a general principle of contract law laying down a general duty to give notice within a reasonable period of time after the party knew, or ought to have become aware, of the breach and the remedy sought.[20]

The statutory rules and the general principle of the duty to give notice of breach are not mandatory in commercial transactions. Although contract clauses derogating from the rules are in principle effective, their use in specific cases is likely to be restricted by way of interpretation (or, as a last resort, with reference to the general clause in §36 of the Contracts Act) in order to avoid manifestly unreasonable results such as, e.g., speculation at the expense of the party in breach. Furthermore, a no waiver clause seems to be vulnerable to attack in cases where the conduct of the party in question has given the party in breach the impression that the right or remedy has been given up or that it will not be asserted, i.e., where the general principle of forfeiture of contractual rights by failure to act applies (see above). Although conduct meeting the criteria according to this principle is not tantamount to a binding tacit promise, in most cases, the courts would probably find that the party in breach should be entitled to rely on the conduct.

---

[18] See Gomard, Godsk Pedersen and Ørgaard, *Almindelig Kontraktsret*, pp. 75f.; and Bryde Andersen, *Grundlæggende aftaleret*, p. 228.

[19] See B. von Eyben, P. Mortensen and I. Sørensen, *Lærebog i Obligationsret II*, 3rd edn (Thomson Reuters, 2008), pp. 169–174; and B. Gomard and T. Iversen, *Obligationsret 3. Del*, 2nd edn (Jurist- og Økonomforbundets Forlag, 2009), pp. 265–268.

[20] See Bryde Andersen and Lookofsky, *Lærebog i obligationsret I*, pp. 279–280.

There seems to be no publicised case law on the clause. It has been addressed by only a few commentators stating that the no waiver clause is not likely to be literally enforced.[21]

2.4 Severability

The consequences for the rest of the contract of the invalidity of a certain contract term depend on an evaluation of the individual case. One of the general principles of interpretation speaks in favour of saving the contract by giving the remainder of the contract effect. Alternatively, the contract may not function as intended by the parties without the invalid term, or its absence may disturb the balance between the parties and thus make it unreasonable to do less than setting aside the contract as a whole.

The flexibility of Danish contract law in terms of tailoring the legal effects of voidness has found a marked expression in the general clause in §36 of the Contracts Act (see Section 1 above).The flexibility in this respect is partly based on the realistic view that it is possible, only to a limited degree, to foresee which solutions will meet practical needs in different hypothetical situations. For the same reason, it is hardly possible, without a rather high degree of specification, to derogate totally from this flexibility. A contract clause specifying the effects or lack of effects on the remainder of the contract if a specific term turns out to be invalid (e.g., according to competition law) may have full effect. However, it is not plausible that the courts will respect a clause that generally rules out the possibility that the whole contract is invalid because of the invalidity of one of the terms.[22]

2.5 Conditions

It is a general principle of contract law that the remedy of termination normally presupposes fundamental breach, and that the question of whether this condition is met depends on a comprehensive, actual assessment of the extent and the nature of the breach and its significance to the

---

[21] See B. Saltorp and E. Werlauff, *Kontrakter*, 2nd edn (Jurist- og Økonomforbundets Forlag, 2009), p. 256; and J. Schans Christensen, *Grænseoverskridende virksomhedsoverdragelser. Tilrettelæggelse, Forhandling. Aftaleudarbejdelse og Opfølgning* (GadJura, 1998), p. 265.

[22] See Gomard, Godsk Pedersen and Ørgaard, *Almindelig Kontraktsret*, p. 134; Lynge Andersen and Madsen, *Aftaler og Mellemmænd*, p. 128 (note 30), Bryde Andersen, *Praktisk aftaleret. Aftaleretten II*, p. 360; and Saltorp and Werlauff, *Kontrakter*, p. 256.

party in question, as well as the significance of the termination to the other party. As far as sales of goods between commercial parties are concerned, it follows directly from §21(3) of the Sales of Goods Act that any delay is fundamental. The rule is one of the fairly few examples where the Sales of Goods Act is not in harmony with the general non-statutory principles of contract law. It is the general view in legal theory and practice that the rule is too inflexible and that the threshold for deviating from §21(3) based on an interpretation of the contract is very low.[23]

The same general trend of restrictive interpretation is traceable in the way that courts interpret contracts even though it is, of course, left to the parties to define what they consider to be so fundamental that it can trigger the remedy of termination. If the condition is in fact applied by a contract party as a pretext for not honouring a claim or for activating a legal remedy that is disproportionate compared to the real actual need to protect the party's legitimate interests, the courts are willing to disregard the condition as unreasonable and/or as abuse of legal remedy.[24]

An example to illustrate this point is found in the Supreme Court case reported in *Ugeskrift for Retsvæsen* (herinafter UfR) 1985.766, where an insurance company refused to honour a guarantee covering the debtor's payments under a mortgage deed because the transfer of the mortgage deed to the insured party was not registered. According to information provided by the association of insurance companies, this condition was found in most insurance companies' guarantees and was in fact enforced by the companies. Whereas the High Court gave judgment in favour of the insurance company with a brief reference to the fact that registration of the transfer was made a clearly expressed condition for coverage under the guarantee, the Supreme Court decided the case in favour of the insured party. It held that the failure to register the transfer had had no influence on the risk evaluation and no significant detrimental effects on the insurance company's interests. This being the case, non-coverage under the guarantee would be such a disproportionate effect of the failure to register that it would not be reasonable if the insurance company could be released from the contract with reference to this condition.

---

[23] See Bryde Andersen and Lookofsky, *Lærebog i Obligationsret*, pp. 214–215; and Gomard, *Obligationsret 2. Del*, p. 91.

[24] See Bryde Andersen and Lookofsky, *Lærebog i Obligationsret*, pp. 215–225; and Ewald, *Retsmisbrug I formueretten*, p. 201.

2.6   Sole remedy

The freedom of commercial contract parties to decide the remedies applicable in case of breach of the contract is respected by the courts, although not without modifications. One modification is based on the general notion that each party to a contract should have an adequate remedy at his or her disposal in all cases of the other party's breach of the contract. If the sole remedy of the contract turns out not to protect the interests of a party in a way that is adequate and reasonable in the given situation, then that party has the right to activate the remedies authorised in the general rules of contract law. This is a well-established principle in case law. As far as warranties stipulating repair as the sole remedy in case of non-conformity of a product are concerned, the innocent party, after having given the other party sufficient opportunity to attempt (unsuccessfully it turns out) to eliminate the defects by repair, is entitled to terminate the contract if the non-conformity is fundamental,[25] or to claim damages[26] or a proportional price reduction according to the general rules of contract law.[27]

Other modifications follow from the general principles developed in the case law concerning the interpretation and voidability of contract clauses excluding or limiting liability to pay damages. According to the case law, in order to have effect on liability founded in negligence, such exclusion/limitation clauses must clearly state so. Furthermore, exclusion/limitation clauses are unenforceable in cases where the liable party caused the damage deliberately or, as a main rule, by gross negligence. As indicated, this is not without exceptions – see the Supreme Court judgment reported in UfR 2006.632 concerning a clause limiting the amount of damages to be paid for goods stolen while they were in the possession of a cargo freight company which had acted with gross negligence. The liability clause was part of the General Conditions of Nordic Freight Forwarders (NSAB 2000) and the only exception, according to the wording of the terms, was deliberately caused damage. The Supreme Court stated that the terms were based on negotiations between trade organisations representing freight forwarders and their customers, and that the limitation clause, together with various other terms, was part of the set of standard terms which were presumed to be the result of an

---

[25] See Supreme Court judgment reported in UfR 1969.152.
[26] See Supreme Court judgment reported in UfR 1986.654.
[27] See Gomard, *Obligationsret 2. Del*, pp. 55–56; and Bryde Andersen and Lookofsky, *Lærebog i Obligationsret*, pp. 406 and 420.

overall trade-off, considering, inter alia, the insurance options. Therefore, the court found no basis for setting aside the clause according to the general clause in §36 of the Contracts Act.

The groups of modifications mentioned above also apply to contracts defining the payment of a certain amount ('konventionalbod')[28] as the sole remedy. Generally, a contract term authorising this remedy is likely to be interpreted as substituting the remedy of damages so that the entitled party cannot claim damages according to general rules[29] unless the modifications mentioned above apply or the amount defined in the contract is unreasonable according to §36 of the Contracts Act.

2.7   Subject to contract

If a term negotiated, seen in isolation, contains a binding promise, its binding effect is not automatically excluded by the fact that other elements of the document point in the opposite direction. In that case, as in other cases of mutually conflicting contract elements, the result depends on interpretation, taking into account all facts of the individual case. See, e.g., the Supreme Court decision reported in UfR 1994.470 about a document with the title 'letter of intent', which stated: 'In view of the fact that [the Bank] has placed credit facilities at the disposal of the [subsidiary company], the undersigned [parent company] hereby declares . . . that we shall if required transfer [to the subsidiary company] sufficient liquid funds to make sure that the subsidiary company will at all times be able to fulfil its obligations towards the bank.' The majority of the Supreme Court decided that the parent company had made a clear and unconditional promise. On the basis of the above quotation, there was, irrespective of the title of the declaration, a presumption that the parent company was bound in accordance with the contents. The fact that during prior negotiations with the bank, the parent company had refused to act as guarantor for the subsidiary company was not sufficient reason to establish that the bank had accepted that the declaration was not to be considered legally binding. The reason for this was that refusal to act as guarantor is (for accounting reasons) the typical reason for the

---

[28] Equivalent to liquidated damages – see Section 3.1 below for details.

[29] See Bryde Andersen and Lookofsky, *Lærebog i Obligationsret*, p. 422; and Bryde Andersen, *Praktisk aftaleret. Aftaleretten* II, pp. 395–396, but in the opposite direction J. Nørager-Nielsen, S. Theilgaard, M. Bjerg Hansen and M. Hørmann Pallesen, *Købeloven*, 3rd edn (Thomson, 2008), p. 493.

use of a 'comfort letter', as in this case. In the Supreme Court case reported in UfR 1998.1289, the result was the opposite. Here the parent company in a 'letter of comfort' had declared 'to support [the subsidiary company] financially with a view to enable the company to fulfil its obligations towards [the bank]'. A majority of judges stated that the declaration, in contrast to that in the 1994 case mentioned above, did not expressly state an obligation for the parent company to transfer liquid funds to the subsidiary company, and that the declaration could be complied with without such a transfer. The minority could find no sufficient basis for making such a distinction between the declaration in question and that of the 1994 case, and therefore voted for the same result as in the 1994 decision.

If a party to a non-binding preparatory agreement, e.g., a letter of intent to continue negotiations in order to reach a final agreement, does not participate in a loyal way in the continued process, that party may incur a liability to pay damages covering the other party's costs (i.e., the negative interest) caused by negligence (*culpa in contrahendo*) founded in the manifest violation of the general principle of loyalty.[30] In its decision of the case reported in UfR 2007.3027, the Supreme Court held that a trading agreement was a framework agreement only for a future partnership based on a common expectation that one of the parties would develop measuring equipment and that that party was under no obligation to develop such equipment. The Court stated that, within the scope of the agreement, it was a consequence of the agreement that both parties were obliged to honour loyal conduct and to inform each other of facts pertinent to the planned partnership (*in casu*, the failure to develop the measurement equipment), and that violation of this duty of loyalty could lead to liability for payment of damages, which was, in fact, the outcome.

If the (rather strict) conditions for liability to pay damages for failure to reach a final agreement due to disloyal conduct are met, a subject to contract clause, not explicitly stating that it excludes liability in case of negligence, is not likely to have that effect.[31]

---

[30] See Bryde Andersen and Lookofsky, *Lærebog i Obligationsret*, pp. 242–244; Bryde Andersen, *Grundlæggende aftaleret*, pp. 94ff.; Lynge Andersen and Madsen, *Aftale og mellemmænd*, p. 109; and Gomard, Godsk Pedersen and Ørgaard, *Almindelig Kontraktsret*, p. 89.

[31] See the general principles developed in case law concerning the interpretation and voidability of contract clauses excluding or limiting liability to pay damages. See Section 2.6 above.

2.8   Material adverse change

According to the general principles of contract law, the significance of altered circumstances to the binding effect of contractual obligations is usually dealt with primarily under the doctrine of failure of assumptions.[32] The basic conditions for the release of the promisor from the promise required by the doctrine are that the assumption in question was fundamental to the promise and that this was perceptible to the promisee. Furthermore, it is a condition that it is just and reasonable to put the risk of the failure of the assumption upon the promisee, taking into account which of the parties had, in the given situation, the better reason and the better possibility to investigate the circumstances, and thus clarify the validity of the assumption in question, their insurance possibilities, etc. Such factors in general indicate that the risk should lie with the promisor, but there are also specific cases where the risk should typically lie with the promisee. The release of the promisor in commercial situations normally requires subsequent events of a quite extraordinary nature and beyond normal commercial calculation.

To the extent that material adverse change clauses specify what constitutes material changes making the contract not binding, they make the doctrine of failure of assumptions redundant, whereas imprecise clauses are likely to be interpreted in line with that doctrine. Furthermore, courts, generally speaking, tend to put a rather restrictive interpretation on such clauses to the extent that they leave the question of the binding effect of the contract to the discretion of one of the parties. This then counteracts the clause being used as a pretext for withdrawing from the contract in cases where the party in question has no real need to do so[33] or ought to have anticipated the development, or where the change is clearly not affecting that party's interests on a permanent basis. The more precise the clauses are, e.g., in terms of quantifying what constitutes a material change, the less likely the restrictive interpretation will be.[34]

---

[32]   In Danish: *forudsætningslæren*. The introduction of §36 of the Contracts Act in 1975 was expected by some commentators to be the beginning of the end for the doctrine of failure of assumptions, because §36 would make it superfluous in practice. The doctrine is, however, still alive and well alongside §36. See Gomard, Godsk Pedersen and Ørgaard, *Almindelig Kontraktsret*, pp. 199–200; and Lynge Andersen and Madsen, *Aftale og mellemmænd*, pp. 199 and 126.

[33]   Compare this with Section 2.5 above concerning 'conditions'.

[34]   L. Stolze and C. Svernlöv, 'Virksomhedsoverdragelsesskolen', in *Revision & Regnskabsvæsen* (2005), No. 1, 6–13, No. 4, 50–60 and No. 5, 50–56, 54–56; and A. Tamasauskas, *Erhvervslivets lånoptagelse* (Gjellerup, 2006), pp. 555–556.

There seem to be no publicised decisions on the material adverse change clauses.

3 Clauses that use a terminology with legal effects not known to the applicable law

The common intention of the parties when the contract was made is decisive. This also applies to the interpretation of contract clauses containing special terminology, be it technical, legal, in another language, etc. In order to establish the common intention of the parties, the courts will take into account all available pertinent facts and such pragmatic factors as mentioned above in Section 2.1. It does not matter that the common intention of the parties deviates from the authorised or natural understanding of the term in question; *falsa demonstratio non nocet.*[35]

To the extent that it is not possible to ascertain the common intention of the parties, courts tend to interpret/fill out the contract in a way that complies with the general rules and principles of the applicable law, i.e., in the present context, Danish contract law (see above, Section 1). The Western High Court decision reported in UfR 1977.1031 concerned a special delivery clause, 'Jan Fix15/4', that the parties had apparently copied from a department store's contract practice where the clause seemed to have been used to indicate that delivery could take place from a certain point in time (*in casu*, January) and that the goods had to be at the buyer's disposal at the very latest on a certain date (*in casu*, 15 April). The controversy concerned the question of delay. The goods were handed over to the carrier on 14 April and arrived at the buyer's shop on the 17 April. The parties had not discussed the precise meaning of the clause when the contract was made, the clause was not generally used within the trade, and its content was not considered well-established trade usage. The court therefore interpreted the clause in compliance with the concept of delivery of the Sales of Goods Act and accordingly held that delivery had taken place on 14 April. Consequently, there was no delay.

The delivery clause interpreted in the Supreme Court decision reported in UfR 2001.1039 was less exotic and the decision nicely illustrates the basic point.[36] Both the Danish buyer's order and the Italian

---

[35] Gomard, Godsk Pedersen and Ørgaard, *Almindelig Kontraktsret*, p. 178; and Lynge Andersen and Madsen, *Aftaler og Mellemmænd*, p. 388.

[36] In that particular case, Italian law applied to the contract. Therefore, the value of the decision as precedent for Danish courts is doubtful as regards interpretation of contracts under Danish law.

seller's confirmation of the order contained the clause 'franco (the Danish city of) Skanderborg'. The buyer later brought a lawsuit concerning the non-conformity of the goods delivered against the seller in a Danish court, based on the fact that the 'franco' clause, according to Danish default rules,[37] defines the place of delivery and thus meant that Danish courts had jurisdiction under Article 5(1) of the Brussels Convention. The Italian seller argued that the 'franco' clause should be interpreted in accordance with Italian law where the clause concerns costs only and has no relevance to the place of delivery. The Supreme Court stated that it was not established that the parties had based their business relations on the buyer's interpretation of the 'franco' clause and, referring to the fact that Italian law was the applicable law to the contract, held that the contract did not show that the parties had agreed that the city of Skanderborg was the place of delivery. Therefore, according to Article 31(a) of the CISG, the place of delivery was in Italy and the Danish courts did not have jurisdiction.

3.1   Liquidated damages

In Danish contract law, there is no sharp distinction between penalty clauses and clauses defining a standardised amount of damages. Both categories are within the scope of '*konventionalbod*'. Before the General Clause of §36 was introduced into the Contracts Act in 1975, §36 contained a rule to the effect that such payment obligations could be set aside to the extent that the payment of the full amount would be manifestly unreasonable. The mixed character (penalty/damage) of this clause found expression in the way the former provision described some of the factors to be taken into account when deciding on the question of reasonableness. Thus, not only the loss suffered but also the interest of the entitled party in the breach in question (together with the other facts of the case) should be taken into account. This provision was repealed and substituted by the General Clause in 1975, but it is the general view that the criteria are, by and large, still the same when the General Clause is applied to such clauses.[38] An illustration is found in the Supreme Court decision reported in UfR 2004.2400 concerning delay of the delivery of

---

[37] See §65 of the Danish Sales of Goods Act.

[38] See Gomard, Godsk Pedersen and Ørgaard, *Almindelig Kontraktsret*, p. 200; and T. Iversen, 'Nogle bemærkninger om dagbøder', in T. Iversen (ed.), *Festskrift til Det Danske Selskab for Byggeret* (Thomson Reuters, 2009), pp. 105–124, 121–124.

elements for air-conditioning systems. The Supreme Court held that the daily amount (50,000 SEK) stipulated in the contract to be paid by the seller in case of delay as well as the total amount claimed (1.4 million SEK) were markedly out of proportion with the contract value (260,000 SEK) and that it was not shown that the buyer would suffer or actually had suffered losses of such a size that the daily amount stipulated and the total amount claimed were proportionate to the losses incurred. Therefore, according to §36, the amount to be paid under the contract clause was reduced considerably (to less than 100,000 SEK).

Generally, the clauses do not apply unless there is a basis for liability to pay damages according to the general rules of contract law.[39] Furthermore, it is the general view that there is a presumption that such clauses should be interpreted as excluding the payment of damages in excess of the stipulated amount.[40] See Section 2.6 above for further details.

4   Clauses that regulate matters already regulated in the applicable law

4.1   Representations and warranties

One important aspect of the general contract law principle of loyalty in contractual relations is the general duty to disclose material facts. This rule is developed in case law and has been embodied in the statutory rules on consumer sales that, in this respect, also reflect the principles that apply to commercial contracts. It follows from §§76 (1) and (3) of the Sales of Goods Act that the goods are not in conformity with the contract if the seller has failed to inform the buyer of circumstances that influenced the buyer's assessment of the goods and which were known, or ought to have been known, by the seller. Breach of the duty to disclose such facts implies negligence and thus, *per se,* a basis of liability to pay damages for breach of contract.[41]

Whereas extensive lists of representations and warranties may reduce the practical need for applying the general principle of the duty to disclose material facts, it is not plausible that such lists will be considered exhaustive in the sense that there will be no duty to disclose other

---

[39]   See Bryde Andersen and Lookofsky, *Lærebog i Obligationsret,* p. 422.
[40]   See *ibid.,* p. 422, but in the opposite direction, Nørager-Nielsen *et al., KøReloven,* p. 493.
[41]   A statutory rule to this effect concerning consumer sales is found in §§80(1) and (3) of the Sales of Goods Act.

material facts known, or which ought to have been known, by the contract party in question.[42] In the case reported in UfR 2004.1784, the Supreme Court held that the buyer was entitled to terminate a contract of transfer of the ownership of a company inter alia, because the seller did not loyally inform the buyer of a significant decline in orders, for at least a six-month period, from one of the company's largest customers.

4.2   Hardship and force majeure

Danish contract law only to a rather limited extent contains precise rules dealing with the legal consequences of supervening external events making performance more onerous to a party, and thus leaves it to the parties to regulate the matter in their contract. In addition to the rather general and vague principles expressed in the doctrine of failure of assumptions[43] and in the General Clause in §36 of the Contracts Act, §24 of the Sales of Goods Act contains a rather precise rule regulating the basis of liability to pay damages for breach of generic obligations, i.e., obligations to supply a given quantity of generically defined, unascertained goods.[44] §24 applies to the seller's delayed delivery of goods only, but embodies a general principle concerning the breach of generic obligations.[45] According to §24, the breach triggers liability unless it is deemed impossible to perform in time due to extraordinary circumstances such as war, import prohibition, etc. Such circumstances are usually (but not in the wording of §24) defined as *force majeure*. In order to exempt the party from liability, the circumstances causing the impossibility must belong to the same category (*ejusdem generis*) as the examples mentioned (war, etc.) and not have been foreseeable to the party when the contract was made.[46] The *force majeure* principle based on §24 concerns the basis of liability to pay damages, but also applies to the party's obligation to perform, in that the obligation is suspended temporarily or brought to an end by the same circumstances.[47]

It is the general view that there is a presumption that clauses referring to *force majeure* should be interpreted in accordance with the principle in §24. This implies that, for want of evidence pointing in another direction, *force majeure* clauses stipulating examples of exemptions other than

---

[42] See Schans Christensen, *Grænseoverskridende virksomhedsoverdragelser*, p. 194.
[43] See Section 2.8 above.   [44] Another example is Article 79 of the CISG.
[45] Gomard, *Obligationsret 2. Del*, p. 161.   [46] See *ibid.*, pp. 163ff.
[47] See *ibid.*, p. 35.

those mentioned in §24 (labour disputes, bad weather, etc.) in all other respects are interpreted in compliance with the principle in §24. In addition, as far as the legal effects of an exemption are concerned, there is a general presumption that such clauses should be interpreted as dealing only with remedies of liability to pay damages and the obligation to perform.[48]

4.3   Clauses on contractual liability and/or product liability

One special feature of Danish law is the status of the rules on product liability, i.e., the liability for personal injury and damage caused to property (other than the dangerous/defective product itself). The product liability rules are constructed in a way that can cause problems concerning the interpretation and validity of contract clauses dealing with limitations of a seller's or a service provider's liability. Under Danish law, personal injury and damage caused to property (other than the defective product itself) are outside the scope of the seller's liability for breach of contract. No explicit rule to this effect is found in the Sales of Goods Act, but the Act has been, and still is, understood in this way by the courts.[49] An exception to this is found *e contrario* in Article 5 of the CISG, concerning damage to the buyer's property in international non-consumer sales contracts.

The liability of producers and suppliers of dangerous/defective products and services is based on fault (*culpa*) following the non-statutory principles of tort law with the extra refinement that professional suppliers have a vicarious liability for product liability incurred by previous links in the chain of production or distribution. The principle of vicarious liability is developed by the courts and it is usually justified by the consideration that the professional supplier is regularly in a better position than the injured party to influence and to seek recourse against the producer and other previous links in the chain of distribution. In addition to the court-developed principles, rules on product liability are

---

[48] See *ibid*, p. 168; and Nørager-Nielsen *et al.*, *Køberloven*, p. 434.

[49] This interpretation has been based mainly on the preparatory works of the Sales of Goods Act (from 1906). Although it may be doubtful that the preparatory works of the Act were actually meant to be understood in this way (see T. Iversen, 'Produktansvar og ansvarsbegrænsningen', *Juristen*, 6 (2008), 188–193, 190), it has for a long time been an established fact that the Act does not apply to product liability, See Justitsministeriet, København, *Betænkning 1502/2008 om visse køberetlige regler om sikkerhedsmangler om visse køberetlige regler om sikkerhedsmangler*, p. 74.

found in the Product Liability Act[50] implementing the Product Liability Directive.[51] These impose a strict (no-fault) defect liability on the 'producer' (with a development risk defence) and codify the pre-existing principle of professional suppliers' vicarious liability for product liability incurred by fault by a previous link in the chain of production and distribution.[52] As is the case with the Directive, the scope of the Product Liability Act is personal injury and damage to consumers' property. Thus, both the court-developed rules and the rules of the Product Liability Act apply to personal injury and damage to consumers' property, whereas only the court-developed rules apply to damage to non-consumer property.

The Product Liability Act is mandatory not only to the benefit of the injured party[53] but also to the benefit of a supplier who has paid damages to the injured party according to §10a of the Product Liability Act, i.e., on the basis of the supplier's vicarious liability for fault-based liability of a previous link – see §12 of the Act.[54] This means that contract terms excluding or limiting liability claims between commercial parties are not binding on suppliers seeking recourse against a previous link in the chain of distribution. The mandatory rule applies within the scope of the Product Liability Act, i.e., only in cases of personal injury and damage

---

[50] Act No. 371/1989.

[51] Council Directive 85/374/EEC of 25 July 1985 on the approximation of the laws, regulations and administrative provisions of the Member States concerning liability for defective products, OJ 1985 No. L210/29.

[52] Originally, the Product Liability Act stipulated that suppliers were also vicariously liable for the producers' strict liability. In its preliminary ruling in Case C-402/03, *Skov Æg v. Bilka Lavprisvarehus* [2006] ECR I-199, the European Court of Justice found that the supplier's vicarious liability for the producer's no-fault liability was in conflict with the Product Liability Directive. The vicarious liability rule of the Danish Act was amended accordingly to the effect that suppliers are now vicariously liable for the producers' (and other previous links') fault-based liability only – see §10a of the Act. The net result of *Skov Æg* was that the protection of consumers was lowered, and the Danish Minister of Justice therefore appointed a committee to consider a possible amendment of the Sales of Goods Act in order to improve the protection of consumers without laying disproportionate burdens on the sellers. In its report, the committee recommended an amendment of the Sales of Goods Act to the effect that the seller's liability for damage caused by nonconforming goods includes personal injury and damage to property: see *Betænkning 1502/2008 om visse køberetlige regler om sikkerhedsmangler*.

[53] I.e., the victim of personal injury or the owner of the consumer property damaged.

[54] See J. Langemark and H. Jørgensen, 'Regresaftaler vedrørende produktansvar', *Ugeskrift for Retsvæsen*, B (1997), 65–69; and M. Samuelsson, 'Ansvarsfraskrivelse og produktansvar', in *Forsikrings- og Erstatningsretlige Skrifter* I:2000 (Forsikringshøjskolens Forlag, 2000), p. 248. According to Article 8(1), the Directive does not prejudice national law concerning the right of contribution and recourse.

to consumers' property. Damage to non-consumer property is outside the scope of the Act and accordingly, beyond the reach of the mandatory rule. Furthermore, as a result of *Skov Æg,* the supplier's vicarious liability is no longer extended to the producer's non-fault based liability. Conversely, the mandatory rule also applies in cases where a vicariously liable supplier seeks recourse against another supplier who is also vicariously liable for fault-based liability incurred by the producer.

Another point to be made goes beyond the Product Liability Act, in that it concerns the distinction between contract law rules on non-conformity and rules on product liability in general. As mentioned above, personal injury and damage to property (other than the non-conforming/defective good itself) are traditionally considered to be outside the scope of the liability rules of the Sales of Goods Act. Accordingly, there seems to be a basis for a general assumption that clauses in sales contracts that do not unambiguously refer to product liability rules but to sales law concepts are to be understood as dealing with matters within the scope of the Sales of Goods Act only. Thus, clauses limiting the liability for, e.g., 'non-conformity' of the object of sale or 'breach' of the contract do not have any effect on the liability for physical damage caused by the object of sale.[55]

The Supreme Court judgment reported in UfR 1999.255 provides a basis for an assumption to this effect. A Danish supplier who had delivered pipes to a municipal heating scheme had incurred vicarious liability for damage caused to other parts of the pipeline by a leak in welded steel pipes produced by a German company who had sold the pipes to the Danish supplier. The German producer had incurred fault liability vis-à-vis the municipality under the court-developed rules on product liability. The sales contract between the German seller and the Danish supplier referred to the seller's general conditions of delivery and payment, which contained a choice-of-law clause according to which 'the law of seller's domicile applies to all legal relations between the buyer and us'[56] and a clause concerning notification of defects using contract law terminology ('conformity', 'non-conformity', 'replacement'), and stating, inter alia, that 'all other claims, including claims for damages, no matter their legal foundation, are excluded'.[57] The Supreme

---

[55] See V. Ulfbeck, *Erstaningsretlige grænseområder. Professionsansvar, produktansvar og offentlige myndigheders erstatningsansvar,* 2nd edn (Jurist- og Økonomforbundets Forlag, 2010), pp. 216–223; and Nørager-Nielsen *et al., Købeloven,* p. 831.

[56] This is my own translation of the Danish translation (found in the decision). The original text in German is not cited in the reported case.

[57] See note 56.

Court held that the question of whether the Danish supplier was entitled to have recourse against the German seller for the liability of the latter to compensate the municipality was not, with a sufficient degree of clarity, within the scope of the choice-of-law clause of the seller's general conditions. Therefore, the clause did not apply to the case. Similarly, the Supreme Court held that the supplier's claim of recourse was not within the scope of the seller's 'general conditions' clause on notification of defects.

The Supreme Court judgment reported in UfR 2006.2052 shows how a liability limitation can be drafted in order to make sure that both contractual liability and product liability are within its scope. In this case, the clause stipulated that the seller, in case of non-conformity and damage caused by the product, was liable only if the non-conformity or the damage was caused by failure or negligence by the seller.

It should be noted that neither the 1999 case nor the 2006 case concerned liability under the Product Liability Act but damage to non-consumer property falling outside the scope of the Act, and that the cases were consequently dealt with under the court-developed rules on product liability. Although the same principles of interpretation are likely to apply in cases that are within the scope of the Product Liability Act, the main emphasis in such cases is typically on the fact that the victim's and supplier's right of recourse are protected by mandatory rules.[58]

As mentioned above, the sharp distinction between contract law liability and product liability was originally founded in the preparatory works of the Sales of Goods Act. Nevertheless, a similar interpretation to the one applied by the Supreme Court in UfR 1999.255 seems to apply to the interpretation of contract law clauses outside the scope of sales law, i.e., normally in areas of the law where there are no statutory rules.[59] See the Supreme Court judgment in UfR 2008.982. This case arose from a fire in a power plant caused by a negligently installed safety membrane. The claim in question concerned consequential loss caused by the fire. A clause found in a widely used agreed document, the General Conditions for Turnkey Contracts (ABT 93), was part of the contract. The clause stipulates that:

> §35. The contractor shall be liable for compensation of losses suffered due to non-conformity[60] of the work where such non-conformity is caused by

---

[58] See §12 of the Act and the text above.
[59] The general principles of Danish contract law are not codified. See Section 1 above.
[60] The Danish term used is 'mangler', which is contract law terminology. In the English translation available at http://servicebutik.danskbyggeri.dk, the term used is 'defect'.

errors or negligence on the part of the contractor, or where they relate to properties the presence of which has been guaranteed in the contract.

Subsection 2. The contractor shall not be liable for operational losses, loss of profit or other indirect losses.

The Supreme Court stated that the case did not concern the contractor's contractual liability for the non-conforming installation but rather the product liability (outside the scope of the Product Liability Act), and that the clause in §35 applies to contractual liability only. Therefore, the liability for operational losses was not excluded by sub-section 2 of the clause.

In summary, the interpretation and validity of contract terms excluding or limiting liability sometimes depend on whether the basis of the liability in question is found in contract and/or in tort law rules. A last example mentioned here to illustrate the rather delicate difference between contractual liability and product liability (outside the scope of the Product Liability Act) is found in a Supreme Court judgment reported in UfR 2010.1360. In this case, the producer of a gas engine used by a power plant was not liable to compensate the power plant's operational losses caused by the breakdown of the gas engine. The breakdown was due to a defective thread in a connecting rod made and installed in the engine by the same producer. The damage to the gas engine caused by the faulty connecting rod was not within the scope of the product liability rules, i.e., damage to other property, but damage to the product itself, and was thus a consequence of non-conformity of the gas engine.

The Nordic tradition: application of boilerplate clauses under Finnish Law

GUSTAF MÖLLER

1 Introduction

The general starting point in Finnish contract law, as it usually is in countries with market economies, is *pacta sunt servanda* and that each party must carry his or her own risk as to how the contracted obligations will develop. The Finnish Contracts Act of 1929 is almost completely identical to the Danish, Norwegian and Swedish Contracts Acts, which have served as models for the Finnish Contracts Act. Moreover, the Sales of Goods Acts in Finland, Norway and Sweden are, with the exception of some minor differences, identical. However, Finland has no comprehensive civil code like, e.g., the German BGB or the French Civil Code. Instead, the general principles of contract law are not codified, which makes case law and doctrine important as legal sources in the field of contract law in Finland. In substance, the principles of Finnish law on contracts are the same as in the other Scandinavian countries.

The basic principles of Finnish contract law that seem relevant in this context are good faith and loyalty in contractual relationships and fairness. The underlying idea is to conceive a contractual relationship as a cooperative project for the parties instead of an arrangement which entitles a party to a contract to pursue only his or her own interests. In general, these principles impose a duty to also take into consideration the interests of the other party. These principles may prevent the full implementation of clauses aiming at detaching the contract from Finnish law, which is presumed to be the governing law. First, the parties cannot, at least not fully, exclude liability for fraud or gross negligence. Nor is a party under Finnish law allowed to exploit a contract to his or her own advantage. Secondly, pursuant to §36 of the Contracts Act, an agreed-upon term may be amended or disregarded if it is deemed unfair or

unreasonable, or if its application in a given case would be unfair or unreasonable. In considering whether a term is unreasonable, the court shall take into account the whole contract, the situation of the parties when the contract was entered into and the situation of the parties thereafter, as well as other circumstances. If the term is such that because the amendment of the term makes it no longer reasonable for the contract to remain in force, then other parts of the contract can also be amended or the contract terminated. §36 is very rarely applied by the courts to commercial relations. Under Finnish law, it is clear that the parties cannot completely renounce their duty to disclose information. Liability for fraudulent and grossly negligent information that falls within §§30 (fraud) or 33 of the Contracts Act cannot be contracted out:
§30 provides:

> Where a person in relation to whom a legal act is performed has fraudulently represented or withheld facts which may be presumed to be material in relation to the act, such person shall be deemed to have thereby induced the legal act, unless it is shown that such legal act was not influenced by fraud.

§33 provides as follows:

> A legal act which would otherwise be deemed valid may not be relied upon where the circumstances in which it arose were such that, having knowledge of such circumstances, it would be inequitable to enforce the legal act, and where the party in respect of whom such legal act was performed must be presumed to have had such knowledge.

Whether or not there is a duty to disclose depends on both objective and subjective circumstances, and the evaluation of whether it would be inequitable to enforce a legal act shall be done taking into account the principle of loyalty and §33 of the Contracts Act. There are two sets of principles that may apply in situations of supervening circumstances affecting the balance in the parties' agreement. First, there is the doctrine of failed assumptions. Secondly, there is the aforementioned mandatory rule in §36 of the Contracts Act (the 'general clause'). However, the influence of the doctrine of failed assumptions has been rather limited in Finland, at least in comparison to what has been the case in Denmark, Norway and Sweden. It has been submitted that the doctrine of the right to be discharged from obligations under the contract because of factual (physical) or economic impossibility can sometimes also be used in these situations. Moreover, since 1983, there is even less need for the doctrine of failed assumptions, because §36 of the Contracts Act is no longer limited to penalty clauses, as was originally the case.

In commercial settings, the threshold for setting aside or amending contracts under §36 will be similar to that under the doctrine of failed assumptions in Sweden and Norway. In reality, however, where the risk for failed assumptions has been allocated in the agreement, there is little room left for the application of §36 of the Contracts Act.

As to interpretation, a court is likely to choose the alternative that is seen as the most 'fair and reasonable' option. This is supported by the general duty of loyalty in contracts under Finnish law and the standard for fairness in §36 of the Contracts Act. It is likely that the considerations of fairness and reasonableness will depend on the specific circumstances of the case. Sometimes non-mandatory legislation, e.g., the Sales of Goods Act, is used in practice as a yardstick for fairness or reasonableness. Exemption clauses and other clauses excluding liability are construed narrowly. In addition, the *in dubio contra stipulatorem sive proferentem* rule is a well-established rule in Finnish contract law. Surprising and onerous clauses are usually narrowly construed.

2   Clauses aiming at fully detaching the contract from the applicable law

2.1   Entire agreement

An entire agreement clause does not, under Finnish law, mean that all sources of law other than the contract would be excluded. Thus, it does not have the consequence that a contract in writing is regarded as an exhaustive regulation of the contractual relationship. It does not prevent a party from invoking practices or usages that they may have established between themselves, unless this has been explicitly mentioned in the clause. However, there can be no doubt that the clause has the effect that the parties' precontractual conduct and agreements are of minor relevance for the interpretation of the contract. The clause would most probably, except perhaps in very rare and exceptional cases, prevent corrective interpretation based on precontractual circumstances. Most probably, the parties' precontractual assumptions will be of little relevance when it could reasonably be expected that the question was regulated in the contract. Circumstances arising subsequently to entering into a contract are probably not affected by the clause.

An entire agreement clause probably has only minor effects when it is necessary to fill a gap in a contract. However, it may prevent supplementation of the agreement when supplementation is not required for the contract to function. If, e.g., the parties have on a previous occasion agreed upon certain specifications for certain products but have not incorporated these specifications into the present contract, the contract probably could not, because of the entire agreement clause, be interpreted in the light of the previously agreed specifications.

It seems obvious that it cannot be deemed unfair or unreasonable according to §36 of the Contracts Act that certain precontractual circumstances are precluded from having legal effect. The courts are, as mentioned above, rather reluctant to apply §36 to commercial relations. However, the potential unreasonableness that may be occasioned by the clause may, in very exceptional circumstances, justify the application of this mandatory rule.

2.2 No waiver

A clause, according to which failure by a party to exercise a right or remedy that he or she has under the contract does not constitute a waiver thereof, would certainly thus not be invalid under Finnish law. Under Finnish law, the right to use a remedy will be lost because of the rules on the duty to give notice of the breach or because of the general rules on the effect of passivity, unless the parties have agreed otherwise. However, the validity of a no waiver clause is limited by the principle of loyalty in contractual relationships. The clause may be disregarded if it would violate the principle of good faith or the duty of loyalty to the extent that it would allow disloyal behaviour by the party invoking it. Thus, for instance, in some cases, it may be unreasonable if the party against whom the clause is invoked could not, in spite of the clause, trust that he or she has waived the right to exercise a right or remedy because of the other party's conduct. However, when a party's conduct is considered disloyal, a no waiver clause may have the effect that the threshold becomes higher.

If the contract gives one party the right to terminate in case of delay in the delivery and the delivery is late, but the party does not terminate until after a considerable time and the real reason for the termination is not the delay but the fact that the market has changed and the contract is no longer profitable, the old delay probably cannot be invoked as a ground for termination; to do so would be regarded as disloyal behaviour.

2.3 No oral amendments

Under Finnish law, a no oral amendments clause cannot prevent the parties from entering into other agreements orally. As long as the separate agreement does not contradict the original contract with a no oral amendments clause, the clause cannot prevent that separate agreement from being valid and enforceable. A possibility for the parties to restrict their own ability to enter into future agreements does not seem to conform to the principle of freedom of contract. If the parties enter into an oral agreement amending the original agreement, the clause will probably be regarded as being waived implicitly, unless the whole contract is found to be rescinded and is then replaced with a new contract.

The principles of good faith and loyalty in contractual relationships under Finnish law may also prevent a party from invoking a no oral agreement clause. For instance, if the parties to a written construction contract have later orally agreed on extra construction work, the client cannot deny the contractor's claim for compensation for that work.

However, a no oral amendments clause will probably create a presumption that the parties did not definitively intend to vary the contract in a way that would be legally binding. This presumption may often be difficult to rebut.

2.4   Severability

A severability clause allows that, even when a provision of an agreement is or becomes illegal, invalid or unenforceable, the validity or enforceability of any other provision of the agreement shall not be affected, and therefore other provisions or the entire contract itself would not be disregarded. This is also the general rule under Finnish law. However, a literal interpretation of the clause may lead to an unbalanced contract if the provision that becomes invalid or unenforceable has significance for the interests of only one of the parties. Therefore, in such cases, the court may, pursuant to §36 of the Contracts Act, find that because a provision in the agreement is or becomes illegal, invalid or unenforceable, other parts of the contract may also be amended or the contract terminated.

2.5   Conditions

A clause according to which certain obligations regulated in a contract are fundamental and according to which any breach thereof shall amount to a fundamental breach of the contract is thus valid under Finnish law. This clause may often be interpreted as meaning an 'absolute' right to rescind the contract if there is a breach, not because the term is regarded as a condition but because the parties have expressed the opinion that the obligation is important. Even though the provision as such would be valid under Finnish contract law and the parties need to have such a regulation, the parties cannot, in all cases, be certain that the phrase gives an 'absolute' right to rescind if there is a breach of the obligation. It may well be that a Finnish court would give the clause a restrictive interpretation. Thus, for example, if the contract defines delay in delivery as a fundamental breach and if there is a delay, but the delay has only insignificant (if any) consequences for the other (innocent) party, it may well be that a Finnish court may find that reliance on the clause would be against the principles of good faith and loyalty in contractual relationships. The clause on fundamental breach could certainly not be invoked if it is established that the real reason for the termination is not the delay but the change in the market.

2.6   Sole remedy

A clause that defines that the payment of a certain amount shall be the buyer's sole remedy for any delay in delivery for which the seller is responsible under the agreement is thus certainly not invalid under Finnish law. However, if the damage clause limits the liability and can be regarded as an exemption clause, it may be disregarded pursuant to §36 of the Contracts Act. Thus, if the non-defaulting party is able to prove that the breach has caused a damage considerably larger than the agreed amount, the courts would probably often disregard the clause. Exemption clauses, especially those that cover gross negligence or intentional breaches, are traditionally set aside by the courts, as they may encourage disloyal behaviour. Since the principles of good faith in contract and the principle of loyalty in contractual relationships have a foothold in Finnish contract law, the courts are not likely to promote the possibility of disloyal behaviour.

2.7   Subject to contract

A document which provides that it does not represent a binding agreement between the parties and that neither party shall be under any liability to the other party in case of failure to enter into the final agreement is normally given full effect under Finnish law. However, the principles of good faith and loyalty in contractual relationships may have the effect that such a clause is disregarded. Thus, for instance, if the parties enter into a letter of intent specifying that failure to reach a final agreement will not expose any of the parties to liability, a party who refuses to enter into a final agreement may be liable to compensate the other party for his or her losses, in particular if it is established that he or she never really intended to enter into a final agreement and used the negotiations only to prevent the other party from entering into a contract with a third party.

2.8   Material adverse change

The intended effect of material adverse change clauses is presumably to protect a contracting party from unknown risks by allowing that party to walk away from the transaction in case of a material adverse change event. If one party invokes this clause to avoid a deal that it has lost interest in and it is established that the real reason is not a change in external circumstances but in the party's own evaluation thereof, he or she could probably not successfully rely on the clause; to do so would be against the principle of good faith and loyalty in contractual relationships.

3   Clauses that use a terminology with legal effects not known to the applicable law

3.1   Liquidated damages

Finnish law permits the parties to agree on contractual penalties. These may be cumulated with reimbursement of damages. Under Finnish law, there is no clear distinction between liquidated damages and penalties. Finnish law does not consider the compensatory nature of damages as mandatory. So-called penalty clauses relating to pre-estimation of damages fill both the purposes of compensating for and deterring from breach. In addition, they usually make any evidence of the amount of the damage superfluous.

Finnish law does not consider the compensatory nature of damages as mandatory. If the parties agree to a penalty, they are, in principle, allowed to do so without concealing it as compensatory liquidated damages. However, Finnish courts have been able to attack the misuse of penalties pursuant to §36 of the Contracts Act ever since the enactment of that Act.

The use of the English term 'liquidated damages' under Finnish law would most probably create a presumption that the amount contractually stipulated is intended to be a reasonable estimation of the actual damages to be recovered by one party if the other party breaches. Thus, 'liquidated damages' may not usually be cumulated with reimbursement of actual damages.

Under Finnish law, a liquidated damage clause is usually presumed to be exclusive. In particular, this is the case in construction contracts regarding 'daily fines' for delay. However, this presumption is probably not likely to be upheld if the breach is intentionally committed by the defaulting party or because of gross negligence. If the actual loss is much bigger than the liquidated damages, the courts have the discretion of adjusting the damages using §36 of the Contracts Act. This will especially be the case if the bigger loss is due to the fact that the defaulting party's conduct was disloyal towards the innocent party, even though there is no intentional breach.

If the liquidated damages clause limits the liability and can be regarded as an exemption clause, it can be set aside pursuant to §36 of the Contracts Act. As mentioned above, exemption clauses, particularly those that cover gross negligence or intentional breaches, are traditionally set aside by the courts, as they may encourage disloyal behaviour. The principles of good faith in contractual relationships have a foothold in Finnish contract law and the courts are not likely to promote the possibility of disloyal behaviour.

It is not entirely clear under Finnish law whether the principle of good faith has the consequence that the duty to mitigate damages also applies to 'liquidated damages'.

3.2 Indemnity

If an indemnity clause was triggered by a breach of contract and the law applicable to the contract is Finnish law, the indemnity clause would probably just be understood to mean that damages have to be paid in case of a breach of contract. If the contract uses the term 'indemnity' to designate a guaranteed payment, it is a question of interpretation as to whether it prevents the guaranteed payment when no actual damage has occurred. Thus, if it is clear that the term 'indemnity' has been used only to designate a guaranteed payment, the use of the term does not, as such, prevent the guaranteed payment when no actual damage has occurred.

4   Clauses that regulate matters already regulated in the applicable law

4.1   Representations and warranties

Under Finnish law, there is no general requirement to disclose information. However, the parties shall disclose such information that it would be dishonest to withhold. In addition, the principles of good faith and loyalty may require information to be disclosed. The parties have a general duty to bargain in good faith, which means that the parties have a precontractual duty to disclose such information that is relevant for the opposite party. The duty to disclose information varies somewhat depending on the type of contract, but generally it is strict in situations where it is difficult or impossible for a party to the contract to conduct an inspection of the trade object and thus is without information that would be within the knowledge of the opposite party. Therefore, it is clear that the parties cannot completely renounce their duty to disclose information. Liability for fraudulent or grossly negligent behaviour and situations that fall within §33 of the Contracts Act cannot be contracted out of. This is also the case with certain remedies for breach of contract. Beyond this, the answer is more uncertain and depends on the principles of loyalty and good faith and the criteria of unfairness in §36 of the Contracts Act.

Whether or not liability can be contracted out of depends on which of the parties, after a concrete assessment according to the aforementioned rules and principles, is to have responsibility for disclosing information.

One more general point can probably be stated, which is that even though it is not possible to contract out of all liability for the duty to disclose information, the fact that the parties have included such an extensive and detailed list of representations and warranties in the contract will probably affect the extent of the duty to disclose other information that is not written into the contract. Beyond this, the answer must be found by assessing each case concretely and individually.

As a primary conclusion here, it must be said that the parties should specify more explicitly in their contract that they wish to limit the responsibility for withheld or disclosed information. A list of representations and warranties does not give grounds for a presumption that the parties have meant to exclude liability.

With regard to the information that is typically included in the list of representations and warranties, it is not possible to give a general answer as to when the parties will be objectively liable. However, it is probable that this will be the case for much of the information contained in the list. When the information which is 'warranted' concerns specified attributes, is detailed and amounts to substantial information, and in some cases also concerns 'core' attributes, it is probable that the disclosing party will be objectively liable for damages. With respect to contracts concerning the sale and purchase of businesses, it is often held that the main function of representations and warranties is to impose objective liability on the party disclosing the information.

4.2 Hardship

There is no general provision in Finnish law that specifically regulates the consequences of supervening, external events that make the performance excessively onerous for one party. The only general provision concerning contractual relations and supervening events is the aforementioned provision in §36 of the Contracts Act providing that, in considering whether a term is unreasonable, the court shall take into account not only the whole contract and the situation of the parties when the contract was entered into, but also the situation of the parties thereafter. If the parties regulated the matter in their contract, this does not mean that the contract regulation will be the only applicable regulation, but it will be integrated in the applicable law.

Thus, §36 of the Contracts Act may be applied despite the hardship clause in the contract.

4.3 Force majeure

Until the Sales of Goods Act was adopted in 1987, there were no provisions in Finnish law on *force majeure*. §§27 and 40 of the Sales of Goods Act provide that a party is not liable for a failure to perform any of his or her obligations if he or she proves that the failure was due to an impediment beyond his or her control and that he or she could not reasonably have been expected to take the impediment into account at the time of conclusion of the contract, or to have avoided or overcome it or its consequences. These two provisions are identical to Article 79(1) of the CISG. The same rule has later been included in some other new legislation relating to the delivery of goods. A clause that describes as *force majeure* such events that are beyond the control of the parties and that may not be reasonably foreseen or overcome would, at least normally, be valid under Finnish law. If the law applicable to the contract is Finnish law, however, it would not be applied independently of Finnish law. Thus, an impediment or event within a party's own organisation is not regarded to be beyond the control of that party. Nor is an impediment or event beyond the control of a party if the impediment or event is, e.g., due to the fact that the party's subcontractor or his or her supplier has not fulfilled its obligation, unless this is due to an impediment or event beyond the sub-contractor's or supplier's control that he or she could not reasonably have been expected to take into account at the conclusion of the contract, or if the event could not have been avoided or its consequences overcome. For an impediment or event to be beyond the control of a party, it is thus not sufficient that a party has been diligent and has acted in good faith.

The parties may, of course, validly agree that a *force majeure* clause shall apply even when the impediment could reasonably have been taken into account at the time of conclusion of the contract, or even if the consequences of the impediment could have been avoided. In addition, the use of the word 'event' instead of the word 'impediment' would probably mean that the *force majeure* clause would apply in cases in which the provisions on *force majeure* in the Sales of Goods Act and the CISG would not apply.

The Nordic tradition: application of boilerplate clauses under Norwegian law

VIGGO HAGSTRØM

1 The Scandinavian law of obligations – and of contracts – is a part of the law with old traditions[1]

From a Norwegian perspective, a modern law of obligations and of contracts was launched in the early 1850s, with the publication of a textbook incorporating the existing statutes and court decisions. By the 1870s, the law of obligations was a well-established discipline, both academically and in legal practice. The law of obligations was strengthened at the same time by the establishment on a governmental level of Scandinavian cooperation on legislation in the field of the law of obligations. One of the best known fruits of this is the joint Scandinavian Sales of Goods Act (1905–1907). It was not, however, a wholly Scandinavian invention, but was to a large extent a pragmatic simplification of concepts from English, French and German law. It can be noted that this pragmatic legislation was one of the cornerstones for CISG; it was very familiar to Ernst Rabel, who had initiated the publication of a German version of Tore Almén´s extensive commentary on the Sales of Goods Act.[2]

Thus, Scandinavian law has long been regarded as a separate entity from English, French and German law, a law family of its own.[3] The law of contracts is the main core of Scandinavian private law, and textbooks and court decisions from one of the countries is regarded more or less as on the same level as internal sources of law. Even though Norway has a

---

[1] V. Hagstrøm, 'The Scandinavian Law of Obligations', *Scandinavian Studies in Law*, 50 (2007), 113–124, 117ff.

[2] V. Hagstrøm, *Kjøpsrett* (Universitetsforlaget, 2005), pp. 23f.

[3] K. Zweigert and H. Kötz, *An Introduction to Comparative Law*, 3rd ed. (Oxford University Press, 1998) pp. 276ff.

small population and thus not a large number of court decisions on contract law, sources from Denmark, Sweden and later on also from Finland have supplemented the Norwegian sources to a large extent. From this perspective, Norwegian law is not something provincial, but a part of the Scandinavian legal family, having taken concepts from various legal families and transplanted them in Scandinavian soil.

There has been no political proposal to reform the Norwegian law of contract. When the United Nations (Vienna) Convention on Contracts for the International Sale of Goods ('CISG') was ratified, the Nordic countries enacted new laws for internal sales that differed only slightly from the CISG. This was not a large step, because the Nordic Sales of Goods Act (1905–1907) was very similar to the CISG. It follows from this that the UNIDROIT Principles of International Commercial Contracts ('UPICC') and Principles of European Contract Law ('PECL') are a familiar landscape to a Norwegian lawyer, and they are also widely used in internal transactions. Likewise, Books II and III of the Draft Common Frame of Reference ('DCFR') are close to the Nordic tradition, although the abstraction following from the incorporation of not only contracts but other obligations as well makes the DCFR a bit unfamiliar.

In summary, the law of contracts has a long tradition in Scandinavia, and over the years it has been enriched by English, French and German law, but has nonetheless maintained its individuality. It has functioned fairly well. It is also in line with recent international developments. One might therefore wonder how the present anglification of the law of contracts came about. I think it is due in part to worldwide economic development, with the USA as the dominating economic power and the City of London as the international economic centre, and, to a certain extent, to sociology, rather than to the superiority of the common law itself.

2   The way commercial contracts are drafted in Norway has changed considerably during the past twenty to thirty years

Since the beginning of the nineteenth century, Norway has had an industrial sector dominated by engineers. Most of them were educated at the Technical University in Trondheim, still an elite institution today. These men were familiar with all stages of production in their companies. They preferred to draft their company´s contracts themselves as they had a thorough understanding of the production process, the products and the markets. In many instances, lawyers were not consulted at all. Even when they were, the contracts still tended to be rather brief and straight-forwardly written in the Scandinavian style. One might wonder, of course, how this could have worked. To a large extent, the contracts relied on supplements found in the default rules of the law of obligations, and this actually worked well.

A new area in the industrial sector began in the early 1970s, with the advent of oil production in the North Sea. As Norwegian companies had little, if any, competence and experience in oil production, the operators of the oil fields were international oil companies. Their contractual agreements came mostly from a common law tradition and all contracts were therefore drafted in this tradition, even though the governing law, as stipulated in the concessions, should be Norwegian. This practice was also followed in relation to suppliers, so that common law contract models permeated an important part of the Norwegian industrial sector. There was a subsequent development: the leaders of the companies were no longer primarily recruited from the ranks of engineers, but rather, to a large extent, from pools of economists. Through their education, the economists had close ties to the USA and England. They were strongly influenced by the ideas of commerce in the Anglo-American world. As a result, globalisation brought the common law to the forefront. During the last decades of the twentieth century, the drafting of contracts changed in Norway and influences for these changes clearly came from common law.

This development was linked to fundamental changes in the law firms. At the beginning of the 1980s, law firms in Norway tended to be rather small, reflecting the demand for legal services from the business sector. But then there was a demand for more sophisticated services, especially in drafting contracts, often written in English and in the common law tradition, even though both parties to the agreement were Norwegian. This development largely contributed to a huge growth in law firms, whose staff tended to look to common law models when drafting con-tracts. These contracts regularly incorporated standard contract clauses. Moreover, whole procedures were transplanted from common law, for example, the due diligence process, without the question ever being raised as to whether such costly procedures were necessary, not to mention the added security that Norwegian law could provide. In a nutshell, this is the development that has taken place in Norway.

In my opinion, this development has not been satisfactory in every respect. One aspect is quite apparent: from an economic point of view, transaction costs have risen considerably. The rise in costs cannot be said to have added significant foreseeability and security for the clients; in many instances, the opposite is true. By introducing common law contract models, an uncertainty is often created. As already mentioned, the Norwegian contract law has its roots in civil law traditions, especially German law. It is widely accepted that the common law tradition is not compatible with the civil law tradition – and therefore with the Scandinavian tradition – on major issues. As will be discussed later, many of the contract clauses that are now widely used in contracts with Norwegian law as the governing law stem from common law. In many instances, these clauses are not in accordance with the governing law. The aim of introducing common law contract clauses is obviously to secure foreseeability, a phenomenon widely recognised as a characteristic of English law. But when common law concepts are taken out of their context and transplanted into a system such as that in Norway, uncertainty may very well be the result.

3   Clauses aimed at fully detaching the contract from the applicable law

3.1   Entire agreement

One evident example is the concept of entire agreement clauses. These clauses are connected to the procedural rule of parol evidence in English law, which has no counterpart in Norwegian law. A contract in writing does not bar evidence prior to contract; there is no such procedural rule in Norway. Understood on the basis of their common law background, the clauses would have no meaning and therefore would be devoid of any force. However, when the parties have inserted such a clause in their contract without having any mutual understanding, one might expect that Norwegian law would tend to solve the problem in line with the regulation in Article 2(1)(17) of the UNIDROIT Principles 2004, which states: 'A contract in writing which contains a clause indicating that the writing completely embodies the terms on which the parties have agreed cannot be contradicted or supplemented by evidence of prior statements or agreements. However, such statements or agreements may be used to interpret the writing.' By so doing, the clause would be given an effect that, it must be presumed, is in line with the intentions of the parties.[4]

---

[4] V. Hagstrøm, *Obligasjonsrett* (Universitetsforlaget, 2003), pp. 63f. See also H. W. Bjørnstad, *Entire Agreement Clauses*, Publications Series of the Institute of Private Law No. 177 (University of Oslo, 2009), pp. 201f.

In this instance, we see that the clause only creates a slight degree of uncertainty. It must be added, though, that it is not clear that Norwegian law would accept such a strict solution as is laid down in the UNIDROIT Principles. The need to append special supplements to the contract could be the next recourse.

3.2   No waiver

The no waiver clause, expressing that failure by a party to exercise a right or remedy that it has under the contract does not constitute a waiver thereof, is much more problematic.[5] A central concept under Norwegian contract law is the duty of loyalty and good faith. If a no waiver clause is invoked, although it would be against good faith to do so, then it is not likely that the courts would apply the clause. For example, if a delivery is late but the party does not terminate until after a considerable length of time and changes in the market, and the latter is the real reason for termination, Norwegian courts would not give the no waiver clause effect. But the duty of loyalty goes beyond preventing mere speculation at the other party's risk. It would be deemed that a party is under a duty to give notice about a breach within a reasonable time, even though no loss is incurred.[6] A no waiver clause must therefore be presumed to be without effect if a party demonstrates passivity in a situation where this is contrary to good faith.

3.3   No oral amendments

The no oral amendments clause has another position. Business contracts in Norway are most frequently made in writing, apart from such specialised areas as, for example, the sale of stocks. Even without an express contract clause, the courts would be very reluctant to accept mere oral changes to a written contract, as they tend to give the written contract considerable weight.[7] It must follow from these decisions that the need for clarity and foreseeability leads to the need for the interpretation to be based on the written contract and not on oral statements and

---

[5] F. Skribeland, *No waiver-klausulen*, Publications Series of the Institute of Private Law No. 176 (University of Oslo, 2009), pp. 117ff.

[6] Hagstrøm, *Obligasjonsrett*, pp. 339ff.

[7] See Rt. 1994, p. 581; Rt. 2000, p. 806; Rt. 2002, p. 1155; Rt. 2003, p. 1132 (Rt.= supreme Court Reporter).

assumptions. Therefore, in principle, the no oral amendments clause does not add very much. However, if a party has reasonably relied on an oral statement, then the other party may be precluded by its own conduct from invoking the clause. This solution is in line with Article 2(1)(18) of the UNIDROIT Principles.[8]

3.4 Severability

Severability clauses express that if a provision in the agreement is or becomes illegal, invalid or unenforceable, this will not affect the validity or enforceability of any other provision of the agreement. Partial invalidity is a well-known feature in Norwegian contract law.[9] As a point of departure, these clauses do not add much to the applicable law. The difference is that while the severability clause declares that illegality, invalidity or unenforceability shall have no effect on any other provision of the agreement, it is nevertheless at the court´s discretion to make decisions pursuant to Norwegian contract law. Therefore, minor discrepancies may arise where the clause adds something.

3.5 Conditions

The conditions clause, meaning that any breach of a described duty is a fundamental breach, has its counterpart in Norwegian contract law ('betingelser').[10] Thus, as a starting point, this clause does not add anything new. However, whereas the clause is rarely used in practice in contracts made in the Norwegian tradition, apart from the clause 'time is of the essence', it seems to be more widely used in contracts drafted in the common law tradition.[11] In a Norwegian contract, only terms of utmost importance would be made conditions, if ever, whereas other terms might be made conditions in a contract based on the common law tradition. Thus, it might be said that if Norwegian law is the governing law, the clause itself may not be a problem, but rather its use would be. If terms other than those of utmost importance are made conditions, one can envisage that a minor breach would give the other party a right to

---

[8] J. C. Westly, *No Oral Amendments klausler*, Publications Series of the Institute of Private Law No. 178 (University of Oslo, 2009), pp. 171ff.
[9] J. Hov and A. P. Høgberg, *Alminnelig avtalerett* (Papinian, 2009), p. 316.
[10] Hagstrøm, *Obligasjonsrett*, pp. 412f.
[11] T. Sandsbraaten, *The Concepts of Conditions, Warranties and Covenants*, Publications Series of the Institute of Private Law No. 179 (University of Oslo, 2009), pp. 21ff.

terminate the contract. This could lead to highly unfair results. The Norwegian courts have never been willing to accept this. The leading case in point is Rt. 1922, p. 308, where the seller in a commercial transaction was delayed in supplying the goods. The buyer terminated the contract pursuant to the Sales of Goods Act 1907, which deemed that any delay should be regarded as a fundamental breach in a commercial sale. Even though the buyer had the right to terminate pursuant to the wording of the Sales of Goods Act, the Supreme Court would not accept a result leaving the seller with costly equipment tailored specially for the buyer, while the buyer was hardly affected by the delay, and held that such a result could not have been the parties' intention. As there was no evidence of the parties' intention in this regard, it is recognised that the decision was based on public policy considerations. As Rt. 1922, p. 308 concerns the application of a law, the considerations would apply even more so to a contract clause.

3.6   Sole remedy

What has been said about conditions could also apply to clauses on sole remedy. The concept is well known and widely used in many commercial contracts, for example, in cases where a party is entitled only to a certain amount of liquidated damages in the event of a breach of contract.[12] Normally, such clauses will be respected. They are much more common and germane to Norwegian law than clauses containing conditions. Only in more exceptional instances would one expect a sole remedy clause to be set aside pursuant to the general clause against unfair contract terms in §36 of the Contracts Act 1918.

3.7   Subject to contract

The subject to contract clause is quite well known in Norwegian contract law. Basically, and in general, such clauses will be respected and upheld by the courts. The parties are free to negotiate. Since it is often arguable whether the parties entered into a contract through negotiations, the clause is designed to make the position clear. In the introduction to Part 3 of this book, an unusual situation is described: the parties have entered into a letter of intent, while the one party never intended to enter into a final agreement and used the negotiations only to prevent the other party

---

[12]   Hagstrøm, *Obligasjonsrett*, pp. 651ff.

from entering into a contract with a third party. If such intentions could be proven, it is not likely that the party could find a formal shield against liability in the subject to contract clause. Such behaviour would surely constitute an abuse of the freedom of contract and is not worth protecting, even though the contractual arrangement was clear.

3.8 Material adverse change

The material adverse change clause is not unknown in Norwegian law, although change in circumstances is usually treated within the framework of the theory of failed assumptions mostly developed through case law in Scandinavia. As this protects the party at loss to a certain extent, it is not usual to insert a material adverse change clause in the contract. However, assuming the clause is included, the introduction to Part 3 then describes the situation where a party invokes the clause in order to avoid the deal, in which it has lost interest. A point of departure in Norwegian law would be that if the clause is effective, it is not up to the courts to evaluate the party´s behaviour. This would be a moral judgment, not a judgment based on law.[13] But if it must be deemed that the party abused his or her contractual right, the party cannot rely on the material adverse change clause.

4 Clauses with legal effects not known to the applicable law

4.1 Liquidated damages

A clause pertaining to this category is the liquidated damages clause. In Norwegian law, this clause will not create confusion or problems. However, the well-known distinction between liquidated damages and penalty clauses in English law has no parallel in Norwegian law. According to Norwegian law, the parties are free to agree on contractual penalties, even though the liquidated damages do not correspond to an actual loss – or no loss at all.[14] If Norwegian law is the applicable law, one would not apply the common law rules on penalty clauses unless it is deemed that it was the parties' intention to invoke this particular doctrine. A further question is whether or not liquidated damages may be cumulated with the reimbursement of damages. In principle, there are no obstacles to such cumulation in Norwegian contract law.[15] However, the

---

[13] *Ibid.*, pp. 303ff.   [14] *Ibid*, p. 652.   [15] *Ibid*, p. 653.

question is a matter of interpretation. A liquidated damages clause is normally inserted into the contract to avoid responsibility exceeding the liquidated damages. If this is the case, no cumulation is relevant. One will assume that the parties intended to maximise the limit of responsibility to the sum held as liquidated damages.

4.2   Indemnity

Another clause within this category is the indemnity clause. In common law, this assumes that damage has in fact occurred. If Norwegian law is the applicable law and the contract is drafted in English using the expression 'indemnity', one must assume that an actual loss must be suffered and that it does not cover mere guaranteed payment. The very term 'indemnity' suggests an actual loss and that the promisor should have the privilege of subsidiarity. But this is only a matter of interpretation.

5   Clauses that regulate matters already regulated in the applicable law and how these interact with each other

5.1   Representations and warranties

The first issue is a contract containing representations and warranties. In Norwegian contracts inspired by common law clauses, such clauses regularly appear in acquisitions.[16] They rarely add anything to Norwegian law, under which one party has a duty to inform the other party of important matters about which the other party has a reasonable expectation to be informed.[17] This is a general duty and is not restricted to instances of misrepresentation. The duty to inform is a cornerstone of Norwegian contract law and is a part of the more extensive duty of good faith. It is also accepted that the parties may regulate this duty in their contract. In regular sales, an 'as is' clause can be mentioned as an example; it follows from this clause that the duty to inform is then restricted to what the seller knew about, not what he or she ought to have known; see §19 of the Sales of Goods Act 1988. When a contract contains an extensive list of representations and warranties, the question arises as to whether this list shall be regarded as exhaustive, whereby the

---

[16] M. B. Christoffersen, *Kjøp og salg av virksomhet* (Gyldendal Akademisk, 2008), pp. 215–216.

[17] Hagstrøm, *Obligasjonsrett*, pp. 135ff.

other party waives the protection pursuant to the principles of the right to be informed. In Norway, a list of representations and warranties would normally be regarded as giving the other party a protection not necessarily granted by the ordinary rules. Generally, such representations and warranties should therefore be integrated by the duty to give information stemming from the general rules. It is difficult to envisage that a party may limit its duty to inform according to Norwegian law by using representations and warranties.

5.2   Hardship

The second issue is contracts containing a hardship clause, raising the question of whether such a clause in a contract would exclude other regulations. Hardship, that is, a duty to renegotiate contracts which, because of supervening events, makes performance onerous for the other party, is not a general part of contract law in Norway. The situations usually covered by hardship clauses are normally dealt with by §36 of the Contracts Act 1918 and the general principles of failed assumptions. Pursuant to these rules, a party may claim that the contract must be altered or that he or she should be relieved from all his or her duties. Thus, a hardship clause brings in a new element, namely that the other party has a duty to cooperate and to renegotiate the contract in a given situation. This can be regarded as a procedural rule, the aim of which is to ensure that the parties find a balanced solution in the changed circumstances. A hardship clause would not, as a general rule, be interpreted as excluding the said §36 and the principles of failed assumptions. One would normally regard such a provision as adding something to the general rules. If a party fails to fulfil his or her duty to renegotiate, this would be an argument for applying §36, even if the threshold is not met.[18]

5.3   Force majeure

Force majeure clauses give rise to several questions. Unknown in English law, *force majeure* is a well-established concept in Norwegian law. Stemming from civil law, the concept has been developed considerably through court decisions. Of course, classical events like war, civil war, acts of sabotage, natural disasters, explosions, fires, boycotts, strikes,

---

[18]   *Ibid.*, pp. 292ff.

lock-outs and acts of authority are recognised as *force majeure*. However, the courts have gone further. Rt. 1970, p. 1059 established that failure to deliver on the part of the seller's supplier constituted *force majeure* for the seller. Therefore, events outside the control of a party must normally be considered as *force majeure*. However, it is not enough that a party has been diligent and has acted in good faith. 'Beyond the control' presupposes that some external event has occurred constituting an impediment to the fulfilment of the contract. Furthermore, *force majeure* presupposes that the party could not be reasonably expected to have taken the impediment into account at the time of the conclusion of the contract – see Rt. 1962, p. 165. However, the fact that the impediment could not have been foreseen is not relevant.[19] It is also expected that the party could not have avoided or overcome the impediment or its consequences.

On this background, *force majeure* clauses written in a common law tradition could create uncertainty, as they are usually much narrower in their description of *force majeure* than in Norwegian contract law. The question then arises as to whether the clause should be regarded as exhaustive or whether it should be interpreted in line with Norwegian case law. Thus, a *force majeure* clause based on a common law model could clearly create the opposite of what was intended – namely confusion.

---

[19] *Ibid.*, p. 271.

The Nordic tradition: application of boilerplate clauses under Swedish law

LARS GORTON

1   General background

Scandinavian law is often regarded by comparative lawyers as one particular group under the civil law family. There is no common Scandinavian law, except for particular parts of contract law and the law of obligations. There is a common Scandinavian approach in several respects and there is thus some common legislation. This is particularly true within parts of private law, the particular area of law covered in this book.

Following Nordic legislative cooperation at the end of the nineteenth and the first half of the twentieth centuries, a substantial amount of private law legislation from this period is common or similar in the different Scandinavian countries. Thus, for example, the Maritime Codes from the 1890s, the Sales of Goods Acts from the early-twentieth century, the Contracts Acts from around 1915–1920 and the Acts on Promissory Notes from the end of the 1930s were more or less common.[1] Apart from the Maritime Codes of the 1990s, which are largely common for all the Nordic countries, the situation has partly changed. Thus, for example, in spite of all Nordic countries having adhered to the United Nations (Vienna) Convention on Contracts for the International Sale of Goods (CISG), there are currently differences between the Nordic Sales of Goods Acts.[2] Some amendments have been made to the Contracts Acts, the most important amendment being that regarding §36, the

---

[1] The reason for not giving any exact dates is that the various pieces of legislation were introduced at different times in each of the Nordic countries.

[2] Particularly with respect to the National Sales of Goods Acts, there are differences between the solutions chosen. Denmark decided to maintain the old Sales of Goods Act from 1905. See, inter alia, J. Herre and J. Ramberg, *Allmän köprätt*, 5th edn (Norstedts Juridik, 2009), pp. 25ff.

so-called general clause. In Sweden, this amendment was made in 1976. This provision has given the courts in Scandinavia rather wide discretion to amend or set aside 'unreasonable' clauses or even contracts. In spite of the common legislation in the fields involved here, Scandinavian case law shows that there are certain differences in approach, and there also seem to be some differences in approach with respect to §36 of the Contracts Act in relation to commercial contracts.

The object of this book is to cover various contractual clauses, clauses related to negotiations before the contracting, as well as clauses related to the performance of the contract. Some of these clauses form part of the *boilerplate clauses* that evolved primarily in Anglo-American law.[3] Due to the impact of Anglo-American contract practice, such boilerplate clauses have also come to form part of contracts drafted by lawyers in the Nordic countries, where English or American law is not applicable to the contract. The impact of the Anglo-American contract tradition on contracts drafted by Scandinavian lawyers leads to a considerable increase in the text usually employed in a contract. Part of the explanation for this development is that English lawyers need to be more specific, since there is less legislation to fall back on. English and American law have become more important as applicable law when drafting international business contracts. The effect has been more lengthy contracts, where certain contractual clauses are not necessary when the contract is subject to another law. The contractual solution may even be in conflict with a corresponding regulation in the law chosen for the contract. On the whole, I think that there are some merits to the use of more comprehensive contracts, although there is also a risk that an Anglo-American clause might create difficulties when considered by a court in, say, Norway or Germany.

This chapter comments from a Swedish point of view on the clauses listed in the introduction to Part 3, but will cover some of them more extensively than others. The clauses that will be focused on are entire agreement, no oral amendments, material adverse change, liquidated damages and hardship. The reason for this choice is that these contractual provisions seem to be more frequently discussed in Swedish legal doctrine than the others. There is limited Swedish case law with respect to many of the clauses in question and to the various solutions in use. The various clauses are known and disputes are known, but case law from courts involving them is sparse.

---

[3] See, for example, L. Gorton, 'Boilerplateklausuler', *Erhvervsjuridisk Tidsskrift* (2009), 170–188, with references.

Although the similarities are considerable between different jurisdictions with respect to fundamental contract law principles, there are differences with respect to the principles on how and when a contract is entered into, when a contract is or is not enforceable, etc. The Nordic Contracts Acts have four chapters: Chapter 1, covering the formation of a contract; Chapter 2, dealing with authority; Chapter 3, concerning the invalidity of contracts; and Chapter 4, setting out certain general provisions. However, interpretation of contracts has developed entirely in case law and in the legal doctrine.

Again, it has to be underlined that Swedish contract law is not the same as, but is rather close to, other systems in the Scandinavian legal family. The Nordic Contracts Acts are more or less equal, but in case law certain differences appear.[4] That being said, it must also be borne in mind that in many areas, Swedish case law is not abundant and sometimes Swedish lawyers or courts may try to find guidelines from solutions arrived at in other Nordic legal systems.[5]

2   Contractual principles and contractual considerations

Certain general principles are still regarded as fundamental in contract law, although they have been gradually narrowed down. One of them is freedom of contract (the parties are free to contract with whomever they wish and on whichever terms that they want, etc.) and the other is the sanctity of contracts (meaning that the parties are bound by what they have agreed to).[6]

---

[4] It could, for example, be mentioned that §37 of the Contracts Acts has been completely deleted in Danish and Norwegian law, whereas in Swedish and Finnish law, the part concerning *lex commissoria* still remains.

[5] A particular phenomenon that is gradually becoming more obvious is that Swedish courts, at least to some degree, are more open to consider solutions developed in other jurisdictions with solutions adopted in various international or European collections of principles. In a recent judgment rendered 2010–01021 (No. T 9904–08), the Swedish Supreme Court used as part of its reasoning the solution chosen in the Draft Common Frame of Reference ('DCFR') with respect to the right to terminate a distributorship agreement. In Swedish law, there is no particular provision in this respect and there was no contractual solution. In the choice between making an analogy from other pieces of legislation or other contractual solutions, the Supreme Court, without much hesitation, adopted the solution developed in the DCFR.

[6] These principles also appear in the UNIDROIT Principles of International Commercial Contracts ('UPICC'), (International Institute for the Unification of Private Law, 2004), inter alia, Articles 1.1 and 1.3; the Principles of European Contract Law ('PECL'), Parts I and II; O. Lando and H. Beale, (eds.), *Principles of European Contract Law*, Parts I and II

Another important contractual principle which has developed is the *clausula rebus sic stantibus*, meaning that a contract should be performed in accordance with the conditions and circumstances that are prevailing at the time of the conclusion of the contract. However, it seems unlikely that a legal system would be based on this latter doctrine. This principle seems, rather, to have evolved in cases where, due to changed circumstances, a court may adjust the contractual undertaking of a party. A general loyalty (good faith) principle has also developed in some jurisdictions.[7]

Another general principle seems to be that only rarely is a particular form required in order to make a contract binding. For example, this is the case in all the Nordic legal systems.

The above principles mean that contractual parties, particularly in commercial relations, may have incentives to create by agreement a different or more precise contractual regulation than that provided by law.[8] Following the principle of freedom of contract, parties are generally (but within limits) allowed to set the contractual framework within which they carry out their negotiations and perform their contractual undertakings.

This also implies that rules set out in the legislation need to be filled out in various ways in order to determine when a contract has come into being, and also the principles to be applied for such determination. Sometimes and in different contexts, as well as in various ways, the parties themselves introduce one or more clauses, changing the pattern given in law. The parties may also introduce into their agreement particular clauses setting out agreed interpretation provisions.

Parties may thus agree on certain parameters which determine how and when a contract shall be regarded as entered into and binding upon the parties. Thus, in the contract, there may be various reservations or conditions precedent before the contract shall be regarded as

---

(Kluwer Law International, 2002), Article 1:102; as well as the DCFR, Study Group on a European Civil Code/Research Group on EC Private Law (eds.), *Principles, Definitions and Model Rules of European Private Law – Draft Common Frame of Reference (DCFR)* (Sellier, 2009).

[7] Thus, German law seems to have gone furthest in establishing such principle in §242 of the Bürgerliches Gesetzbuch (BGB). English law does not recognise a general good faith principle. The Nordic countries have a rather broad provision in the Contracts Act through the general clause in §36, giving courts considerable discretion to meddle in contractual relations. There is also some recognition of a loyalty principle.

[8] In business-to-consumer relations, the situation is different in that the legislator, to a greater degree, has introduced contractual elements to protect the consumer.

finally binding on both parties.[9] However, in practice, it may be hard to determine whether at a certain point a binding agreement may have come into existence between the parties, not least for evidentiary reasons.

The research project upon which this book is based showed that there may be tensions between various legal rules and principles related to the contractual framework, but equally also with respect to business organisation and business efficacy. Various legal principles have developed gradually, not necessarily at the same time, following agreed contractual solutions. The legislator,[10] the courts and the contract draftsmen could therefore be seen as carrying forward the development of contract law together.

3   Different parameters

When discussing some of the points below, it may be useful to set them against a certain factual background. Contracts may differ in various ways depending on the particular parameters taken into consideration, and these different parameters (having some importance in Scandinavian law) may have as a consequence substantial variations in the contractual procedure when it comes to the determination of the obligations of the parties, as well as their liability. Some of these differences may be summed up in the following way:

a) Two connected principles in contract law have evolved, namely contractual freedom and the binding nature of the contract.
b) Another principle with different implications is the Roman law principle *clausula rebus sic stantibus*.
c) In some legal systems, the principle of good faith and fair dealing has fundamental roots. In a number of jurisdictions, contract clauses exempting the performing party from its liability are not enforceable in the event of intent or gross negligence.
d) Gradually, more rules and principles of a general character have been developed in order to protect weaker parties, in particular consumers/private persons, but also in, e.g., agency law and the law of carriage of goods.

---

[9] Such clauses are frequently used in commercial contracts and, particularly in loan agreements, conditions precedent clauses are used as requirements for a lender being bound to pay out the loan amount.

[10] In Scandinavian legal doctrine, 'legislator' seems to be the concept used instead of 'legislature' in this connection, 'legislature' being a more legal technical term.

e) A distinction could be made between spot contracts and cooperation contracts. Such distinctions are also often parallel to 'result oriented contracts' and contracts based on 'best efforts'.

f) To a growing extent, business is conducted in corporations and thus business organisation plays a growing role, affecting and also involving questions of representation and agency. From a contractual perspective, this has a bearing on such contractual uses as inserting clauses that subject the effectiveness of the contract to some form of approval (generally to the approval by the board of each of the parties), no oral amendments clauses, etc.

g) To a growing extent, contracts are made in an international environment.

Related questions also lead to various observations concerning contractual methods, the standardisation of contracts, the understanding and construction of contracts, and the relations in the contract.

Therefore, it may be important to see how these different parameters are treated by the legislator, the courts and the contract draftsmen in different jurisdictions. It may be that there are some different approaches applied in different jurisdictions. It is evident that the various parameters concerned have an impact on the development of the various clauses. In short, we may say that the different parameters discussed here concern the parties (who are they?), the time frame (short term or long term), the type of contract (type of business and type of functions) and the geographical area (local, regional, global).

4 The organisational/agency aspect – the use of representatives

There is thus an expected structure in many contracts, and there is also an expected structure in relations and in many business organisations with respect to decision making. To what extent will a decision actually be made by the board of a company? Will some decision powers follow from an organisation plan? To what extent will a certain position in an organisation entail power of decision (power of position, ostensible authority or apparent authority)? These questions have relevance for the particularities of an individual contract relation. A business organisation consists of many individuals and requires an organisational structure, and there is generally a need for instructions regarding who in the organisation may make what decision. These parameters may have some legal impact when it comes to the question of power given and authority possible to act on and bind the business entity.

Will a person or a team negotiating for a company have a right to negotiate for, or sign for, and bind the company with respect to the final agreement? Some power will follow from law. Sometimes, such powers follow from particular acts (the giving of a power of attorney).

The relation between the contractual parameters and the organisational aspects becomes obvious when dealing with such clauses as subject to approval, no oral amendments and entire agreement, mainly because decision makers in a business organisation wish to maintain the decision-making power at certain levels. Such clauses mirror the efforts to maintain the decision power on a certain level or within a certain group of people in the organisation. Such practical control does not necessarily reflect the principles as developed by the legislator or the courts. The effect will, in practice, sometimes be that practices of business administration and legal frames of contract law do not always go hand in hand.

The various clauses used mirror different phases in the contracting, and some of the clauses are geared to a specific phase of negotiation such as the entering into the contract (conditions precedent, subject to approval, entire agreement), whereas others are geared towards the performance phase (no oral amendments, no waiver, impossibility, *force majeure*, hardship and material adverse change). Some of the latter clauses are related to changed circumstances.

The subject to approval clause is often drafted to create contractual asymmetry and binds one of the parties, while allowing the other party some time to consider before the subject is lifted. Such clauses are basically allowed and recognised in commercial relations, but they may generally be looked upon less favourably by courts in consumer relationships.

5   Contract phases

5.1   *Some general points*

The various clauses will be discussed below in relation to the particular contract phase to which they are most relevant. Do they mainly apply during the negotiation phase or rather during the performance phase? The clauses may often be geared to one or the other phase, but they may also have relevance to both phases. The various clauses may have an implication with respect to where they appear in the contractual framework.

Disregarding the marketing phase, the borderlines between the negotiation phase and the contract performance phase will be addressed.

5.2 Negotiation phase

5.2.1 General remarks

A contract is often preceded by negotiations leading up to the binding agreement. Even in commercial contracts, there is not always a very clear point at which the borderline between the negotiation and the contracting is passed (due to evidentiary problems), but there is a principle borderline, which will often have to be established in hindsight, where there is either no contract at all or else there is a binding contract. Some legal systems recognise also a principle of *culpa in contrahendo*.

Once the parties have agreed, they are bound by that agreement. Normally there is no requirement of form. Depending upon the wide variety of situations, it may in practice turn out not to be so easy to determine if the borderline has been passed or not.

In hindsight, it is also often hard to determine the actual meaning of a contract when considering the circumstances. It may even be the case that one of the parties at a later stage comes to the conclusion that there was no binding contract. The parties may thus have agreed to use various measures to safeguard the contract being upheld in accordance with what was agreed by them.

The parties may, for different reasons, decide to set the frame for the binding nature of the contract by introducing clauses such as conditions precedent, subject to approval and entire agreement in order to create a more solid basis of predictability and to prevent a court from introducing its own approach in this respect. By using these contractual devices, the parties may agree that certain prerequisites should be fulfilled before the binding contract is settled. In connection with commercial contracts, it is not uncommon that the parties use letters of intent or letters of commitment as a step in the contractual negotiations. In Swedish law, there is little case law with respect to these various clauses.[11]

---

[11] Generally, there is a lack of Swedish case law with respect to commercial cases. This is mainly an effect of the choice of the parties to insert jurisdiction clauses into their contracts referring disputes to arbitration for settlement rather than to courts.

Another feature of practical importance is the use of standard form contracts, which have, over time, caused various legal considerations. Standard contracts may be of different kinds and may serve different purposes, either as a model form for negotiation or as a take-it-or-leave-it part of the contract package.

5.2.2   Conditions precedent and subject to approval

Conditions precedent seem to be used primarily in loan agreements and acquisition contracts (the purchase of businesses) setting out certain requirements to be reached before there is a binding contract (a distinction is made between resolutive conditions and suspensive conditions).[12] A seller of a business may have to provide certain financial statements, auditors' reports, etc., and there may be similar requirements on the borrower in a loan agreement (covering, for example, documentation to be presented, showing sufficient insurance, legal opinions, etc.).

Another related item is that the agreement may have a provision saying something along the lines of 'the contract is subject to board approval, which shall be lifted at the latest . . . failing which this contract shall be null and void'. This is a very common clause in many individually negotiated contracts and also in some standard contracts, and the different reservations may vary. In the legal doctrine, there is a discussion on the understanding and the application of such clauses, not least from a good faith point of view.[13]

5.2.3   No oral contracts

The question of written contracts is often discussed in the legal doctrine. Although there are few requirements in law for a contract to be in writing, in practice, parties often agree specifically that there will be a binding agreement only when both parties have signed the contract.[14]

---

[12] See in Swedish law, inter alia, A. Adlercreutz, *Avtalsrätt I*, 12th edn (Studentlitteratur, 2002), pp. 109ff.; K. Grönfors, *Avtalsgrundande rättsfakta* (Thomson Fakta, 1993), pp. 74ff.; and C. Ramberg and J. Ramberg, *Allmän avtalsrätt*, 8th edn (Norstedts Juridik, 2010), pp. 95ff.

[13] See NJA 1995, p. 437, where it was discussed whether a subject to board's approval clause would apply with respect to small companies with a small board of directors and few owners, when the particular physical person involved in the negotiation/contracting has a decisive influence on the company. Related questions are also connected with the use of letters of intent and (particularly in loan agreements) the use of letters of commitment.

[14] See, for instance, in Swedish contract law, A. Adlercreutz, 'Om den rättsliga betydelsen av avtalad skriftform och om integrationsklausuler', in U. Bernitz, K. Grönfors, J. Hellner, J. Kleinemann, J. Sandström and J. Herre, *Festskrift till Jan Ramberg*

The parties are free to agree to such a clause, but certain problems may arise when it comes to its application in the individual case.

It is important to note that there are different situations that are often related to questions of evidence. If it has been made clear between the parties that only a written contract between them shall be regarded as a binding contract, then that shall prevail. There may also be a custom between the parties or a custom of the trade to the same effect.

However, the situation in practice appears somewhat differently. If one of the parties sends over to the other the contract for signing to confirm their agreement, then there is already a binding agreement between the parties. For evidence reasons, one of the parties may wish to have a signed contract and if the other party does not respond and it later becomes clear that the failing party does not perform, then the question will arise as to whether there was already a binding contract and also what the terms of the contract were. If, after the contract has been concluded, one of the parties sends over a signed contract to be signed and returned by the party, this would be regarded as proof only of the contractual terms, not as a prerequisite for the contract coming into being.[15]

5.2.4   Entire agreement

5.2.4.1 Reasons for the use of entire agreement clauses   Entire agreement clauses stem from English and American contract practice.[16] In English law, the doctrines of parol evidence and *stare decisis* have been recognised for a long time.[17] These are doctrines which are not applied in Scandinavian law. Entire agreement clauses were introduced in contracts subject to English law in order to persuade the courts to uphold the parol

---

(Juristförlaget, 1996), pp. 17–29.; Adlercreutz, *Avtalsrätt I*, pp. 85ff.; and Ramberg and Ramberg, *Allmän avtalsrätt*, p. 94. This is also a situation close to the discussion of incorporation of standard contracts; see, inter alia, NJA 2007, p. 562, referred to in Ramberg and Ramberg, *Allmän avtalsrätt*, p. 142 and in A. Adlercreutz and L. Gorton, *Avtalsrätt II*, 6th edn (Juridiska föreningen i Lund, 2010), p. 76, as well as in U. Bernitz, *Standardavtalsrätt* (Norstedts Juridik, 2008), pp. 52 and 58.

[15] See, for instance, the discussion in Adlercreutz, *Avtalsrätt*, pp. 78ff.; Adlercreutz, 'Om den rättsliga betydelsen', pp. 17ff.; and Adlercreutz and Gorton, *Avtalsrätt II*, pp. 89ff.

[16] These clauses are also known as merger clauses or integration clauses; see for example, L. Gorton, 'Merger Clauses in Business Contracts', *Erhversretslig Tidsskrift* (2008), 344–360, with references.

[17] C. Mitchell, *Interpretation of Contracts* (Routledge-Cavendish, 2007), pp. 35f. and 137f. See, from a Swedish perspective, J. Hellner, 'The parol evidence rule och tolkningen av skriftliga avtal', in A. Agell (ed.), *Festskrift till Bertil Bengtsson* (Stockholm Nerenius & Santérus, 1993), pp. 185–205.

evidence rule, namely that only what appears in the contract (within the four corners of the contract) shall be considered by the court. In Scandinavian law, also including Swedish law, there is instead a procedural principle to the effect that the courts are allowed to consider any evidence presented by the parties, including documents and statements preceding the final contract.

It has thus been discussed in Swedish law whether and to what extent a court would take an entire agreement clause into consideration. Therefore, some main principles collide, namely that of freedom of contract, the binding nature of a contract and the freedom of the courts to apply any evidence presented.

5.2.4.2 Entire agreement clauses – drafting and application   Entire agreement clauses are now found fairly frequently in international business contracts, often in the standard form but also in individually negotiated contracts, a development which, in turn, led to a situation where the courts also had to interpret the particular clause.[18]

The fairly new contract form 'Newbuildcon'[19] contains the following provision in clause 47 under the heading 'sundry':

> This Contract constitutes the entire agreement between the Parties, and no promise, undertaking, representation, warranty or statement by either Party prior to the date of this Contract stated in Box 1 shall affect this Contract. Any modification of this Contract shall not be of any effect unless in writing signed by or on behalf of the Parties.

This particular provision deals with two aspects: the entire agreement aspect as well as the modification (no oral amendments) aspect. The two parameters are often dealt with in conjunction with each other. They deal with different aspects but are both connected with contractual stability.

As mentioned previously, Swedish procedural law is based on the idea that courts shall consider all evidence when judging a case. This means that there are basically no restrictions on how courts may deal with evidence. When it comes to the construction and interpretation of contracts, Swedish law has gradually moved towards a model where a court will not search for the subjective intention of the parties but rather will

---

[18] These questions have been discussed in depth by Mitchell, *Interpretation*, pp. 129ff. See also Hellner, 'The parol evidence rule', pp. 185f.

[19] This is a contract drafted by BIMCO in relation to shipbuilding and it is used here as an example not because shipbuilding is the most important business, but because it is an established international business.

determine its object from the contract. In connection with an entire agreement clause, there is an inherent conflict between the liberty of the court to consider evidence presented and the rights of the parties to make their own choice (within the freedom of contract framework) with respect to those parameters that the court should take into consideration.

5.2.4.3 Swedish case law   As mentioned above, Swedish case law in this area is rather limited. The few cases reported that relate to entire agreement clauses where Swedish courts/arbitrators have been involved have been discussed by, among others, Erik Sjöman.[20]

In the first case there was an Entire Agreement clause stating:

> Complete regulation.
>   This agreement is the complete agreement by the parties of all questions concerned by the Agreement. All written or oral covenants and representations preceding the agreement shall be substituted for by the contents of this agreement.

The dispute in the case concerned how the contract, lacking a clause on the right of termination, should be interpreted and applied.[21]

In the contract, there was a catalogue of representations and covenants, the breach of which would lead to a price reduction. The particular deficiency which the buyer referred to was not part of the catalogue but was mentioned in an information memorandum. The purchaser based its claim on the Swedish Sales of Goods Act and its rules. The seller referred to the entire agreement clause, alleging that the Sales of Goods Act should be disregarded. If the view of the seller prevailed, the buyer would have been cut off from a contractual remedy. Without discussing the applicability of the entire agreement clause, the arbitrators found that a price reduction would be allowed.

The second case is a case from the labour court, AD 2007, No. 86.[22] This case concerned whether an employer had a good reason for dismissal of an employee who had used the credit card of the employer for withdrawal of money for private use (this was only provisional as he was later going to reimburse and did reimburse the employer). The employer

---

[20] See E. Sjöman, 'Integrationsklausulen och dispositive rätt' (2002–2003) *Juridisk Tidskrift*, 935–941; and E. Sjöman, 'Ett rättsfall om integrationsklausuler' (2008) *Svensk Juristtidning*, 571–577.

[21] See Gorton, 'Boilerplateklausuler', 178ff.

[22] The labour court is a special court and its judgments have to be evaluated with some caution in civil law matters.

was of the opinion that the employee was not entitled to such use of the credit card, but the employee did not share this view. The written employment contract did not contain any particular provision to this effect. In this case, there had been a transfer of ownership and the contract had an entire agreement clause, which prescribed that the written agreement was the complete regulation of the contractual relations between the parties, that the agreement replaced all previous oral and written undertakings, agreements and arrangements, and that all amendments should be in writing. According to the employer, the clause meant that previous benefits which were not set out in the written agreement, such as the right to use the credit card, were no longer applicable.

In its judgment, the labour court noted that the typical aim of entire agreement clauses is to eliminate or at least reduce the importance of such oral or written statements, and to make sure that amendments to the agreement would have to be in writing in future. The labour court also noted that there is no authoritative case law available to illustrate the correct interpretation of such a clause. It also discussed the role of the entire agreement clause as a standard clause which had not been noticed by that party who had not drafted the agreement. The court did not delve further into that question but it found, instead, that the application of the clause was also dependent on the general principles of interpretation. Reference was made to the fact that the employee had actually used the credit card without any objection of the employer and also other benefits, although not specifically mentioned, had been maintained.

The employer had thus itself not upheld the entire agreement clause during the course of the employment. Under the circumstances in the case, the court found that the aim of the clause was not to extinguish all employment benefits which had not been set out in the employment agreement. The clause could therefore not be understood to mean that the employee would not be entitled to use the credit card as he had done.

5.2.4.4 Some final observations on the entire agreement clause

To sum up, there are some differences between the Scandinavian approach and the original purpose of entire agreement clauses under English law, where, due to procedural rules, we may presume that Swedish courts will have to find a balance between the binding force of the contract and the wide scope of the court in procedural law to take all evidence into consideration when judging a dispute. It is hardly likely that Swedish courts/arbitrators would follow only the principle of freedom of contract.

A further point could also have importance, namely whether the entire agreement clause is a standard clause or whether it is an individually negotiated clause.

A final observation is that it is not unlikely that Swedish lawyers would, when considering an entire agreement clause, apply an approach similar to that expressed in Article II – 4:104 of the DCFR with respect to the understanding of a merger clause:

1) If a contract document contains an individually negotiated clause stating that the document embodies all the terms of the contract (a merger clause), any prior statements, undertakings or agreements which are not embodied in the documentation do not form part of the contract.

2) If the merger clause is not individually negotiated, it establishes only a presumption that the parties intended that their prior statements, undertakings or agreements were not to form part of the contract. This rule may not be excluded or restricted.

3) The parties' prior statements may be used to interpret the contract. This rule may not be excluded or restricted except by an individually negotiated clause.

4) A party may by statements or conduct be precluded from asserting a merger clause to the extent that the other party has reasonably relied on such statements or conduct.[23]

5.3   Performance phase

5.3.1   Some general remarks

Following the principle that a contract, once entered into by the parties, shall be binding upon them in accordance with what they agreed, the parties are regarded to be bound by the contract as it stands once it is entered into.

Law itself may prescribe certain deviations from this principle, due to, for example, impossibility, *force majeure* and frustration (in common law). In some legal systems, there may be provisions allowing for renegotiation in case of hardship.

In some legal systems, a principle of good faith (loyalty) may be used to prevent the parties from abusing subsequently arising events in order

---

[23] Similar solutions are found in Article 2:105 of the PECL and in Article 2.1.17 of the UPICC.

to maintain that the contract shall be performed as once agreed upon, irrespective of the circumstantial development, and in the Scandinavian countries, §36 of the Contracts Act may also be used.

5.3.2   No oral amendments

No oral amendments clauses are fairly frequent in commercial contracts. They are often – but by no means always – combined with modification clauses, i.e., where the parties have agreed that modifications of the contract shall be allowed but only on certain grounds. They are quite common in long-term contracts such as construction contracts and shipbuilding contracts.

The no oral amendments clause may set out that a change in the contract may only be made in accordance with certain formal requirements, for example, only in writing or when signed by a person duly authorised to do so or who is on the same level in the organisation hierarchy as the person originally signing the contract (organisational formality). As already mentioned, the no oral amendments clause is often combined with the entire agreement clause.[24]

The no oral amendments clause is thus one of the clauses which serve to create foreseeability in the contract relation. A party seeking to apply the clause too strictly in accordance with its wording may find that a Swedish court comes to the conclusion that such use of the clause would contravene good faith (or the court may interpret the clause to such effect or possibly use § 36 of the Contracts Act).

5.3.3   Change of circumstances

5.3.3.1 Generally   It is also common that the parties, through various contract clauses related to changed circumstances, open up the possibility for changes to be taken into consideration. Such clauses may concern various matters and they may be geared to physical events, political events, financial events, etc. The contractual solutions may also be of a different nature, in some cases rather narrow and precise, and in other cases broader and of a more general nature.

Depending upon what the parties set out as their agreement, a contract may provide that under certain circumstances a court may modify certain provisions of the agreement, or the contract may instead open up the possibility for a particular right to deviate from the original text when the circumstances so demand. There are various contractual

---

[24] See, for example, the BIMCO clause above in Section 5.2.4.2.

solutions designed to serve as an object to achieve the effects when this particular doctrine is applied (under headings such as *force majeure*, hardship, indexing, escalation, etc.). The effects of such clauses may vary. Some clauses allow a court to set a certain provision in the contract aside, while other clauses allow a court to declare the whole contract void, and some clauses allow the adjustment of a contract.

The UPICC, the PECL and the DCFR have provisions concerning *force majeure* and hardship.[25]

5.3.3.2 Force majeure   In most commercial contracts, there are *force majeure* clauses based either on a model that is rather close to the control provision of the CISG or on a broader traditional *force majeure* clause.[26]

Rather than delving into the variety of *force majeure* clauses in use, we instead refer to Article 79 of the CISG, which is based on control liability. Under Article 79, the seller is exempted from liability if an impediment occurs that is beyond the control of the seller and that was unforeseeable at the time of conclusion of the agreement. Some new *force majeure* clauses seem to adapt the pattern of the CISG provision, but there are also several *force majeure* clauses in use that are broader and allow for more events to be covered.

Swedish courts are likely to take into some consideration the solution appearing in §27 of the Swedish Sales of Goods Act (1990: 931) or §79 in the Swedish legislation based on the CISG (1987: 222) when judging *force majeure* clauses, although they will undoubtedly utilise the wording used in the particular clause as the starting point.

5.3.3.3 Cost increase and hardship   Sometimes, the parties introduce particular clauses mirroring cost increases into their contracts. The price agreed is then the basic price, whereas the price that will actually be paid will depend on various factors. A particular question that could be discussed concerns whether Article 79 of the CISG is also applicable to hardship events, that is, price-related changes. There is German and Swiss case law showing that hardship events may be covered by Article 79, but to my knowledge there is, so far, no case where Swiss or German

---

[25] Articles 7.1.7 and 6.2.3 of the UPICC; see also DCFR III – 3:104 and III – 1:110 and Articles 3:108 and 6:111 of the PECL.

[26] In Swedish case law, there are a number of decisions related to *force majeure* questions. This discussion goes back to the Sales of Goods Act of 1905. One later case that was at its time much discussed is NJA 1970, p. 478, also involving a *force majeure* clause.

courts have applied the control liability provision of the CISG for a price increase.[27]

There may be an automatic variation in the price depending on particular price increases. The parties may have agreed that the price shall follow an index,[28] certain price increases reported in a certain publication, labour costs, material costs, etc. The cost increase may be applied automatically or it may be a basis for negotiations. Furthermore, there may be clauses dealing with changes in the foreign exchange rates having an impact on the price agreed.[29]

The hardship clause is drafted differently and normally it is separate from the *force majeure* clause. Hardship clauses are primarily related to circumstances which have changed the agreed parameters for the price calculation, mainly due to substantial cost increases. The hardship clause normally gives rise to renegotiation between the parties.[30]

Swedish case law in this area is again rather limited, but there are cases illustrating how courts may take into consideration substantial changes with respect to the duty to perform. There may also have been a certain change in view over time. The Supreme Court has thus in some cases accepted substantial cost increases as a basis for an adjustment of hire.[31] In a couple of later cases, it applied §36 in the Contracts Act to amend very long contracts.[32]

5.3.3.4 Material adverse change

The material adverse change (MAC) clause seems to appear most frequently in loan agreements and in

---

[27] See, for example, I. Schwenzer, '*Force Majeure* and Hardship in International Sales Contracts' (2009) 39 *Victoria University of Wellington Law Review*, 709–725. In Swedish law, there are some old cases where economic *force majeure* was discussed; see NJA 1918, p. 20 and NJA 1923, p. 20.

[28] For example, NJA 1953, p. 301 and NJA 1983, p. 385.

[29] See E. M. Runesson, 'Bidrag till frågan om existensen av en omförhandlingsplikt och dess innehåll', in B. Flodgren, L. Gorton, B. Nyström and P. Samuelsson (eds.), *Vänskrift till Axel Adlercreutz* (Juristförlaget i Lund, 2007), pp. 451–462, 451, with references.

[30] See Articles 6.2.1–6.2.3 of the UPICC and Article 6.111 of the PECL (using the terminology change of circumstances).

[31] In NJA 1946, p. 679, the Supreme Court decided that there was a continued right to buy tickets from a railway at a certain price (agreed in connection with the purchase of land for the building of houses) even though there had been substantial price increase since the agreement was made. For a further discussion, see J. Hellner, 'Jämkning av långvarigt avtal' (1994–1995) *Juridisk Tidskrift*, 137–141.

[32] In NJA 1983, p. 385, the Supreme Court amended the contract, but in NJA 1979 p. 731, it did not make any further amendment than what the contract party had already accepted. In NJA 1994, p. 359, §36 was used to limit in time an agreement 'for eternity'.

mergers and acquisitions (M&A) transactions. This clause could be seen as incorporating the effects of the legal doctrine of failed assumptions ('förutsättningsläran') that, in Scandinavian law, is one of several legal methods that could be used by a court or by arbitrators in certain cases of changed circumstances.[33] It could be seen as one of the doctrines developed in order to balance out some effects of the *pacta sunt servanda* principle. When circumstances have changed at the time of performance of the contract, as compared to those prevailing at the time of the conclusion of the contract, courts may, in some cases, declare that the contract is no longer binding upon the parties. The doctrine of failed assumptions has developed differently and is applied somewhat differently in the various Scandinavian countries. In Swedish law, courts used to be more reluctant to apply this doctrine than Norwegian judges, but there currently seems to be some more readiness among Swedish judges to apply the doctrine.[34]

The MAC clause has some objects of a rather similar nature as those covered by this doctrine. When used in M&A agreements, the MAC clause is generally inserted to release a buyer of a company from its promise to buy in the event that material adverse changes have occurred. It is often drafted as a renegotiation clause. Loan agreements often have one MAC clause geared at the phase prior to drawdown and another applicable to the loan period. With respect to the first period, the MAC clause may be used as a reason for the lender not to advance the loan amount and, with respect to the loan period, the clause may be used as a particular event entitling the lender to early termination of the loan agreement.[35]

Depending on their drafting, MAC clauses may be applicable in relation to the particular financial situation of the borrower or in relation to a general economic downturn, which may also affect the financial activities of the prospective borrower. Lacking precise parameters for its application, a MAC clause may turn out to be difficult to use in the

---

[33] See, for example, B. Lehrberg, *Förutsättningsläran* (Iustus, 1989).

[34] This may be an effect of the study by Lehrberg opening up for a broader discussion of the related matters.

[35] In Swedish legal doctrine, the MAC clause has been discussed by L. Gorton, 'Material Adverse Change-klausuler', in Flodgren *et al.*, *Vänskrift till Axel Adlercreutz*, pp. 117–132.

Although the expression 'early termination' is not generally recognised in different European legal systems, it is used here because it seems to be the term normally applied in this type of agreement. International loan agreements are also often drafted on the basis of model forms drafted under Anglo-American law.

individual situation, but it may also prove to be useful for the opening up of renegotiation of an agreement.

As far as I know, there is no case involving the interpretation or the application of a MAC clause in Swedish court practice.

6   Compensation clauses

6.1   General background

I have chosen to delve somewhat into the question of compensation clauses, since this is an area where there is some legal doctrine and some Swedish case law.[36] There are some different solutions in different jurisdictions. As a starting point, the CISG prescribes that the seller has certain rights in case of breach of performance by the seller (Articles 45–52), including the right to claim damages (Articles 74–77).[37]

Parties to a contract may, however, prefer other solutions than those offered in particular legislation. In such a case, they must address the question through contractually agreed clauses. There are several types of compensation clauses in use designed for different purposes and with different effect.

In individual contracts, but often also in standard contracts, the parties frequently determine the character of their contractual under-takings as well as the prerequisites for, and the consequences of, a breach, including the determination of compensation. The parties are basically free to agree on the consequences of a breach, but within a certain framework.[38] §36 of the Nordic Contracts Acts may be used as a balance in case a compensation clause would be deemed to be unreasonable.[39]

---

[36] Again, it must be reiterated that case law from the courts is rather old and present-day disputes are often referred to arbitration, the decisions of which are basically not public.

[37] See, for example, J. Herre and J. Ramberg, *Internationella köplagen (CISG). En kommentar*, 3rd edn (Juristförlaget, 2010), pp. 302ff. and 480ff.

[38] Different legal systems may have different rules regarding how far the parties may use their contractual freedom in this respect. Are they free to agree that a breach entitles the suffering party to retain a prepayment or down payment (forfeiture) and still terminate the contract? Could a compensation clause be used by one party to buy itself out of its contractual obligations? Several different questions may thus arise. Depending on the particular situation, a forfeiture clause may not be acceptable in all legal systems.

[39] See, for example, Statens Offentliga Utredningar (SOU) 1974:84 for a thorough discussion of the ideas behind §36 of the Contracts Act and its use.

6.2   Liquidated damages and penalties

Given an extensive meaning, the term 'compensation clause' may cover clauses of different types, such as forfeiture, limitation of liability, exclusion and liquidated damages. They may be interpreted differently and may be dealt with differently in different legal systems. I mainly focus here on the compensation clause in the more narrow form of a liquidated damages clause.

6.3   The use of compensation clauses

Compensation clauses are more common in commercial contracts than in consumer contracts.[40] In its original form in 1916, the Swedish Contracts Act had an explicit provision (§36) on liquidated damages, allowing a court the discretion to adjust the agreed amount if it appeared 'obviously unreasonable'. The introduction of the provision followed a long discussion in the legal doctrine on the use of such clauses.[41] A large number of cases related to compensation clauses are reported in the years following the introduction of the Contracts Act and there is a comprehensive survey of these cases, including an analysis and a discussion of the principles, in a study by Lena Olsen.[42]

As explained by Almén, these clauses are used in various situations[43] and in connection with different contract types. They may be designed differently, they may be standardised or individually negotiated, they may concern delay but also other types of breach whether of positive or negative type, they may rule out the use of all other consequences of the breach and they may work as an option.[44] This means that the variety is considerable, which also opens up different interpretations. These clauses are quite specific, but also need to be read in their legal context.

Different drafting techniques may thus be used with respect to different types of contracts. Sales contracts often contain standard terms with

---

[40] Courts are rather reluctant to accept compensation clauses in consumer contracts.

[41] T. Almén, *Lagen om avtal och andra rättshandlingar på förmögenhetsrättens område av den 11 julin 1915 samt därav föranledda författningar med litteraturhänvisningar och förklarande anmärkningar* (P. A. Norstedt & Söners Förlag, 1916).

[42] L. Olsen, *Ersättningsklasusuler. Vite och andra avtalade klausuler vid kontraktsbrott* (Nerenius & Santérus, 1986); see in particular pp. 70ff. and 93ff.

[43] Almén, *Lagen om avtal*, p. 211.

[44] In later Swedish legal doctrine, the question has been discussed by L. Gorton and P. Samuelsson, 'Kontraktuella viten', in C. Dahlman (ed.), *Festskrift till Ingemar Ståhl. Studier i rättsekonomi*, (Studentlitteratur, 2005), pp. 75–106, Chapters 5–7.

respect to compensation due to the seller's delay. They often spell out that the compensation amount shall be the *only* compensation, but if there is a considerable delay, the buyer shall also be entitled to terminate the contract. In some cases, there may be an option for the suffering party to choose either the agreed compensation or to demand damages, in which case the suffering party will have to prove his or her loss.

In all compensation clauses, there is a particular amount agreed with respect to the particular breach (a certain amount per day of delay, a certain amount per deficiency in speed, etc.), but the contract may also specifically provide that, in case the buyer is entitled to cancel the contract, no liquidated damages will be paid. The rationale for this is that a builder (in a construction contract) will make a considerable loss in case of cancellation and that the buyer should carry some of this burden.

Sales contract compensation clauses are most common in relation to delay in performance. In such cases, the contract normally prescribes that a certain amount shall be paid as compensation to the other party per day, per week or per other specified time unit of delay. In some contracts, a compensation clause with respect to other types of breach of performance may also be inserted. This is particularly the case where the obligation is precise, such as deficiency in a particular warranted quality or characteristic. Sometimes, the compensation clauses are standardised in a contract form, while in other cases, room is left open for the insertion of a certain amount, and in yet other instances, the parties will negotiate the compensation clause individually.

Compensation clauses are often agreed upon with respect to a positive obligation ('we undertake to deliver . . .'), but there are also instances where the compensation clause is agreed upon in relation to a negative undertaking ('we undertake not to disclose . . .'). The question may arise as to whether there is a principal difference between these types when it comes to their interpretation.

In contracts where a party sells a business, the M&A agreement often accompanies a prohibition for the seller to compete with the buyer within the same type of business for a certain period of time, with a compensation clause in case of breach.[45] In addition, in the event that a party has promised not to disclose information received during negotiations, such an undertaking may be underpinned by a compensation

---

[45] This may thus set out that if any information received during the negotiations is abused or disclosed to a third party, a certain amount shall be paid as a penalty.

clause.[46] Certain categories of employees may have a clause in their employment contracts prohibiting them from entering into new employment with a competing business until after a certain period of time. Often, such an undertaking is also coupled with a compensation clause. All these clauses thus cover negative undertakings. In these cases, it may be particularly hard to determine the damages to be paid.

The situation is different if, in connection with the sale of a company, it appears that the economic result of the company is less magnificent than was originally contemplated by the buyer (irrespective of the due diligence carried out). The contract may then set out that the seller will be liable up to a certain amount of the economic deficiency. Such liability will normally be valid only for a limited period of time.

Compensation clauses may thus be relevant both with respect to positive undertakings and negative undertakings. In the latter case, it is often very hard in practice to determine the amount of damages to be paid in case of breach of the undertaking, and the compensation amount is therefore often agreed upon depending on how the parties may agree on the financial effect of a breach.

There are some practical considerations with respect to the application of compensation clauses. Agreed compensation amounts with respect to positive undertakings often seem to be somewhat lower than damages that might be determined in the event of open-ended claims for damages.[47] The great advantage of compensation clauses is that the party claiming compensation will not have to prove that it has encountered a loss nor the amount of the loss, but if the prerequisites of the clause are met, then the amount will be paid out. However, this is also where there may be an argument against the application of the clauses by the party in breach, claiming that if there is no loss, then no amount should be paid. At least among Swedish arbitrators, there seems to be a tendency to uphold a compensation clause under such circumstances, and it is likely that Swedish courts will also, to a great extent, accept the compensation clause in such situations.

Another question may be whether a compensation clause shall be considered to be full compensation or whether the suffering party has a choice between using the compensation clause or instead going for full compensation according to general principles on damages, or whether

---

[46] There are several examples, among them negotiations in connection with patent licence agreements or other intellectual property agreements.

[47] This is, of course, a statement which has to be read carefully, since there are a number of situations where the agreed damages give a very good (and sometimes too good) cover.

they may be used in combination. Further, a question could be whether a compensation clause could be used even if the contract is terminated. Often, compensation clauses explicitly state that the only consequence of a breach shall be the agreed compensation. There shall be no further amounts payable and there shall also be no right of termination, unless the discrepancy between the agreed performance and the actual performance is substantial. For example, if there is a very long delay of, say twelve months, there may be a right of termination of the contract, but the right of compensation is then also cut off. The clauses in use are thus normally rather clear on these points.

There are no clear-cut cases in Sweden where courts have come to the conclusion that a deliberate breach of contract shall be treated in the same way if the contract contains a liquidated damages clause as if the contract contains a limitation of liability clause. The following can be used as an example. A Swedish building contract (general standard conditions – AB 2004) contains a provision on liquidated damages payable in case of delay on the side of the construction company. Let us assume that the construction company is offered another contract during the construction with a substantially better earning potential. Even if it would have to pay the full 'penalty' amount to the first buyer, the second contract would render a good profit. Would the construction company then be entitled to claim that they could just pay out the penalty amount and instead carry out the second project, possibly coming back to the first project at a later time?

There are different views on this in Swedish law. One approach is that the construction company in case of intentional breach may not rely on the compensation clause as a limitation amount. The other approach is that the agreed compensation shall be seen as the agreed amount to be paid for a breach.

If Swedish law treated compensation clauses as limitation of liability or exemption from liability, then compensation clauses would not be upheld in the event of intentional breach or gross negligence. Compensation clauses could also be regarded as an agreed compensation for a breach. How then would the difference between the two types of clauses be set out? Would there be a difference between compensation clauses covering positive or negative undertakings?

6.4   Delay interest

A particular item in this connection concerns the delay in payment. The payment debtor, as well as the performance debtor, has a duty to pay within the time agreed. Failing this, there is a breach of his or her obligations and also certain consequences.

The DCFR prescribes in Article III – 3:708 on delay in payment of money:

(i) If payment of a sum of money is delayed, whether or not the non-performance is excused, the creditor is entitled to interest on that sum from the time when payment is due to the time of payment at the average commercial bank short-term lending rate to prime borrowers prevailing for the contractual currency at the place where payment is due.

(ii) The creditor may in addition recover damages for any further loss.

The contractual solution is often an agreed delay interest to be paid in case of delay in payment, but there may also be a particular provision entitling the counterparty to terminate the contract. Delay interest is normally set as a higher interest rate than that quoted as the current interest rate. Legislation in many countries has also often set out a rather high interest to be paid in case of delay in payment.

Delay interest is also a type of compensation clause. In the Nordic countries, particular legislation was introduced several years ago with the specific aim of allowing a high delay interest rate in order to induce debtors to pay in time. Currently, the EU Directive (2000/35/EL) prescribes that delay interest shall be paid in the event of delay in payment.

7 Conclusion

It is not easy to draw general conclusions from the above. Undoubtedly, there are differences between the Scandinavian approach and the interpretation and construction of contracts under English law, which is the original context of the examined clauses. There are also certain differences in approach between the courts in the various Scandinavian countries.

English and American contract practices have come to play a particular role in the drafting of international business contracts. Several different contractual solutions have developed over time that may apply in different phases of the contract (negotiations and performance), and contract draftsmen have introduced several different contractual clauses involving contracting, changes and amendments. Courts and contract draftsmen may not always share the same view on the binding nature of the contract. Whether a principle of good faith and fair dealing may be used to set aside what the parties have agreed upon cannot be generally determined.

In recent Swedish case law, we have seen that a Swedish court will not only glance at other Scandinavian courts for guidance in the application of certain legal rules and principles, but may also take into consideration the development of English case law when determining the construction of a contract which has been drafted according to English law principles even though Swedish law is applicable. In addition, Swedish courts, to a growing extent, consider the various restatements of transnational principles (such as the UPICC, the PECL and the DCFR) when deciding cases under Swedish law.

So far, Swedish courts, in my view for good reasons, have been rather cautious in allowing the extensive use of § 36 of the Contracts Act in commercial relations. However, there has been some growing use of loyalty (good faith and fair dealing) reasoning during the last few years. Generally, two trends seem to have developed: on the one hand, a growing importance of English-American drafting technique and, on the other hand, a growing impact of legal reasoning emanating from European and international principles.

In order to sum up the Swedish aspects, a distinction could be made between boilerplate clauses that hardly have any contractual consequences in Swedish law and those that may have some legal implications. The former category will probably embrace clauses such as 'singular and plural', 'gender', *'pari passu'* and 'partial invalidity'. The second category embraces clauses which will have some, but not always absolutely clear, contractual impact:

Entire agreement: these clauses are common and have been judged in some cases. They have limiting effects on the freedom of a court to consider evidence. They will, however, hardly give rise to the creation of a parol evidence rule situation.

No waiver: the clause is not uncommon and will be given effect. In spite of the clause, the repeated behaviour of a party in contravention of it will probably as a consequence mean that it will lose its impact in the case.

No oral amendments: these clauses, which also serve to create contractual order, will be given effect, but if they are too formalistic, a court may decide to apply the clause somewhat less stringently.

Conditions: Swedish law does not recognise the traditional distinction in common law between conditions and warranties, but some contractual provisions are regarded as rather more fundamental than others.

Sole remedy: this is a provision normally found in connection with liquidated damages clauses and is basically recognised.

Subject to contract: this is a type of clause which is also normally given effect in a contractual relation, but if applied in bad faith, a court may set the clause aside.

Material adverse change: this is a type of clause which is common in certain types of contracts. There is no Swedish case law concerning MAC clauses and it is hard to foresee their limits.

Liquidated damages: these clauses are very common in commercial contracts as a substitute for damages, and also possibly other consequences of a breach of contract. They will generally be given effect, but § 36 of the Contracts Act may be used to modify such a clause or even set it aside. In order for this to happen, the clause has to be regarded as very unreasonable in the circumstances at hand. Very often, a particular sole remedy provision will form part of the liquidated damages clause.

Indemnity, representations and warranties: there is no clear distinction in Swedish law between these types of clauses, but they will be understood and construed in accordance with their wording and the context in which they are used.

Hardship: there is no general exception for hardship events in Swedish law, but economic *force majeure* may be taken into consideration. Also, §36 of the Contracts Act may, under certain circumstances, be used to amend a contract with respect to hardship events. If there is a hardship clause in the contract, this will normally be recognised and upheld by a court.

15

The East European tradition: application of boilerplate clauses under Hungarian law

ATTILA MENYHÁRD

1 Introduction

Commercial law does not exist as a separate branch of law in Hungarian private law. Hungarian private law is built on a unified system where the Civil Code[1] covers the regulation of contracts, including the general framework and limits of freedom of contract for merchants as well as for other parties. As commercial contracts are neither defined nor covered by specific legislation, the Civil Code is to be applied to commercial contracts as well. There is specific legislation for contracts of foreign trade[2] providing more liberal regulation compared to the Civil Code, but the applicability of this law decree – still in force as one of the reminders of the socialist legislation – is in question, as in defining its scope it refers to the Foreign Trade Act, which is no longer in force. There is ongoing reform aimed at recodification of Hungarian private law, which would abolish this regulation discrepancy. The New Hungarian Civil Code – expected to come into force in about 2013 – would provide unitary (monistic) legislation and would cover commercial transactions as well.

As a main rule, the provisions of the Civil Code concerning the rights and obligations of the parties are default rules which become the content of the contract insofar as the parties did not agree otherwise. The paradigm of Hungarian contract law is freedom of contract, which necessarily implies that contract law rules are not mandatory. The non-mandatory character of regulation of contract law is provided in §200(1) of the Hungarian Civil Code, which explicitly provides that the parties to

---

[1] Act No. IV of 1959 on the Civil Code of the Republic of Hungary (Ptk.).
[2] Law-Decree No. 8 of 1977 on Application of the Civil Code in Foreign Business Relationship.

a contract are free to stipulate the content of their contract and that they shall be entitled, upon mutual consent, to deviate from the provisions pertaining to contracts insofar as such deviation is not prohibited by the law. Although sometimes it is not clear whether certain rules are of a mandatory character, one has to assume that provisions concerning contractual rights and obligations – insofor as not otherwise provided by the law – are of a non-mandatory character. Provisions of other types, like the definition of structural concepts of contract law (grounds and consequences of invalidity, termination, frustration, etc.) covering the construction of contracts or rules which entitle the court to intervene in the area of contractual rights and obligations of the parties (judicial amendment of contracts, judicial reduction of obligations of the parties, etc.), are mandatory rules which cannot be overruled by the parties. The same holds true for provisions that are implied as general clauses of the Civil Code, like the requirement of good faith and fair dealing.[3]

The central issue of dispute resolution in contractual relationships is the construction of the contract. The Hungarian Civil Code provides for a general norm concerning the construction of contractual statements by the parties. According to this rule, the contract is to be construed with regard to the assumed intent of the parties and the circumstances of the case, in accordance with the general accepted meaning of the words used in the contract. If the contract was concluded on the basis of standard contract terms or is a consumer contract, and if the meaning of a standard contract condition or the contents of a consumer contract cannot be clearly established by the application of the main rule of construction, the construction which is more favorable to the consumer or to the party entering into a contract with the person imposing such contractual terms or conditions shall prevail. Should a person waive his or her rights in part or in full, such a statement cannot be broadly construed. The parties' secret reservations or concealed motives will be irrelevant.[4] This rule of construction is to be considered mandatory, as it does not design and allocate the rights and obligations of the parties, but gives guidelines to the courts and other third parties concerning the construction of the contract.

---

[3] §4(1) of the Hungarian Civil Code. The general principles of private law (good faith and fair dealing, prohibition of abuse of rights, *nemo turpitudinem suam*) are covered by the introductory provisions of the Civil Code and are to be applied for all forms of private law relationships, including contracts.

[4] §207(1), (2), (4) and (5) of the Hungarian Civil Code.

The Hungarian arbitration and court practice in commercial dispute resolutions seem to tend to follow a flexible approach. As – in line with the non-mandatory character of regulation – normally the validity of undertaking contractual obligations in commercial law does not depend on compliance with normatively defined types, forms or categories of obligations, and covenants may have a valid cause even if they are atypical.[5] Thus, contractual obligations may be valid even if they do not correspond to normative types insofar as they do not violate mandatory rules or prohibitions in the regulation of contracts.

Imported contract clauses are widely used in Hungarian practice as well, mostly but not exclusively in transactions involving foreign investors. They still remain largely untested in Hungarian court practice. That is why analysing them can only rest on analysing the context provided by legislation and court practice. This makes the conclusions to be reached somewhat restricted or limited, especially where the result would depend on the standardised construction of typical clauses or where the starting points in court practice or regulation are completely missing. Although the clauses analysed here are to be held as enforceable on the basis of freedom of contract and parties are to be held as free in negotiating them, sometimes they may result in an unequal bargain which comes under the general control of private law and therefore may come up against the general limits of freedom of contract. It is not the aim of this chapter to give a detailed analysis of these situations. On the one hand, in commercial transactions on which this chapter focuses, these limits are relatively flexible and the courts would presumably be inclined to enforce the agreement of the parties as far as possible. On the other hand, such analysis would certainly go too far beyond the scope and limits of the aims of this chapter. The general tools for controlling unequal bargaining and preventing unacceptably unequal situations or abuse of rights in Hungarian private law are the general clauses of private law, especially the prohibition of abuse of rights and the requirement of good faith and fair dealing, as well as the grounds for invalidity of contracts contained in contract law regulation.

The requirement of good faith and fair dealing expresses the principle of mutual trust and shall be understood as a general standard of conduct set by the overall moral values accepted in society.[6] It is a general clause

---

[5] Supreme Court, Legf. Bír. Gfv. I. 33.312/1997. sz. – BH 1998. No. 440.

[6] A. Földi, *A jóhiszeműség és tisztességesség elve; intézménytörténeti vázlat a római jogtól napjainkig* (Publicationes Instituti Iuris Romani Budapestiensis fasc. 9, published by the

which, in its normative form, has been formulated among the introductory provisions of the Civil Code. It can and shall be applied in private law as a whole. Thus, the scope of the requirement of good faith and fair dealing shall not be restricted to contract law. The requirement of good faith and fair dealing is a fundamental principle underlying the private law in general. Its role and meaning is similar to that of *Treu und Glauben* in §242 of the German BGB. Article 1.7 of the UNIDROIT Principles of International Commercial Contracts and Article 1.106 of the Principles of European Contract Law formulate good faith and fair dealing as a fundamental principle to be applied overall within the scope of the Principles.[7]

At the heart of preventing and controlling unequal bargaining in contract law regulation lie the prohibition of immoral contracts (contracts contrary to public policy are to be understood as 'immoral' as well),[8] the prohibition of usury,[9] as well as the possibility of avoiding contracts with a striking imbalance between the performance and the counter-performance (§201(2) of the Civil Code)[10] and the control of standard contract terms.[11] The analysis provided here could not extend

---

Roman Law Department of ELTE Law Faculty, 2001), p. 90; and L. Vékás, in G. Gellért (ed.), *A Polgári Törvénykönyv Magyarázata* (Complex Kiadó, 2008), 4. §2.

[7] See the comments to Article 1.107 of the UNIDROIT Principles and the comments to Article 1.106 of the European Principles.

[8] §200(2) of the Hungarian Civil Code.

[9] Usury is a wide-ranging concept referring to excessive and abusive benefit. §202 of the Hungarian Civil Code provides that if a contracting party has stipulated a striking disproportionate advantage at the conclusion of the contract by exploiting the other party's situation, the contract shall be null and void (usurious contract).

[10] §201(2) of the Hungarian Civil Code provides the substantive justice in contracts. According to this provision, if, at the time of concluding the contract, there is a striking difference between the value of the two performances, without one of the parties having the intention of giving a gift, the aggrieved party is entitled to avoid the contract.

[11] As is provided in §209(1) and (2) of the Hungarian Civil Code, a standard contract term or a contractual term of a consumer contract which has not been individually negotiated shall be regarded as unfair if, contrary to the requirement of good faith and fair dealing, it caused a significant and unjustified imbalance in the parties' rights and obligations arising under the contract to the detriment of the other contractual party entering into a contract with the person imposing such a contractual term or condition. The unfairness of a contractual term shall be assessed, taking into account the nature of the services for which the contract was concluded and by referring, at the time of conclusion of the contract, to all the circumstances relating to the conclusion of the contract and to all the other terms of the contract or of another contract on which it is dependent. §209/A(1) of the Civil Code provides for the avoidability of unfair standard contract terms, while §209/A(2) makes them null and void in consumer contracts.

to all the possible aspects of limits of freedom of contract. Some of these grounds of unenforceability are referred to where the court practice, the regulation or the contracting situation in the context of the clause indicates its specific role and importance. It is, however, to be established in general that if the specific circumstances of the case call for the application of these norms and the limits of freedom of contract they imply, the otherwise-allowed contract clauses may be held as unenforceable in the given case and under the given circumstances.

2 Entire agreement

As far as defining the rights and obligations of the parties is concerned, such clauses are to be held as valid and enforceable between the parties on the basis of freedom of contract because they do not violate any mandatory rule. From this follows that, when the contract contains this clause, prior negotiations, representations, undertakings and agreements may not be held as part of the contract.[12] Conversely, if there are *lacunae* that require construction of the contract, such clauses could not prevent the judge from interpreting the contract – according to §207 of the Hungarian Civil Code – as it had to be understood by the other party. Thus, the contract can and is to be interpreted in the light of the previous statements, representations and undertakings of the parties.[13] The question of whether certain previously agreed specifications are to be held as parts of the parties' contractual obligations is to be answered according to the result of the interpretation. If the entire agreement clause is to be interpreted as excluding the application of these specifications, they are not to be held as part of the contract (although they may be implied by the court as gap-filling terms, e.g., as usual standards of quality in commerce). If that is not the case, these specifications may be referred to in the course of constructing the parties' assumed and expressed contractual will, as the parties may not restrict the courts in applying and interpreting the rules on construction of contracts, as is provided in §207 of the Hungarian Civil Code.

---

[12] This is suggested in the context of Hungarian private law as well by Kisfaludi: A. Kisfaludi, 'A teljességi záradék', *Gazdasági és Jog*, 11 (1995), 7.

[13] This conclusion is not only a logical consequence of interpreting the law, but is also the suggested solution for the New Hungarian Civil Code. L. Vékás (ed.), *Szakértői Javaslat az új Polgári Törvénykönyv tervezetéhez* (Complex Kiadó, 2008), p. 774.

3   No waiver

The Hungarian Civil Code does not provide that failure by a party to exercise a right or remedy should constitute a waiver thereof. Thus, it seems that such clauses neither amend the content of the contract to be implied by the provisions of the Civil Code nor affect the position of the parties under the governing law. However, in the absence of such a clause, the court may conclude that not exercising the right of termination within a reasonable time period constitutes a waiver of the right of termination on the basis of the requirement of good faith and fair dealing, or that referring to it would be an abuse of right which results in preventing the party from exercising the right.[14] If, however, the parties stipulated a no waiver clause in a commercial contract, normally there should be less room for the courts to imply limits concerning the exercising of this right on the basis of general clauses of the Civil Code, although such an implication of waiver, primarily on the basis of the requirement of good faith and fair dealing, may not be excluded. The general clauses of the Civil Code – among them the requirement of good faith and fair dealing or the prohibition of abuse of rights – are mandatory rules establishing implied obligations and requirements that the parties cannot contract out of. It follows from this that in the event that a no waiver clause is stipulated in a commercial contract, if, e.g., the contract gave the right to the party to terminate in case of delay in delivery and, in spite of the late delivery, the party did not terminate until after a considerable amount of time had passed, citing changes in the market, the termination is to be held basically as lawful, provided that the law or the contract allowed termination on this ground and the parties did not agree otherwise. The court, however, may come to the conclusion – especially if the delay in exercising the right might have created a protected interest (trust) of the party in breach – that exercising the right would be a violation of the implied duty of compliance with good

---

[14] A. Menyhárd, 'Protection of Legitimate Expectations in Hungarian Private Law', in B. Fauvarques-Cosson (ed.), *La Confiance Légitime et l'Estoppel* (Société de Législation Comparée, 2007), p. 278. A very recent development of court practice is that the court may reject the claim of the owner of a pre-emption right to enforce the contract concluded between the defendants if he or she knew that the defendants concluded the contract violating his or her rights but delayed enforcing his or her rights for a considerable time and could not provide acceptable explanation for this delay. Supreme Court, Legf. Bír. Pfv. VI. 20.492/2004. sz. – BH 2005 No. 320.

faith and fair dealing and may hold the termination, in spite of the no waiver clause, unlawful, barring the party from referring to it.

4 No oral amendments

§217(2) of the Hungarian Civil Code explicitly provides that the parties may agree that their contract shall be valid only in the agreed form. The form – including written form – is a precondition of validity of a contract if the parties expressly stipulated this. In such cases, however, the contract shall become valid by acceptance of performance or partial performance, even if a formal requirement had been stipulated but the parties failed to comply with it. Amendments to a contract, which are themselves contracts, are also to be covered by this provision of the Civil Code. It follows from this that no oral amendments clauses are valid under Hungarian law, and by such a clause an agreement on the amendment of the contract shall be valid in an oral form only if one of the parties accepted the – at least partial – performance of the other according to the orally agreed terms. The basis of this rule[15] is that if the party, in spite of the agreed form, accepted performance according to orally agreed terms, the performance from the one side and the acceptance of that on the other side shall be understood as mutual confirmation of the oral agreement. Thus, with performance and acceptance of performance, the parties set aside the agreed form by mutual consent.

On this ground, in the context of Hungarian contract law, it can be concluded that if the parties agree on an oral amendment, the party to the contract shall be entitled to refuse performance simply by invoking the no oral amendments clause and he or she could not be enforced to accept performance according to the orally agreed terms.

However, it is not clear whether the Hungarian courts would be inclined to construe the oral amendment – or a tacit agreement concluded by a conduct – as if the parties did set aside the no oral amendments clause by mutual consent. Such an interpretation – i.e., that oral agreement with mutual consent in spite of the no oral amendments clause implies agreement for setting aside the no oral amendments clause itself – could not be excluded in Hungarian contract law, although such a

---

[15] Motivation of the Draft for the Hungarian Civil Code of 1959, motivation to §217. *A Magyar Népköztársaság Polgári Törvénykönyve. Az 1959. évi IV. tv. és a javaslat miniszteri indokolása* (Közgazdasági és Jogi Könyvkiadó, 1963), p. 242.

conclusion has not been confirmed, up to now, in Hungarian court practice.

5   Severability

There is a general provision provided in the Hungarian Civil Code for partial invalidity. As it is provided in §239 of the Hungarian Civil Code for non-consumer contracts, in the event of partial invalidity of a contract, the entire contract shall fail only if the parties would not have concluded it without the invalid part. As far as consumer contracts are concerned, in the event of partial invalidity, the entire contract shall fail only if the contract cannot be performed without the invalid part. There is no specific rule in Hungarian private law providing that the invalidity of certain contract terms renders the whole contract invalid. Thus, the severability clause does not seem to conflict with the regulation and is to be construed as if the parties declared that none of the terms and conditions of their contract should be considered to be so fundamental that they would not have contracted in the event of its unenforceability. The rule provided in §239 of the Hungarian Civil Code seems to be open enough to allow the parties to define clauses whose invalidity shall lead to the invalidity of the entire agreement. If the severability clause resulted in an unbalanced contract, that will be controlled with general clauses (such as the invalidity of contracts contrary to good moral public policy) of the Civil Code or with other grounds of invalidity. If, e.g., the severability clause in standard contract terms or in a non-individually negotiated consumer contract is unfair, it is unenforceable.[16]

6   Conditions

'Fundamental breach' is not listed in the Hungarian Civil Code as a ground for termination of the contract. Generally, breach of contract

---

[16] According to §209 of the Hungarian Civil Code, a standard contract term or a contractual term of a consumer contract which has not been individually negotiated shall be regarded as unfair if, contrary to the requirement of good faith and fair dealing, it caused a significant and unjustified imbalance in the parties' contractual rights and obligations to the detriment of the party entering into the contract with the person imposing such a contractual term or condition. The unfairness of a contractual term shall be assessed, taking into account the nature of the services for which the contract was concluded and by referring, at the time of conclusion of the contract, to all the circumstances relating to the conclusion of the contract and to all the other terms of the contract or of another contract on which it is dependent.

has consequences like overdue interest, damages, agreed penalties, etc. At the centre of defining cases of breach of contract which provide a ground for termination by the aggrieved party is the concept of frustration of interests in performance.

In the event of delay, the obligee shall be entitled to terminate the contract if his or her interests in performance have been frustrated. The obligee shall be entitled to terminate the contract in the absence of proving the frustration of his or her interests in performance if, according to the agreement of the parties or due to the imminent purpose of the service, the contract had to be performed at a definite time and no other, or if the obligee has stipulated a reasonable peremptory term for the delayed performance and this period elapsed without result.[17] This means that in the context of delay, the parties are free to stipulate the undertaken deadline as a fixed one giving the right to the obligee to terminate the contract on the sole ground of missing the deadline; otherwise, the frustration of interest must be proven or an adequate peremptory period must be given to, and again missed by, the obligor as a prerequisite of termination.

In the event of defective performance, the obligee shall be entitled to terminate the contract if he or she was entitled to neither repair nor replacement, or if the obligor refused to provide repair or replacement, or was unable to complete the repair or replacement within a reasonable period of time and without any significant inconvenience, taking account of the nature of the goods and the purpose for which the consumer required the goods. The obligee shall not be entitled to have the contract terminated if the defect is minor.[18]

Thus, a clause saying simply that certain obligations are fundamental and any breach thereof shall amount to a fundamental breach of the contract has no meaning in the context of Hungarian contract law. In general, however, parties are free to provide grounds of termination in the contract according to their mutual will. Freedom of contract includes the freedom to design rights of termination and provide the prerequisites for exercising these rights in the contract. Thus, parties are free to stipulate that a fundamental breach is a basis for termination and they are free to define fundamental breach or to circumscribe the situations to be qualified as a fundamental breach. If they agree that the aggrieved party shall be entitled to terminate the contract if the other party breached the contract and the breach is a fundamental one

---

[17] §300 of the Hungarian Civil Code.   [18] §306 of the Hungarian Civil Code.

according to the contract, this agreement shall be enforceable. In this context, if the parties agreed that a fundamental breach is a ground for termination and the contract defines delay in delivery as a fundamental breach, this shall be enforceable as well. If the delay occurred, it means that the agreed prerequisite of an agreed remedy (i.e., termination) occurred and this shall give the right to the other party – independently of the actual consequences of the delay – to terminate the contract. With such an approach, termination may be seen not as a remedy but simply as a right given to the party for a condition (delay) that has been fulfilled. As in the contract the party undertook the risk of termination in case of delay, in commercial relationships, the courts presumably would not consider if it was an abuse of rights or incompliance with the requirement of good faith and fair dealing to exercise the right in the absence of any adverse consequences, but because, e.g., the market has changed and the contract is no longer profitable.

To sum up, in the context of Hungarian contract law, there is no point in defining contractually which breaches are to be deemed fundamental as regulation does not attach any consequences to fundamental breach. The parties are, however, free to give the right of termination to each other and may describe the prerequisites of exercising the rights or the cases and situations when the right of termination may be exercised, including defining cases of fundamental breach and giving the right of termination in these cases. If the right of termination provided to the parties or to one of the parties resulted in an imbalance between the rights and obligations of the parties, is abusive or does not comply with the requirement of good faith and fair dealing, the general tools for control of enforceability of a contract are to be applied. The right of termination in this case – as with the content of the contract – is a negotiated right provided to the party. If the negotiated prerequisites are fulfilled and have opened up the possibility of exercising the right, the clause should be enforceable, regardless of the real reason for exercising the negotiated right. In commercial relations, courts would presumably be reluctant to go into the real motives of conduct if the parties themselves defined the conduct as lawful.

7 Sole remedy

A sole remedy clause restricting the party's remedies to liquidated damages is a limitation of liability for breach of contract in two ways. On the one hand, it deprives the aggrieved party of other remedies provided by the regulation, such as claiming that the contract should be enforced in kind,[19] the right to terminate the contract, claiming overdue interest (if the missed obligation is paying a sum) or, if applied in the context of defective performance, of repair or replacement. On the other hand, it limits the liability for damages to a certain negotiated sum even if the suffered loss exceeded the agreed amount.

Both ways of limitation of liability fall under the application of §314 of the Hungarian Civil Code, which provides the limits for exclusion and limitation clauses. According to this provision, the liability for breach of contract – insofar as it is not explicitly prohibited – can be excluded or limited only if the disadvantage of limitation of liability was compensated by an adequate reduction of the price or other countervalue, or by providing another benefit. Liability for breach of contract caused deliberately, by gross negligence or by crime, or which caused damage to life, health or physical integrity cannot be validly excluded. The provision shall not be applicable in foreign commercial relations of Hungarian companies falling under a special regime of Law Decree No. 8 of 1978 (§15). Thus, a sole remedy clause in the context of the application of the Hungarian Civil Code shall be held enforceable if it has complied with the two-step test of §314 of the Hungarian Civil Code: first, the breach of contract was not grossly negligent, was not a crime, was not deliberate

---

[19] §277(1) of the Hungarian Civil Code provides that contracts shall be performed as stipulated at the place and in the time set forth and in accordance with the quantity, quality and range specified therein. This provision of the Civil Code underlies one of the basic principles of the rules of performance which may be called the principle of 'real performance'. The general rule of the Civil Code is specific performance and this is expressly provided in §300, which regulates the consequences of a breach of contract when the breach consists of a delay in performance: if the party to the contract fails to perform his or her obligation as it falls due, the aggrieved party shall have the right to claim performance of the contractual obligation. Monetary compensation (damages) shall replace enforced performance only if the performance in kind is impossible or if it would be against the interests of the creditor. The general principle of enforced performance is supported by other provisions of the Civil Code as well. It follows from the provisions and the structure of the rules covering the remedies for breach of contract in Ptk. that if the performance becomes impossible, the party who was responsible for it shall be obliged to pay damages to the other party. This means that impossibility excludes specific performance. If performance is possible but the debtor is in delay, the creditor has the right to demand enforced performance or to repudiate the contract (§300), and if the debtor refuses to fulfil his or her obligation, the creditor may choose between the consequences of delay (demanding enforced performance) and the consequences of impossibility (§313) (i.e., claiming damages instead of specific performance). If the contractual obligation of the party is providing a declaration, the court may rectify it with its judgment (§295).

and did not cause damage to life, health or physical integrity; and, second, the disadvantage of the exemption clause was compensated for by the adequate reduction of the price or other countervalue, or by providing another benefit. It seems to be generally accepted that the compensation – the price reduction or any other benefit – must be proportional to the detriment deriving from the exemption clause. The proportionality must be assessed *at the time of the conclusion of the contract*, according to the ratio of the compensation and the risk deriving from the exemption clause (it should not be assessed after the breach of contract, according to the ratio of the caused damage and the given compensation).[20] The adequate compensation not only can be provided as a price reduction, but also in the form of any other benefit. In a chain of contracts or in special constructions like a financial lease, the assignment of the rights from remedies can also be an adequate compensation.[21] The solution, making the enforceability of exclusion clauses dependent on providing adequate compensation, has been strongly criticised in the Hungarian literature. It has been argued that adequate reduction of the counterperformance could provide a proper result only if the value of the counterperformance would be objectively determinable, which is normally not the case. Since the stipulation of the price is up to the parties, the test of adequate compensation can easily be evaded by formally setting a higher price and ostensibly 'reducing' it to the amount that the seller originally wanted to get for the goods.[22] In cases of defective performance, it is widely accepted that the compensation is adequate if the price is reduced to the value of the defective good but if the defective good's value remains much lower than the reduced price, the exemption of liability is unenforceable.[23]

If it is assumed that parties with equal bargaining power consented freely and consciously to clauses drawing the boundary of their liabilities, there does not seem to be a reasonable ground for distinguishing between definition clauses and exemption clauses. This would limit the parties'

---

[20] F. Petrik, *Szavatosság, jótállás és fogyasztóvédelem* (Közgazdasági és Jogi Könyvkiadó, 1995), p. 24.

[21] E.g., in a financial lease, the lessor can validly exclude his or her liability regarding the subject of the lease if he or she assigns his or her rights against the supplier to the lessee if the assignment provided real and complete compensation for the disadvantage. See, e.g., the opinion of the County Court of Csongrád No. 3 of 2000, 21 June 1996.

[22] A. Kisfaludi, *Az adásvételi szerződés* (Budapest: Közfazdasági és Jogi Könyvkiadó, 1999), p. 205.

[23] Petrik, *Szavatosság*, p. 24. See also Gellért, *A Polgári Törvénykönyv Magyarázata*, §314.

freedom of contract in spite of the non-mandatory character of contract law. In commercial transactions, regulatory limitations on exclusion clauses – like §314 of the Civil Code in Hungarian law – restrict the freedom of the parties to agree upon lump-sum damages, making the boundaries of the obligation undertaken as the result of the bargain clear. This is also a question of pricing: the price the party would ask for his or her performance is normally adjusted to the risk imposed on him or her by the law and by the contract. Statutory restrictions on exclusion clauses also restrict the playing field of the parties for the bargain, as this way the law simply prevents the parties from agreeing freely regarding the risks to be undertaken for the agreed price. In commercial transactions, this does not seem to be reasonable and this led the Hungarian legislator to abandon this restriction (i.e., requiring an adequate price reduction as a prerequisite of the enforceability of exclusion clauses) in the New Civil Code, at least as far as damage to property was concerned.[24]

Thus, the enforceability of sole remedy clauses depends on the compensation provided for the disadvantage it creates. Providing adequate compensation can make the sole remedy clause enforceable concerning both restricting the available remedy to the liquidated damages and the limitation of liability to the agreed sum as liquidated damages. In the absence of adequate compensation, in cases of personal injury or if the breach of contract was a result of gross negligence, deliberateness or crime, the sole remedy clause is unenforceable. If the sole remedy clause had not been made enforceable by adequate compensation, the aggrieved party may claim full compensation and may exercise all the rights he or she is provided by regulation irrespective of the sole remedy clause and liquidated damages.

8   Subject to contract

In Hungarian legal doctrine, a contract is the result of the mutual expressed will of the parties to create legally binding promises. Whether the contract is concluded between the parties depends on the construction of their expressed will in the course of the contracting process. If, according to the rule of construction (§207 of the Hungarian Civil Code), the conclusion of contract as an exchange of legally binding promises cannot be established, there is no contract between the parties.

---

[24] L. Vékás (ed.), *Szakértői Javaslat az új Polgári Törvénykönyv tervezetéhez* (Complex Kiadó, 2008), p. 818.

The parties may bind themselves to conclude a contract with a certain content, but such a 'preliminary' contract must also be concluded with a mutual consent of undertaking the legally binding obligation to make a contract in the future. If the parties expressed their intent to conclude a contract without expressing that they hold themselves as legally bound to do so, such an expression of intentions cannot create contractual rights and obligations between the parties. Hungarian court practice and regulation make a clear distinction between expressing intent without making legally binding promises to contract, the 'preliminary' contract creating legally enforceable obligations for the parties to conclude the contract and the contract itself. Expressed intent to contract does not create legally binding obligations and cannot be enforced either as a contract or as a preliminary contract. On the basis of letters of intent, neither the obligations to be undertaken in the final contract (e.g., payment or performance of other contractual obligations)[25] nor the conclusion of a contract according to the letters of intent can be enforced.[26] If the parties agreed to conclude a contract in the future, they are obliged to conclude the contract with the agreed content according to their preliminary contract. If a party refuses to conclude the (final) contract on the basis of the preliminary contract, the court shall – on the basis of the claim of the aggrieved party to the preliminary contract – create the final contract and determine its content with the judgment.[27] Letters or

---

[25] Supreme Court, Legf. Bír. Gfv. X. 30.072/2002. sz. – BH 2003. No. 203, Supreme Court, Legf. Bír. Pfv. VIII. 22.912/1996. sz. – BH 1998. No. 229.

[26] §295 of the Hungarian Civil Code under enforcement of contracts – as a normatively provided method of specific performance of contractual promises – makes it possible to substitute the legal acts that a party was contractually obligated to make with a court decision. Under this rule, however, Hungarian court practice substitutes only declarations undertaken in a contract but not on the basis of a letter of intent. Court practice seems to be consequent in rejecting such claims on the basis of a letter of intent or other declaration of an intent. Supreme Court, Legf. Bír. Pfv. VI. 22.060/2006. – BH 2007. No. 368, Regional Court of Budapest, Fővárosi Ítélőtábla 7. Pf. 21 108/2003/5. – BDT2004. No. 1011.

[27] The court shall also be entitled to establish a contract if the preliminary contract does not contain an agreement concerning the key issues of the contract, provided that, in due consideration of the interests of the parties and the national economy, the content of the contract can be determined on the basis of the parties' negotiations and pre-existing contracts, and all of the circumstances of the case. Under special circumstances, the court may bring a contract into existence by modifying the terms specified in the preliminary contract if it is justified by the interests of the national economy or any interest of the parties deserving special consideration. Either party shall be entitled to refuse to conclude a contract if it provides proof of inability to perform the contract by virtue of a circumstance that has occurred after the conclusion of the preliminary contract or if the performance of the contract would be detrimental to the national economy, or if, on the

other forms of declaration of intent do not in themselves create a preliminary contract.[28] In order to establish that a preliminary contract is concluded between the parties, it is necessary to express a contractual will of entering such a contract and exchanging legally binding promises to conclude the final contract at a certain point of time in the future. Expressing intents is certainly not enough to establish this.

Thus, a letter of intent or the parties' mutual declaration that a document signed by them does not represent a binding agreement between the parties and that neither party shall be under any liability to the other party in the event of failure to enter into the final agreement cannot, in Hungarian law, create legally binding promises between the parties and cannot be enforced as a contract.

However, this does not mean that the trust created by the party by such an expression of intent cannot establish legally protected interests and that the party cannot be held liable for the legitimate expectations he or she induced. Either the general rules of liability in tort or a specific provision of the Hungarian Civil Code (§6) may establish an obligation to provide compensation for a frustrated trust.

The basic norm of liability in tort is provided by §339(1) of the Hungarian Civil Code, which establishes that if a person caused damage to another unlawfully,[29] he or she shall be liable for that and can exonerate himself or herself from liability by proving that he or she acted as would be generally expected under the given circumstances. Hungarian tort law regulation is a system of open rules which provides the courts with great power and allows them to establish and use the proper guidelines to assess tort cases. Accordingly, Hungarian tort law as a law in action is a flexible system.[30] The result of this system is that a large part of the Hungarian tort law is

---

basis of such a circumstance, avoidance or termination of the contract might apply. Concerning other issues, the provisions pertaining to a contract to be concluded on the basis of an agreement in principle shall be duly applied regarding the preliminary contract (§ 208 of the Hungarian Civil Code).

[28] Supreme Court, Legf. Bír. Pfv. V. 20.261/1995.sz. – BH 1996. No. 421.

[29] Unlawfulness is a wide-ranging concept in Hungarian tort law and does not infer wrongful interference with protected interests defined or circumscribed by the law. Although courts often try to find a certain legal norm which had been interfered with by the tortfeasor in order to establish liability, this would not be a necessary requirement of liability. G. Eörsi, *A polgári jogi kártérítési felelősség kézikönyve* (1966, Közgazdasági és Jogi Könyvkiadó), No. 221.

[30] For the concept of a flexible system, see W. Wilburg, *Entwicklung eines beweglichen Systems im Bürgerlichen Recht* (Rede gehalten bei der Inauguration als Rector magnificus der Karl-Franzes Universität in Graz am 22 November 1950, 1950) and *Zusammenspiel der Kräfte im Aufbau des Schuldrechts* [163 AcP (1964)], p. 364.

judge-made law built upon a complex system of criteria to assess and decide tort law cases and to draw the boundaries of liability. The basis of liability under §339(1) of the Hungarian Civil Code is fault, where fault is a conduct which did not meet the requirement of general required conduct, i.e., generally expected behaviour in the given circumstances. In this flexible system, the court may establish the liability in tort of those who falsely create an expectation or an appearance. Hungarian courts most often choose fault-based tort liability to provide compensation for victims of falsely created expectations. Since not only the concept of fault but also causation are very open concepts in this system, the indirect nature of causation does not preclude establishing liability of the tortfeasor for frustrated expectations.

§6 of the Hungarian Civil Code provides a specific norm and basis of claims for compensating damage suffered by induced conduct and created expectations. According to this specific provision of the Hungarian Civil Code, someone who with intentional conduct induced another person in good faith and with good reason to act in a certain way may be held fully or partly liable to compensate that person for the damage he or she suffered through no fault of his or her own because he or she relied on the inducement of the former. This provision of the Civil Code establishes an obligation that is not based on liability: neither fault on the defendant's part nor the unlawfulness of their conduct is a precondition of the obligation to compensate the victim. The rule aims at protecting reliance interests – just like estoppel in common law systems – and allocating the risk of the plaintiff's conduct. §6 of the Hungarian Civil Code provides a general remedy for suffering harm as a consequence of reliance on the conduct of another. The provision is very specific from a theoretical as well as from a practical point of view. The theoretical starting point of the legislator was providing a remedy for the consequences of behaviour which is neither unlawful (unlawfulness would establish liability in tort) nor lawful (lawful behaviour shall not be sanctioned) and does not consist of a breach of a contractual promise. It follows from this that this provision cannot be applied if the conduct triggers liability in tort or establishes liability for breach of contract. In such a case, the victim is entitled to remedy in tort or breach of contract. The conduct on which the aggrieved person relies is neither prohibited, nor does it express contractual will.[31] The conjunctive prerequisites of

---

[31] Motivation to the Bill of the Act of IV 1959 on the Civil Code of Hungarian Republic, p. 39. See also T. Lábady, *A magyar magánjog (polgári jog) általános része*, 3rd edn (Dialóg Campus, 2002), p. 304.

responsibility for such behaviour under §6 of the Hungarian Civil Code are: intentional conduct (which does not necessarily aim at influencing the behaviour of the aggrieved person);[32] the aggrieved person acting in good faith; the aggrieved person acting in good faith relying on the conduct and that conduct inducing him or her – with reasonable justification – to act;[33] the aggrieved person suffering harm as a result of his or her own conduct induced by the other; and the aggrieved person suffering harm through no fault of his or her own.

These prerequisites do not necessarily establish the obligation of the person to compensate the aggrieved person: according to §6 of the Hungarian Civil Code, the court *may* oblige the person inducing the other to act to compensate fully or in part the aggrieved person, who suffered harm. The court has wide discretionary powers to decide whether to order compensation or not at all and, if it does so, to what extent the aggrieved party's loss shall be compensated.[34] The Hungarian court practice seems to be restrictive in the course of the application of §6 of the Civil Code. Courts consequently reject the claims based on §6 of the Civil Code if a contract exists between the parties,[35] even if this would not follow from the norm itself. There is a general tendency for courts to apply this specific provision as a means of risk allocation – which reflects the actual function of the provision – and to be reluctant to shift the risk of one's own act to another person. The general approach, which has been reinforced in the Supreme Court's guidelines relating to economic cases,[36] is that an enterprise basically shall bear the risk of its own activity. If an enterprise fails to foresee the possibility that an event that falls within the definition of a normal business risk might occur, it may not argue that it relied on the assumption that the event would not occur in order to claim the fulfilment of the other party's performance. In such a case, the fault of the aggrieved party excludes the compensation under §6 of the Civil Code.[37] This is also the case for reliance on information provided by the other party. In commercial cases, the starting

---

[32] Actually, it is not clear what the scope of the intent of the person should be in order to establish the application of §6 of the Hungarian Civil Code.

[33] There must be a causal link between the conduct and the acting of the aggrieved party. Supreme Court, Legf. Bír. Pfv. V. 22.772/1995. sz. – BH 1997. No. 275.

[34] K. Benedek and M. Világhy, *A Polgári Törvénykönyv a gyakorlatban* (Közgazdasági és Jogi Könyvkiadó, 1965), p. 38

[35] Supreme Court, Legf. Bír. Pf. I. 20 157/1992. sz. – BH 1992. No. 385.

[36] Legfelsőbb Bíróság GK 14. sz. gazdasági kollégiumi állásfoglalás (Supreme Court, Statement No. GK. 14 of the College for Commercial Cases).

[37] Supreme Court, P. törv. I. 20 289/1985. sz. – BH 1986. No. 319. G. Légrádi, Az utaló magatartás (biztatási kár) a Ptk.-ban és a bírói gyakorlatban, *Polgári Jogi Kodifikáció* 2003/4, p. 22.

point is that even if the party has been induced by another's representation, the consequences of its acts shall remain within its own risk.[38]

Thus, if the parties entered into a letter of intent specifying that failure to reach a final agreement will not expose any of the parties to liability, there is no legally binding promise between the parties on the basis of the letter of intent. The risk that the other party fails to adhere to the expressed intent shall be regarded as the business risk of the aggrieved party. If, however, it turned out that one party never really intended to enter into a final agreement and used the negotiations only to prevent the other party from entering into a contract with a third party, this is not considered to be part of the business risk of the parties. In such a case, the aggrieved party may claim compensation for damages on the basis of tort law or §6 of the Hungarian Civil Code, which provides compensation for induced and frustrated reliance.

9   Material adverse change

Establishing conditions precedent to closing should be construed as an atypical enforceable agreement between the parties. Such agreements – although not typical – are not incompatible with the regulation of contracts provided for in the Hungarian Civil Code, and there is no ground to hold them as invalid. As the agreement on conditions precedent is enforceable, the party shall be entitled to invoke the clause to avoid a deal if any of the circumstances circumscribed in the conditions precedent occurred. As in the case of a legal dispute, the burden of proof concerning the occurrence of the referred circumstance is shifted to the person relying on this; the party invoking the clause has to prove that the event referred to actually did occur. The risk to be borne by the party invoking the clause is that it will be the subject of an *ex post* evaluation if it got out of the transaction lawfully or if it is in breach of the contract. From this point of view, the evaluation of the party seems to be irrelevant – the question would be whether the change in external circumstances giving the right to the party to avoid concluding the contract actually did occur.

10   Liquidated damages

In commercial contracting practice, parties usually try to standardise the compensation the obligor has to pay in the event of breach of contract. By

---

[38] Supreme Court, GK 14.

doing so, they try to make their obligations foreseeable and pre-estimate the undertaken risk. Liquidated damages in Hungarian contract law are not a regulated remedy. A penalty is the typical regulated remedy for breach of contract provided by contract law regulation. Penalty clauses have a double function, as they provide lump-sum compensation to the aggrieved party and also provide a repressive sanction in the event of breach of contract, even in the absence of damage, in order to enforce the party to perform if breaching the contract would be more efficient for him ot her. A penalty in Hungarian contract law is a contractual secondary obligation. According to §246 of the Civil Code, under a penalty clause stipulated in the contract, the obligor has to pay a certain sum of money if he or she failed to perform the contract or if his or her performance does not conform with the contract for reasons attributable to him or her (default penalty). The payment of a penalty does not relieve the party of his or her contractual obligation because, according to §246(2) of the Hungarian Civil Code, the obligor shall be entitled to claim damages exceeding the penalty as well as enforcing other rights resulting from a breach of contract (however, by claiming a default penalty, he or she loses the right to claim performance in kind). The obligee shall be entitled – in accordance with the relevant regulations – to demand compensation for damages caused by the breach of contract, even if he or she has not enforced his or her claim for a default penalty. Penalty is one-sided: it relieves the obligee of the burden of proving the loss he or she suffered as far as the penalty extends, but it would not limit the obligations of the obligor. In this way, the penalty fixes only the minimum amount to be paid in the event of a breach but does not set the maximum, so it is not a proper tool for standardising damages and providing the proper allocation of risks.

Liquidated damages clauses are surely the most reasonable and optimal method of risk allocation in commercial relationships. They make the risks of the obligor as well as the recovery of the obligee predictable and help to avoid the costs of a later dispute emerging from the uncertainties relating to the necessity of proving the loss of the aggrieved party. This is why liquidated damages clauses are frequently applied in commercial transactions in Hungarian contractual practice. As atypical guarantees are enforceable in Hungarian law,[39] liquidated damages clauses are basically to be held as enforceable agreed remedies. There are, however, two great ambiguities concerning their enforceability.

[39] Supreme Court, Legf. Bír. Gfv. I. 33.312/1997. sz. – BH 1998. No. 440.

One ambiguity is the risk that the courts may construe the liquidated damages clause as a penalty. For example, if the parties agree that in the event of a breach of contract, the party in breach shall pay to the aggrieved party a certain sum specified in the contract, the court may come to the conclusion that the parties agreed to a penalty. In the course of construing the contract, the Hungarian Supreme Court seems to be inclined to come to the conclusion that a stipulated sum to be paid as a consequence of the breach of the other contracting party is to be qualified as a penalty.[40]

The other ambiguity is that if the actual loss of the aggrieved party exceeded the sum of the agreed remedy, the actual effect of the liquidated damages clause would be a limitation of liability. Limitation of liability shall be enforceable only if it complies with the test provided in §314 of the Hungarian Civil Code, i.e., the breach was neither intentional nor the result of gross negligence or a crime, it did not involve personal injury and the party relying on the liquidated damages clause in order to avoid paying more than the agreed sum provided adequate compensation for the limitation.

Thus, although liquidated damages clauses are to be enforceable in spite of their atypical character in Hungarian law, there is a considerable risk of them being construed as penalty clauses or deemed to be exclusion clauses falling under the limits of enforceability, i.e., they cannot be enforced in cases of breach of contract with intentional conduct, gross negligence or crime, or in order to limit liability for personal injury and – in cases of patrimonial damage – if adequate compensation was not provided for the limitation. In both cases, the result is that – as a remedy for breach of contract – the aggrieved party is not prevented from claiming compensation for the loss exceeding the liquidated damages in spite of the agreement.

11 Indemnity

Atypical obligations in Hungarian court practice are accepted as enforceable promises. Undertaking an obligation to pay a certain sum to the other party if agreed circumstances occur (e.g., the failure of payment of a certain sum by another person to the obligee) is normally held to be

---

[40] The Hungarian Supreme Court seems to be inclined to follow this interpretation: Supreme Court Legf. Bír. Pfv. IX. 21.385/2008. – BH 2010. No. 16 and Supreme Court, Legf. Bír. Gfv. X. 33. 092/1994. sz. – BH 1995. No. 722.

enforceable by Hungarian courts.[41] Such promises are construed as atypical guarantees. Court practice accepts them as contractual obligations that are binding and enforceable upon the terms agreed by the parties.[42] Such guarantees are construed according to their content. The use of terminology that assumes damage actually has occurred does not necessarily prevent the guaranteed payment when no actual damage has occurred if, upon the agreed terms, the agreement of the parties shall be construed as not assuming actual loss to be enforced.

12   Representations and warranties

Allocation of information is one of the most complex problems of contract law. The decision of an uninformed party is not a free decision, which might mean that the market constituting the economic environment of the contract is imperfect. Thus, sustaining the freedom of decisions and market mechanisms would justify a requirement placing the parties in the same informed situation. Information asymmetry may be seen as a market failure which should be corrected. On the other hand, a general obligation to share all the information a party has would discourage investment in the production of information, which would have the consequence of halting innovation. All of the legal systems, to a certain extent, provide – impliedly or explicitly – for establishing a duty to speak or a duty to inform before contracting, while setting the boundaries of this obligation.

In the Hungarian Civil Code, there are additional provisions establishing a duty to cooperate and a duty to inform the other party of circumstances relevant to the contract. At the centre of this is the general requirement of good faith and fair dealing (§4), which is also to be applied in this context and which may be a general source of an obligation of a duty to disclose.

§205(4) of the Hungarian Civil Code explicitly requires that parties shall inform each other of all the relevant circumstances of the contract. If there is an infringement of this duty, this may be a ground for avoidance of the contract because of mistake or misrepresentation and/ or it may be a basis for damages in tort or a remedy for breach of contract as an alternative to avoidance for mistake or misrepresentation. According to §210(1) of the Civil Code, if a party concludes the contract

---

[41] Supreme Court, Legf. Bír. Pf. IV. 20 561/1991. sz. – BH 1992. No. 239.
[42] Supreme Court, Legf. Bír. Gfv. I. 33.312/1997. sz. – BH 1998. No. 440.

by erring on a substantial circumstance of the contract, and the other party caused or should have recognised the mistake, the contract may be avoided by the aggrieved party (mistake and/or misrepresentation). If the parties shared the same mistake, either of them shall be entitled to avoid the contract. If a party convinces the other to contract through deceit, the contract may be avoided by the aggrieved party. The same rule shall be applied if the deceit was carried out by a third party and the contracting party knew or should have known this to be the case (§210(4) of the Hungarian Civil Code). The avoidance of the contract does not prevent the aggrieved party from claiming damages on the basis of liability in tort (§339) or under §6. In cases where the party (typically the seller) provided information regarding the product to be the subject of the contract, the information may be implied as a contractual term and part of the contract according to §277(1)(b) of the Hungarian Civil Code.[43] This construction establishes the contractual liability of the party if the product fails to meet the alleged quality. In these cases, avoidance of the contract (on the ground of mistake, misrepresentation or deceit) and remedy for breach of contract are alternative claims for the plaintiff. Avoidance of the contract excludes the liability for breach of contract – however, avoidance of the contract does not exclude the establishment of a claim of liability in tort or based on §6 of the Hungarian Civil Code.

Incompliance with the required standard of good faith and fair dealing, the duty to cooperate or disclosure may also result in liability in tort,[44] independently of other consequences relating to the enforceability

---

[43] Even without this explicit provision, the construction of the contract may lead (and might have led) to the same result in practice.

[44] Liability consequences of failure to fulfil the obligation of the duty to speak may be presented by the following decision of the Hungarian Supreme Court. In this case, the plaintiff bought a building site and built a house directly next to the public railway line between Budapest and Hegyeshalom, because he relied on the railway reconstruction plans, according to which the railway would have been relocated about one kilometre further away. After the building of the house, these reconstruction plans were altered and the programme of relocating the railway was also cancelled. It also turned out that the plan was only in a very early phase and there was only a concept without a final decision. The plaintiff claimed for damages on the ground that he had relied on the information about the railway relocation plans and had bought plots of land and built houses near the railway because he assumed that the railway would be moved. The defendants were the Hungarian State Railway Company and the local government, who sold the land as the seller. The Supreme Court decided in favour of the plaintiff and ordered the local municipality to pay damages at about 60:40 ratio, where the defendant had to pay the larger amount. The claim against the State Railway Company was rejected. The court declared that the buyer had also contributed to his own loss because, before contracting,

of the contract. Liability in tort is one of the basic consequences of incompliance with these duties according to §339 of the Hungarian Civil Code. Eörsi, whose theory deeply influenced modern Hungarian tort law theory and regulation, emphasises that in Hungarian tort law, there is no gap that should be filled with the *culpa in contrahendo* doctrine. He explicitly refers to §339 of the Civil Code (the basic norm of liability), the principle of good faith and fair dealing and the duty to cooperate in §4(2) to establish liability for cases qualified as *culpa in contrahendo* in German court practice and literature.[45]

To sum up, representations and warranties describing facts, circumstances, expectations, etc., which are made relevant by the parties for their contracting may basically result in the following consequences, depending on the construction of the representations and warranties and the agreement of the parties:

1) Facts, circumstances, expectations, etc., described in the representations and warranties are made part of the contract and part of

> he should have investigated the stability and finality of these reconstruction plans more thoroughly. His contribution should reduce the damages to be paid by the defendants by 20 per cent. According to the decision, the defendant failed to provide the proper information to the buyer regarding the railway reconstruction. The basis of their obligation to do so was the requirement of good faith and fair dealing. The damage was the depreciation in value of land due to the abandoning of the reconstruction plans. The liability of the seller for false information was established here on non-contractual grounds. Until this decision, such cases concerning liability for information were relatively rare in Hungarian court practice. In the present case, the court shifted the risk of the realising of the reconstruction plans to the defendant. Another line of argument, according to which it should have been the risk of the buyer, also sounds correct, since the court did not investigate whether the contractual will of the buyer was and to what extent it was influenced by these plans; thus, one could argue that this was a kind of speculation relying on the planned reconstruction to buy a plot of land cheaply and later on, after the railway relocation, to have a more valuable plot. It also should have been taken into account whether or not the planned reconstruction was a factor affecting the price of the plot of land when the buyer bought it. These factors – especially the risk allocation element – seem to fall outside the arguments of the court. The damage was the fall in the value of the land, which occurred at the moment when it turned out that the reconstruction would not be realised. The plaintiff was not the only one affected; there were other adversely affected owners who could have sued in separate cases. Supreme Court, Legf. Bír. Pfv. IX. 20.130/2001. sz. – BH 2003. No. 195.

[45] According to Eörsi, in German legal theory and practice, it was necessary to develop such a doctrine because of the gap in the rules of liability for tort and for breach of contract left in the BGB. Because of the general clause of liability in §339 of the Hungarian Civil Code, such a gap does not exist in Hungarian private law. Since these cases are covered by §339 of the Civil Code, it was not necessary to develop such a doctrine. G. Eörsi, *Elhatárolási problémák az anyagi felelősség körében* (Közgazdasági é s Jogi Könyvkiadó, 1962), p. 181.

the party's contractual duty. Incompliance with them is a breach of contract and the remedies are the agreed or statutory remedies for breach of contract, including contractual liability.

2) Facts, circumstances, expectations, etc., described in the representations and warranties are the agreed basis of the contract. If they prove to be false or frustrated, this may result in the unenforceability of the contract either by making the contract voidable on the basis of mistake or deceit, or by resulting in frustration of purpose, which terminates the contract and turns into the liability of the party responsible for the deceit or the frustration.[46]

3) If the facts, circumstances, expectations, etc., described in the representations and warranties do not become part of the contract and they prove to be false or frustrated, this may result in liability in tort of the party declaring, confirming or undertaking them.

Whether representations and warranties shall be held as a closed list of relevant matters concerning the basis and the content of the contract or the expectations of the parties protected by the contract depends on the construction of the representations and warranties clauses of the contract. If the list is not construed as a closed one according to the agreement of the parties, the matters left out fall under the general duty of disclosure. If the list is construed as a closed one, matters left out shall be deemed as explicitly declared irrelevant by the parties, which may result in the parties being considered to have waived the legal protection otherwise provided by the law. As, however, waiver of rights is to be narrowly construed (§207(4) of the Hungarian Civil Code), the court would presumably hold the list to be a closed one, resulting in a waiver of the legal protection otherwise provided by the law if the parties explicitly agreed on this. There is no standardised interpretation concerning the exhaustive nature of the list or whether it is to be held as integrated by the information duties under contract law regulation.

---

[46] According to §312 of the Hungarian Civil Code, if performance has become impossible for a reason that cannot be attributed to either of the parties, the contract shall be held as terminated. If performance has become impossible for a reason for which the obligor is liable, the obligee may claim damages for breach of contract. If performance has become impossible for a reason for which the obligee is liable, the obligor shall be relieved of his or her obligation and shall be entitled to demand damages therefrom. If performance of any of the alternative services becomes impossible, the contract shall be limited to the other services.

13   Hardship

The change of circumstances that make the performance excessively onerous for the party may have an impact on the enforceability of the contract in two basic ways.

First, supervening or external events that make the performance excessively onerous for a party may result in physical or economic impossibility of the contract. *Ex post* impossibility terminates the contract if performance has become impossible for a reason that neither of the parties is responsible for. If performance has become impossible for a reason for which the obligor is liable, the obligee may claim damages for breach of contract. If performance has become impossible for a reason for which the obligee is liable, the obligor shall be relieved of his or her obligation and shall be entitled to claim damages therefrom.

Secondly, on the basis of the claim of the party, the court may amend a contract regulating a long-term relationship if, as a result of changed circumstances of contracting, the performance of the contract became excessively onerous for one of the parties (§241 of the Hungarian Civil Code). A similar rule is to be applied if the external circumstance making the contract excessively onerous for the party is an *ex post* statutory amendment (§226(2)). A party is prevented from claiming a judicial amendment of the contract on the ground of realisation of a risk allocated to him or her by the contract, or if the change of circumstances could have been foreseen at the time of the conclusion of the contract.[47]

Whether a detailed definition of such changed circumstances in the contract prevents a court from considering the other circumstances provided for by contract law depends on the result of construction of the parties' agreement on hardship. There is no generally accepted standardised approach in Hungarian court practice and theory concerning this. The parties are to be held as basically free in their agreement to determine circumstances that may be relevant from this point of view, but as the result would restrict the parties' opportunities concerning judicial amendment, such a construction is to be held as a waiver to be construed narrowly. This may lead the court to the conclusion that the list provided by the parties in the contract describing the circumstances that may be relevant in the context of hardship is to be construed as the sole applicable regulation only if the parties explicitly agreed to this.

---

[47] Supreme Court, Legf. Bír. Pfv. II. 21.281/2003. sz. – BH 2005. No. 347.

14 *Force majeure*

Force majeure, as a ground for relief of the contractual obligation or as a prerequisite of exoneration, is not used in contract law regulation. In Hungarian private law, the policy underlying tort law regulation of the Civil Code 1959 was to provide a unified system of liability. This idea included the unitary regulation of liability for tort and for breach of contract. According to §318(1) of the Hungarian Civil Code, the rules of delictual (tort) liability are to apply for liability for breach of contract as well, except as otherwise provided by the law. This solution reinforces the idea of a common moral basis of liability – irrespective of whether the obligation that is breached arises out of a contract or is imposed by operation of law – and makes the system a simple one, avoiding borderline problems and the constant necessity of classifications. The distinction made by the Hungarian Civil Code (§318(1)) is that liability for breach of contract cannot be reduced on equitable grounds (which is allowed in the event of delictual liability according to §339(2)) and there are differences in the preconditions of the validity of exclusion clauses and the liability for third persons as well. The earlier court practice in Hungary was somewhat confusing, since decisions were often based on the basic rule of liability (§339) instead of referring to the special rule for contractual liabilities (§318) in cases of remedies for breach of contract. At the beginning of the 1970s, a tendency towards preferring the contractual basis could be detected,[48] and this tendency has developed into a clear standpoint today. If there is a concurrence of contractual and non-contractual (tort) liability, the courts refer to the special rule of liability for breach of contract provided in §318 and decide the case on the basis of contractual liability.[49] One obvious and significant difference has, however, been clearly developed in court practice and this is the different measures for exculpation: in contractual cases, the courts apply stricter tests in assessing whether the party was at fault and allow exculpation only if the party can prove that the harm in the given circumstances was unavoidable. Thus, the level of the required standard of conduct in contractual liability is higher than in tort cases, as the party shall be liable for breach of contract insofar as the breach (i.e., the cause of the

---

[48] A. Harmathy, *Felelősség a közreműködőért* (Közgazdasági és Jogi Könyvkiadó, 1974), p. 202.

[49] J. Gyevi-Tóth, 'A szerződéses és a deliktuális felelősség egymáshoz való viszonya', in A. Harmathy (ed.), *Jogi Tanulmányok* (ELTE, 1997), p. 178.

breach) was avoidable.[50] This approach provides a wider relief of liability as the unavoidable circumstances will not necessarily fall outside the scope of the party's activity in order to lead to exoneration, but presupposes that it fell beyond the control of the party, which seems to be a wider circle than in cases of *force majeure*.

However, the parties shall be free in defining and designing their requirements as they do not limit their liability (which falls under the test of §314 of the Hungarian Civil Code). *Force majeure* clauses in this context may be construed in two ways, depending on the content of the agreement of the parties. Either they specify the cases where the party shall not be liable for breach of contract and provide a closed exhaustive list of the circumstances relieving the party of the obligation he or she undertook in the contract, or they simply mention cases where the party certainly shall not be liable even if there may also be cases of unavoidable events providing relief to the party. Both of the possible constructions are enforceable under Hungarian contract law. The result of the first construction (an exhaustive list of relief of obligations) is that the contract makes the liability of the party stricter than would be the case under the general statutory regime of liability for breach of contract. In this way, *force majeure* clauses do not change the statutory system of liability, but instead specify it. Neither under the statutory regime nor under the application of *force majeure* clauses is it enough for the party to prove that he or she was diligent and acted in good faith in order to be relieved of liability for breach of contract; rather, he or she has to prove that under the given circumstances, it was not possible to avoid a breach.

---

[50] I. Kemenes, 'A gazdasági szerződések követelményei és az új Polgári Törvénykönyv', *Polgári Jogi Kodifikáció*, 1 (2001), 9.

16

The East European tradition: application of boilerplate clauses under Russian law

IVAN S. ZYKIN

1 Introductory remarks

In line with the general topic of this book, the purpose of the present chapter is to ascertain to what extent different terms of a commercial contract based upon the concepts of Anglo-American law are compatible with Russian law, if the latter is applicable. This chapter focuses mainly on substantive law issues, leaving aside the issues of Russian private international law (PIL).[1]

Naturally, Russian law is influenced to a certain extent by the laws of other countries, Anglo-American law not being an exception. Contracts of finance lease, agency, franchise and entrusted management of property governed by the Civil Code of the Russian Federation (RCC) may be cited as examples. However, Russian legal rules dealing with such contracts are adapted to the continental law system, to which Russia belongs.

Another channel for such an influence is the international conventions in which Russia participates. The most notable example here is the 1980 United Nations (Vienna) Convention on Contracts for the International Sale of Goods ('CISG'). The impact of Anglo-American legal concepts can be traced in some provisions of the CISG. When the currently-in-force RCC was elaborated in the 1990s, the CISG was taken into account not only with regard to sales contracts, but also when drafting the general provisions of contracts.[2]

---

[1] The main body of PIL rules in Russia is found in Division VI (Articles 1186–1224) of the Civil Code of the Russian Federation (the RCC).

[2] See A. L. Makovskiy, 'The Influence of the 1980 Vienna Convention on the Development of Russian Law', in A.S. Komarov (ed.), *The Vienna Convention on Contracts for the International Sale of Goods. Practice of Application in Russia and Abroad* (Wolters Kluwer, 2007), pp. 123–131 (in Russian); M.I. Braginskiy, 'The 1980 Vienna Convention and the RCC', in M.G. Rozenberg (ed.), *The 1980 Vienna UN Convention*

Nevertheless, one has to admit that the degree of influence of Anglo-American legal concepts upon Russian law is rather limited and should not be overestimated.

The CISG applies to contracts for sale of goods between the parties whose places of business are in different states: (a) when the states are participants of it; or (b) when the rules of PIL lead to the application of the law of a state participating in the CISG (Article 1(1)). If Russian law is the applicable law by virtue of Article 1(1)(b), it entails the application of the CISG, which actually replaces the relevant provisions of the RCC, which could then be applied only subsidiarily. This holds true not only where the conflict of law rules point to the application of Russian law, but also where the parties agree to apply Russian law without expressly excluding the application of the CISG. Therefore, it should be borne in mind that Article 1(1)(b) of the CISG considerably widens the sphere of its application and respectively narrows the sphere of application of the relevant national law that is otherwise applicable, namely Russian law.[3]

The RCC has special provisions on the interpretation of a contract. According to Article 431, a court should first be guided by a literal meaning of a contract term, taking into account, if necessary, other terms of the contract and the sense of the whole contract. If the meaning of the contract term could not be thus established, then the real common will of the parties must be ascertained, taking into account the purpose of the contract and all associated circumstances.[4] However, Article 431 does not say what legal meaning should be attributed to the contract

---

on *Contracts for the International Sale of Goods. The Ten Years of Application by Russia* (Statut Publishing House, 2002), pp. 14–17 (in Russian).

[3] See M. G. Rozenberg, 'Application of the 1980 Vienna Convention in the Practice of the ICAC at the RF CCI', in A. S. Komarov (ed.), *International Commercial Arbitration. Modern Problems and Solutions* (Statut Publishing House, 2007), pp. 336–340 and the literature cited therein (in Russian). See also P. Schlechtriem and I. Schwenzer (eds.), *Commentary on the UN Convention on the International Sale of Goods (CISG)*, 2nd edn (Oxford University Press, 2005), pp. 15–40, 90–92.

[4] Article 431 of the RCC states:

> In the interpretation of the terms of a contract a court shall take into account the literal meaning of the words and expressions contained in it. The literal meaning of a term of a contract, in case the term is not clear, shall be established by comparison with the other terms and the sense of the contract as a whole.
>
> If the rules contained in the first part of the present Article do not allow the determination of the content of the contract, the real common will of the parties must be ascertained, taking into account the purpose of the contract. In such a case all surrounding circumstances shall be taken into account, including negotiations and correspondence preceding the

term in situations where such a term is based upon the concepts of a foreign law. The problem here is to determine how the given term should be classified or qualified on the basis of the legal concepts or categories of the applicable law.

A similar issue arises in the sphere of PIL, where it is called the problem of characterisation and is known to be a fundamental problem. The core of the problem is that the terms used in a conflict-of-law rule may be understood quite differently from country to country, and a proper interpretation of the term becomes essential for the determination of the applicable law. The problem of characterisation is specifically addressed in some national laws[5] and there exists abundant literature on the subject.[6]

Once the applicable law is determined, the meaning and legal effect of a particular contractual term is to be established on the basis of the legal concepts or categories of the applicable law.[7] In contrast with the issue of characterisation in PIL, the problem of proper determination of the effect of contractual terms inspired by foreign law on the basis of Russian substantive law is not adequately studied in Russian doctrine. The existing literature on comparative law, specifically in Russia, does not help much. This literature focuses on a comparison between the legal concepts and rules of different countries, whereas in a given case the task is to determine how certain contractual terms are compatible with the national law in question. The fact that those contractual terms also find their basis in law (though a foreign one) does not overshadow the

---

contract, the practice established in the mutual relations of the parties, the customs of commerce, and the subsequent conduct of the parties.

See Peter B. Maggs and Alexei N. Zhiltsov (eds. and translators into English), *The Civil Code of the Russian Federation*, parallel Russian and English texts (Norma Publishing House, 2003). Further, the translation of the RCC made by these authors is used.

[5] E.g., see Article 1187 of the RCC, 'Characterization of Legal Concepts in the Determination of the Applicable Law'. See, inter alia, L. Collins LJ, C. G. J. Morse, D. McClean, A. Briggs, J. Harry and C. McLachlan (eds.), *Dicey, Morris & Collins on the Conflict of Laws*, 14th edn, 2 vols. (Sweet & Maxwell, 2006), vol. I, pp. 37–52 and the literature cited therein.

[6] See, inter alia, Collins *et al.*, *Dicey, Morris & Collins*, vol. I, pp. 37–52 and the literature cited therein.

[7] This approach is widely shared by Russian scholars. See M. M. Boguslavskiy, *Private International Law*, 6th edn (Norma Publishing House, 2009), pp. 113–115 (in Russian); V. P. Zvekov, *Conflict of Laws in Private International Law* (Wolters Kluwer, 2007), pp. 180–190 (in Russian); and V. A. Kanashevskiy, *Foreign Economic Transactions: Substantive and Conflict of Laws Regulation* (Wolters Kluwer, 2008), pp. 165–166 (in Russian).

situation that here the task is to juxtapose the contractual terms (a category quite different from legislation) and the law.

The mere fact that certain contractual terms are based on foreign law concepts unknown to Russian law obviously does not mean that their legal force is not recognised *per se*. According to Article 6(1) of the RCC, if civil law relations 'are not directly regulated by legislation or agreement of the parties and there is no custom of commerce applicable to them, then civil legislation regulating similar relations (analogy of statute) shall be applied to such relations, if it does not contradict their nature'. Article 6(2) of the RCC provides further guidance. If it is impossible to resort to the analogy of statute, 'the rights and obligations of the parties shall be determined proceeding from the general principles and sense of civil legislation (analogy of law) and the requirements of good faith, reasonableness, and justice'. It should be added that the application of the analogy of statute or the analogy of law could be quite a difficult task from a practical point of view, with a result which is hard to foresee.

Under Article 1(2) of the RCC, the parties 'are free in the establishment of their rights and duties on the basis of contract and in determining any conditions of contract *not contradictory to legislation*' (emphasis added). According to Article 422(1), 'a contract must comply with rules obligatory for the parties established by a statute and other legal acts (imperative norms)'. Subject to those mandatory rules, 'the terms of the contract shall be determined at the discretion of the parties' (Article 421(4)).

Therefore, as a minimum test, contractual terms should not contradict the mandatory rules of Russian legislation. Russian law, judicial practice and doctrine do not recognise such a phenomenon as a self-regulatory contract being totally detached from the mandatory provisions of the applicable law.

Russian law imposes certain general restrictions aimed at a proper exercise of civil law rights. Those restrictions are laid down in Article 10 of the RCC.[8] It prohibits abuse of a legal right in any form. The concept of

---

[8] Article 10 of the RCC, entitled 'Limits of Exercise of Civil-Law Rights', runs as follows:

1. Actions of citizens and legal persons taken exclusively with the intention to cause harm to another person are not allowed, nor is abuse of a legal right allowed in other forms.
    Use of civil-law rights for the purpose of restricting competition is not allowed, nor is abuse of one's dominant position in the market.
2. In case of failure to observe the requirements provided by Paragraph 1 of the present Article, the court, commercial court, or arbitration tribunal may refuse the person protection of the rights belonging to him.

abuse of rights is rarely applied by Russian courts. The current legislation does not establish a formal general requirement to act in good faith, though it is set forth in certain specific instances.[9] In practice, a rather broad notion of the prohibition of abuse of a legal right somehow partly compensates for the relatively limited ambit of the good faith requirement.[10] The proposed reform of the Russian civil legislation envisages a considerable enlargement of the ambit of the good faith requirement as a general overriding principle applicable both when a contract is being negotiated and after its conclusion.[11]

The answer to the issues considered herein might depend upon a number of factors. The specific circumstances of a particular case are one of the most important factors of that sort. The degree of acquaintance of a particular law-applying body with the relevant foreign legal concepts or categories might also come into play.[12]

The foregoing general starting considerations are better understood when applied to particular contractual terms, which are dealt with below.

2   Some particular contract clauses[13]

2.1   Entire agreement

Similar clauses are frequently encountered in contracts entered into by Russian parties and normally do not create serious problems. The issue

---

3. In cases when a statute places protection of civil-law rights in dependence upon whether these rights were exercised reasonably and in good faith, the reasonableness of actions and the good faith of the participants in civil legal relations shall be presumed.

[9]   E.g., according to Article 53(3) of the RCC, 'a person who, by virtue of a statute or the founding documents of a legal person, acts in its name must act in the interests of the legal person represented by him in good faith and reasonably'.

[10] See Informative Letter of the Presidium of the RF Supreme Arbitrazh Court, dated 25 November 2008, No. 127, entitled 'A Review of the Practice of Application by Arbitrazh Courts of Article 10 of the Civil Code of the Russian Federation'. Arbitrazh courts are specialised state commercial courts which, in spite of a misleading similarity of the name with commercial arbitration bodies, should not be confused with the latter. Informative letters of the Supreme Arbitrazh Court are regarded as a summary of good judicial practice and are normally followed by lower commercial courts.

[11] See *The Concept of Development of the Civil Legislation of the Russian Federation* (Statut Publishing House, 2009), pp. 30–31. The concept was adopted by the RF President on 13 October 2009 and is being implemented now.

[12] This, in turn, is linked with the frequency of dealing with international commercial transactions by such a body. The most experienced in the field in Russia is the International Commercial Arbitration Court ('ICAC') at the RF Chamber of Commerce and Industry ('CCI') with nearly eighty years of practice and a considerable case load.

[13] For the text of the clauses analysed here, see the introduction to Part 3 of this book.

that does arise is whether prior negotiations, representations, undertakings and agreements could still be taken into account when interpreting the contract irrespective of the express provision that they are
superseded by the contract.

Article 431 of the RCC[14] does not exclude this possibility, namely
when the literal meaning of contractual terms is not clear and there is a
need to ascertain the real common will of the parties. According to the
language of Article 431(2), in such a case, all surrounding circumstances
should be taken into account, including, inter alia, negotiations and
correspondence preceding the contract and the practice established in
the mutual relations of the parties.

The wording of the contractual clause limits the possibility of relying
upon prior negotiations, representations, undertakings and agreements.
Yet the possibility to take them into account, in my view, is not completely ruled out. This might be true where they do not contradict the
terms of the contract and help to establish the real common will of the
parties, which would otherwise remain obscure. In other words, prior
negotiations, representations, undertakings and agreements might be of
relevance to the extent that they make it possible to ascertain the meaning of the terms of the existing contract. There may be no other way for a
court to achieve a satisfactory result. However, much depends upon the
circumstances of a particular case.

2.2   No waiver

The Anglo-American legal concept of a waiver is not recognised by
Russian civil law.[15] From the point of view of Russian law, one could
regard as superfluous the contractual provision that a failure by a party to
exercise a right or remedy the party has under the contract does not
constitute a waiver thereof. According to the general rule of Article 9(2)
of the RCC, even a waiver by persons to exercise rights belonging to them
should not entail the termination of those rights, unless otherwise stipulated by statute.

---

[14] Cited in note 4 above.
[15] This concept is embodied in Article 4 of the 1993 Russian Law on International
Commercial Arbitration, which is completely identical to Article 4 of the UNCITRAL
Model Law on International Commercial Arbitration. However, it covers a distinct and
limited area of international commercial arbitration. It may be noted in general that the
1993 Russian Law closely follows the UNCITRAL model.

Thus, for example, even if a party exercises its right with a considerable delay, this usually does not lead to relinquishment of the right. The claim may be time-barred, but that is another matter.

2.3   No oral amendments

The clause stipulating that no amendment of the contract will take effect unless it is done in writing fully corresponds to Russian law. Article 162 (3) of the RCC contains a mandatory requirement that a foreign economic transaction should be made in writing. The violation of this requirement renders the transaction invalid, and such a transaction is void. To ensure the application of this rule, Article 1209(2) of the RCC provides that Russian law shall govern the form of a foreign economic transaction in which at least one of the parties is Russian.[16]

There is no legal definition of a foreign economic transaction. For practical purposes, it would be enough to say that international commercial contracts between Russian and foreign parties fall under this category.

The written-form requirement is equally applicable to any amendments and supplements to such contracts. This requirement is strictly followed by Russian state courts and arbitral tribunals sitting in Russia.[17]

2.4   Conditions

The concept of fundamental breach is embodied in Article 450(2) of the RCC. Fundamental breach of a contract by a party entitles the other party to rescind the contract. Under Russian law, the same remedy is also available to the aggrieved party in other cases, as provided by statute or contract.

The wording of the contractual clause may be different. It may be stipulated that certain obligations are regarded by the parties as fundamental and any breach thereof should amount to a fundamental breach of the contract. The contract may simply state that in the event of a breach of certain obligations by a party, the other party is entitled to

---

[16] Some eminent Russian scholars regard Articles 162(3) and 1209(2) of the RCC as overriding mandatory provisions with extra-territorial effect (see Boguslavskiy, *Private International Law*, pp. 131 and 298; Zvekov, *Conflict of Laws*, pp. 294–295; and others).

[17] See M .G. Rozenberg, *International Sale of Goods. Commentary to Legal Regulation and Practice of Dispute Resolution*, 3rd edn (Statut Publishing House, 2006), pp. 64–77 (in Russian).

terminate the contract. The effect would be the same as where a commercial contract provides for the possibility of rescinding the contract unilaterally, no matter how substantial the breach is. The freedom of the parties' will is respected, unless it otherwise follows from statute or the nature of the obligation (Article 310 of the RCC).

If, under the circumstances, a party attempts to rescind the contract despite such a remedy being manifestly disproportional to the consequences of the breach, the opposite party might rely in its defence upon the prohibition of abuse of a legal right set forth in Article 10 of the RCC (see above).

2.5   Liquidated damages

In Russian practice, contractual clauses providing that, upon a failure of performance by one party, that party is obliged to pay an agreed sum to the other party are very common. International commercial contracts concluded by Russian entities with foreign companies do not constitute an exception in this regard.[18] As is well known, the legal concept of agreed and liquidated damages in English law and American law is not identical to the legal concept of penalty in continental laws, including Russian law.

Irrespective of the existing differences, the concept of agreed and liquidated damages is more similar to the concept of penalty in Russian law than to any other concept of that law. Consequently, the relevant contractual clause would normally be interpreted as a penalty clause under Russian law. A penalty is defined in Article 330(1) of the RCC as 'a monetary sum determined by a statute or a contract that the debtor must pay to the creditor in case of non-performance or improper performance of an obligation, in particular in case of a delay in performance'. Like the position of English law and American law, it is further added that when claiming payment of a penalty, the creditor does not have a duty to prove that he or she sustained losses.

Another alternative is to qualify such a clause as a provision specifying the amount of *damages* to be paid in case of a breach of an obligation. Russian law does not prohibit the parties from reaching such an agreement. As stated in Article 15(1) of the RCC, an aggrieved person is

---

[18] Very often, such contracts made in two languages use different legal terms to designate the said sum: agreed and liquidated damages in English and penalty ('neustoika') in Russian, thus creating some additional uncertainty.

entitled to full compensation of the damages suffered, unless a statute or a contract provides for a lesser amount of compensation. However, under Russian law, damages should be proved. The author is of the opinion that, in contrast with a penalty clause, the use of the adjectives 'agreed and liquidated' before the term 'damages' is not sufficient to abolish the requirement to prove the damages (see Article 330(1) of the RCC cited above). Therefore, the qualification of the clause as the damage clause under Russian law would defeat one of the main purposes of the clause, i.e., to relieve the creditor of the obligation to prove damages, which may be quite a difficult task. That is why, in my view, the analysed alternative is not a proper option.

Under English law and American law, when a contractual clause provides for payment of a sum which is manifestly excessive and unreasonable, it is then regarded as a penalty and is unenforceable. As follows from the above, in Russian law, the term 'penalty' has a broader and more neutral meaning, and denotes the clause as such, irrespective of whether the sum due is grossly excessive or not. Under Russian law, the clause providing for payment of a disproportionate sum is not void. However, a court has the right to reduce the penalty if the sum subject to payment is clearly disproportionate to the consequences of violation of an obligation (Article 333 of the RCC). The court could also exercise this power where the respondent does not make such a request. Article 333 of the RCC is a very important rule aimed at safeguarding the principle of the compensatory nature of liability for violation of obligations.[19] This very principle is characteristic of English law and American law.

One of the most notable differences of the Russian law approach to such clauses is that, as a general rule, the actual sum of compensation is not limited to the agreed sum. According to Article 394(1) of the RCC: 'If a penalty is provided for non-performance or improper performance of an obligation, then losses shall be compensated in the part not covered by the penalty.' The parties to an international commercial contract may provide otherwise in their agreement. Does the use of the English terminology 'liquidated damages' exclude the possibility of claiming damages? The answer is linked to the two alternatives to qualifying the clause (see above). I am inclined to answer the question in the negative. It could be recommended to the parties to expressly provide in their contract that a

---

[19] See also Informative Letter of the Presidium of the RF Supreme Arbitrazh Court, dated 14 July 1997, No. 17, entitled 'A Review of the Practice of Application by Arbitrazh Courts of Article 333 of the Civil Code of the Russian Federation'.

claim for damages is ruled out, in order to achieve the same result as where English law or American law is applied.

2.6   Sole remedy

Russian law permits the inclusion of sole remedy clauses in commercial contracts (see, in particular, Articles 15, 394, 397, 397 and 400 of the RCC). Hence, such a contract could provide for the payment of a certain amount as the sole remedy in case of a breach. Even if the aggrieved party is able to prove that the breach has caused much more substantial damage than the agreed sum, the liability of the debtor would be limited to the agreed amount. As expressly stated in Article 394(1) of the RCC, a contract may provide that recovery only of a penalty but not of losses is allowed.

However, it should be borne in mind that 'an agreement concluded in advance for eliminating or limiting liability for the intentional violation of an obligation is void' (Article 401(4) of the RCC). This is a mandatory requirement applicable to all obligations. It should be added that Article 10 of the RCC, which prohibits the abuse of a legal right, might also be applicable if the clause is manifestly unfair.[20]

2.7   Subject to contract

It is often the case that prior to concluding the main contract, the parties sign certain documents aimed at facilitating the reaching of a final agreement. The name of such documents might be different (a letter of intent, a memorandum of understanding, a protocol of negotiations, etc.). When determining whether these documents are binding on the parties, it is not their title but the contents showing the parties' intent that is of primary importance.

Under Russian law, the parties are free to enter into a preliminary contract whereby they have, in the future, a duty to conclude the main contract on the terms provided for by the preliminary contract (Article 429 of the RCC). The preliminary contract creates legal obligations and entails liability in the event of its breach.

---

[20] See note 8 above. See also Kanashevskiy, *Foreign Economic Transactions*, p. 166; O. N. Sadikov, *Damages in the Civil Law of the Russian Federation* (Statut Publishing House, 2009), pp. 133–157 (in Russian).

Suppose that the parties executed an instrument specifying that the failure to reach a final agreement will not expose any of them to liability. What happens if one party never really intended to enter into a final agreement and used the negotiations only to prevent the other party from entering into a contract with a third party? Russian law does not have specific provisions in this regard. The well-known Russian scholars arrive at the conclusion that the liability in such a case could be based on the general rules of the law of torts (Articles 1064–1083 of the RCC). The aggrieved party might also rely upon Article 10 of the RCC, which prohibits the abuse of a legal right in any form.[21] As stated above, the future reform of the Russian civil legislation envisages the application of the principle of good faith to the relations of the parties at the precontractual stage (see Section 1 above).

2.8 Representations and warranties

It is impossible to find direct general legal equivalents in Russian law to the notions of representations and warranties in English law and American law. Still, in certain particular instances, some equivalents could be found. The most notable examples in this regard are Article 470, 'Guarantee of Quality of the Goods', and Article 722, 'Guarantee of Quality of the Work', of the RCC. Normally, clauses providing for representations and warranties are not found in domestic commercial contracts in Russia, one notable exclusion again being provisions concerning the guarantee of quality of goods and works.

The clauses analysed under this heading often vary considerably in substance. Sometimes they are formulated in such a way that one may even doubt whether they have any legal effect under Russian law at all. Not being in a position to examine each and every clause of this kind, the discussion here will be limited to a more general legal assessment.

The legal effect of the clauses in question depends upon whether they may be qualified as an obligation. The obligation may arise from a contract and from other grounds provided by the law (Articles 8(1)

---

[21] M. I. Braginskiy and V. V. Vitrianskiy, *Contract Law*, Book 1, 2nd edn (Statut Publishing House, 1999), pp. 229–239 (in Russian). See also A. N. Kucher, *Theory and Practice of the Pre-Contractual Stage: The Legal Aspects* (Statut Publishing House, 2005), pp. 29–31, 210–296 (in Russian). Article 10 is reproduced in note 8 above.

and 307 of the RCC). The substance and the language of the clause may count in order to determine the existence of the obligation.

Two situations should be distinguished further in case of a breach by a party of the representations and warranties having legal effect. First, when the contract remains valid, the aggrieved party is then entitled to damages and other available remedies (Articles 15, 309–310, 393–396 and 453(5) of the RCC). Secondly, when the contract is invalid, this generally entails restitution (Article 167)[22] and the application of the rules on unjust enrichment (Articles 1102–1109).

Two more articles of the RCC dealing with specific grounds of invalidity of a transaction are directly relevant: Article 178 on the invalidity of a transaction made under the influence of misapprehension;[23] and Article

---

[22] Article 167 of the RCC runs as follows:

1. An invalid transaction does not entail legal consequences other than those that are connected with its invalidity and is invalid from the time of its making.
2. In case of the invalidity of a transaction, each of the parties has the duty to return to the other everything received under the transaction and in case of the impossibility of returning what was received in kind (including when what was received consisted of the use of property, work done, or services provided) to compensate for its value in money, unless other consequences of the invalidity of the transaction are provided by a statute.
3. If from the content of a voidable transaction it follows that it may only be terminated for the future, the court, declaring the transaction invalid, shall terminate its effect for the future.

It should be pointed out that the RCC does not envisage the application of the law of torts in such cases. As a general rule, this code makes it possible to claim full compensation for harm from the tortfeasor.

[23] Article 178 of the RCC states:

1. A transaction made under the influence of a misapprehension having a substantial significance may be declared invalid by a court on suit of the party that acted under the influence of the misapprehension.
   A misapprehension has a substantial significance if it is with respect to the nature of the transaction or of the identity or other qualities of its subject that significantly reduce the possibility of using it for its purpose. A misapprehension concerning the motives of the transaction does not have a substantial significance.
2. If a transaction is declared invalid as made under the influence of a misapprehension, the rules provided by Paragraph 2 of Article 167 of the present Code shall be applied correspondingly.

In addition, the party on whose suit the transaction was declared invalid shall have the right to claim from the other party compensation for the actual damage caused to it if it proves that the misapprehension arose due to the fault of the other party. If this is not proved, the party, on whose suit the transaction was declared invalid, shall be obligated to compensate the other party on its demand for the actual damage caused to it, even if

179, which envisages in particular invalidity of a transaction made under the influence of fraud.[24] Under these articles, the aggrieved party may seek from the other party not only a restitution of everything received by the latter under the transaction, but also a recovery of actual damage. However, a recovery of lost profit is not allowed.

It is widely recognised in Russian legal literature that a misapprehension and a fraud may take place both in an active manner (i.e., by making misleading and false statements) and in a passive manner (i.e., by a failure to disclose certain facts).[25] In line with this approach, according to my analysis, even if a contractual list of representations and warranties does not provide some information, this in itself would not serve as a bar for a court to declare the transaction invalid due to being made under the influence of misapprehension or fraud. Thus, though the legislation does not expressly establish that the parties are obliged to inform each other about all relevant material facts concerning the conclusion of the contract, such a duty may be drawn from Articles 178 and 179 of the RCC.[26]

2.9   Force majeure *and hardship*

Russian law bears express provisions dealing with these legal categories (Articles 401(3),[27] 416, 417 and 451 of the RCC). *Force majeure* clauses

---

the misapprehension arose due to circumstances not depending upon the misapprehended party.

[24] Article 179 provides in the relevant parts for the following:

1. A transaction made under the influence of a fraud ... may be declared invalid by a court on suit of the victim.
2. If a transaction is declared invalid by a court on one of the bases indicated in Paragraph 1 of the present Article, then the other party shall return to the victim everything it received under the transaction and, if it is impossible to return it in kind, its value in money shall be compensated. Property received under the transaction by the victim from the other party and also due to it in compensation for that transferred to the other party shall be transferred to the income of the Russian Federation. If it is impossible to transfer the property to the income of the state in kind, its value in money shall be taken. In addition the victim shall be compensated by the other party for the actual damage caused to him.

[25] See Braginskiy and Vitrianskiy, *Contract Law*, pp. 813–815; Kucher, *Theory and Practice of the Pre-Contractual Stage*, pp. 228–239, 244–246 and the literature cited therein.

[26] Kucher, *Theory and Practice of the Pre-Contractual Stage*, p. 235.

[27] Article 401(3) of the RCC states: 'Unless otherwise provided by a statute or the contract, a person who has not performed an obligation or has performed an obligation in an improper manner in the conduct of entrepreneurial activity shall bear liability unless he proves that proper performance became impossible as the result of *force majeure*,

are often inserted into commercial contracts signed by Russian companies. To the extent that the above provisions are of a non-mandatory
character (actually most of them), parties could depart from them in
their contracts. However, this does not mean that the contract clauses
automatically become the only applicable regulation, but rather that they
should be interpreted and applied within the framework of the governing
law. The parties are free to establish in their contract an exhaustive list of
force majeure circumstances, thus assuming liability if events not mentioned in the clause occur.

It may be added that if a contract makes reference to circumstances
beyond the party's reasonable control that it could not reasonably be
expected to have taken into account at the time of the conclusion of the
contract or to have avoided or overcome, the effect of such circumstances
comes very close to the CISG, in which Russia participates (see Section 1
above). Such a clause also corresponds in principle to the definition of
force majeure in Article 401(3) of the RCC. Hence, such a clause would be
unlikely to create practical difficulties.

When the parties provide that events beyond their control relieve
them of liability, they agree upon less stringent requirements to be
applied since, under Russian law, *force majeure* is defined as 'extraordinary circumstances unavoidable under the given conditions' (Article 401
(3) of the RCC). Such a provision could give rise to some questions.
Much depends upon the wording of the particular clause. If a contractual
provision is qualified as the *force majeure* clause, then the specific
circumstances mentioned therein should meet the legal criteria of *force
majeure*.[28]

As a general legal rule, a person bears liability in the event of fault
(intent or negligence) unless a statute or contract provides other grounds
of liability (Article 401(1) of the RCC). In commercial relations, parties
bear liability irrespective of their fault and are relieved of liability in the
event of *force majeure* (Article 401(3)). This is an important exclusion
from the above general rule. Since the above rule is of non-mandatory
nature, the parties could provide in their contracts for liability in case of
fault. If a contractual clause provides that events beyond the control of

---

i.e., extraordinary circumstances unavoidable under the given conditions. Such circumstances do not include, in particular, violation of obligations by contract partners of the
debtor, absence on the market of goods necessary for performance, nor the debtor's lack
of the necessary monetary assets.'

[28] See Rozenberg, *International Sale of Goods*, pp. 341–346; Kanashevskiy, *Foreign
Economic Transactions*, pp. 169–173.

one party relieve it of liability, such a clause could be interpreted as an agreement on liability in case of fault. Then a party who violated an obligation must prove an absence of fault to be relieved of liability.[29]

Russian law allows transactions made on a condition (Article 157 of the RCC). According to Article 157(2): 'A transaction shall be considered made on a condition subsequent, if the parties have placed the termination of rights and duties in dependence upon a circumstance with respect to which it is unknown whether it will occur or not occur.' It could be argued that a certain circumstance not meeting the requirements of *force majeure* is to be regarded in appropriate instances as a condition subsequent. The legal consequence of an occurrence of such a circumstance is the termination of the transaction.

To sum up, the mere fact that a specific circumstance does not meet the criteria of *force majeure* does not necessarily mean that an occurrence of such a circumstance would not relieve the party from liability, as other concepts might turn out to be applicable.

---

[29] 'A person is recognized as not at fault, if with the degree of care and caution that was required of him by the nature of the obligation and the conditions of commerce, he has taken all measures for the proper performance of the obligation' (Article 401(1), the second passage).

Conclusion: the self-sufficient contract, uniformly interpreted on the basis of its own terms: an illusion, but not fully useless

GIUDITTA CORDERO-MOSS

The analysis carried out in this book shows that there is a gap between the way in which international contracts are written on the one hand and the way in which they are interpreted and enforced on the other. Contracts are often written as if the only basis for their enforcement were their terms and as if contract terms were capable of being interpreted solely on the basis of their own language. However, as Part 3 of this book showed, the enforcement of contract terms, as well as their interpretation, is the result of the interaction between the contract and the governing law. Considering contracts to be self-sufficient and not influenced by any national law, as if they enjoyed a uniform interpretation thanks to their own language and some international principles, thus proves to be illusionary. This contract practice may lead to undesired legal effects and is not optimal when examined from a legal point of view. Seen from a wider perspective, however, it may turn out to be more advantageous than employing large resources in order to ensure legal certainty.

1 International commerce fosters self-sufficient contracts

The gap between the parties' reliance on the self-sufficiency of the contract and the actual legal effects of the contract under the governing law does not necessarily derive from the parties' lack of awareness of the legal framework surrounding the contract. More precisely, the parties may often be conscious of the fact that they are unaware of the legal framework for the contract. The possibility that the wording of the contract is interpreted and applied differently from what a literal application would seem to suggest may be accepted by some parties as a calculated risk.

As David Echenberg shows in Chapter 1, a contract is the result of a process, in which both parties participate from opposite starting points. This means that the final result is necessarily a compromise. In addition, time and resources are often limited during negotiations. This means that the process of negotiating a contract does not necessarily meet all the requirements that would ideally characterise an optimal process under favourable conditions. What could be considered as an indispensible minimum in the abstract description of how a legal document should be drafted does not necessarily match with the commercial understanding of the resources that should be spent on such a process. This may lead to contracts being signed without the parties having negotiated all the clauses or without the parties having complete information regarding each clause's legal effects under the governing law. What may appear, from a purely legal point of view, as unreasonable conduct is actually often a deliberate assumption of contractual risk.

Considerations regarding the internal organisation of the parties are also a part of the assessment of risk. In large multinational companies, risk management may require a certain standardisation, which in turn prevents a high degree of flexibility in drafting the single contracts. In balancing the conflicting interests of ensuring internal standardisation and permitting local adjustment, large organisations may prefer to enhance the former, as described in Chapter 2 by Maria Celeste Vettese.

In other words, it is not necessarily the result of thoughtlessness if a contract is drafted without having regard for the governing law. Nor is it the symptom of a refusal of the applicability of national laws. It is the result of a cost-benefit evaluation, leading to the acceptance of a calculated legal risk.

Acknowledging this circumstance is important when international contracts are interpreted. A judge or an arbitrator who assumes that all contracts are always written following the optimal process may assume a will by the parties to comply with the applicable law and may react to the lack of correspondence between the contract terms and the applicable law by proposing ingenious constructions in an attempt to reconcile the two. However, the parties may have taken a calculated risk that there was no compliance; the ingenious reconciliation may come as a bigger surprise than the incompatibility with the applicable law. Also, observers may induce from the practice whereby contracts are drafted without considering the applicable law that international contract practice refuses national laws. On this assumption, observers may propose that contracts should be governed by transnational rules instead of national laws. However, that the parties may have disregarded the applicable law as a result of a cost-benefit evaluation does not necessarily mean that they want to opt out of the applicable law. The parties are still interested in enforcing their rights, and enforceability is ensured only by the judicial system of the applicable law.

2   Detailed drafting as an attempt to enhance the self-sufficiency of contracts

To minimise the risk of the governing law interfering with the contract, international contracts are drafted in a style that aims at creating an exhaustive, and as precise as possible, regulation of the underlying contractual relationship, thus attempting to render any interference by external elements redundant, be it the interpreter's discretion or rules and principles of the governing law.

To a large extent, this degree of detail may achieve the goal of rendering the contract a self-sufficient system, thus enhancing the impression that if only they are sufficiently detailed and clear, contracts will be interpreted on the basis of their own terms and without being influenced by any governing law.

However, this impression is proven to be illusionary and not only because governing laws may contain mandatory rules that may not be derogated from by contract.

As a matter of fact, not many mandatory rules affect international commercial contracts; therefore, this is not the main aspect that this book focuses on (there are, however, important mandatory rules, particularly in the field of liability, that are also relevant in the commercial context). What mostly interests us here is the spirit underlying general contract law. This will vary from legal system to legal system and will inspire, consciously or otherwise, the way in which the contract is interpreted and applied. Notwithstanding any efforts by the parties to include as many details as possible in the contract in order to minimise the need for interpretation, the governing law will necessarily project its own principles regarding the function of a contract, the advisability of ensuring a fair balance between the parties' interests, the role of the interpreter in respect of obligations that are not explicitly regulated in the contract, the existence of a duty of the parties to act loyally towards each other, and the existence and extent of a general principle of good faith – in short, the balance between certainty and justice. The clauses analysed in this book were chosen with the purpose of highlighting the relevance of the governing law in these respects. With these clauses, the parties try to take into their own hands those aspects where the balance between certainty and justice may be challenged.

The drafting impetus may reach excesses that are defined as 'non-sensical' by Edwin Peel in Chapter 7 on English law,[1] such as when, among the matters that the parties represent to each other, the ubiquitous representations and warranties clause lists that their respective obligations under the contract are valid, binding and enforceable. This representation and warranty is itself an obligation under the contract and is itself subject to any ground for invalidity or unenforceability that might affect the contract, so what value does it add? It is particularly interesting that this observation is made by an English lawyer, because it shows that the attempt to detach the contract from the governing law may go too far even for English law, and this notwithstanding the fact that the drafting style adopted for international contracts is no doubt based on the English and American drafting tradition. Extensive contracts do not reflect the tradition of civil law: a civilian judge reads the contract in the light of the numerous default rules provided in the governing law for that type of contract, so extensive regulations are not needed in the contact.[2] In turn, the common law drafting tradition requires extensive contracts that spell out all obligations between the parties and leave little to the judge's discretion or interpretation, because the common law judge sees it as his or her function to enforce the bargain agreed upon between the parties, not to substitute for the bargain actually made by the parties, one which the interpreter deems to be more reasonable or commercially sensible.[3] Thus, the English judge will be reluctant to read into the contract obligations that were not expressly agreed to by the parties. Since the English judge often affirms that a sufficiently clear contract wording will be enforced, parties are encouraged to increase the level of detail and to circumvent legal obstacles by formulating clauses that will not fall within the scope of

---

[1] Chapter 7 of this book, note 160.

[2] For a more extensive argument and references, see G. Cordero-Moss, 'International Contracts between Common Law and Civil Law: Is Non-state Law to be Preferred? The Difficulty of Interpreting Legal Standards such as Good Faith', *Global Jurist (Advances)*, 7, 1 (2007), Article 3, 1–38.

[3] *Charter Reinsurance, Co. Ltd* v. *Fagan* [1997] AC 313.

the problem.[4] This enhances the impression that a well-thought-out formulation may solve all problems. When adopting the common law style, however, drafters may apparently be tempted to overdo and to write regulations that tend to elevate the contract to the level of law,[5] such as the above-mentioned representation and warranty. This clause, as noted above, seems nonsensical even in an English law context, because a contract obligation does not have the power to determine whether it is valid or enforceable – it is for the law to decide what is valid and enforceable. This clause is, though, symptomatic of the intense desire to detach the contract from the applicable law so that it becomes its own law.[6]

---

[4] The liquidated damages clause, for example, is designed to escape the common law prohibition of penalty clauses. In addition, this clause and the possibility of converting it into a price-variation clause provide a significant example of how drafting may be used to achieve a result that otherwise would not be enforceable. This is defined as the possibility for the parties to manipulate the interpretation in order to avoid the intervention of the courts; see Chapter 7, Section 2.7.

[5] A similar attempt to elevate the contract to the level of law may be found in the assumption that the contract's choice-of-law clause has the ability to move the whole legal relationship beyond the scope of application of any law but the law chosen by the parties. However, the choice of law made by the parties has effect mainly within the sphere of contract law. For areas that are relevant to the contractual relationship but are outside the scope of contract law, the parties' choice does not have any effect. Areas such as the parties' own legal capacity, company law implications of the contract or the contract's effects towards third parties within property law are governed by the law applicable to those areas according to the respective conflict rule, and the parties' choice is not relevant. A research project that I run at the University of Oslo assesses such limitations to party autonomy, particularly in connection with international arbitration: more information on the project may be found at www.jus.uio.no/ifp/english/research/projects/choice-of-law, last accessed 6 October 2010. See also G. Cordero-Moss, 'International Arbitration and the Quest for the Applicable Law', *Global Jurist (Advances)*, 8, 3 (2008), Article 2, 1–42; and G. Cordero-Moss, 'Arbitration and Private International Law', *International Arbitration Law Review*, 11, 4 (2008), 153–164.

[6] A representation on the validity and enforceability of the contract is a typical part of boilerplate clauses. See, for example, Section 5.2, Article V, Form 8.4.01 (Form Asset Purchase Agreement); and M. D. Fern, *Warren's Forms of Agreements*, vol. 2 (LexisNexis, 2004). This is also the first representation recommended in the Private Equity Law Review, 'Representations and Warranties in Purchase Agreements', Section 2.1 (www.privateequitylawreview.com/2007/03/articles/for-private-equity-sponsors/deal-documents/acquisition-agreement/representations-and-warranties-in-purchase-agreements/, last accessed 23 May 2010). See also Sample Representations and Warranties, 3.2, Documents for Small Businesses and Professionals, www.docstoc.com/docs/9515308/Sample-Representations-and-Warranties, last accessed 23 May 2010). Numerous examples of the actual use of this representation may be found in the contracts filed with the US Securities and Exchange Commission; for example, Section 25.1.3 of the contract dated 21 November 2004 between Rainbow DBS and Lockheed Martin Commercial Space

The representation on the validity and enforceability of the contract is not the only attempt to detach the contract from the governing law: other clauses analysed in this book regulate the interpretation of the contract and the application of remedies independently of the governing law.

Interestingly, some of these clauses do not seem to achieve the desired results even under English law. As noted by Edwin Peel in Chapter 7, observers may tend to overestimate how literally English courts may interpret contracts. Be that as it may, contract practice shows that it is based on the illusion that it is possible, by writing sufficiently clear and precise wording, to draft around problems and circumvent any criteria of fairness that the court may find relevant. Peel's chapter actually shows that this is supported indirectly by English courts themselves, who often based their decisions on the interpretation of the wording rather than on a control of the contract's substance. In respect of some contract clauses, which interestingly attempt to regulate the interpretation of the contract precisely, it seems that the drafting efforts are not likely to achieve results that might be considered unfair by the court, no matter how clear and precise the drafted wording, and in spite of the courts' insisting on making this a question of interpretation. In respect of other clauses analysed in this book, the criteria of certainty and consistency seem to be given primacy by the English courts. This ensures a literal application of the contract notwithstanding the result, as long as the clause is written in a sufficiently clear and precise manner.

The treatment of boilerplate clauses by English courts has great relevance to the subject matter of this book: the assumption that a sufficiently detailed and clear language will ensure that the legal effects of the contract will be only based on the contract itself and will not be influenced by the applicable law was originally encouraged by English courts, and was then exported to contracts to which other laws apply.

The project upon which this book is based was intended to demonstrate the thesis that this assumption is not fully applicable under systems of civil law, because traditionally these systems are held to be based on principles (good faith and loyalty) that contradict this approach. The research in the project not only demonstrated the thesis, but even showed that the assumption is not always correct even under English law.

Systems for the construction of up to five television satellites (www.wikinvest.com/stock/ Cablevision_Systems_(CVC)/Filing/8-K/2005/F2355074, last accessed 23 May 2010) and Section 5.02 of the merger agreement dated 14 May 2007 between eCollege.com and Pearson Education, Inc. and Epsilon Acquisition Corp. (www.wikinvest.com/stock/ ECollege.com_(ECLG)/Filing/DEFA14A/2007/F4972482, last accessed 23 May 2010).

3   No real alternative to the applicable law

Before some concluding observations on the effects of the analysed clauses in the various legal systems, a brief comment should be made regarding the lack of alternatives to applying a national governing law.

Legal models do circulate and the European integration enhances this circulation, as Jean-Sylvestre Bergé shows in Chapter 6;[7] therefore, it is not necessarily problematic that contracts modelled on a certain law are governed by another law. However, as incisively formulated by Gerhard Dannemann in Chapter 4, these contracts suffer a loss of context and may (not necessarily always) presume the existence of legal institutions that cannot be found in the governing law, write around problems that do not exist in the governing law (or vice versa) or write on the basis of certain remedies that may not be available under the governing law.[8] Chapter 4 shows various examples of the consequences that may follow a loss of legal context, and so does Chapter 2.[9]

The question of what can go wrong if a contract is based on a law but is subject to the law of another system[10] requires various observations regarding the method and the sources applied in the analysis.

Courts seem to have had a less than consistent approach to the question, with results that may sometimes appear to be artificial.[11]

The question of which law applies to a contract is approached through private international law (conflict of laws). As the analysis in Chapter 3 shows, the simple use of a drafting style that is loosely inspired by the common law is not a sufficient connecting factor to determine the governing law, nor is the use of the English language.[12] Therefore, international contracts drafted according to the common law tradition and written in English will be subject to the law chosen on the basis of the applicable conflict rule, just like any other international contract. As such, a governing law may be selected that does not belong to the common law legal family.

The analysis made in Chapter 3 also shows that there are no real alternatives to a state governing law when it comes to principles of general contract law upon which the interpretation and application of the agreed wording is based. Restatements of soft law, compilations

---

[7] Chapter 6, Section 1.   [8] Chapter 4, Section 2.   [9] Chapter 2, Section 2.

[10] In this phrase, Dannemann summarises the purpose of this book; see Chapter 4, Section 2.

[11] Chapter 4, Section 4.

[12] Chapter 3, Section 1. This is also confirmed by Dannemann in Chapter 4, Section 1 and Magnus in Chapter 8, Section 3.1.2.

of trade usages, digests of transnational principles and other international instruments, sometimes invoked as appropriate sources for international contracts,[13] may be invaluable in determining the content of specific contract regulations, such as INCOTERMS are for the definition of the place of delivery in international sales.[14] However, these sources do not, for the moment, provide a sufficiently precise basis for addressing the questions that are focused on in this book regarding the function of a contract, the advisability of ensuring a fair balance between the parties' interests, the role of the interpreter in respect of obligations that are not explicitly regulated in the contract, the existence of a duty of the parties to act loyally towards each other, and the existence and extent of a general principle of good faith. As Chapter 3 shows, some of the previously mentioned transnational sources solve these questions by making extensive reference to good faith; however, good faith is a legal standard that requires specification and there does not seem to be any generally acknowledged legal standard of good faith that is sufficiently precise to be applied uniformly and irrespective of the governing law, as the analysis of the material available on the entire agreement clause shows.[15]

Not much help can be found in the observation that legal systems converge on an abstract level and that very similar results may thus be achieved in the various systems, albeit by applying different legal techniques. As Edward T. Canuel shows in Chapter 5, convergence cannot be said to be full. Even within one single legal family, there are significant differences, for example, between US and English law regarding exculpatory clauses. Moreover, even within the same system, there may be divergences, as the same clause may have different legal effects in the different states within the US.[16] Morevoer, reducing the divergence to a mere question of technicalities misses the point – it is precisely the different legal techniques that matter when a specific wording has to be applied. It would not be of much comfort for a party to know that it could have achieved the desired result if only the contract had had the correct wording as required by the relevant legal technique. The party is interested in the legal effects of the particular clause that was written in the contract, not in the abstract possibility of obtaining the same result by a different clause.

---

[13] See, for example, Magnus in Chapter 8, Section 2.

[14] However, INCOTERMS do not cover all legal effects relating to the delivery: for example, they do not determine the moment when title passes from the buyer to the seller, as pointed out by Vettese in Chapter 2, Section 2.

[15] Chapter 3, Section 2.4.   [16] Chapter 5, Section 2.

An observer may be tempted to dismiss these considerations with a pragmatic comment: most international contracts contain an arbitration clause, and therefore disputes arising in connection with them will be solved by arbitration and not by the courts. International arbitration is a system based on the will of the parties, and arbitrators are expected to abide by the will of the parties and not apply undesired sources that bring unexpected results. Moreover, arbitral awards enjoy broad enforceability and the possibility of courts interfering with them is extremely limited, so that the court's opinion on the legal effects of the contracts becomes irrelevant.[17] While all these observations are correct, they do not necessarily affect the research conducted here.

It is true that an arbitral award will be valid and enforceable even though it does not correctly apply the governing law. Not even the wrong application of mandatory rules of law is a sufficient ground to consider an award invalid or unenforceable. Therefore, arbitral tribunals are quite free to interpret contracts and to decide how (and if at all) these contracts shall interact with the governing law.

This, however, will not supply the arbitral tribunal with a sufficient answer to the question of how to interpret the contract. This is not a mere question of verifying whether mandatory rules have been complied with. It is a deeper and more subtle question, and it regards the values upon which interpretation should be based.

The interpreter's understanding of the relationship between certainty and justice (described above as regarding the function of a contract, the advisability of ensuring a fair balance between the parties' interests, the role of the interpreter in respect of obligations that are not explicitly regulated in the contract, the existence of a duty of the parties to act loyally towards each other, and the existence and extent of a general principle of good faith) may lead to an interpretation of the contract that is more literal or more purposive. Some judges or arbitrators may be unaware of the influence that the legal system exercises on them: they may have internalised the legal system's principles in such a way that interpretation based on these principles feels like the only possible interpretation. Others, and particularly experienced international arbitrators, may have been exposed to a variety of legal systems and thus have acquired a higher degree of awareness that the terms of a

---

[17] On the enforceability of international awards and the scope within which national courts may exercise a certain control, see Cordero-Moss, 'International Arbitration'; and Cordero-Moss, 'Arbitration and Private International Law'.

contract do not have one natural meaning, but that their legal effects depend upon their interaction with the governing law. These aware interpreters face a dilemma when confronted with a contract drafted with a style extraneous to the governing law: on the one hand, they do not want to superimpose on the contract the principles of a law that the parties may not have considered during the negotiations; on the other hand, they have no uniform set of principles permitting them to interpret a contract independently of the governing law. Particularly if one of the parties invokes the governing law to prevent a literal application of the contract (notwithstanding that it might not have been aware of it during the negotiations), the dilemma is not easy to solve, not even for an arbitrator.

The clauses selected in this book and the cases proposed to highlight the interpretative challenges that may be faced are intended as an illustration of the dilemma faced by the interpreter.

4   The differing legal effects of boilerplate clauses

The analysis undertaken in this book shows that it is not possible to rely on one uniform interpretation of boilerplate clauses. Having the purpose of highlighting the possible influence that the governing law has on the interpretation and application of their wording, the book has divided the selected clauses into three groups: (i) clauses aiming at creating a self-sufficient system that does not depend upon the governing law for the interpretation or exercise of remedies; (ii) clauses that regulate mechanisms or use terminology that is not part of the governing law; and (iii) clauses that regulate matters already regulated by the governing law. For all these groups, cases have been proposed that put a strain on the literal application of the wording and highlight the impact of the governing law. The text of the clauses and the cases are listed in the introduction to Part 3. An analysis of the legal effects of these clauses under the various laws is given in Part 3. Some concluding observations follow below.

4.1   Clauses aiming at fully detaching the contract
from the applicable law

4.1.1   Entire agreement

The purpose of an entire agreement clause is to isolate the contract from any source or element that may be external to the document. This is also often emphasised by referring to the four corners of the document as the borderline for the interpretation or construction of the contract. The parties' aim is thus to exclude the possibility that the contract is integrated with terms or obligations that do not appear in the document.

The parties are obviously entitled to regulate their interests and to specify the sources of their regulation. However, many legal systems provide for ancillary obligations deriving from the contract type,[18] from a general principle of good faith[19] or from a principle preventing abuse of rights.[20] This means that a contract would always have to be understood not only on the basis of the obligations that are spelled out in it, but also in combination with the elements that, according to the applicable law, are integrated into it. A standard contract therefore risks having different content depending upon the governing law; the entire agreement clause is meant to avoid this uncertainty by barring the possibility of invoking extrinsic elements. It creates an illusion of exhaustiveness of the written obligations.

This is, however, only an illusion: first of all, ancillary obligations created by the operation of law may not always be excluded by a contract.[21]

Moreover, some legal systems make it possible to bring evidence that the parties have agreed upon obligations that are different from those contained in the contract.[22]

Furthermore, many civilian legal systems openly permit the use of precontractual material to interpret the terms written in the contract.[23]

---

[18] See, for France, Chapter 9, Section 2, as well as the general considerations on Article 1135 of the Civil Code in Section 1; for Italy, see Article 1347 of the Civil Code and Chapter 10, Section 1; for Denmark, see Chapter 11, Section 1.

[19] See the general principle on good faith in the performance of contracts in §242 of the German BGB. See Chapter 4, Sections 3.2 and 3.3 for examples of its application by the courts.

[20] See, for Russia, Chapter 16, Section 1.

[21] See, for France and Italy, note 18 above. For Finnish law, see Chapter 12, Section 2.1.

[22] See, for Germany, §309 No. 12 of the BGB, prohibiting clauses which change the burden of proof to the disadvantage of the other party: see Chapter 8, Section 5.1.1.1. Italy, on the contrary, does not allow oral evidence that contradicts a written agreement, see Chapter 10, Section 1.

[23] In addition to Germany (see previous note), see, for France, Chapter 9, Section 2; for Italy, Chapter 10, Section 4; for Denmark, Chapter 11, Section 2.1; for Norway, Chapter 13, Section 3.1; for Hungary, Chapter 15, Section 2; and for Russia, Chapter 16, Section 2.1 The situation seems to be more uncertain in Sweden (see Chapter 14, Section 5.2.4.2) and more restrictive in Finland (see Chapter 12, Section 2.1).

Finally, a strict adherence to the clause's wording may, under some circumstances, be looked upon as unsatisfactory even under English law. English courts, despite insisting that a properly drafted entire agreement clause may actually succeed in preventing any extrinsic evidence from being taken into consideration, interpret it so as to avoid unreasonable results. The motivation given by the courts in the decisions may create the impression that a proper drafting may achieve the clause's purpose, but the ingenuity of the courts' interpretation gives rise to the suspicion that a drafting would never be found to be proper if the result were deemed to be unfair.[24]

The entire agreement clause is an illustration of a clause by which the parties attempt to isolate the contract from its legal context, which is not completely successful and cannot be fully relied upon.

Incidentally, a literal application of this clause would not be allowed under the UPICC or the PECL either, both of which are based on a strong general principle of good faith that, furthermore, is specified by an express rule for the entire agreement clause.[25]

4.1.2 No waiver

The purpose of a no waiver clause is to ensure that the remedies described in the contract may be exercised in accordance with their wording at any time and irrespective of the parties' conduct. The parties try, with this clause, to create a contractual regime for the exercise of remedies without regard to any rules that the applicable law may have on the time frame within which remedies may be exercised and the conditions for such exercise. Many legal systems have principles that protect one party's expectations and prevent the abuse of formal rights. These rules may affect the exercise of remedies in a way that is not visible from the language of the contract. The no waiver clause is inserted to avoid these 'invisible' restrictions to the possibility of exercising contractual remedies.

The parties are, of course, at liberty to regulate the effect of their conduct. However, under some circumstances, this regulation could be used by one party for speculative purposes, such as when a party fails for a long time to exercise its right to terminate and then exercises it when it sees that new market conditions make it profitable to terminate the contract. The real reason for the termination is not the other party's old default that originally was the basis for the right of termination, but

---

[24] See Chapter 7, Section 2.1.   [25] See Chapter 3, Section 2.4.

the change in the market. The no waiver clause, if applied literally, permits this conduct. A literal interpretation of the clause in such a situation is allowed in some systems,[26] but would in many legal systems be deemed to contradict principles that cannot be derogated from by contract: the principle of good faith in German law that prevents abuses of rights,[27] the same principle in French law that prevents a party from taking advantage of a behaviour inconsistent with that party's rights[28] and the principle of loyalty in the Nordic countries[29] that prevents interpretations that would lead to an unreasonable result in view of the conduct of the parties.[30] The clause may have the effect of raising the threshold of when a party's conduct may be deemed to be disloyal,[31] but it will not be able to displace the requirement of loyalty in full. Furthermore, in this context, a literal application of the clause would also be prevented by the UPICC and by the PECL, both of which assume good faith in the exercise of remedies.[32]

Also in the case of this clause, as seen above in connection with the entire agreement clause, English courts argue as if it were possible for the parties to draft the wording in such a way as to permit results that would be prevented in the civilian systems due to them being contrary to good faith or loyalty. However, the English courts' decisions leave the suspicion that even an extremely clear and detailed wording would not be deemed to be proper if its application would lead to unfair results.[33]

Thus, the no waiver clause promises self-sufficiency in the regime for remedies that may not be relied upon.

4.1.3   No oral amendments

The purpose of a no oral amendments clause is to ensure that the contract is implemented at any time according to its wording and irrespective of what the parties may have agreed later, unless this is recorded in writing. This clause is particularly useful when the contract is going to be exposed to third parties, either because it is meant to circulate, for example, in connection with the raising of financing or

---

[26] Neither in Hungarian nor in Russian law would the principle of abuse of right have the effect of depriving a party from its remedy in spite of a considerable delay in exercising the remedy: see, respectively, Chapter 15, Section 3 and Chapter 16, Section 2.2.

[27] See note 19 above.   [28] See Chapter 9, Section 3.

[29] See, for Denmark, Chapter 11, Section 2.3; for Finland, Chapter 12, Section 2.2; and for Norway, Chapter 13, 3.2.

[30] See Chapter 11, Section 2.3.   [31] See Chapter 12, Section 2.2.

[32] See Chapter 3, Section 2.4.   [33] See Chapter 7, Section 2.2.

because its performance requires the involvement of numerous officers of the parties, who are not necessarily all authorised to represent the respective party. In the former scenario, third parties who assess the value of the contract must be certain that they can rely on the contract's wording. If oral amendments were possible, an accurate assessment of the contract's value could not be made simply on the basis of the document. In the latter scenario, the parties must be certain that the contract may not be changed by agreement given by some representatives who are not duly authorised to do so. In a large organisation, it is essential that the ability to make certain decisions is reserved for the bodies or people with the relevant formal competence.

Therefore, the clause has a legitimate purpose and the parties are free to agree to it. Under some circumstances, however, the clause could be abused – for example, if the parties agree on an oral amendment and afterwards one party invokes the clause to refuse performance because it is no longer interested in the contract after the market has changed.

A strict application of the written form requirement is imposed in Russia by mandatory legislation.[34] An application of the clause, even for a speculative purpose, would be acceptable under French law, which has a rule excluding the possibility of bringing oral evidence in contradiction to a written agreement.[35] A similar rule is also present in Italian and Hungarian law, although case law on the matter seems to be unsettled.[36] In German law, the opposite approach applies: German law does not allow the exclusion of evidence that could prove a different agreement by the parties and does not permit terms of contract that disfavour the other party in an unreasonable way.[37] The Nordic systems would give effect to the wording of the clause by raising the threshold for when it can be considered as proven that an oral amendment was agreed upon. However, once such an oral agreement is proven, it would be considered enforceable due to the principle of *lex posterior*,[38] loyalty[39] or good faith.[40]

Even under English law, in spite of the alleged primacy of the contract's wording, it is uncertain whether the clause would be enforced if there was evidence that the parties had agreed to an oral variation.[41]

---

[34] See Chapter 16, Section 2.3.   [35] See Chapter 9, Section 4.

[36] See Chapter 10, Section 3 and Chapter 15, Section 4.

[37] See Chapter 8, Section 5.1.2.1.   [38] See, for Denmark, Chapter 11, Section 2.2.

[39] See, for Finland, Chapter 12, Section 2.3; and for Norway, Chapter 13, Section 3.3.

[40] See, for Sweden, Chapter 14, Section 5.3.2.   [41] See Chapter 7, Section 2.3.

The no oral amendments clause is yet one more example of a clause that will not necessarily always be applied in strict accordance with its terms.

4.1.4   Severability

The purpose of a severability clause is to regulate the consequences for the contract if one or more provisions of the contract are deemed to be invalid or illegal under the applicable law. The clause aims at excluding the possibility that the effects of an external source rendering a provision ineffective spread to the rest of the contract. As already mentioned in respect of the previous clauses, the parties are free to determine the effects of their contract. However, a literal application of this clause may have effects that seem unfair if the provision that became ineffective had significance for the interests of only one of the parties, and the result is that the remaining contract is unbalanced.

There does not seem to be abundant case law on this matter; however, the material analysed in Part 3 shows that the clause would be disregarded in France, in case the invalid provision should be deemed to be essential or if the situation affected the economic balance of the contract.[42] In addition, in the Nordic systems, the general power of the courts to determine in their discretion the consequences of the inefficacy of a provision cannot be derogated from by contract if this creates an imbalance.[43]

4.1.5   Conditions/essential terms

The purpose of a conditions/essential terms clause is to give one party the power to terminate the contract early upon breach by the other party of specific obligations, irrespective of the consequences of the breach or of the early termination. By this clause, the parties attempt to avoid the uncertainty connected with the evaluation of how serious the breach is and what impact it has on the contract. This evaluation is due to the requirement, to be found in most applicable laws, that a breach must be fundamental if the innocent party shall be entitled to terminate the contract. By defining in the contract certain terms as essential or by spelling out that certain breaches give the innocent party the power to terminate the contract, the parties attempt to create an automatism

---

[42] See Chapter 9, Section 5.
[43] See, for Denmark, Chapter 11, Section 2.4; for Finland, Chapter 12, Section 2.4; and for Norway, Chapter 13, Section 3.4.

instead of allowing an evaluation that takes all circumstances into consideration.

As already mentioned above, it falls within the parties' contractual freedom to regulate their respective interests and to allocate risk and liability. Among other things, this means that the parties are free to determine on which conditions the contract may be terminated early. However, a literal interpretation of the clause may lead to unfair results, such as when the breach under the circumstances does not have any consequences for the innocent party, but this party uses the breach as a basis to terminate a contract that it no longer considers profitable, for example, after a change in the market.

In this context, the assumed primacy of the contract's language seems to be confirmed by English courts. If it is not possible to avoid unfair results by simply interpreting the clause, English courts are inclined to give effect to the clause according to its terms, even though the result under the circumstances may be deemed to be unfair. English courts do so, even if with evident reluctance, to ensure consistency in the law underlying the repudiation and termination of the contract.[44] In this context, therefore, properly drafted language achieves the effects that follow from a literal application of the clause even if these effects are unfair. The same result could be obtained under Hungarian law.[45]

Conversely, the other systems analysed here would not allow a literal application of the clause if this had consequences that may be deemed to be unfair, because of the general principle of good faith and loyalty[46] or under the assumption that parties cannot have intended such unfair results.[47]

This clause is an illustration of contractual regulation that may be applied literally when subject to English law, whereas it has to be applied in combination with the governing law when subject to most civil law systems.

4.1.6   Sole remedy

The purpose of a sole remedy clause is to ensure that no remedies other than those regulated in the contract will be available in case of breach of

---

[44] See Chapter 7, Section 2.4.   [45] See Chaper 15, Section 6.

[46] See, for Germany, the principle of good faith in the performance contained in §242 of the BGB; for France, Chapter 9, Section 6; for Denmark, Chapter 11, Section 2.5; and for Finland, Chapter 12, Section 2.5. The same would be obtained under Russian law, based on the principle prohibiting abuse of rights: see Chapter 16, Section 2.4.

[47] See, for Norway, Chapter 13, Section 3.5.

contract. Like the clauses mentioned earlier, this is also an attempt to insulate the contract from the legal system to which it is subject. Rather than relating to the applicable law's remedies and the conditions for their exercise, which may differ from country to country, the parties define in the contract the applicable remedies, the conditions for their exercise and their effects, thus excluding the applicability of any other remedies. Also in respect of this clause, it must first be recognised that it is up to the parties to agree on what remedy to exercise. However, a literal interpretation of this clause could lead to a situation where one party is prevented from claiming satisfactory remedies: assume, for example, that the sole remedy defined in the contract is the reimbursement of damages; if the amount of the damage is quantified in advance in a liquidated damages clause that determines a very low sum, the innocent party would not have any satisfactory remedy available.

This is another illustration of clauses that, in civil law, may not be applied literally but have to be integrated by the applicable law. In particular, the clause may be disregarded if the default was due to gross negligence or wilful misconduct by the defaulting party;[48] moreover, the clause may be disregarded if it has the effect of limiting the defaulting party's liability in such a way that it deprives the contract's essential obligations of their substance.[49] Another line of argument is that the clause may not deprive the innocent party of adequate remedies, in which case the remedies available by the operation of law will be applicable notwithstanding the clause's attempt to exclude them.[50]

Under English law, assuming that the clause is drafted in such a clear and precise language that the courts do not have leeway in their interpretation of it, nothing at common law will limit the parties' freedom to regulate their interests in this context. However, under statutory law, the clause may be subject to control as if it were a limitation of liability clause.[51]

---

[48] See, for France, Chapter 9, Section 7; for Denmark, Chapter 11, Section 2.6; for Finland, Chapter 12, Section 2.6; for Hungary, Chapter 15, Section 7; and for Russia, Chapter 16, Section 2.6.

[49] See, for France, Chapter 9, Section 7. In Hungary, a similar line of argument requires that the sole remedy clause is accompanied by a corresponding benefit, such as a price reduction: see Chapter 15, Section 7.

[50] See, for Denmark, Chapter 11, Section 2.6. See also, for Sweden, Chapter 14, Section 6.3; and for Italy, Chapter 2, Section 2. The situation is more restrictive in Norway, where the clause may be set aside only under exceptional conditions as unfair; see Chapter 13, Section 3.6.

[51] See Chapter 7, Section 2.5.

4.1.7   Subject to contract

The purpose of a subject to contract clause is to free the negotiating parties from any liability in case they do not reach a final agreement. This clause, like those mentioned above, protects important interests in international commerce: it must be possible for the parties to wait until they have completed all negotiations before they make a decision on whether to enter into the contract. Often, negotiations are complicated and are carried out in various phases covering different areas of the prospective transaction, whereby partial agreements on the respective area are recorded and made 'subject to contract'. When all partial negotiations are concluded, the parties will be able to have a full evaluation and only then will they be in a position to finally accept the terms of the deal.

The parties may freely agree when and under what circumstances they will be bound. However, a literal application of the clause may lead to abusive conducts, such as if one of the parties never really intended to enter into a final agreement and used the negotiations merely to prevent the other party from entering into a contract with a third party.

In this case, as in respect of the clause on termination of the contract, there is a dichotomy between the common law approach and the civil law approach. English law seems to permit the parties to negate the intention to be bound, without concerning itself with the circumstances under which the clause will be applied. English courts seem to show a certain sense of unease when they permit the going back on a deal, but it seems that a very strong and exceptional context is needed to override the clause.[52] On the contrary, civil law, like the UPICC and the PECL, is concerned with the possibility that such a clause may be abused by a party entering into or continuing negotiations without having a serious intention of finalising the deal. Therefore, such conduct is prevented, either by defining the clause as a potestative condition and therefore null[53] or by assuming a duty to act in good faith during the negotiations.[54]

Therefore, parties may generally rely upon the possibility of negating the intention to be bound if the relationship is subject to English law. If

---

[52] See Chapter 7, Section 2.6.

[53] See, for France, Chapter 9, Section 8. Potestative conditions are also null under Italian law: see Article 1355 of the Civil Code.

[54] See, for France, Chapter 9, Section 8; for Denmark, Chapter 11, Section 2.7; for Finland, Chapter 12, Section 2.7; for Norway, Chapter 13, Section 3.7; and for Russia, Chapter 16, Section 2.7. The duty to act in good faith during the negotiations is also spelled out in §311 of the German BGB and in Article 1337 of the Italian Civil Code. See, for the UPICC and the PECL, Chapter 3, Section 2.4. For Hungarian law, see Chapter 15, Section 8.

the applicable law belongs to a civilian system, however, the parties will be subject to the principle of good faith under the negotiations, irrespective of the language they have used to avoid it.

4.1.8   Material adverse change

The purpose of a material adverse change clause is to give one of the parties the discretion to withdraw from its obligations in case of change in circumstances that significantly affect the creditworthiness of the other party or in case of other defined circumstances. As above, this clause serves a useful purpose by permitting agreement in advance on all terms of the transaction, though reserving for events that may have a negative effect and may supervene between the time of the agreement and the time at which the obligations are to become effective. The parties are free to define the list of events that are included in the clause. However, a widely formulated clause may lead to abuse if a party invokes it to avoid a deal in which it has lost interest.

Case law on this clause is not abundant; therefore, it may be difficult to express a definite opinion on the enforceability of the clause under all circumstances.[55] What is clear is that under French law, the clause should be formulated in an objective way, so as to exclude the possibility that a party applies purely subjective criteria, thus rendering it a potestative condition.[56] In some Nordic systems, the principle of good faith[57] would impose a restrictive interpretation of the clause[58] in order to avoid abuse in its application.

Therefore, the language of the clause may not be understood purely on the basis of its terms, and it must be integrated with the principles of the applicable law.

4.2   Clauses using terminology with legal effects not known to the applicable law

4.2.1   Liquidated damages

The liquidated damages clause quantifies the amount of damages that will be compensated and has the purpose of creating certainty regarding

---

[55] On the difficulty of predicting the outcome of a case involving this clause under Swedish law, see Chapter 14, Section 5.3.3.4.

[56] See Chapter 9, Section 9.

[57] See, for Finland, Chapter 12, Section 2.8. Germany also has a principle of good faith in the performance of the contract: see §242 of the BGB.

[58] See, for Denmark, Chapter 11, Section 2.8. See also Hungarian law (Chapter 15, Section 9).

what payments shall be due in case of breach of certain obligations. In many civilian systems, this may be achieved by agreeing on contractual penalties. The liquidated damages clause has its origins in the common law, where contractual penalties are not permitted. The main remedy available for breach of contract in common law is compensation of damages. In order to achieve certainty in this respect, contracts contain clauses that quantify the damages in advance. As long as the clause makes a genuine estimate of the possible damages and is not used as a punitive mechanism, it will be enforceable. The agreed amount will thus be paid irrespective of the size of the actual damage. The common law terminology is also adopted in contracts governed by other laws, even when the applicable law permits contractual penalties. In the intention of the parties to these contracts, these clauses are often assumed to work as penalty clauses. This means that they are not necessarily meant to be the only possible compensation for breach of contract and are to be paid irrespective of the size of the actual damage. However, questions may arise as to the effects of the clause: shall they have the same effects as in English law and make the agreed sum payable in spite of the fact that there was no damage at all, or that the damage had a much larger value, or that the clause was meant to be cumulated with a reimbursement of damages calculated according to the general criteria?

It must be first pointed out that this is one of the clauses that demonstrate the primacy of the contract language in the eyes of the English courts. Structuring the clause as a liquidated damages clauses rather than as a penalty clause makes it possible to avoid the penalty rule under English law. This effect follows appropriate drafting rather than the substance of the regulation. Although the courts have the power to exert control on whether the quantification may be deemed to be a genuine evaluation of the potential damage, they are very cautious in making use of this power, under the assumption that the parties know best how to assess any possible damages.[59] Moreover, the penalty rule applies to sums payable upon breach of contract; an appropriate drafting will make it possible to circumvent these limitations by regulating payments as a consequence of events other than breach, thus excluding the applicability of the penalty rule.[60] This is a good example of how far the appropriate drafting may reach under English law.

[59] See Chapter 7, Section 2.7.   [60] *Ibid.*

In civil law, on the contrary, no matter how clear and detailed the drafting, there are some principles that may not be excluded by contract. Thus, the agreed amount of liquidated damages will be disregarded if it can be proven that the loss actually suffered by the innocent party is much lower[61] or much higher.[62] Under certain circumstances, contractual penalties may be cumulated with other remedies, including the reimbursement of damages.[63] The English terminology that refers to 'damages' may create a presumption that the parties did not intend to cumulate that payment with other compensation. This may come as a surprise to the parties that used the terminology on the assumption that it is the proper terminology for a contractual penalty; however, if it is possible to prove that the parties intended to regulate a penalty and did not intend to exclude compensation for damages in spite of the terminology they used, the presumption may be rebutted.[64]

Relying simply on the language of the contract, and particularly if the contract also contains a sole remedy clause, a party could be deemed to be entitled to walk out of the contract if it pays the agreed amount of liquidated damages. The liquidated damages clause could thus be considered as the price that a party has to pay for its default, and as an incentive to commit one if the agreed amount is lower than the benefit that derives from walking out of the contract. In many countries, however, the principle of good faith prevents the defaulting party from invoking the liquidated damages clause in the event that the default was due to that party's gross negligence or wilful misconduct.[65]

The liquidated damages clause is one more example of the different approach to drafting and interpretation in the common law and civil law traditions. Whereas the former makes it possible to circumvent the law's rules by appropriate drafting, the latter integrates the language of the contract with the law's rules and principles.

---

[61] See, for Germany, Chapter 8, Section 5.2.2.1; for France, Chapter 9, Section 10; for Denmark, Chapter 11, Section 3.1; and for Russia, Chapter 16, Section 2.5.

[62] See, for France, Chapter 9, Section 10; for Finland, Chapter 12, Section 3.1; for Norway, Chapter 13, Section 4.1; for Hungary, Chapter 15, Section 10; and for Russia, Chapter 16, Section 2.5.

[63] See, for Finland, Chapter 12, Section 3.1; for Norway, Chapter 13, Section 4.1; for Hungary, Chapter 15, Section 10; and for Russia, Chapter 16, Section 2.5.

[64] See, for Finland, Chapter 12, Section 3.1; for Norway, Chapter 13, Section 4.1.

[65] See, for France, Chapter 9, Section 10; for Denmark, Chapter 11, Section 3.1; for Finland, Chapter 12, Section 3.1; for Hungary, Chapter 15, Section 10. The law seems to be unsettled on this matter in Sweden: see Chapter 14, Section 6.3.

4.2.2   Indemnity

Indemnity clauses have a technical meaning under English law and, among other things, they assume that there is a liability and that damage actually occurred. However, some contracts use the term 'indemnity' or 'indemnify' to designate a guaranteed payment. The analysis made in Part 3 shows that the simple use of the term does not imply that it shall be understood with the technical meaning that follows from English law. Therefore, if the parties intended the payment to be made irrespective of the occurrence of a damage, it will not be possible to avoid it by invoking the requirements that the technical meaning of indemnities have under English law. The clause will be interpreted in accordance with the substance regulated by the parties and the applicable law.

4.3   Clauses regulating matters already regulated in the applicable law

4.3.1   Representations and warranties

The representations and warranties clause contains a long list of circumstances that the parties guarantee to each other – from the validity of the parties' respective incorporation to the validity of the obligations assumed in the contract and the characteristics and specifications of the contract's object. As was seen above, some of these representations and warranties may not be deemed to have any legal effect, because they fall outside of the parties' contractual power;[66] however, most of the circumstances that are represented or warranted relate to specifications or characteristics of the contract's object. These representations and warranties create an obligation for the party making them and, if breached, will either allow the other party to repudiate the contract or to claim compensation for damages. Therefore, the clause has an important function. This function is particularly important in common law, where the parties are expected to spell out in the agreement their respective assumptions and obligations, and it may be difficult to convince a court to imply specifications or characteristics that were not mentioned in the contract. During contract negotiations, a party is under no duty to disclose matters relating to the contract's object and the representations and warranties clause is usually the occasion for the

---

[66] See Section 2 in this chapter.

parties to list all information that they consider relevant, and where they expect the other party to assume responsibility. Without the representations and warranties clause, there would be no basis for a claim.

On the contrary, in civilian systems, the parties are under extensive duties to disclose any circumstances that may be of relevance in the other party's appreciation of its interest in the bargain. It is not the party interested in receiving the information that shall request the other party to make a list of specific disclosures, it is the party possessing the information that is under a general duty to disclose matters that are relevant to the other party's assessment of the risk and its interest in the deal. This duty of information exists by operation of law even if the contract has no representations and warranties clause.

When the parties insert a long and detailed representations and warranties clause, and carefully negotiate its wording, they may be under the impression that this long list exhaustively reflects what they represent and warrant to each other. This impression is in compliance with the effects of the clause under English law, where accurate wording is crucial in deciding whether a party has a claim or not.[67]

Under civil law, the clause also has effects: if a certain characteristic was expressly represented or warranted in the contract, failure to comply with it will more easily be qualified as a defect in the consent or a breach of contract, without the need to verify whether it had been relied on, whether it was essential, etc. The clause therefore creates certainty regarding the consequences of the breach of the representations and warranties that were made.

However, the clause does not have the reverse effect: if a certain characteristic was not included in the representations and warranties, it does not mean that it may not be deemed to be among the matters that the parties have to disclose or bear responsibility for. The parties may have invested considerable energy in negotiating the list and one party may intentionally have omitted certain matters, under the illusion that this would have been sufficient to avoid any liability in that connection. However, if the matter left out is material, the other party may be entitled to claim the nullity of the contract[68] or compensation for damages.[69] The

---

[67] See Chapter 7, Section 2.9.
[68] See, for France, Chapter 9, Section 12; and for Russia, Chapter 16, Section 2.8.
[69] See, for Denmark, Chapter 11, Section 4.1; and for Russia, Chapter 16, Section 2.8.

duty of disclosure may not be contracted out of[70] and is considered to be such a cornerstone that it applies even to sales that are made 'as is'.[71]

This clause is an example of where an accurate drafting may obtain results if the contract is subject to English law, because English law leaves it to the parties to determine the content of their bargain. Civil law, on the contrary, regulates this area extensively, and the drafting of the parties may not affect this regulation, no matter how clear and detailed it is.

4.3.2 Hardship

The hardship clause regulates, sometimes in detail, under what circumstances and with what consequences the parties may be entitled to renegotiate their contract because of a supervened and unexpected unbalance in the respective obligations. English law does not provide for any mechanism to suspend or discharge the parties from obligations in case the performance, though still possible, becomes more onerous for one party, and nor does French law. On the contrary, other civilian systems permit a party to request a modification to the obligations if changed circumstances seriously affect the balance in the contract.[72] The clause thus gives the parties greater rights than they would have under English or French law, while at the same time it may restrict the rights that the affected party would have under other laws. The parties may have introduced a hardship clause in an attempt to take the regulation of supervening circumstances into their own hands and to exclude the application of corresponding rules in the governing law. A clause permitting the affected party to request renegotiations will be enforced in a system where such a right is not recognised by the general law, because it will simply create a new regulation based on the contract but not prohibited by law. The reverse, however, is more problematic: a detailed hardship clause may restrict the right that the affected party has under the applicable law. For example, the clause may contain an intentionally restrictive definition of the events that trigger the remedy, significantly

---

[70] See, for Finland, Chapter 12, Section 4.1; and for Russia, Chapter 16, Section 2.8. Hungarian law is less absolute: see Chapter 15, Section 12.

[71] Under Norwegian law (see Chapter 13, Section 5.1) – although in the case of sales 'as is', the duty extends only to what the seller had knowledge of.

[72] See, for Denmark, Chapter 11, Section 4.2; for Finland, Chapter 12, Section 4.2; and for Norway, Chapter 13, Section 5.2. For Germany, see §313 of the BGB and for Italy, see Articles 1467–1469 of the Italian Civil Code.

more restrictive than the applicable law's standard of 'more burdensome performance'. Also, the clause may regulate that the only possible remedy is the request of renegotiation without suspending the duty to perform and thus exclude other remedies, such as withholding the performance, which may be permitted by the applicable law.

The parties may actually have written such a restrictive hardship clause with the purpose of limiting the application of the governing law's generous rules. However, the clause will not be understood as the sole regulation in case of supervened imbalance in the contract and will thus be cumulated with the applicable law's rules.[73]

4.3.3   *Force majeure*

This clause is meant to regulate, in detail, under what circumstances a party may be excused for non-performance of its obligations under the contract in case the performance becomes impossible. Corresponding regulations may be found not only in the legal systems that, as seen immediately above, have a regulation for hardship, but also in English and French law. *Force majeure* clauses thus regulate matters that are already regulated by the applicable law. The law's regulation, however, is not mandatory; therefore, it is quite possible for the parties to create a separate contractual regime and allocate the risk of supervened impediments differently from the allocation that follows from the governing law.

Often, *force majeure* clauses are detailed and extensive. This, combined with the above-mentioned non-mandatory nature of the legal regime, gives the impression that these clauses will be applied equally, irrespective of the governing law. However, the principles of the applicable law are likely to influence the understanding of the clause. For example, many *force majeure* clauses describe the excusing impediment as an event beyond the control of the parties that may not be foreseen or reasonably overcome. Different legal systems may have differing understandings of what is deemed to be beyond the control of one party: whereas many systems will consider this wording as an allocation of the risk in the sphere of either party (what is not under the control of one party is under the control of the other one), others may focus more on the

---

[73] See, for Denmark, Chapter 11, Section 4.2; for Finland, Chapter 12, Section 4.2; for Norway, Chapter 13, Section 5.2. See, however, German law and Hungarian law, which allow the parties to derogate from the statutory regulation: see Chapter 8, Section 5.3.2.1 and Chapter 15, Section 13.

conduct of the affected party. If the non-performing party has been diligent and cannot be blamed for the occurrence of the impediment, it will be excused. In the former approach, it may be the case that a party is not excused even though it has acted diligently and cannot be blamed – the basis for liability is that the risk that materialised was deemed to have been assumed by that party. This approach is typical of the common law and may be also found in the CISG.[74] In the latter approach, the party will be excused if it did not have the actual possibility of influencing the circumstances that caused the impediment. This approach may be found in some civilian systems.[75]

The different approaches to what is beyond the control of the parties may be illustrated by comparing how the CISG and Norwegian law deal with a situation where performance is prevented by a failure made by the seller's supplier. The rule on liability for the seller's non-performance has the same wording in both systems: the Norwegian Sales of Goods Act is the implementation of the CISG, and its §27 translated the rule contained in Article 79 of the CISG. In spite of the rule being the same, its application is diametrically different. In the CISG, if the seller is not able to perform because of a failure by its supplier, it will not be excused.[76] The choice of supplier is within the control of the seller, so failure by a supplier may not be deemed to be beyond the control of the seller. Under Norwegian law, on the contrary, failure by the seller's supplier is deemed to be an external event that excuses the seller.[77] As long as the supplier was chosen in a diligent way, the seller may not be blamed for the supplier's failure because it does not have any actual possibility of influencing the supplier's conduct.

---

[74] For a more extensive explanation and bibliographic references, see G. Cordero-Moss, *Lectures on Comparative Law*, Publications Series of the Institute of Private Law No. 166 (University of Oslo, 2004), pp. 156–159, available at http://folk.uio.no/giudittm/ GCM_List%20of%20Publications.htm, last accessed 6 October 2010.

[75] See, for Russia, Chapter 16, Section 2.9. See, for further references, Cordero-Moss, *Lectures on Comparative Law*, pp. 151–156.

[76] The United Nations Secretariat's *Commentary to the UNCITRAL Draft Convention*, adopted at the United Nations Conference on Contracts for International Sale of Goods, Vienna, 10 March–11 April 1980 (A/CONF./97/5), available at www.uncitral. org/uncitral/en/uncitral_texts/sale_goods/1980CISG_travaux.html (last accessed 6 October 2010), is the closest to an official report to the CISG. In the comment to the second paragraph of Article 79 on the use of subcontractors, it specifies that the rule does not include suppliers of raw materials or of goods to the seller: see *Commentary*, p. 172.

[77] See Chapter 13, Section 5.3.

This different understanding of the rule on the supplier's failure is a good illustration of how different legal traditions may affect the interpretation of the same wording.[78]

5   The drafting style does not achieve self-sufficiency, but has a certain merit

The research undertaken in this book shows that the terms of a contract are not detached from the governing law: the governing law will influence the interpretation and application of these terms. To what extent the legal effects differ from what a literal application would suggest varies depending on the governing law.

Therefore, there is no reason to rely on a full and literal application of the contract's wording as if it were isolated from the governing law.

If this is so, why do contract parties go on drafting detailed (and sometimes, as seen above, nonsensical) clauses without adjusting them to the governing law? Why do they engage in extensive negotiations of specific wording without even having discussed which law will govern the contract?

Each of the parties may repeatedly send numerous delegations consisting of financial, marketing, technical, commercial and legal experts to meet and negotiate specific contractual mechanisms and wording to be inserted in the contract. All these people may spend hours and days negotiating whether the penalty for a delay in performance shall be $10,000 or $15,000 a day, or fighting over whether the contract shall include the word 'reasonable' in the clause permitting early termination of the contract in case the other party fails to perform certain obligations. All these negotiations are usually made without even having addressed the question of the governing law. The contract may end up[79] being governed by English law, in which case the clause on penalties will be unenforceable, or by German law, in which case the concept of reasonableness will be part of the contract irrespective of the appearance of the word. All the efforts in negotiating the amount of the penalty or in

---

[78] The interpretation referred to in Chapter 13, Section 5.3 is based on a Supreme Court decision rendered in 1970, long before the implementation of the CISG in the Norwegian system. However, the Supreme Court's decision is still referred to as correctly incorporating Norwegian law after the enactment of the Sales of Goods Act, as the reference made in Chapter 13 confirms (see, for further references, Cordero-Moss, *Lectures on Comparative Law*, pp. 152f.).

[79] Either because the parties chose it or because the applicable conflict rule pointed at it.

rendering the early termination clause stricter will have been in vain. Unfortunately, it is not at all rare that the choice-of-law clause is left as the last point in the negotiations and that it is not given the attention that it deserves.

This does not necessarily mean that the practice of negotiating detailed wording without regard to the governing law is always unreasonable. From a merely legal point of view, it makes little sense, but from an overall economic perspective, it is more understandable, as was seen in Part 1 of this book.

Thus, it is true that clauses, originally meant to create certainty, upon the interaction with the governing law may create uncertainty.[80] The uncertainty about how exactly a clause will be interpreted by a judge is deleterious from a merely legal point of view. However, this uncertainty may turn out to be less harmful from a commercial perspective: faced with the prospects of employing time and resources in pursuing a result that is unforeseeable from a legal point of view, the parties may be encouraged to find a commercial solution. Rather than maximising the legal conflict, they may be forced to find a mutually agreeable solution. This may turn out to be a better use of resources once the conflict has arisen.

In addition, this kind of legal uncertainty is evaluated as a risk, just like other risks that relate to the transaction. Commercial parties know that not all risks will materialise, and this will also apply to the legal risk: not all clauses with uncertain legal effects will actually have to be invoked or enforced. In the majority of contracts, the parties comply with their respective obligations and there is no need to invoke the application of specific clauses. In situations where a contract clause actually has to be invoked, the simple fact that the clause is invoked may induce the other party to comply with it, irrespective of the actual enforceability of the clause. An invoked clause is not necessarily always contested. Thus, there will be only a small percentage of clauses that will actually be the basis of a conflict between the parties. Of these conflicts, we have seen that some may be solved amicably, precisely because of the uncertainty of the clause's legal effects. This leaves a quite small percentage of clauses upon which the parties may eventually litigate. Some of these litigations will be won, some will be lost. Commercial thinking requires a party to assess the value of this risk of losing a lawsuit on enforceability of a clause (also considering the likelihood that it materialises) and compare this

---

[80] This observation is made by Hagstrøm in Chapter 13, Section 2.

value with the costs of alternative conduct. Alternative conduct would be to assess every single clause of each contract that is entered into, verify its compatibility with the law that will govern each of these contracts and propose adjustments to each of these clauses to the various other contracting parties. This, in turn, requires the employment of internal resources to revise standard documentation and external resources to adjust clauses to the applicable law, and possibly negotiations to convince the other contracting parties to change a contract model that they are well acquainted with. In many situations, the costs of adjusting each contract to its applicable law will exceed the value of the risk that is run by entering into a contract with uncertain legal effects.

The sophisticated party, aware of the implications of adopting contract models that are not adjusted to the governing law and consciously assessing the connected risk, will identify the clauses that matter the most and will concentrate its negotiations on those, leaving the other clauses untouched and accepting the corresponding risk.

6   Conclusion

The contract practice described above does not mean that the parties have opted out of the governing law for the benefit of a transnational set of rules that is not easy to define. Just because the parties decided to take the risk of legal uncertainty for some clauses does not mean that the interpreter has to refrain from applying the governing law or that the legal evaluation of these clauses should be made in a less stringent way than for any other clauses. The interpreter should acknowledge the parties' desire that the contract be, to the fullest extent possible, interpreted solely on the basis of its own terms. Therefore, extensive interpretation or integration of terms should be avoided. However, such a literal interpretation of the contract should be made in compliance with the principles underlying the applicable law, as well as its mandatory rules.

Therefore, taking the risk of legal uncertainty does not justify that the drafters neglect being aware of the legal effects that their clause may have under the governing law: a calculated risk assumes a certain understanding of what risk is being faced. Being fully unaware would not permit the drafters to assess the risk and decide which clauses should be adjusted and which ones do not justify using resources in negotiating. In the examples made above, the penalty clause should certainly be adjusted to the governing law in order to permit enforcement, whereas the clause on reasonable early termination does not need to be negotiated because a change in the wording will not affect its enforcement. Knowing the legal effects under the governing law will permit the parties to apply their resources reasonably during the negotiations. This makes it possible to take a calculated risk. On the contrary, ignoring the problems and blindly trusting the effectiveness of the contract's wording resembles recklessness more than a deliberate assumption of risk.

BIBLIOGRAPHY

Adlercreutz, Axel, *Avtalsrätt I*, 12th edn (Studentlitteratur, 2002).

'Om den rättsliga betydelsen av avtalad skriftform och om integrationsklausuler', in Bernitz, Ulf, Grönfors, Kurt, Hellner, Jan, Kleinemann, Jan, Sandström, Jan and Herre, Johnny, *Festskrift till Jan Ramberg* (Juristförlaget, 1996).

Adlercreutz, Axel and Gorton, Lars, *Avtalsrätt II*, 6th edn (Juridiska föreningen i Lund, 2010).

Agell, Anders, *Festskrift till Bertil Bengtsson* (Stockholm Nerenius & Santérus, 1993).

Almén, Tore, *Lagen om avtal och andra rättshandlingar på förmögenhetsrättens område av den 11 julin 1915 samt därav föranledda författningar med litteraturhänvisningar och förklarande anmärkningar* (P. A. Norstedt & Söners Förlag, 1916).

Anwaltkommentar BGB, vol. 1 (Deutscher Anwaltverlag, 2005).

Bamberger, Heinz Georg and Roth, Herbert, *Beckscher Online-Kommentar* (Beck-online, 2007).

Bürgerliches Gesetzbuch mit Nebengesetzen, vol. 2, 2nd edn (C. H. Beck, 2008).

Bar, Christian von and Mankowski, Peter, *Internationales Privatrecht*, vol. I, 2nd edn (C. H. Beck, 2003).

Basedow, Jürgen, Hopt, Klaus and Zimmermann, Reinhard (eds.), *Handwörterbuch des Europäischen Privatrechts*, vol. 1 (Mohr Siebeck, 2009).

Baumbach, Adolf and Hopt, Klaus (eds.), *Handelsgesetzbuch*, 34th edn (C. H. Beck, 2010).

Beale, Hugh, *Chitty on Contracts*, 30th edn (Sweet & Maxwell, 2008).

'General Clauses and Specific Rules in the Principles of European Contract Law: The "Good Faith" Clause', in Grundmann, Stefan and Mazeaud, Denis (eds.), *General Clauses and Standards in European Contract Law* (Kluwer Law International, 2006), pp. 205–218.

Benedek, Károly and Világhy, Miklós, *A Polgári Törvénykönyv a gyakorlatban* (Közgazdasági és Jogi Könyvkiadó, 1965).

Berg, Alan, 'The Detailed Drafting of a Force Majeure Clause', in McKendrick, Ewan (ed.), *Force Majeure and Frustration of Contract*, 2nd edn (Informa Publishing, 1995).

Berger, Klaus Peter (ed.), *Trans-Lex- Law Research*, http://trans-lex.org.

Bernitz, Ulf, *Standardavtalsrätt* (Norstedts Juridik, 2008).

Bernitz, Ulf, Grönfors, Kurt, Hellner, Jan, Kleinemann, Jan, Sandström, Jan and Herre, Johnny (eds.), *Festskrift till Jan Ramberg* (Juristförlaget, 1996).

Biehl, Björn, 'Grundsätze der Vertragsauslegung', *JuS* (2010), 195–200.

Birks, Peter (ed.), *Wrongs and Remedies in the Twenty-First Century* (Clarendon Press, 1996).

Bjørnstad, Henrik W., *Entire Agreement Clauses, Publications Series of the Institute of Private Law No. 177* (University of Oslo, 2009).

Bogdan, M., *Comparative Law* (Kluwer Law International, 1994).

Boguslavskiy, M. M., *Private International Law*, 6th edn (Norma Publishing House, 2009) (in Russian).

Bonell, Michael J., *Unilex- International Case Law and Bibliography on CISG & UNIDROIT Principles*, http://www.unilex.info/, last accessed 6 October 2010.

Braginskiy, M. I., 'The 1980 Vienna Convention and the RCC', in M. G. Rozenberg (ed.), *The 1980 Vienna UN Convention on Contracts for the International Sale of Goods. The Ten Years of Application by Russia* (Statut Publishing House, 2002), pp. 14–17 (in Russian).

Braginskiy, M. I., and Vitrianskiy, V. V., *Contract Law*, Book 1, 2nd edn (Statut Publishing House, 1999) (in Russian).

Bredow, Jens and Seiffert, Bodo, *INCOTERMS 2000* (Economica Verlag, 2000).

Bruett, Keith, 'Can Wisconsin Businesses Safely Rely upon Exculpatory Contracts to Limit their Liability?', *Marquette Law Review*, 81 (1998), 1081.

Bryde Andersen, Mads, *Grundlæggende aftaleret. Aftaleretten I*, 3rd edn (Gjellerup, 2008).

Praktisk aftaleret. Aftaleretten II, 2nd edn (Gjellerup, 2003).

Bryde Andersen, Mads and Lookofsky, Joseph, *Lærebog i Obligationsret I*, 3rd edn (Thomson Reuters, 2010).

Burrows, Andrew and Peel, Edwin (eds.), *Contract Formation and Parties* (Oxford University Press, 2010).

(eds.), *Contract Terms* (Oxford University Press, 2007).

Campbell, Dennis (ed.), *Legal Aspects of Doing Business in Western Europe* (Kluwer, 1983).

Cappalli, Richard B., 'Open Forum: At the Point of Decision: The Common Law's Advantage over the Civil Law', *Temple International and Comparative Law Journal*, 12 (1998), 87.

Cendon, Paolo (ed.), *I contratti in generale*, vol. IV, *Clausole abusive* (UTET, 2001).

Chen-Wishart, Mindy, 'Controlling the Power to Agree Damages', in Birks, Peter (ed.), *Wrongs and Remedies in the Twenty-First Century* (Clarendon Press, 1996).

Christoffersen, Margrethe Buskerud, *Kjøp og salg av virksomhet* (Gyldendal Akademisk, 2008).

Clarke, M., 'Notice of Contractual Terms' [1976] CLJ 51.

Collins, Lawrence, Lord Justice, Morse, C. G. J., McClean, David, Briggs, Adrian, Harry, Jonathan and McLachlan, Campbell (eds.), *Dicey, Morris & Collins on the Conflict of Laws*, 14th edn, 2 vols. (Sweet & Maxwell, 2006).

Commission of the European Communities, *European contract law and the revision of the acquis: the way forward*, COM (2004) 651 final.

Green Paper on the conversion of the Rome Convention of 1980 on the law applicable to contractual obligations into a Community instrument and its modernisation, 14.1.2003, COM (2002) 654 final.

Comoglio, *Le prove civili* (Wolters Kluwer Italia, 1999).

Coote, Brian, *Exception Clauses* (Sweet & Maxwell, 1964).

Corbin, Arthur L., *Corbin on Contracts*, 15 vols., Joseph Perillo (ed.), (Matthew Bender and Company, 2002).

Cordero-Moss, Giuditta, *Anglo-American Contract Models and Norwegian or other Civilian Governing Law*, Publications Series of the Institute of Private Law No. 169 (University of Oslo, 2007).

'Arbitration and Private International Law', *International Arbitration Law Review*, 11, 4 (2008), 153–164.

'Consumer Protection Except for Good Commercial Practice: A Satisfactory Regime for Commercial Contracts?', in Schulze, Reinar (ed.), *CFR and Existing EC Contract Law* (Sellier, 2009), pp. 63–92.

'The Function of Letters of Intent and their Recognition in Modern Legal Systems', in Schulze, R. (ed.), *New Features in Contract Law* (Sellier, 2007), pp. 139–159.

'Harmonized Contract Clauses in Different Business Cultures', in Wihelmsson, T., Paunio, E. and Pohjolainen, A. (eds.), *Private Law and The Main Cultures of Europe* (Kluwer International, 2007), pp. 221–239.

'International Arbitration and the Quest for the Applicable Law', *Global Jurist (Advances)*, 8, 3 (2008), Article 2, 1–42.

International Commercial Law, 2nd edn, Publications Series of the Institute of Private Law No. 185 (University of Oslo, 2010).

'International Contracts between Common Law and Civil Law: Is Non-state Law to be Preferred? The Difficulty of Interpreting Legal Standards such as Good Faith', *Global Jurist (Advances)*, 7, 1 (2007), 1–38.

Lectures on Comparative Law, Publications Series of the Institute of Private Law No. 166 (University of Oslo, 2004).

Dahl, Børge, Melchior, T. and Tamm, D. (eds.), *Danish Law in a European Perspective*, 2nd edn (Thomson, 2002).

Dahlman, Christian (ed.), *Festskrift till Ingemar Ståhl. Studier i rättsekonomi* (Studentlitteratur, 2005).

Dainow, Joseph, 'The Civil Law and the Common Law: Some Points of Comparison', *American Journal of Comparative Law*, 15 (1967), 419–435.

Dannemann, Gerhard, *Die ungewollte Diskriminierung in der internationalen Rechtsanwendung. Zur Anwendung, Berücksichtigung und Anpassung von Normen aus unterschiedlichen Rechtsordnungen* (Mohr Siebeck, 2004).

'Sachrechtliche Gründe für die Berücksichtigung nicht anwendbaren Rechts', in Hohloch, Gerhard, Frank, Rainer and Schlechtriem, Peter (eds.), *Festschrift für Hans Stoll zum 75. Geburtstag* (Mohr Siebeck, 2001), pp. 417–436.

David, René and Brierly, John E. C., *Major Legal Systems in the World Today* (Stevens and Sons Publishing, 1985).

De Nova, Giorgio, *Il contratto alieno*, 2nd edn (Giappichelli, 2010).

DiMatteo, Larry A., 'An International Contract Law Formula: The Informality of International Business Transactions Plus the Internationalisation of Contract Law Equals Unexpected Contractual Liability', *Syracuse Journal of International Law and Commerce*, 23 (1997), 67–111.

Eidenmüller, Horst, Faust, Florian, Grigoleit, Hans Christpoh, Jansen, Nils, Wagner, Gerhard and Zimmermann, Reinhard, 'The Common Frame of Reference for European Private Law – Policy Choices and Codification Problems', *Oxford Journal of Legal Studies*, 28, 4 (2008), 659–708.

Eörsi, Gyula, *A polgári jogi kártérítési felelősség kézikönyve* (Közgazdasági és Jogi Könyvkiadó, 1966).

Elhatárolási problémák az anyagi felelősség körében (Közgazdasági és Jogi Könyvkiadó, 1962).

Ewald, Jens, *Retsmisbrug i formueretten* (København: Jurist- og Økonomforbundets Forlag, 2001).

Ewald, William, 'What's So Special about American Law?', *Oklahoma City University Law Review*, 26 (2001), 1083–1115.

Eyben, Bo von, Mortensen, Peter and Sørensen, Ivan, *Lærebog i Obligationsret II*, 3rd edn (Thomson Reuters, 2008).

Farber, Daniel A., 'Book Review: The Hermeneutic Tourist: Statutory Interpretation in Comparative Perspective', *Cornell Law Review*, 81 (1996), 513–529.

Farnsworth, E. Allan, *Farnsworth on Contracts*, 3 vols. (Aspen Publishers, 1998).

Feingerts, Bruce L., Stein, Mark S. 'Exculpatory Provisions in Towage Contracts', *Tulane Law Review*, 49 (1975), 392.

Fern, Martin. D., *Warren's Forms of Agreements*, vol. 2 (LexisNexis, 2004)

Filthaut, Werner, *Haftpflichtgesetz*, 6th edn (C. H. Beck, 2010).

Flodgren, Boel, Gorton, Lars, Nyström, Birgitta and Samuelsson, Per (eds.), *Vänskrift till Axel Adlercreutz* (Juristförlaget i Lund, 2007).

Földi, András *A jóhiszeműség és tisztességesség elve; intézménytörténeti vázlat a római jogtól napjainkig* (Publicationes Instituti Iuris Romani

Budapestiensis fasc. 9, published by the Roman Law Department of ELTE Law Faculty, 2001).

Fontaine, Marcel and De Ly, Filip, *La redazione dei contratti internazionali*, Italian translation by Renzo Maria Morresi (Giuffrè Editore, 2006).

Freisen, Jeffery L., 'When Common Law Courts Interpret Civil Codes', *Wisconsin International Law Journal*, 15 (1996), 1.

Gabrielli, Enrico (ed.), *I contratti in generale*, vol. II, 2nd edn (UTET, 2006).

Garner, Bryan A. (ed.), *Black's Law Dictionary* (West Publishing, 1999).

Gellért, György (ed.), *A Polgári Törvénykönyv Magyarázata* (Complex Kiadó, 2008).

Giuliano, Mario and Lagarde, Paul, Report on the Convention on the law applicable to contractual obligations, OJ C 282, 31.10.1980.

Glendon, M. A., Gordon, M. W. and Osakwe, C., *Comparative Legal Traditions* (West Publishing, 1994).

Gomard, Bernhard, 'Aftalelovens §36 og erhvervskontrakter', *Erhvervsjuridisk Tidsskrift* (2008), 14–26.

Obligasjonsret 2.Del, 3rd edn (Jurist- og Økonomforbundets Forlag, 2003).

Gomard, Bernhard and Iversen, Torsten, *Obligationsret 3.Del*, 2nd edn (Jurist- og Økonomforbundets Forlag, 2009).

Gomard, Bernhard, Pedersen, Godsk, Viggo, Hans and Ørgaard, Anders, *Almindelig aftaleret*, 3rd edn (Jurist- og Økonomforbundets Forlag, 2009).

Gomard, Bernhard and Rechnagel, Hardy, *International Købelov* (Jurist- og Økonomforbundets Forlag, 1990).

Goode, Roy, 'Usage and its Reception in Transnational Commercial Law', 46, 1 (1997) *International and Comparative Law Quarterly*, 1–36.

Goode, Roy, Kronke, Herbert, McKendrick, Ewan and Wool, Jeffrey, *Transnational Commercial Law – Text, Cases and Materials* (Oxford Univeristy Press, 2007).

Gorton, Lars, 'Boilerplateklausuler', *Erhvervsjuridisk Tidsskrift* (2009), 170–188.

Material Adverse Change-klausuler, in Flodgren, Boel, Gorton, Lars, Nyström, Birgitta and Samuelsson, Per (eds.), *Vänskrift till Axel Adlercreutz* (Juristförlaget i Lund, 2007), pp. 117–132.

'Merger Clauses in Business Contracts', *Erhversretslig Tidsskrift* (2008), 344–360.

Gorton, Lars and Samuelsson, Per, 'Kontraktuella viten', in Dahlman, Christian (ed.), *Festskrift till Ingemar Ståhl. Studier i rättsekonomi* (Studentlitteratur, 2005), pp. 75–106.

Grassetti, Cesare, *L'interpretazione del negozio giuridico* (CEDAM, 1983).

Grönfors, K., *Avtalsgrundande rättsfakta* (Thomson Fakta, 1993).

Grosheide, Willem, 'The Duty to Deal Fairly in Commercial Contracts', in Grundmann, Stefan and Mazeaud, Denis (eds.), *General Clauses and Standards in European Contract Law* (Kluwer Law International, 2006), pp. 197–204.

Gruber, Joachim 'Auslegungsprobleme bei fremdsprachigen Verträgen unter deutschem Recht', *Deutsche Zeitschrift für Wirtschatfs- und Insolvenzrecht* (1997), 353–359.

Gruber, Urs Peter, *Methoden des Internationalen Einheitsrechts* (Mohr Siebeck, 2004).

Grundmann, Stefan and Mazeaud, Denis (eds.), *General Clauses and Standards in European Contract Law*, (Kluwer Law International, 2006).

Guinchard Serge *et al.* (eds.), *Droit processuel*, 4th edn (Précis Dalloz, 2007).

Gyevi-Tóth, Judit, 'A szerződéses és a deliktuális felelősség egymáshoz való viszonya', in A. Harmathy (ed.), *Jogi Tanulmányok* (ELTE, 1997), pp. 153–185.

Hagstrøm, Viggo, *Kjøpsrett* (Universitetsforlaget, 2005).

Obligasjonsrett (Universitetsforlaget, 2003).

'The Scandinavian Law of Obligations', *Scandinavian Studies in Law*, 50 (2007), 113–124.

Harmathy, Attila, *Felelősség a közreműködőért* (Közgazdasági és Jogi Könyvkiadó, 1974).

Hartkamp, Arthur and Hesselink, Martijn (eds.), *Towards a European Civil Code* (Kluwer Law International, 1998).

Hayek, Friedrich A., *Law, Legislation and Liberty*, vol. I, *Rules and Order* (University of Chicago Press, 1973).

Heidel, Thomas, Hüsstege, Rainer, Mansel, Heinz-Peter and Noack, Ulrich (eds.), *Anwaltkommentar BGB*, vol. 1 (Deutscher Anwaltverlag, 2005).

Hellner, Jan, 'Jämkning av långvarigt avtal', *Juridisk Tidskrift* (1994–1995), 137–141.

'The parol evidence rule och tolkningen av skriftliga avtal', in A. Agell (ed.), *Festskrift till Bertil Bengtsson* (Stockholm Nerenius & Santérus, 1993).

Herbots, Jacques, 'Interpretation of Contracts', in Smits, Jan M. (ed.), *Elgar Encyclopedia of Comparative Law* (Edward Elgar Publishing, 2006), pp. 325–347.

Herre, Johnny and Ramberg, Jan, *Allmän köprätt*, 5th edn (Norstedts Juridik, 2009).

Internationella köplagen (CISG). En kommentar, 3rd edn (Juristförlaget, 2010).

Hertz, Ketilbjørn and Lookofsky, Joseph, *EU-PIL. European Union Private International Law in Contract and Tort* (DJØF Publishing, 2009).

Hesselink, Martijn, *The New European Private Law: Essays on the Future of Private Law* (Kluwer Law International, 2002).

Hohloch, Gerhard, Frank, Rainer and Schlechtriem, Peter (eds.), *Festschrift für Hans Stoll zum 75. Geburtstag* (Mohr Siebeck, 2001).

Holmes, Oliver Wendell, *The Common Law* (Little Brown, 1881).

Honnold, John and Flechtner, Harry (eds.), *Uniform Law for International Sales under the 1980 United Nations Convention*, 4th edn (Kluwer Law International, 2009).

Hov, Jo and Høgberg, Alf Petter, *Alminnelig avtalerett* (Papinian, 2009).

International Institute for the Unification of Private Law (UNIDROIT), *Principles of International Commercial Contracts* (International Institute for the Unification of Private Law, 2004), available at http://www.unidroit.org/ english/principles/contracts/principles2004/integralversionprinciples2004-e.pdf, last accessed 6 October 2010.

Iversen, Torsten, 'Produktansvar og ansvarsbegrænsningen', *Juristen*, 6 (2008), 188–193.

Iversen, Torsten, 'Nogle bemærkninger om dagbøder', in Iversen, Torsten (ed.), *Festskrift til Det Danske Selskab for Byggeret* (Thomson Reuters, 2009), pp. 105–124.

Jansen, Nils and Zimmermann, Reinhard, '"A European Civil Code in All But Name": Discussing the Nature and Purposes of the Draft Common Frame of Reference' (2010) 69 *CLJ*, 98–112.

Justitsministeriet, København, *Betænkning 1502/2008 om visse køberetlige regler om sikkerhedsmangler*.

Kanashevskiy, V. A., *Foreign Economic Transactions: Substantive and Conflict of Laws Regulation* (Wolters Kluwer, 2008), pp. 165–166 (in Russian).

Karayanni, Michael Mousa, 'The Public Policy Exception to the Enforcement of Forum Selection Clauses', *Duquesne Law Review*, 34 (1996), 1009.

Kaufmann, Sebastian, *Parol Evidence Rule und Merger Clauses im internationalen Einheitsrecht* (Peter Lang, 2004).

Kegel, Gerhard, Schurig, Klaus, *Internationales Privatrecht*, 9th edn (C. H. Beck, 2004).

Kemenes, István, 'A gazdasági szerződések követelményei és az új Polgári Törvénykönyv', *Polgári Jogi Kodifikáció*, 1 (2001), 9–31.

Kisfaludi, András, *Az adásvételi szerződés* (Közgazdasági és Jogi Könyvkiadó, 1999).

'Teljességi záradék', *Gazdasági és Jog*, 11 (1995), 3–7.

Komarov, Alexander S., (ed.) *International Commercial Arbitration. Modern Problems and Solutions* (Statut Publishing House, 2007) (in Russian).

(ed.), *Vienna Convention on Contracts for the International Sale of Goods. Practice of Application in Russia and Abroad* (Wolters Kluwer, 2007) (in Russian).

Kritzed, Albert H., 'Pre-Contract Formation', editorial remark on the Internet database of the Institute of International Commercial Law of the Pace University School of Law, www.cisg.law.pace.edu/cisg/biblio/kritzer1.html, last accessed 6 October 2010.

Kropholler, Jan, *Internationales Einheitsrecht* (J. C. B. Mohr, 1975).

Kucher, A. N., *Theory and Practice of the Pre-Contractual Stage: The Legal Aspects* (Statut Publishing House, 2005).

Lábady, Tamás, *A magyar magánjog (polgári jog) általános része*, 3rd edn (Dialóg Campus, 2002).

Lando, Ole, 'CISG and its Followers: A Proposal to Adopt Some International Principles of Contract Law', *American Journal of Comparative Law*, 53 (2005), 379–401.

Lando, Ole and Beale, Hugh (eds.), *Principles of European Contract Law, Parts I and II* (Kluwer Law International, 2002).

  (eds.), *Principles of European Contract Law, Part III* (Kluwer Law International, 2003).

Langemark, Jesper and Jørgensen, Henrik, 'Regresaftaler vedrørende produktansvar', *Ugeskrift for Retsvæsen*, B (1997), 65–69.

Larenz, Karl and Wolf, Manfred, *Allgemeiner Teil des Bürgerlichen Rechts*, 9th edn (C. H. Beck, 2004).

Lao Tzu, 'Tao Te Ching', in Emily Morrison Beck (ed.), *Bartlett's Familiar Quotations* (Little, Brown and Company, 1980)

Le Tourneau, Philippe, *Juris-Classeur Civil App. Articles 1131–1133* (LexisNexis).

Lego Andersen, Eigil, 'Hvorledes indgår erhvervslivet aftaler?', *Erhvervsjuridisk Tidsskrift* (2008), 34–39.

Légrádi, Gergely, 'Az utaló magatartás (biztatási kár) a Ptk.-ban és a bírói gyakorlatban', *Polgári Jogi Kodifikáció*, 4 (2003), 20–27.

Legrand, Pierre, 'Against a European Civil Code', *Modern Law Review*, 60 (1997), 44.

  Fragment on Law-as Culture (W. E. J. Tjeen Willink, Schhordijk Institute, 1999).

Lehrberg, Bert, *Förutsättningsläran* (Iustus, 1989).

Leible, Stefan (ed.), *Das Grünbuch zum Internationalen Vertragsrecht* (Sellier, 2004).

Lewison, Kim, *The Interpretation of Contracts*, 3rd edn (Sweet & Maxwell, 2007).

Lookofsky, Joseph, 'Desperately Seeking Subsidiarity', in *Center for International & Comparative Law Occasional Papers vol. 1: The Annual Herbert L. Bernstein Memorial Lecture in Comparative Law. The First Six Years* (Durham, 2009), pp. 111–130, also available at www.law.duke.edu/cicl/ciclops, last accessed 6 October 2010.

Lookofsky, Joseph and Møgelvang-Hansen, Peter, 'Ny indenlandsk købelov: KBL III?', *Ugeskrift for Retsvæsen*, B (1999), 240–252.

Lüderitz, *Auslegung von Rechtsgeschäften – Vergleichende Untersuchung anglo-amerikanischen und deutschen Rechts* (Karlsruhe, 1966).

Lynge Andersen, Lennart and Madsen, Palle Bo, *Aftaler og Mellemmænd*, 5th edn (Thomson, 2006).

Maggs, Peter B. and Zhiltsov, Alexei N. (eds. and translators into English), *The Civil Code of the Russian Federation*, parallel Russian and English texts (Norma Publishing House, 2003).

Makovskiy, A. L., 'The Influence of the 1980 Vienna Convention on the Development of Russian Law', in Komarov, Alexander S. (ed.), *The Vienna Convention on Contracts for the International Sale of Goods.*

Practice of Application in Russia and Abroad (Wolters Kluwer, 2007), pp. 123–131 (in Russian).

Mankowski, Peter, 'Stillschweigende Rechtswahl und wählbares Recht', in Leible, Stefan (ed.), *Das Grünbuch zum Internationalen Vertragsrecht* (Sellier, 2004), pp. 63–108.

'Überlegungen zur sach- und interessengerechten Rechtswahl für Verträge des internationalen Wirtschaftsverkehrs', *Recht der internationalen Wirtschaft* (2003), 2–14.

Marston, G., 'The Parol Evidence Rule: The Law Commission Speaks' [1986] CLJ 192.

Mattei, Ugo, Monti, Alberto, 'Abstract: Comparative Law and Economics' (1999), available at http://encyclo.findlaw.com/0560book.pdf, last accessed 6 October 2010.

Maxeiner, James R., 'Standard-Terms Contracting in the Global Electronic Age: European Alternatives', *Yale Journal of International Law*, 28, 1 (2003), 141–156.

Mazza, F., 'Merger clause (o clausola di completezza)', in Cendon, P. (ed.), *I contratti in generale*, vol. IV, *Clausole abusive* (UTET, 2001), pp. 725–755.

McKendrick, Ewan (ed.), *Force Majeure and Frustration of Contract*, 2nd edn (Informa Publishing, 1995).

McMeel, Gerard, *The Construction of Contracts: Interpretation, Implication and Rectification* (Oxford University Press, 2007).

Menyhárd, Attila, 'Protection of Legitimate Expectations in Hungarian Private Law', in Fauvarques-Cosson, B. (ed.), *La Confiance Légitime et l'Estoppel* (Société de Législation Comparée, 2007), pp. 277–294.

Merryman, John Henry, *The Civil Law Tradition* (Little, Brown and Company, 1985).

The Loneliness of the Comparative Lawyer and Other Essays in Foreign and Comparative Law (Kluwer Law International, 1999).

Meyer, Olaf, 'Die privatautonome Abbedingung der vorvertraglichen Abreden – Integrationsklauseln im internationalen Wirtschaftsverkehr', *Rabels Zeitschrift für ausländisches und internationales Privatrecht*, 72 (2008), 562–600.

Mitchell, Andrew D., 'Good Faith in WTO Dispute Settlement', *Melbourne Journal of International Law*, 7 (2006), 339–373.

Mitchell, Catherine, *Interpretation of Contracts* (Routledge-Cavendish, 2007).

Møgelvang-Hansen, Peter, 'Contracts and Sales in Denmark', in Dahl, Børge, Melchior, T. and Tamm, D. (eds.), *Danish Law in a European Perspective*, 2nd edn (Thomson, 2002), pp. 237–276.

Monateri, Pier Giuseppe, 'Lex Mercatoria e competizione fra ordinamenti', *Rivista di Sociologia del Diritto*, 2, 3 (2005), 229–240.

Moss, Giuditta Cordero – *see* Cordero-Moss, Giuditta

Münchener Kommentar zum Bürgerlichen Gesetzbuch, vol. 1/1, 5th edn (C. H. Beck, 2010).

Münzer, Cornelia, *Handeln unter falschem Recht* (Peter Lang, 1992).

Mustill, Lord Justice, 'The New Lex Mercatoria: The First Twenty-Five Years', *Arbitration International*, 4, 2 (1987), 86–119.

Nicola, Fernanda, 'Book Review: *The Enforceability of Promises in European Contract Law* (ed. by James Gordley)', *Harvard International Law Journal*, 44 (2003), 597.

Nørager-Nielsen, Jacob, Theilgaard, Søren, Bjerg Hansen, Michael and Hørmann Pallesen, Martin, *Købeloven*, 3rd edn (Thomson, 2008).

Nottage, Luke, 'Comment on Civil Law and Common Law: Two Different Paths Leading to the Same Goal', *Victoria University of Wellington Law Review*, 32 (2001), 843–851.

Olsen, Lena, *Ersättningsklasusuler. Vite och andra avtalade klausuler vid kontraktsbrott* (Nerenius & Santérus, 1986).

Palandt, BGB, 69th edn (C. H. Beck, 2010).

Palmer, N. E., 'Negligence and Exclusion Clauses. Again' [1983] LMCLQ 557.

Parks, Alex L. and Cattell, Edward V. Jr. (eds.), *The Law of Tug, Tow and Pilotage* (Schiffer Publishing, 1994).

Pejovic, Caslav, 'Civil Law and Common Law: Two Different Paths Leading to the Same Goal', *Victoria University of Wellington Law Review*, 32 (2001), 817–842.

Peel, Edwin, 'Agreements to Negotiate in Good Faith', in Burrows, Andrew and Peel, Edwin (eds.), *Contract Formation and Parties* (Oxford University Press, 2010).

   'Whither *Contra Proferentem*', in Burrows, Andrew and Peel, Edwin (eds.), *Contract Terms* (Oxford University Press, 2007).

Petrik, Ferenc, *Szavatosság, jótállás és fogyasztóvédelem* (Közgazdasági és Jogi Könyvkiadó, 1995).

Prausnitz, *The Standardisation of Commercial Contracts* (Sweet & Maxwell, 1937).

Rainey, Simon, *The Law of Tug and Tow (and Allied Contracts)* (LLP, 2002).

Ramberg, Christina and Ramberg, Jan, *Allmän avtalsrätt*, 8th edn (Norstedts Juridik, 2010).

Ramberg, Jan, *INCOTERMS 2000*, ICC Publication No. 620 (1999).

Reithmann, Christoph and Martiny, Dieter (eds.), *Internationales Vertragsrecht*, 6th edn (Verlag Dr. Otto Schmidt, 2004).

Rogers, Cathrine A., 'Review Essay: Gulliver's Troubled Travels, or the Conundrum of Comparative Law', *George Washington Law Review*, 67 (1998), 149–190.

Rogers, W. V. Horton, *Winfield & Jolowicz on Tort*, 17th edn (Sweet & Maxwell, 2006).

Rozenberg, M. G., 'Application of the 1980 Vienna Convention in the Practice of the ICAC at the RF CCI', in Komarov, Alexander S. (ed.) *International Commercial Arbitration. Modern Problems and Solutions* (Statut Publishing House, 2007), pp. 336–340 (in Russian).

International Sale of Goods. Commentary to Legal Regulation and Practice of Dispute Resolution, 3rd edn (Statut Publishing House, 2006) (in Russian).

(ed.), *The 1980 Vienna UN Convention on Contracts for the International Sale of Goods. The Ten Years of Application by Russia* (Statut Publishing House, 2002) (in Russian).

Runesson, Eric M., 'Bidrag till frågan om existensen av en omförhandlingsplikt och dess innehåll', in Flodgren, Boel, Gorton, Lars, Nyström, Birgitta and Samuelsson, Per (eds.), *Vänskrift till Axel Adlercreutz* (Juristförlaget i Lund, 2007), pp. 451–462.

Sacco, Rodolfo, 'Legal Formants: A Dynamic Approach to Comparative Law', *American Journal of Commercial Law*, 39 (1991), 1–34, 343–402.

'One Hundred Years of Comparative Law', *Tulane Law Review*, 75 (2001), 1159–1176.

Sadikov, O. N., *Damages in the Civil Law of the Russian Federation* (Statut Publishing House, 2009) (in Russian).

Saltorp, Bjørn and Werlauff, Erik, *Kontrakter*, 2nd edn (Jurist- og Økonomforbundets Forlag, 2009).

Samuel, Geoffrey, *Law of Obligations and Legal Remedies*, 2nd edn (Cavendish Publishing, 2001).

Samuelsson, Morten, 'Ansvarsfraskrivelse og produktansvar' *Forsikrings-og Erstatningsretlige Skrifter* I:2000 (Forsikringshøjskolens Forlag, 2000).

Sandsbraaten, T., *The Concepts of Conditions, Warranties and Covenants*, Publications Series of the Institute of Private Law No. 179 (University of Oslo, 2009).

Schadbach, Kai, 'The Benefits of Comparative Law: A Continental European View', *Boston University International Law Journal*, 16 (1998), 331–422.

Schans Christensen, Jan, *Grænseoverskridende virksomhedsoverdragelser. Tilrettelæggelse, Forhandling. Aftaleudarbejdelse og Opfølgning* (GadJura, 1998).

Schelhaas, Harriët, 'The Judicial Power to Reduce a Penalty', *Zeitschrift für Europäisches Privatrecht* (2004), 386–398.

Schlechtriem, Peter, 'The Functions of General Clauses, Exemplified by Regarding Germanic Laws and Dutch Law', in Grundmann, Stefan and Mazeaud, Denis (eds.), *General Clauses and Standards in European Contract Law* (Kluwer Law International 2006), pp. 41–55.

Schlechtriem, Peter and Schwenzer, Ingeborg (eds.) *Commentary on the UN Convention on the International Sale of Goods (CISG)*, 2nd edn (Oxford University Press, 2005).

(eds.), *Kommentar zum Einheitlichen UN-Kaufrecht – CISG*, 5th edn (C. H. Beck, 2008).

Schmidt-Kessel, Martin, 'Articles 8–9', in Schlechtriem, Peter and Schwenzer, Ingeborg (eds.), *Kommentar zum Einheitlichen UN-Kaufrecht – CISG*, 5th edn (C. H. Beck, 2008), pp. 163–197.

Schmitthoff, Clive M., 'The Unification or Harmonisation of Law by Means of Standard Contracts and General Conditions', *International & Comparative Law Quarterly*, 17, 3 (1968), 551–570.

Schulze, Reiner (ed.), *CFR and Existing EC Contract Law*, 2nd revised edn (Sellier 2009).

(ed.), *New Features in Contract Law* (Sellier, 2007).

Schwenzer, Ingeborg, '*Force Majeure* and Hardship in International Sales Contracts', *Victoria University of Wellington Law Review*, 39 (2009), 709–725.

Scognamiglio, Claudio, '*L'interpretazione*', in Gabrielli, Enrico (ed.), *I contratti in generale*, vol. II, 2nd edn (UTET, 2006), pp. 1035–1146.

Sellers, Mortimer, 'The Doctrine of Precedent in the United States of America', *American Journal of Comparative Law*, 54 (2006), 67–88.

Simon, Denys, *Le système juridique communautaire*, 3rd edn (PUF, 2001), No. 335.

Sjöman, Erik, 'Ett rättsfall om integrationsklausuler', *Svensk Juristtidning* (2008), 571–577.

'Integrationsklausulen och dispositive rätt', *Juridisk Tidskrift* (2002–2003), 935–941.

Skribeland, Fredrik, *No waiver-klausulen, Publications Series of the Institute of Private Law No. 176* (University of Oslo, 2009).

Smits, Jan M., (ed.), *Elgar Encyclopedia of Comparative Law* (Edward Elgar Publishing, 2006).

Soubelet, Laurent, 'Le rôle conféré par le droit communautaire aux droits nationaux des États membres', *Chronique de droit européen*, III, Université de Paris Ouest Nanterre La Défense, *Les Petites Affiches*, 19 May 2003, No. 99.

Spencer, J. R., 'Signature, Consent and the Rule in *L'Estrange v Graucob*' [1973] CLJ 104.

Staudingers Kommentar zum Bürgerlichen Gesetzbuch mit Einführungsgesetz und Nebegesetzen (Sellier, 2003).

Staughton, Sir C., 'How Do Courts Interpret Commercial Contracts?' [1999] CLJ 303.

Stein, Peter G., 'Relationships among Roman law, Common Law, and Modern Civil Law: Roman Law, Common Law, and Civil Law', *Tulane Law Review*, 66 (1992), 1591–1603.

Stolze, Lars and Svernlöv, Carl, 'Virksomhedsoverdragelsesskolen' (2005) *Revision & Regnskabsvæsen*, No. 1, 6–13, No. 4, 50–60, No. 5, 50–56.

Study Group on a European Civil Code/Research Group on EC Private Law (eds.), *Principles, Definitions and Model Rules of European Private Law – Draft Common Frame of Reference (DCFR)* (Sellier, 2009).

Sweeney, Joseph C., 'Collisions Involving Tugs and Tows', *Tulane Law Review*, 70 (1995), 581.

Tamasauskas, Andreas, *Erhvervslivets lånoptagelse* (Gjellerup, 2006).

Teske, Wolfgang, *Schriftformklauseln in Allgemeinen Geschäftsbedingungen* (Hetmanns, 1990).

Trebilcock, M. J., 'The Doctrine of Inequality of Bargaining Power', *University of Toronto LJ*, 26 (1976), 359.

Treitel, Guenter H. and Peel, Edwin, *The Law of Contract*, 12th edn (Sweet & Maxwell, 2007).

Triebel, Volker and Balthasar Stephan, 'Auslegung englischsprachiger Vertragstexte unter deutschem Vertragsstatut – Fallstricke der Art. 31, 32 I Nr. 1 EGBGB', *Neue Juristische Wochenschrift* (2004), 2189–2196.

Twigg–Flesner, Christian, *The Europeanization of Contract Law* (Routledge-Cavendish, 2008).

Ulfbeck, Vibe, *Erstaningsretlige grænseområder. Professionsansvar, produktansvar og offentlige myndigheters erstatningsansver*, 2nd edn (Jurist- og Økonomforbundets Forlag, 2010).

Ulmer, Peter, Brandner, Erich and Hensen, Horst-Diether, *AGB-Gesetz.: Kommentar zum Gesetz zur Regelung des Rechts der Allgemeinen Geschäftsbedingungen*, 9th edn (Verlag Dr. Otto Schmidt, 2001).

The United Nations Secretariat's *Commentary to the UNCITRAL Draft Convention*, adopted at the United Nations Conference on Contracts for International Sale of Goods, Vienna, 10 March–11 April 1980 (A/CONF./97/5), available at http://www.uncitral.org/uncitral/en/uncitral_texts/sale_goods/1980CISG_travaux.html, last accessed 6 October 2010.

Vékás Lajos (ed.), *Szakértői Javaslat az új Polgári Törvénykönyv tervezetéhez* (Complex Kiadó, 2008).

Vogenauer, Stefan 'Auslegung von Verträgen', in Basedow, Jürgen, Hopt, Klaus and Zimmermann, Reinhard, (eds.), *Handwörterbuch des Europäischen Privatrechts* vol. 1 (Mohr Siebeck, 2009), pp. 134ff.

Voß, Stefan, *Warranties in Unternehmenskaufverträgen – Struktur und Wirkungsweise anglo-amerikanischer Gewährleistungskataloge in Unternehmenskaufverträgen, die deutschem Recht unterliegen* (MVK, Medien-Verl. Köhler, 2002).

Weick, Günter, 'Zur Auslegung von internationalen juristischen Texten', in Köbler, Gerhard, Heinze, Meinhard and Schapp, Jan (eds.), Geschichtliche Rechtswissenschaft, *Freundesgabe für Alfred Söllner zum 60. Geburtstag am 5.2.1990* (Giessener rechtswissenschafliche Abhandlungen, 1990), pp. 607–628.

Westermann, Harm Peter, *Erman, Bürgerliches Gesetzbuch*, 12th edn (Verlag Dr. Otto Schmidt, 2008).

Westphalen, Graf von, *Vertragsrecht und AGB Klauselwerke* (C. H. Beck, 2003).

Westly, Jens Christian, *No Oral Amendments klausler, Publications Series of the Institute of Private Law* No. 178 (University of Oslo, 2009).

Whittaker, Simon, 'Termination Clauses', in Burrows, Andrew and Peel, Edwin (eds.), *Contract Terms* (Oxford University Press, 2007).

Wilburg, W., *Entwicklung eines beweglichen Systems im Bürgerlichen Recht* (Rede gehalten bei der Inauguration als Rector magnificus der Karl-Franzes Universität in Graz am 22 November 1950: 1950).

Zusammenspiel der Kräfte im Aufbau des Schuldrechts [163 AcP (1964)] 346–379.

Wilhelmsson, Thomas, Paunio, Elina and Pohjolainen, Annika (eds.), *Private Law and the Main Cultures of Europe* (Kluwer Law International, 2007).

Wolf, Manfred, Horn, Norbert and Lindacher, Walter (eds.), *AGB-Gesetz: Gesetz zur Regelung der Allgemeinen Geschäftsbedingungen*, 4th edn (C. H. Beck, 1999).

Wurmnest, Wolfgang, 'Die Mär von der mahr – Zur Qualifikation von Ansprüchen aus Brautgabevereinbarungen', *Rabels Zeitschrift für Ausländisches und Internationales Privatrechts*, 71 (2007), 527–558.

Yassari, Nadjma, 'Die Brautgabe im iranischen Recht', *Das Standesamt* (2003), 198–201.

Yates, David and Hawkins, A. J., *Standard Business Contracts* (Sweet & Maxwell, 1986).

Zakrzewski, Rafal, 'The Nature of a Claim on an Indemnity', *Journal of Contract Law*, 22 (2006), 54.

Zimmermann, Reinhard and Whittaker, Simon, *Good Faith in European Contract Law* (Cambridge University Press, 2000).

Zvekov, V. P., *Conflict of Laws in Private International Law* (Wolters Kluwer, 2007) (in Russian).

Zweigert, Konrad and Kötz, Hein, *Introduction to Comparative Law*, translated by Tony Weir, 3rd edn (Oxford University Press, 1998).

INDEX

absolute contracts, doctrine of 175–176
'abuse of law' defence 74
abuse of right 53, 332–333, 354, 356
  see also good faith
Acceptance Certificate, issue of
    121–122, 166
accounting, standardisation of 21
'acts of God' 205–206
  see also natural disasters
Acts on Promissory Notes, 1930s
    (common to all Scandinavian
    legislatures) 276
advertising 91
Aikens LJ 145–146
Almén, Tore 265, 295
alternative regulations 123–125
amendments 215, 326
  requested on grounds of hardship
    367–368
  see also 'no oral amendments'
ammunition, undeclared
    transportation 73–74
Angola 16, 18
applicable law
  departures from 116–117
  exceptions 41–43
  flexible approach 42–43
  fundamental principles, effect on
    contractual interpretation
    117–118, 245, 254, 346–347,
    368–369
  ignored by drafters 1, 64, 345,
    370–371
  independence of contracts from, see
    self-sufficiency
  interaction with transnational
    sources 47–52, 61

mandatory rules 346
matters already regulated by, clauses
    relating to 127–128, 203–207,
    247–253
  nature of interaction with contract
    344, 360, 372
  provisions compatible with 116
  relevance of non-applicable laws/
    systems 68
  terms unknown to 199–203
  see also choice of applicable law;
    incompatibility; interpretation;
    names of jurisdictions; national
    legal systems
arbitration 210, 216, 283, 352
  enforceability of awards 352
Arbitrazh Courts (Russia) 333
Arden, Lady Justice 59–60
'as is' clause 273
autonomous contract, see
    self-sufficiency
autonomous interpretation,
    requirement of 47, 54, 185

Bentham, Jeremy 160–161
'best endeavours', clauses/translations
    213
Bingham LJ 134–135, 164, 165, 173
boilerplate clauses 3, 4, 23, 277
  counterproductivity 371–372
  derivation 131
  differing legal effects 353–370
  failure to achieve desired results 349
  lesser importance in negotiation
    process 14
  negotiation of precise content 131
  problems of literal application 51–52

types 24–27, 49–52, 118–125, 178, 353
  specific clause types
Bonell, M. 57
borderline statements 27
Brandon, Lord 65
breach of contract 25–26, 127, 173
  caused deliberately 312–313
  common law remedies 363
  duty to give notice 238
  in German law 66
  in Hungarian law 327–328
  minor, disproportionate results
      270–271
  sanctions other than damages 218
  types 150–151
  see also default; fundamental breach;
      repudiatory breach
Bridge LJ 157
Brightman J 157
Brimham LJ 56
brokerage 75
Brussels Convention 246
Buxton LJ 162

Canadian law 97
caveat emptor principle 50–51
change of circumstance clauses, in
      Scandinavian systems
      290–291
  see also hardship
characterisation, problem of 331
choice of applicable law 35,
      37–43, 61, 183–184, 208,
      330–331, 350
  despite incompatibility with contract
      drafting 62
  exceptions to general rules 188
  in ignorance of incompatibility with
      contract drafting 63
  overruled by legal requirements 63–64
  partial 63
  principles 188
  by seller 13
  when not chosen by parties 184
  see also choice-of-law clauses;
      incompatibility; interpretation;
      tacit choice of law
choice-of-law clauses 38–39, 75–76, 348

Churchill, Winston 98
CISG, *see* United Nations (Vienna)
      Convention on Contracts for
      the International Sale of Goods
civil disturbance, impact on
      contractual obligations 123, 124
civil law
  clause specifying choice of 38
  disclosure obligations 366–367
  impact on liquidated damages 364
  judicial traditions 347
  see also applicable law; common law,
      compared with civil law;
      incompatibility
Civil Liability (Contribution) Act 1978
      (UK) 167
clausula rebus sic stantibus principle
      279, 280
clerical error 156
closest connection, principle of 41–43
  case law 42
  restrictive application 42–43
code of conduct 15
Colman J 162
common core, *see* convergence
common law
  compared/contrasted with civil
      systems 23–24, 56, 82–83, 84,
      88, 134–135, 207, 225, 347–349,
      361–362, 363, 365–366
  convergence with civil law 88
  differences between systems 40,
      97–98, 102
  evolution 94–95
  influence on other systems 329–330
  internal comparisons/divergences
      83–84, 351
  interpretation of exculpatory clauses 2
  see also common law contract
      models; English law; US law
common law contract model(s)
  prevalence 1, 9–10, 30, 50–51, 115,
      266, 267–268, 277, 299–300, 347
  problems of interpretation 22–23, 29
  termination, clauses/consequences
      25–26
  transplantation to civil legislatures
      2–3, 22

common law contract model(s) (cont.)
  disadvantages 79
  ease of 66
  see also incompatibility
common sense, overriding of literal
    interpretation 75
companies
  internal regulation 1, 29–30, 281
  use of representatives 281–282
  see also small businesses
comparative law 80–81, 101–103,
    111–112
  method 81–85
compensation, claims for 67
compensation clauses 294–299
  delay interest 298–299
  drafting techniques 295–296
  and full compensation 297–298
  general background 294
  nature of undertaking 296–297
  not limited to agreed sum
    337–338
  practical application 297
  specification of amount
    payable 296
  types 295
  use 295–297
competition, restrictions 131
'concessions', use in negotiation
    process 14
conditions 49–50, 119, 126,
    358–359
  case law 149, 151–152, 240
  defined 148
  in English law 148–152
  express stipulation 149
  in French law 217–218
  in Hungarian law 309–311
  literal interpretation 359
  problems of application 51
  purpose 358–359
  restrictive interpretation 259
  in Russian law 335–336, 343
  in Scandinavian systems 239–240,
    258–259, 270–271, 279–280,
    282, 283, 284, 300–301
consequential obligations 27–29,
    212–213

changes in common law clauses
    28–29
  need for clarification 28–29
consideration, doctrine of 64–65
construction clauses 184
construction contracts 26–27, 75–76,
    129–130, 298
Consumer Credit Act 1974 (UK) 152
consumers, protection 279
contra preferentem principle 132–133,
    167–168, 211
contracts
  addition of terms 58–59
  binding nature 280
  construction 303
  establishment 315–316
  extension of scope 116–117
  'lawless' 210
  non-negotiated 17–18
  obligation to fulfil 122
    relief from 124–125
  range of types/involved entities 11
  role in company relations 23–24
  spot vs. cooperation 281
  'tough' vs. 'dewy' 23–24
  see also amendments; drafting;
    enforceability; interpretation;
    provisions; self-sufficiency;
    standard international
    contracts; wording
Contracts Acts 1915–1929 (common to
    Scandinavian legislatures)
    233–234, 235–236, 238,
    239, 244, 246, 254–256, 257,
    263, 274, 276–277, 278,
    294, 300
conventions, *see* interpretation; *names
    of specific instruments*
convergence/convergence theory 2,
    80–103, 351
  defined 80
  evaluation 81, 83–85
  shortfall 101
  within US system 86–92
conveyancing 157
Corbin, Arthur L. 85, 87
cost-benefit analysis 4
crime, breach caused by 312–313

damages
  breach of contract 25, 127
  compensatory 260–261, 312,
    317–318, 363
  definitions, divergences between
    27–29
  limitation 166
  liquidated 120–121, 160–165,
    200–201, 202–203, 222,
    246–247, 260–261, 272–273,
    295, 319–321, 336–338, 348,
    362–364
  relief of liability for 125
  specification of amount payable
    336–337
  standardisation problems 27–29
  warnings (in German law) 76
Danish law 3, 118, 233–253
  compared with other Scandinavian
    systems 255
  conditions 239–240
  contractual interpretation 245–247
  'entire agreement' clauses 236–237
  force majeure/hardship 248–249
  fragmentary nature of contract law
    233
  general principles 234–236, 243
  'liquidated damages' clauses
    246–247
  'material adverse change' clauses
    244–245
  'no oral amendments' clauses 237
  'no waiver' clauses 238–239
  product liability 249–253
  relationship with EU law 234
  representations and warranties
    247–248
  severability clauses 239
  'sole remedy' clauses 241–242
  'subject to contract' clauses 242–243
  terminology 252
default, wilful 223
  incentives to 364
definition clauses 313–314
delay, contractual provisions/remedies
    126, 246–247, 257, 296, 310
  compensation clauses 298–299
  see also time stipulations

delivery clauses 245–246
Diplock, Lord 130–131, 153, 160–161
disclosure, duty of 171–172, 173–175,
    255, 262–263, 273–274
  absence 365–366
  possibility of contracting out 262
  see also information; good faith
drafting (of contracts) 1, 346–349
  driving forces 30
  methodology 1–2, 35–36, 37–61
  style of, implications for applicable
    law 2, 35, 61, 116–118, 370–372
  see also tacit choice of law
due diligence 267
'duty to read' 87–92

ECJ (European Court of Justice)
    104–106, 107–108, 110–112,
    250
  clarification of issues 109
  procedure 110–111
educational level (of contracting
    parties) 91
electronic documentation, validity
    216–217
employment contracts 297
enforceability (of contractual
    provisions) 11, 13–14, 91–92,
    315–316
  common law provisions in civil
    systems 24
  parties' lack of concern for 15
  supervisory role of courts 161–162
engineering
  contracts 213
  role in Norwegian economy 266–267
England/English law 3, 118, 129–178,
    351
  applicability in foreign courts 69–71
    rejection 69
  application in English courts 63–64
  as basis of contracts 3–4, 9–10, 40,
    127, 189–190
  central principles 129–130, 135–136
  compared with Scandinavian/
    Eastern European systems
    288–289, 299–300, 336–338
  conditions 148–152, 359

England/English law (cont.)
  content 129–132
  domination of sea trade/law 63
  'entire agreement' clauses 136–143,
    194–196, 355, 356
  exculpatory clauses 95–101, 102
  force majeure/hardship 175–178,
    205–206, 207, 367, 368
  foreign experts in 67
  good faith 56, 134–135
  handling of German law-based
    contracts 64–65, 370
  indemnity clauses 165–170, 365
  inflexibility 132
  interpretation of contracts 59–60,
    132–134, 181–182
  liquidated damages 160–165, 203, 363
  marine insurance 40
  'no oral amendments' clauses
    146–147, 198, 357
  'no waiver' clauses 144–146
  references to ECJ 104–105, 110, 112
  representations and warranties
    170–175, 339, 347–349,
    366–367
  'sole remedy' clauses 152–154, 360
  'subject to contract' clauses 154–160,
    361–362
  tensions 130–131
  translation/equivalents of terms 211,
    213
English (language), contracts written
    in 9–10, 16, 41, 75, 179,
    191–192, 363
'entire agreement' clauses 49, 119, 126,
    227–228, 353–355
  additional wording 140–141
  aims 138, 140, 193, 214–215,
    285–286, 288, 353–354
  case law 59–60, 138–139, 142–143,
    287–288
  changes to standard form 139–141
  CISG provisions 230–231
  comparison of national approaches
    194–197, 288–289
  drafting/application 286–287
  in English law 136–143, 146, 147
  in French law 214–215

  in German law 192–197
  in Hungarian law 306
  in Italian law 229–232
  limitations 256, 354–355
  narrow vs. wide 136
  overriding 140
  problems of application 51, 214–215
  recognition in the UPICC 58–59
  in Russian law 333–334
  in Scandinavian systems 236–237,
    256–257, 268–269, 282, 283,
    285–289, 300
  side-letters 138–139
  standardisation of wider sense 141
  validity 193–194, 229–230
Eörsi, Gyula 324
'equity', varying uses of 212
equivalence principle 106
essential obligations/terms
  in French law 217–219
  see also conditions
estoppel 75, 142–143, 160
European Union/EU law 2, 36,
    104–112, 183, 234
  comparative method 112
  competition law 109
  DCFR (Draft Common Frame of
    Reference) 44, 47, 60, 266, 289,
    291, 299, 300
  harmonisation measures 21–22,
    80, 350
  implementation of national laws 111
  Member State jurisdictions 106
  nuanced rereading of national laws
    110–112
  relationship with national systems
    105–112
  stereotypical perceptions 107
  see also Rome I Regulation
exclusion clauses 26–27, 168,
    169–170, 321
  in Danish law 241–242, 253
    non-binding 250–251
  in German law 76–77, 78–79
exculpatory clauses 2, 35–36,
    80–81, 84
  assent to 87–92
  case law 88–91, 93–101

comparison of different systems 101–103
construction 92
defined 85
enforceability 90–91, 92
in towage contracts 93–101
exemption clauses 84, 256, 259, 261, 298, 313–314
defined 85
non-enforcement 92
see also exculpatory clauses
exhaustiveness, intention of 116–117

failure of assumptions, doctrine of 244, 248, 255–256, 293
see also hardship
fair dealing, *see* good faith
Farnsworth, E. A. 86, 87
fault-based liability 204, 249, 317, 342–343
FIDIC (Fédération Internationale des Ingénieurs-Conseils) 179, 187
Finnish law 3, 118, 254–264
conditions 258–259
'entire agreement' clauses 256–257
force majeure 263–264
general principles 254–256
hardship 263
indemnity clauses 261
'liquidated damages' clauses 260–261
'material adverse change' clauses 260
'no oral amendments' clauses 257–258
'no waiver' clauses 257
representations and warranties 262–263
severability clauses 258
'sole remedy' clauses 259
'subject to contract' clauses 259–260
fire, damage by/liability for 205, 252–253
flexibility, in Scandinavian legal systems 235–236, 239
'flow down' contracts 15
food, contamination 90–91

force majeure 123–125, 128, 178, 204–206, 368–370
case law 176–178
defined 342
'election' element 176
in English law 175–178
in French law 226
in Hungarian law 327–328
purpose of clause 368
in Russian law 341–343
in Scandinavian systems 248–249, 263–264, 274–275, 282, 291
temporary 125
France/French law 3, 13–14, 118, 210–226
additional obligations 214
Civil Code 210–213, 216, 224
conclusion of contracts 220
conditions 217–218
construction of contracts 210–214
fact vs. law-based 211
'entire agreement' clauses 214–215
force majeure 226, 368
good faith 356
hardship 225–226, 367
indemnity clauses 222–223
interpretation of contracts:
non-mandatory rules 210–211, 213, 221
'liquidated damages' clauses 222
'material adverse change' clauses 221–222, 362
'no oral amendments' clauses 216, 357
'no waiver' clauses 215
relationship with EU 111–112
representations and warranties 223–225
severability clauses 216–217, 358
'sole remedy' clauses 218–220
'subject to contract' clauses 220–221
translation/equivalents of English terms 213
Frankfurter, Justice 89, 94, 96
fraud 255, 262, 341
free competition, law of 107
free movement, principle of 107

freedom of contract, principle of 84,
        89–90, 129–130, 135, 161, 178,
        332, 359
    in Hungarian law 302–303, 313–314
    in Scandinavian systems 278, 279,
        280, 294
    see also good faith
frustration, discharge by 175–177,
        205–206
fundamental breach 126, 239–240,
        258–259, 335–336
    in English law 133, 149
    non-recognition in Hungarian law
        309–311

GENCON form 72, 187
General Conditions for Turnkey
        Contracts (ABT 93) 252–253
General Conditions of Nordic Freight
        Forwarders (NSAB 2000)
        241–242
general principles, see transnational
        law
German law/courts 2, 3, 35, 62–79, 118,
        179–209
    applicability of foreign laws 63–64
    case law 67–77, 189–190
    choice-of-law clauses 75–76
    Civil Code (BGB) 66–67, 70, 74,
        76–77, 180–181, 193–194, 279,
        305, 354
    Commercial Code (HGB) 70, 71,
        189–190
    compared with other jurisdictions
        194–197, 198–199, 279, 324
    conflict of law rules 71
    criticisms 190–192
    demands on judiciary 79
    'entire agreement' clauses 192–197
    good faith 356
    handling of common law-based
        contracts 66–79, 370
    hardship 206–207, 291–292
    indemnity clauses 199–202
    influence on other systems 268
    influences 179
    interpretation of contracts 180–182,
        208–209

law of obligations/force majeure
        204–205, 206
'liquidated damages' clauses
        202–203
neutral arbitration 67
'no oral amendments' clauses
        197–199, 357
private international law 39
tension between contract
        construction and applicable law
        179–180, 189–192
terms unknown to 199–203
treatment of specific clauses 192–207
understanding of English terms 190
use of standard terms 186–187
Germany, import/export balance 179
Giuliano-Lagarde Report 40
globalisation 80
good commercial practice, see self-
        sufficiency
good faith 48–49, 354, 359, 364
    application in practice 58–59
    case law 211–212
    in common law systems 134–136,
        159, 299–300
    common law vs. civil law 56, 84, 88,
        134–135
    definition of scope 211
    in French law 211–212, 215, 221
    in German law 74–75, 76–77, 354, 356
    in Hungarian law 303, 304–305,
        323–324
    in Italian law 230
    lack of specific criteria 55–57, 61
    in Russian law 333
    in Scandinavian systems 254, 258,
        261, 262, 269, 279, 280, 289–290
    standards, degree of uniformity
        54–57
    in transnational instruments 52–57
    omission 56–57
governmental actions, impact on
        contractual obligations 123,
        124, 166
Griffiths J 178
gross negligence 219, 223, 255, 262,
        312–313
    see also negligence

hardship 122–123, 128, 206–207
  alternative regulations 123
  comparison of different approaches
    367–368
  defined 122–123
  in English law 175–178
  in French law 225–226
  in Hungarian law 326
  in Russian law 341–343
  in Scandinavian systems 248–249,
    263, 274, 282, 291–292, 301
harmonisation
  contractual attempts at 48
  problems of 46–47
  see also transnational law
Hayek, F. A. von 29
Hill, Mr Justice 96–97
hire, contracts of 169–170
  default in payment 151–152
Hoffmann, Lord 65, 156, 171, 181–182
holding fees 164–165
Holmes, Oliver Wendell 25
Hungarian law 3, 118, 302–328
  atypical obligations 321–322
  central principles of contract law
    302–306, 312
  Civil Code 302–303, 304–306,
    307–309, 312–313, 314, 315,
    316–319, 320, 322–325, 326,
    327–328
  compensatory damages 317–318
  conditions 309–311, 359
  court practice 304, 307, 318–319,
    323–324, 327–328
  criticisms 313
  discretionary powers of courts 318
  'entire agreement' clauses 306
  force majeure 327–328
  foreign trade regulation 302,
    312, 313
  hardship 326
  indemnity clauses 321–322
  information provisions 322–324
  'liquidated damages' clauses
    319–321
  'material adverse change' clauses 319
  'no oral amendments' clauses
    308–309, 357

'no waiver' clauses 307–308, 356
  ongoing reforms 302
  partial invalidity 309
  penalties 320
  representations and warranties
    322–325
  severability clauses 309
  'sole remedy' clauses 311–314, 360
  'subject to contract' clauses
    314–319
  tort law regulation 316–318,
    327–328
  use of imported clauses 304
hypothetical choice theory 39

IFRS (International Financial
    Reporting Standards) 21
illegal agreements 105, 110–111
immoral contracts, prohibition under
    Hungarian law 305
imperfect information, contracts based
    on 15–17
implied obligations 214, 232
impossibility, of contractual
    performance 282, 312,
    325, 326
  see also force majeure; hardship
in-house lawyers, perspective on
    contract drafting 29–31
  see also standardisation, corporate
    trend towards
inactivity, forfeiture of rights by 238
inclusio unius est exclusio alterius
    principle 116
incompatibility (of contract provisions
    with applicable law) 48–49, 61,
    63, 115, 344–353
  in German law 179–180,
    188–192
  inconsistency of approach 350
  loss of legal context 79, 350
  problems of 64–67, 208, 350–353
  resolution of conflicts 125–128,
    345–346
  see also choice of applicable law
incorporation, method of 132, 135
INCOTERMS (International
    Commercial Terms) 24–25, 44,

45, 47–48, 186–187, 188, 208, 351
integration with applicable law 48
indemnity clauses 69–71, 121–122, 127, 168, 190, 365
  case law 167–170
  comparison of national approaches 202
  English style 71, 72–73, 165–170, 201–202
  in French law 222–223
  in German law 199–202
  in Hungarian law 321–322
  sample 165–166
  in Scandinavian systems 261, 273, 301
  variations in form/wording 166–167, 200–202
indirect losses/obligations, *see* consequential obligations
industrial action, impact on contractual obligations 123, 124
information
  allocation 322
  duty of 212, 322–323
  undertaking not to disclose 296–297
  see also disclosure; good faith
innominate terms, defined 148
insurance 98–101, 102–103, 172, 223
  refusal of claim 240
intellectual property 297
intention (of contracting parties)
  declarations of 180
  and 'entire agreement' clauses 196–197
  as principle of interpretation 207, 245
  and 'subject to contract' clauses 155–156, 220, 315–316
  see also letters of intent
international commercial law 2
international law, *see* international commercial law; private international law
interpretation (of contracts) 1–3, 54–55, 118, 345–346, 352–353, 372
  antithetic 116–117

applicable law 182–188
  coverage by international conventions 184–186, 188
  in Danish law 245–247
  in English law 132–134, 135, 149–150, 153–154, 156
  in German law 180–182, 186, 190–192
  international 208
  literal 56, 349
  principles 207–209
  restriction of general principles 236–237
  separate law of 191–192
  uniform method 185–186
  see also common law contract models; common sense; incompatibility
Islamic law, marriage contracts 199
Italian law 3, 118, 227–232
  adaptation of Anglo-American model 228
  applicability in foreign courts 245–246
  Civil Code 227, 229–230, 231–232
  consequential losses, non-recognition of 28–29
  'entire agreement' clauses 229–232
  'no oral amendments' clauses 228–229, 357
  standardisation legislation 21
  termination remedies 26–27
  traditional approach 227

labour law 287–288
land sale contracts 155
language(s)
  common, need for 21
  dual 336
  national legal requirements 18–19
  relationship with applicable law 9–10, 16, 41
Lao Tzu 81
Law Commission 138
law firms, changing nature 267
lease, contracts of 88–91, 313
legal culture, defined 21
legal realism 135

Legrand, Pierre 21
letters of intent 126–127, 220, 242–243, 315–316, 319, 338
lex mercatoria, see transnational law
liability
  conflicts of rules 250
  consequent on failure to fulfil obligations 323–324, 341–342
  for failure to reach agreement 243
  limitation 121, 218–220, 222, 241–242, 252, 261, 298, 311–314, 321, 328
  obligation not based on 317–318
  in tort law 316–317, 323–324
    unified system 327–328
  total negation 159
  vicarious 249–252
  see also exclusion clauses; fault-based liability; negligence; product liability; strict liability
'liquidated damages' clauses 71, 120–121, 127, 200–201, 202–203, 348, 360, 362–364
  benefits 320
  case law 161–165
  comparison of different approaches 363–364
  in English law 160–165
  exclusiveness 261
  in French law 222
  in Hungarian law 319–321
  latitude 161–162
  loss greater than agreed remedy 321
  purpose 362–363
  redrafting 164
  restrictions 163–164
  in Russian law 336–338
  in Scandinavian systems 246–247, 260–261, 272–273, 295, 298, 301
  striking down 162
Lloyd's of London 40, 187
loan agreements 162
lock-in agreements 160
loyalty principle, in Scandinavian legal systems 243, 254, 255, 257, 258, 262, 269, 279, 356
  see also good faith
Luxembourg 108

Mansfield, Lord 50
Maritime Codes (Scandinavian) 276
Martiny, Dieter 68
'material adverse change' clauses 120, 127, 136, 362
  exceptions 120
  in French law 221–222
  in Hungarian law 319
  purpose 362
  in Scandinavian systems 244–245, 260, 272, 282, 292–294, 301
  specification of applicability 244–245
misapprehension, in Russian law 340–341
misrepresentation, claims for 173
Misrepresentation Act 1967 (UK) 141–142, 143
models (legal), circulation of 36, 104–112, 350
Monateri, Pier Giuseppe 23–24
monopoly 96–97
Mummery LJ 59
Mustill, Lord 57

national legal systems 2–3
  ambiguities/contradictions 16–17
  applicability to international contracts 37–43, 60–61, 104
  decreasing influence 30
  differences between, impact on contract interpretation 30–31
  failure to incorporate requirements of 17, 18–19
  interpretation methods 207–208
  lack of alternatives to 350–353
  responsibilities/applicability within EU 106, 108–110
  semi-autonomous 108–110
  underlying ethos 54–55, 346–347
  see also applicable law; European Union; *names of countries*
natural disasters, impact on contractual obligations 123, 124
negligence
  English vs. German approach 77
  and exculpatory clauses 93–95, 99–100

negligence (cont.)
  exemptions from liability 91–92,
    241–242
  inclusion of term in contract 170
  lack of specific reference to 90–91
  shifting liability 102–103
  see also gross negligence
negotiations 1, 11–17, 283–289, 345
  absence of 17–18, 345
  boilerplate clauses 14
  borderline with contracting
    phase 283
  as dynamic process 15
  imperfect information 15–17, 345
  role of compromise 14, 18, 345
  starting without serious intent 53
  strategies 14
  time/resources required for 17
New York State, choice as applicable
    law 15
'no oral amendments' clauses 49, 59,
    119, 126, 227–229, 356–358
  comparison of national approaches
    198–199, 357–358
  in English law 146–147
  in French law 216
  in German law 197–199
  in Hungarian law 308–309
  in Italian law 228–229, 231–232
  limitations 198
  overriding 147
  problems of application 51
  purpose 356–357
  in Russian law 335
  in Scandinavian systems 237,
    257–258, 269–270, 281, 282,
    284–285, 290, 300
'no representation' clause 143
'no waiver' clauses 49, 119, 126,
    355–356
  aims 355
  case law 144–146
  'clear and unequivocal' criterion 144
  in English law 144–146
  forms 144
  in French law 215
  in Hungarian law 307–308
  literal interpretation 356

  problems of application 51
  in Russian law 334–335
  in Scandinavian systems 238–239,
    257, 269, 282, 300
  validity 257
non-conformity, Danish rules on 234,
    251–252
non-reliance clauses 140
Norwegian law 3, 83, 118, 265–275
  compared with other Scandinavian
    systems 255–256
  conditions 270–271
  'entire agreement' clauses 268–269
  evolution 266–268
  force majeure 274–275, 369, 370
  hardship 274
  indemnity clauses 273
  law of obligations 265–266
  'liquidated damages' clauses
    272–273
  'material adverse change'
    clauses 272
  'no oral amendments' clauses
    269–270
  'no waiver' clauses 269
  practitioners 267
  representations and warranties
    273–274
  severability clauses 270
  'sole remedy' clauses 271, 360
  standard ship sales contract 187
  'subject to contract' clauses
    271–272
nullity/nullification (of contract)
    104–105, 224–225

oil industry 176–177, 267
Olsen, Lena 295
'onerous' contracts/clauses
  in French law 217
  'or unusual' (as criterion) 132
oral agreements, validity 129–130, 147,
    237, 257–258, 308–309
  see also 'no oral amendments'
    clauses
Ottawa Conventions on International
    Factoring/Financial Leasing
    1988 186

pacta sunt servanda principle 254, 293
parol evidence rule 137–138, 181, 195, 268
  exceptions 196
  problems 137
  purpose 137–138
  see also 'entire agreement' clauses
party autonomy principle 38, 191
PECL (Principles of European Contract Law) 44–45, 52, 53–55, 57, 60, 266, 291, 300, 305, 355, 361
penalty, concept in Russian law 336–337
penalty clauses 65, 78, 200, 272–273, 320, 321, 348
  distinguished from liquidated damages 203, 260–261
  in French law/language 222
  invalidity under English law 69, 71–74, 161–162, 337, 363
'Peril of Navigation excepted' clauses 68–69
personal injury, liability for 121, 165, 219, 249, 250–251
Piper Alpha oil rig 167–168
planning permission 159–160
Port of London Authority 95–96
Post Office 145–146
power
  failure, impact on contractual obligations 123, 124
  supply contracts 177–178
precedent 82–83
prices
  increase, measures to prevent 26–27, 292
  reduction 287
private international law 2, 37–38, 45–47, 207, 331, 350
  in Germany 62, 179–180
privity, doctrine of 65
procedural autonomy, principle of 106
  as bridge between EU and national law 109–110
  effectiveness 110–112
  exceptional/subsidiary nature 107–108

product liability, in Danish law 249–253
  case law 251–253
  distinguished from contract law liability 252–253
Product Liability Act 1989 (Denmark) 249–251, 252
property, damage to 249, 250–251, 252
proportionality principle 313, 336
provisions, contractual
  change of meaning in translation 199–202
  'deal breakers' 13
  differing degrees of importance 11, 12–15
  implied 182
  invalidity 126
  second rank 14–15
  specific to a given law 187–188
  'unreasonable disadvantage' criterion 76–77
  see also boilerplate clauses; standard terms
public policy, as grounds for judgments 94, 95, 96–97, 214

Rabel, Ernst 265
railway construction/routing 323–324
Rattee J 139
reasonableness, principle of 132, 133–134, 158, 213
  in Scandinavian countries 234–236, 254–255, 256
  see also unfairness; unreasonable disadvantage
Reid, Lord 133–134, 149
Reithmann, Christoph 67–68
representations and warranties 115–116, 122, 127–128, 348–349, 365–367
  consequences 324–325, 339–341
  contractual 172
  in English law 170–175, 347–349
  exhaustiveness 325, 347–349
  in French law 223–225
  function 365–366, 367
  in Hungarian law 322–325
  need for 171–172

representations and warranties (cont.)
   precontractual 172–173
   redundant 171
   in Russian law 339–341
   in Scandinavian systems 247–248,
       262–263, 273–274, 301
   see also information
representatives
   companies' use of 281–282, 370–371
   negotiating powers 282
repudiatory breach 150–151, 153
   see also conditions
restraint of trade 160–161
restriction clauses 169–170
revision (of contracts) 123
risk(s)
   allocation 24, 27, 29–31, 318, 320,
       368–369
   legal 371–373
   management 345
Rome Convention 42–43, 182–183, 191
Rome I Regulation 38–43, 46, 62,
       63, 183
   'closest connection' rule 41–43
Russian law 3, 118, 329–343
   Civil Code 329–343
   civil law rights 332–333
   conditions 335–336, 343
   contract interpretation provisions
       330–331
   'entire agreement' clauses 333–334
   establishment of significance of
       contractual terms 331–332
   force majeure/hardship 341–343
   influences 329–330, 332–333
   International Commercial
       Arbitration Court (ICAC) 333
   invalid transactions 340
   Law on International Commercial
       Arbitration 334
   linguistic requirements 18–19
   'liquidated damages' clauses
       336–338
   'no oral amendments' clauses 335,
       357
   'no waiver' clauses 334–335, 356
   representations and warranties
       339–341

'sole remedy' clauses 338
'subject to contract' clauses 338–339

safety, obligation of (in French law) 212
sale of goods, contracts of 129, 149,
       184–186, 219–220, 230–231
   compensation clauses 296–297
Sale of Goods Act 1979 (UK) 149
Sales of Goods Acts 1905–7 (common
       to all Scandinavian legislatures)
       233–234, 240, 245, 248, 249,
       250, 251, 252, 254, 263–264,
       265–266, 273, 276, 287, 291, 369
'satisfaction' clauses/translations 213
Scandinavian legal systems 82–83, 356
   change of circumstance clauses
       290–291
   comparison with common law
       approaches 288–289, 299–300
   cooperation/common legislative
       measures 233–234, 254,
       265–266, 276–278
   'material adverse change' clauses 362
   'no oral amendments' clauses 357
   parameters 280–281
   performance phase clauses 289–294
   severability clauses 358
   vocabulary 280
   see also names of individual countries
Schiemann LJ 147
sea, carriage by, *see* shipping
securities, financial 74
self-sufficiency (of contracts) 3–4, 48,
       118, 125–127, 344–346
   failure to achieve 344, 370–372
   provisions aiming at 236–245,
       346–349
sellers
   failure to deliver 160–161
   strength of bargaining position 12
severability clauses 49, 119, 126,
       136, 358
   case law 217
   in Danish law 239
   in Finnish law 258
   in French law 216–217
   in Hungarian law 309
   in Norwegian law 270

problems of application 51
purpose 358
Shaw, George Bernard 98
shipbuilding contracts 286
shipping contracts 63, 65, 221
  case law 68–74
Sjöman, Erik 287
small businesses
  courts' attitude to 86
  differing approach from large 12
'sole remedy' clauses 50, 119, 126,
    359–360, 364
  case law 153–154
  enforceability 314
  in English law 152–154
  in French law 218–220
  in Hungarian law 311–314
  problems of application 51
  purpose 359–360
  restrictions 218–220, 241
  in Russian law 338
  in Scandinavian systems 241–242,
    259, 271, 301
  specification of amount payable 242
specific performance requirements/
    remedies 25–26, 30–31, 312
  in German law 66
standard international contracts 20–31,
    40–41, 85, 187
  development 20–22
standard terms
  in English law 130–178
  in German law 67, 76–77, 78–79,
    186–187
  types 130–131, 148
  see also boilerplate clauses
standardisation
  corporate trend towards 20–22
  damages, as problem area 27–29
  legal, problems of 22–29
  legislative measures 21–22
standby letters of credit 74
state-owned companies, project
    tenders 17
Steyn, Lord 136, 158
storage contracts 77
strict liability 66–67, 249–250
stylistic clauses 228

'subject to approval' clauses 281, 282,
    283, 284
'subject to contract' clauses 50, 120,
    126–127, 361–362
  abuses 155, 361
  agreement vs. intention, as point at
    issue 155–156
  breakdown of negotiations 160
  case law 155–160, 242–243
  clerical error 156
  comparison of different approaches
    361–362
  effect of negating laibility 159–160
  in English law 154–160
  expunged by implication 156–158
  in French law 220–221
  in Hungarian law 314–319
  implications of inclusion/exclusion
    52, 53, 154–155
  literal application 361
  mutual consent 315–316
  purpose 361
  in Russian law 338–339
  in Scandinavian systems 242–243,
    259–260, 271–272, 301
  waiving 158
subsidiarity principle 109
substantive justice, aim to provide 305
substantive law 62
Suez Canal 176–177
Swedish law 3, 118, 276
  adoption of solutions from other
    jurisdictions 278
  compared with other Scandinavian
    systems 255–256
  compensation clauses 294–299
  conditions precedent 284
  'entire agreement' clauses 285–289
  force majeure 291
  general principles 278–280
  hardship 291–292
  implication of boilerplate clauses
    (summarised) 300–301
  'liquidated damages' clauses 298
  'material adverse change' clauses
    292–294
  'No oral amendments' clauses
    284–285, 290

Swedish law (cont.)
  procedural 286–287
Swiss law 291–292

tacit choice of law 38–41, 42, 61, 191
  examples 40
  insufficient basis for 43
  validity 39–40
technicalities, legal, contractual
    significance 85, 98–101,
    102, 351
termination
  benefit derived from 125
  clauses 25–26, 153
  early 293
  modes of 150
  right of 13, 66, 123, 125, 144, 148,
    150–151, 257, 310–311
    delay in exercising 355–356
    waiver 307
terms (of contract), *see* provisions;
    standard terms
terms of purchase 12
terrorism, acts of 123, 124
third parties, default by 123, 124, 166
'time is of the essence', *see* conditions
time stipulations 149, 150
Toulson J 142–143
towage contracts 84, 93–101
  collisions between vessels 94–95, 96
transaction costs, rise/restriction 130,
    267–268, 291–292
transfer of title clauses 24–25
transnational law 43–60, 61
  binding instruments 44–45
  case law 57–60
  choice of 46–47
  force of law 45–47, 61
  general principles 44, 45, 48–52,
    55–57, 350–351
  lack of uniform standards 52–60, 61
  limitations 351
  non-binding (soft) law 44–45, 47–52
  sources 44–45
  specific regulation 47–48
  see also applicable law
transportation contracts 212
Tunisia 16–17

UCP 600 (Uniform Customs and
    Practice for Documentary
    Credits) 44, 45, 74
uncertainty, and risk assessment
    371–372
UNCITRAL 58
  Model Law on Commercial
    Arbitration 44, 46, 334
unconscionability 86–87, 131,
    160–161, 162
  defined 86
  procedural vs. substantive 87
  subversion of duty to read 88–90
unequal relationship (of parties to
    contract) 89–90, 94, 110–111
Unfair Contract Terms Act 1977 (UK)
    97, 131, 134, 139–140, 143, 154,
    167, 168, 170, 178
unfairness (of contractual terms) 140,
    150–151, 305, 309
  see also reasonableness
unforeseeability 225–226, 275, 342
UNIDROIT 58
  see also UPICC
UNILEX 58–60
United Nations (Vienna) Convention
    on Contracts for the
    International Sale of Goods
    (CISG) 44–45, 56–57, 184–186,
    230–231, 233–234, 237, 266,
    276, 291, 294, 329–330, 369
unknown factors 11
unlawfulness, concept of (in Hungarian
    law) 316
'unreasonable disadvantage' criterion
    76–77
UPICC (UNIDROIT Principles of
    International Commercial
    Contracts) 44–45, 46, 52–55,
    57–60, 182, 208, 230, 266,
    268–269, 270, 291, 300, 305,
    355, 361
URDG (Uniform Rules for Demand
    Guarantees) 74
US law
  as basis of contracts 40, 191, 266
  compared with other jurisdictions
    96–102, 336–338

'entire agreement' clauses 138,
195–197
exemption/exculpatory clauses 84
force majeure 206
hardship 207
indemnity clauses 201–202
internal convergence 86–95
internal variations 101, 196, 351
'no oral amendments' clauses
198–199
penalty clauses 203
representations and warranties 339
role of precedent 82–83
UCC (Uniform Commercial Code) 86
usury, prohibition of 305

waiver
by election 144

non-recognition of concept
334–335
of recourse 223
of subrogation 99–100
total 144
see also 'no waiver' clauses
Walker, Lord 157–158
war, impact on contractual obligations
120, 123, 124
warranties
(alleged) breach 174–175
remedies 173
defined 148
in English law 173–175
implied 171
see also representations and
warranties
wording (of contracts) 2–3